Legislating Morality
Private Choices on the Public Agenda

Kim Ezra Shienbaum, Editor

SCHENKMAN BOOKS, INC.,
Rochester, Vermont

Copyright © 1988

Schenkman Books, Inc.
Main Street
Rochester, Vermont 05767

Library of Congress Cataloging-in-Publication Data

Legislating morality.

　　1. Sex and law--United States.　2. Sex and law.
I. Shienbaum, Kim Ezra.
KF9325.L44　1988　　　　344.73'054　　88-4592
ISBN 0-87073-689-2　　　　347.30454
ISBN 0-87073-690-6 (pbk.)

Printed in the United States of America.

CONTENTS

Overview:
Perspectives on Sex, the State and Public Policy
Kim Ezra Shienbaum

Until recently, public debates over government intervention in matters as personal as contraception, conception, abortion, and homosexuality were fairly rare in America. This is not to imply that political decisions affecting private choices have never been on the governmental agenda. Governmental decision-making in these matters, however, has always been hesitant, uncoordinated, and often indirect—through tax policy, for example. Unlike comparable industrial democracies, such as France and West Germany, the United States still does not have an official "population policy"[1], although attempts have been made as recently as 1981 to create one.

In recent years, however, not only are these questions on the national political agenda, but the public is calling for more, rather than less, regulation—a trend running counter to governmental deregulation in other areas. Our purpose here is to explain the reasons behind these trends.

Factors Inhibiting a Governmental Policy Response

A major factor inhibiting a national governmental response to sexual questions has been that certain matters are, in the bluntest terms, not considered the government's business. Moreover, those matters with which government did concern itself in the past, such as homosexuality and prostitution, were simply declared illegal

Kim Ezra Shienbaum is an associate professor of political science at Rutgers University-Camden.

and left to state and local governments to regulate. Leona Baumgartner writes:

> In the United States, the history of governmental involvement [in personal matters] must be viewed in the light of the pioneer past of this country, in which the individual assumed responsibility for whatever personal health service his family needed and did not look to the government to help him, and in the light of our Puritanical and Victorian heritages, which frowned on matters related to sex.[2]

Government, in other words, had very limited social responsibilities, particularly in those matters considered to be family matters. That this view prevailed until relatively recently is clearly indicated by President Eisenhower's statement in 1959 that "birth control . . . is not our business. I cannot imagine anything more emphatically a subject that is not a proper political or governmental function or responsibility."[3] Despite increasing governmental involvement through the last three decades, the distaste for that role still lingers, even today. Two examples are illustrative. In the 1982 hearings before the House Sub-Committee on Census and Population, which was considering a bill introduced by Rep. Richard Ottinger (D., NY) to establish an Office of Population Policy, committee chair Rep. Robert Garcia (D., NY) in his prefatory comments took special note of the fear Americans had about the government as Big Brother "tampering with the family."[4] In 1985, the House Select Committee on Children, Youth and Families, evaluating the problem of teen pregnancy, acknowledged in their report that:

> Not all solutions to the problems of teen pregnancy and parenting will, or should, involve the federal government, or any government.[5]

Simultaneously, the Puritanical element Baumgartner refers to made many sexual practices illegal (it did not matter whether these were family concerns or "deviant" behavior). For example, it was not until 1971 that it became legal to send contraceptive material through the mails, an act classified as "obscene" by the nineteenth century Comstock Laws. The Judeo-Christian ethic permeated what policy there was on matters as diverse as abortion, artificial insemination, homosexuality, and pornography. For example, Andrea Bonnicksen notes in Chapter 1 that in the matter of artificial insemination, the courts tended to follow the Catholic Church's proscription of the practice on the grounds that it was "immoral," the very same argument used against homosexuality. In testimony before the 1982 House hearings on the Civil Rights Amendments Act of 1981, homosexuality was characterized by church groups as an act as immoral as wife-beating.[6]

Nevertheless, since 1960, the government has begun to play a larger role. Phyllis Piotrow has identified three phases of governmental response: *debate* on the relevance of a policy response, the *feasibility* of various responses and the *implementation* of particular policies. She emphasizes the role of the United Nations in recognizing a world-wide population explosion in the early 1960s, and it is important to note that America's first response to matters such as family planning came via congressional support for *international* programs. While the U.S. was willing to endorse and to fund "population programs" for other countries (by 1969 the U.S. was the principal source of funding for family planning programs throughout the world), it was not until 1970 that Congress passed the Family Planning and Services Act which provided funding for *domestic* family planning programs.[7]

Another factor prodding the federal government to intervene to change public policy was the women's liberation movement, which demanded governmental responses not just to contraception and conception, but also to abortion. By the late 1970s Medicaid was funding abortions for poor women and providing them with contraception services, as well as with supplemental food under the WIC (Women, Infants and Children) program.

The governmental response, though spearheaded by Congress, was soon joined by a more permissive and liberal Supreme Court, which liberalized rules for abortion (*Roe v. Wade*, 1973) and contraception (*Griswold v. Connecticut*, 1965; *Eisenstadt v. Baird*, 1972) and, as Eric Hoffman points out in Chapter 12, developed what many consider to be too restrictive a definition of pornography in *Roth v. the United States*, 1957.

The 1980s have witnessed a counter-trend. Conservative groups, offended by the liberal nature of many decisions in the 1960s and 1970s, have increasingly sought (thus far unsuccessfully) to move the locus of the decision-making back to the states and localities, under the guise of the "New Federalism." For instance, in 1981, during oversight hearings of Family Planning Programs under Title

3

X of the Public Health Service Act, the Commission Chair, Senator Jeremiah Denton (D., AL), expressed dissatisfaction that birth control funds intended for poor women were going increasingly to adolescent teenagers without parental consent. He advocated turning over block grants to states and localities for them to decide how those funds should be disbursed, a suggestion opposed by another member, Senator Howard Metzenbaum (D., OH) who wanted a continuation of categorical grants.[8] On the matter of abortion, it was the desire to turn the issue over to the states that prompted several New Right religious groups to initially favor a "states' rights" amendment which would have allowed the states to legislate as they saw fit, in effect returning to the status quo prior to the *Roe v. Wade* decision.

Sexual Matters on the Public Agenda: Some Reasons Why

Why have private sexual matters recently become the subject of intense public debate with calls for more, rather than less, governmental involvement?

One answer is that, beginning in the 1960s, there have been major expansions of two concepts: "privacy" and "civil rights and liberties." These expansions have led to an explosion of interest group activity spearheaded by "sexual" interest groups. Moreover, the multiplicity of pressure points within the American political system has created a situation of interest group opportunity.

Interest Group Activity: Privacy Rights and Civil Rights

The concept of a constitutionally protected "right to privacy" in sexual matters was first recognized by the Supreme Court in *Griswold v. Connecticut* in 1965. In that instance the Court struck down a Connecticut law which made contraception illegal, even between married couples, and ruled that the "right to privacy" was protected from state infringement by the due process clause of the fourteenth amendment. Then in 1972, the same right to privacy was granted to homosexuals (and other adults) in *U.S. v. Moses*. A Washington, D.C. court concluded that the statutory proscription against "fornication, sodomy and adultery engaged in by consenting adults" was an unconstitutional invasion of the "right of privacy." That same year, a California Superior Court judge in Los Angeles ruled unconstitutional a state law proscribing oral-genital contacts (Section 288a of the California Penal Code), while California voters approved a referendum proposition which added a "right to privacy" to the list of inalienable rights guaranteed by the state constitution."[9] However, in June 1986, a more conservative Supreme Court, in a 5-4 ruling *(Bowers v. Hardwick)*, declared that sodomy between private, consenting adults was *not* protected by a constitutional right to privacy, a marked reversal of direction from previous lower court rulings.

In 1973, the same "right to privacy" argument was used by the Supreme Court in the case of *Roe v. Wade* to strike down restrictive abortion laws enacted by Texas and Georgia. As Marilyn Jane Field notes, a number of states subsequently passed laws in defiance of the court directive, which prohibited interference in a woman's decision to have an abortion in the first trimester of pregnancy. None of these laws, however, has thus far survived court challenges. For example, the New York State law which required a married woman to have her husband's consent, and those under 18 to have parental consent, was struck down on privacy grounds by the Supreme Court in *Planned Parenthood of Central New York v. Danforth* (1976).[10]

A second weapon has been added to the arsenal of those interest groups seeking to expand their sexual rights—the claim that they are entitled to both legislative as well as judicial protection of their "civil rights." The argument is not a new one. In 1942, the Supreme Court ruled in *Skinner v. Oklahoma,* that the "right to procreate" was one of the "basic civil rights of man," and struck down a state statute which permitted the involuntary sterilization of some convicted felons.

Expansions with respect to procreation rights continue. In Chapter 11, Judith Gran examines the legal rights of disabled parents, while in Chapter 7, the reproductive rights of the unmarried are discussed.

By 1981, homosexuals were using the civil rights argument to sponsor a bill, the Civil Rights Amendment Act of 1981, which sought to amend the Civil Rights Act of 1964 to prohibit discrimination on the basis of sexual orientation. In testimony before the

5

House Subcommittee on Employment Opportunities, proponents of the proposed legislation invoked the civil rights argument. For instance, a representative of the United Church of Christ testified that since 1975, the church "has spoken through synod resolutions directed to the civil rights of those persons whose affectional or sexual preference is for those of the same gender. . . . [The United Church of Christ will] work for the enactment of such legislation at the Federal, State and local levels of government that would protect the civil liberties of all persons without discrimination."[11] Church groups opposing the legislation were vehement in their denials that homosexuals should receive constitutional protection for their "civil rights." The following testimony, from the journal *Family Policy Insights*, was introduced before the subcommittee:

> . . . the subject of homosexuality, much like that of abortion, has become inextricably enmeshed in the political rhetoric of rights . . . Anyone whose claim can be asserted on the level of a right therefore gathers a tremendous moral and political impetus for his cause. For this reason, activist homosexuals are attempting to identify themselves as the new civil rights movement.[12]

While on the national level legislation protecting the civil rights of homosexuals foundered, it has met with varying success on the state and local levels. For instance, while in Dade County, Florida, local voters rejected a 1977 referendum that would have granted "basic civil liberties to residents with homosexual or bi-sexual" preferences, the New York City Council passed a law in 1986 prohibiting discrimination against homosexuals.[13]

Women's groups have similarly appropriated the doctrine of civil rights to tackle pornography, although unsuccessfully thus far. For example, an anti-pornography ordinance in Indianapolis, subsequently declared unconstitutional, defined pornography as a "violation of women's civil rights," as did a 1985 anti-pornography ordinance in Minneapolis, which was vetoed by the mayor.[14]

Of late, the New Right, frustrated in their attempts to act through the Congress to turn over sexual legislation to the states and localities, have begun to expropriate the language of civil rights protection for their own purposes. Thus, as Robert Blank explains in Chapter 6, women are finding that their rights to autonomy (and privacy) are being challenged by advocates for the rights of unborn fetuses and embryos. Indeed, as Andrea Bonnicksen points out in Chapter 1, the federal government has declined to fund *in vitro* research due to moral and ethical concerns over the status of the embryo (a concern also voiced by the Warnock Commission in Great Britain, Chapter ?), while state statutes currently weigh the interests of the embryo more heavily than those of infertile couples.

In an attempt to give policy status to this initiative the 1981 Human Life Bill introduced in Congress stated that human life begins at the moment of conception. The intent was to extend statutory "civil rights" to the fetus, and reverse the 1973 ruling by the Court that an embryo or fetus under three months does not have the status or rights of a person.

Civil libertarians (joining "Right-to-Lifers") invoked the civil liberties issue in the Baby Jane Doe case. In this case both parents and doctors had made an informed judgment to withhold treatment of a baby born with severe, and irreparable, birth defects, a decision ultimately upheld by the Courts. Nevertheless, columnist Nat Hentoff wrote:

> As a person under the Constitution, has Baby Jane no rights of her own to live as long as she can? No due process rights? No rights to equal protection under the law?[15]

The Reagan administration subsequently issued a rule which barred hospitals from refusing to treat or feed severely handicapped infants, and a companion requirement that state welfare agencies monitor compliance. The Supreme Court, however, invalidated the "Baby Jane Doe" rule in June 1986, arguing that the administration had failed to give any valid legal justification for the rule.

Thus far, neither homosexuals nor "right to lifers" have been successful on a national level in obtaining either legislative or judicial protection of their respective claims to civil rights protection. The Civil Rights Amendment Act of 1981 did not become law and homosexuals now face new challenges to their civil rights as a result of public concern over the AIDS epidemic, an issue surveyed in Chapter 15, and by Ronald Bayer in Chapter 14. It should be noted that in June 1986, the Justice Department tentatively concluded that people with AIDS were "handicapped individuals" entitled to protection under the federal civil rights laws, but also that employers who feared contagion could fire them for that reason alone. Nor have civil rights, as yet, been extended to fetuses, but the retirement of Chief Justice Warren Burger in 1986 seems to tilt the Court in a more conservative direction, so the case is far from closed.

Expansions of Interest Group Opportunity: Pressure Points in the American Political System

One of the striking characteristics of American public policy generally, and sexual policy in particular, is that there has never been coherence and co-ordination. The reason, of course, is that the American political system is extraordinarily permeable with multiple pressure points existing within the policymaking process. Decisionmaking occurs at several levels, state, local and national as well as executive, legislative and judicial. As a result, the levers of political power are pressed by so many that the appearance is of a government that is working at cross purposes with itself.

Robert Blank confirms this impression in Chapter 10. He points out that Court decisions, made on a case-by-case basis, lack comprehensiveness and may even result in a confusing array of contradictory precedents. Moreover, as Ervin Shienbaum suggests, shifting regulatory responsibilities to states and localities, as proposed by conservatives, would only serve to amplify the contradictions of sexual policy. On the other hand, it is important to emphasize that these same conditions have created myriad opportunities for interest groups to influence the political process.

In addition to the multiple pressure points available, recent developments, such as the decline of parties, have had the effect of paralyzing decision-making at the Congressional level. Hence, both the judiciary and bureaucracy have stepped into this power vacuum, creating even more opportunities for interest groups to influence public policy. Thus, groups stymied at one level can appeal to other, more sympathetic, levels to have those decisions reversed.

In recent years, it has been the courts that have been liberal in many areas, and interest groups have sought their protection from more conservative legislatures. Family planning has been one area that the Courts have zealously protected. As discussed earlier, Title X of the Family Planning and Services Act of 1971 had provided family planning to low income families. Concerned that minors were availing themselves of this, Congress amended Title X via the Omnibus Budget Act of 1981 to require parental notification for minors. Following Congress' instructions, the Department of Health and Human Services in February 1982 proposed requiring that Title X projects notify parents of minors who were receiving contraceptives through federally funded family planning clinics. Final regulations were issued in January 1983 and went into effect the following month. No sooner had this happened than the ruling was challenged by Planned Parenthood and other groups. In March 1983, a U.S. District Court judge issued an injunction forbidding implementation of this rule, a decision upheld on appeal. In this case the court ruled that the administrative decision was contrary to Congress' intent when it enacted Title X.[16]

The conservative battle to corral a liberal judiciary is nowhere as evident as in the abortion controversy. In 1976 Congress passed the Hyde Amendment which restricted government payments for abortions to indigent women under Medicaid (legislation whose constitutionality was actually upheld by the courts). Donald Granberg has pointed out that one of the provisions of the Human Rights Bill introduced in 1981 would have restricted the right of lower federal courts, which had been created by Congress, to review the bill's definition that human life begins at the moment of conception.[17] While the Human Rights Bill has yet to become law, one thing is certain—interest group opportunities to influence the political process ensure that the public debate over "legislating morality" will continue for some time to come.

This book is divided into two sections. Section One, entitled The Family and Social Policy contains material on "normal" sexual matters such as conception, contraception and abortion—issues that in the Eisenhower era would have been considered "family" matters. Section Two, "Sexual Deviancy" and Social Policy, deals with what many consider "deviant" sexual behavior: pornography and homosexuality. The Conclusion examines the administration of sexual policy in the context of increasing state and local activity.

9

Notes

1. See C. Alison McIntosh, *Population Policy in Western Europe: Responses to Low Fertility in France, Sweden and West Germany* (Armonk, New York: M.E. Sharpe Inc., 1983).

2. Leona Baumgartner, "Governmental Responsibility for Family Planning in the United States" in S.J. Behrman, M.D., Leslie Corsa Jr., M.D. and Ronald Freedman, eds., *Fertility and Family Planning—A World View* (Ann Arbor: University of Michigan Press, 1970), p. 435.

3. See Phyllis Tilson Piotrow, *World Population: The Present & Future Crisis* (New York: Foreign Policy Association, 1980), p. x.

4. See U.S. Congress. House. Committee on the Post Office and Civil Service: Subcommittee on Census and Population. *National Population Policy Hearings.* March 10–11, 1982, 97th Congress, 2d Session.

5. U.S. Congress. House. "Teen Pregnancy: What is Being Done? A State By State Look," *Report of the Select Committee on Children, Youth and Families.* p. xi. December 1985, 99th Congress, 1st Session,

6. U.S. Congress. House. Committee on Education and Labor: Subcommittee on Employment Opportunities. *Hearing on the Civil Rights Amendment Act of 1981.* January 27th, 1982, 97th Congress, 2d Session, p. 40.

7. However, it should be noted that Title XIX (Medicaid) of the Social Security Act also permitted doctors to prescribe birth control devices.

8. Hearings on the Civil Rights Amendment Act of 1981, p. xii.

9. For a more detailed discussion see Walter Barnett, *Sexual Freedom and the Constitution* (Albuquerque: University of New Mexico Press, 1973), p. 68–69.

10. See Marilyn Jane Field, *The Comparative Politics of Birth Control: Determinants of Policy Variation and Change in the Developed Nations* (New York: Praeger, 1983). It should be noted that in July 1986, the Supreme Court, by a narrow majority (5–4), struck down a Pennsylvania statute placing restrictions on abortion. Once again, the privacy argument was used by the majority. Justice Harry A. Blackmun announced: "Few decisions are more personal and intimate, more properly private, or more basic to individual dignity and autonomy, than a woman's decision . . . whether to end her pregnancy. . . . A woman's right to make that choice freely is fundamental." See *Newsweek,* June 23, 1986, p. 26.

11. See House Committee on Employment Opportunities, p. 36.

12. *Ibid.*, p. 41.

13. *Ibid.*, p. 36.

14. See Donald Granberg, "The Abortion Controversy: An Overview" in *The Humanist* 41 (July–August 1981), p. 33.

15. Quoted in Arthur Caplan, "Is it a Life?" in *The Nation,* January 21, 1984, p. 37.

16. "Report on Teen Pregnancy . . ."

17. See Granberg, "The Abortion Controversy", p. 33.

Section One:

The Family and Social Policy

1

In Vitro Fertilization, Artificial Insemination, and Individual Rights
A Review of Policy

Andrea Bonnicksen

Alternative conception includes reproductive technologies that allow couples with fertility problems to conceive. It takes place in the absence of sexual intercourse and with the aid of medical professionals. The two most common types of alternative conception are artificial insemination[1] and *in vitro* fertilization.[2] Less established variations include embryo transfer[3] and embryo cryopreservation.[4] The rate of infertility is climbing in the United States.[5] It is expected that more elaborate methods of alternative conception will be developed as reproductive technology becomes increasingly sophisticated and more infertile couples seek help.

Alternative conception holds many promises in a technological age. It offers what is often the last hope for biological parenthood for the one of every six married couples estimated to be infertile.[6] It gives to the general public an object of fascination and curiosity.[7] It also presents to medical researchers the nearly irresistible opportunity to learn about the beginning of life,[8] and allows reproductive specialists to study previously inaccessible processes that will sharpen the ability to treat patients with a wide variety of reproductive disorders.[9]

Andrea Bonnicksen is an associate professor of political science at Eastern Illinois University. This article is based on a paper presented at the Annual Meeting of the American Political Science Association in 1985.

Support is far from universal, however, and detractors of the new conceptions include religious groups[10] and lay persons who fear unbridled technology.[11] Some maintain that alternative conception unethically manipulates nature. Others, acting as advocates of the human embryo, fear that researchers will experiment with spare embryos in a way that contravenes the Western respect for human life. Many detractors believe that once the technology is accepted, other, more frightful applications will follow. This argument, known as the "slippery slope" doctrine, presumes that "once the first step is allowed, there is no way to prevent sliding down to the horrors at the bottom."[12]

Latent in these cautionary arguments is the fear, fueled by Aldous Huxley's *Brave New World* and George Orwell's *1984*, that alternative conception will be used by a dictatorial state and mechanical scientists to foist eugenic principles upon a population in a way that deprives it of autonomy, liberty, and choice. In Huxley's world genetic engineering predestined individuals to be directors, technicians, or elevator operators. In Orwell's world the proletarians were free to copulate as they wished, but party members were subject to stringent anti-sex codes that made procreation an antiseptic, scientific undertaking.

Concerns about the future misuses of alternative conception are appropriate to a point but become counter-productive when they divert attention from real and present weaknesses of today's policy to speculative and remote future dilemmas. Two types of alternative conception, artificial insemination (AID) and *in vitro* fertilization (IVF), are well enough established to warrant an assessment of their application to date. The present paper outlines the perimeters of existing policy related to AID and IVF in order to appraise the demonstrated effects of these two reproductive technologies on individual rights. Although it is possible the Huxlean model is a future prospect, the possibility is extremely remote. An inquiry into present policy reveals no signs of such a scenario. In fact, the opposite appears to be the case. In identifiable ways, the policy resulting from alternative conception has led to an expansion, not a contraction, of individual liberties.

Artificial Insemination by Donor

Artificial insemination is the oldest and simplest form of alternative conception.[13] To inseminate a woman artificially, a physician uses a special instrument to insert motile sperm directly into the uterus of a fertile woman. When done with the husband's sperm, it is known as AIH.[14] When, as is more common, it is done with the sperm of an anonymous donor, it is known as AID. Artificial insemination by donor is indicated when the male partner in a marriage has inadequate or absent sperm or when he has genetic defects he fears passing to his offspring. The success rate for AID is nearly 80 percent if carried out over a period of six or more months.[15] Every year between 10,000 and 20,000 American infants are born as a result of AID.

A negative reaction greeted AID following the establishment of the first commercial facility for handling donated sperm in 1938.[16] By the early 1950s, growing numbers of sperm cryopreservation banks encouraged a wider use of donor sperm for couples in which the male partner was infertile.[17] As early as 1949, however, Pope Pius XII chastised AID, with its use of a third person, as "immoral, and, as such, to be condemned outright."[18] He went on to say that "[t]he husband and wife alone have the reciprocal right over their bodies in order to engender a new life; and this right is exclusive, untransferable, inalienable." Similar moral refrains appeared in public policy as well. One court concluded in 1954 that "a wife who gives birth to a child fathered by a person other than her husband is considered to have committed adultery."[19]

Aside from sporadic judicial decisions that condemned AID and others that condoned it, the greatest reaction to AID was silence. No state had AID laws in the early 1960s;[20] fewer than half had AID laws by the end of that decade. Lacking official legitimation of AID, physicians and couples surreptitiously acted in a policy vacuum, with no clear idea of the rights or responsibilities of interested parties. It was unclear, for example, if physicians were obliged to screen donors for genetic defects or to secure written consent from both the donor and prospective parents. The veil of secrecy surrounding AID was not, in the long run, in the best interest of the involved parties. Physicians who inseminated the wife often deliberately failed to tell the physician who delivered the infant. This allowed the delivering physician, in good faith but erroneously, to put the husband's name on the birth certificate as the natural father. Physicians also used multiple donors within the woman's same cycle to ensure the secrecy of the donor.[21] Although such techniques protected the donor, they arguably endangered the child,

15

since it would be impossible to identify paternity in the event of a serious genetic illness.

Other doctors mixed the donor's and husband's sperm to leave open the chance that the husband might turn out to be the father. Some doctors did this even if it reduced the odds of fertilization when the husband's sperm contraindicated that of the donor.[22] It is not surprising that in this milieu, record-keeping was "woefully deficient."[23] One survey revealed that only 37 percent of AID physicians kept records on the children and only 30 percent kept records on the donor.[24]

By 1980, more accommodating laws and court decisions had emerged, accelerated by AID's growing popularity and by the 1979 publication of a survey that noted the dangers of under-regulation.[25] This evolving policy began to recognize the multiple parties to AID, including parent, child, physician, and donor, and the varied interests of each.

Judicial Decisions

Within the judicial arena, most principles of AID were developed in the context of divorce cases. When a couple that had had a child through AID divorced, the twin questions of paternity and legitimacy of the child were open to legal testing. In an early divorce case, *Strnad v. Strnad*, 190 Misc. 786, 78 N.Y.S.2d 390 (Sup. Ct. 1948), the New York court held that the child was legitimate if the husband consented to AID.[26] It granted to the former husband the same rights a natural father would have following a divorce. Later decisions affirmed this. In *Adoption of Anonymous*, 74 Misc.2d 99, 345 N.Y.S.2d 430 (Sup. Ct. 1973), for example, the court presumed the AID child was legitimate and "entitled to the rights and privileges of a naturally conceived child of the same marriage."

Although most AID decisions followed the tone set by *Strnad*, others left the interests of parties unclear. In the 1954 case of *Doornbos v. Doornbos*, No. 54, S. 1498 (Superior Court, Cook Co., December 13, 1954), an Illinois county court held that an AID child born to a married couple was conceived out of wedlock and therefore was illegitimate. In the 1963 case of *Gursky v. Gursky*, 39 Misc.2d 1083, 242 N.Y.S.2d 406 (Sup. Ct. 1963), a New York court cited *Doornbos* in its conclusion that the AID child, even though conceived with the consent of the husband, was "not the legitimate 'issue' of the husband." The court went on to confer support responsibilities on the husband following the divorce even though it did not treat him as the natural father. Five years later, in *People v. Sorenson*, 68 Cal.2d 280, 66 Cal. Rptr. 7, 437 P.2d 495 (Sup. Ct., 1968), a California court similarly imposed child support obligations on the legal father but declined to give him full father status. It called him the "lawful" father but would not treat him under the law the same as a natural father.[27]

On the whole, court decisions leave some uncertainty about the rights of the parties in AID. Most treat the husband (the legal father) the same as a natural father and most presume the legitimacy of a child born within a marriage through AID. Courts have left largely untouched potential rights of the donor,[28] however, as well as the rights of women to have access to AID.[29] The authority of the cases that have been decided is diminished by the fact that all are limited to the trial court level. To this date there has not "been a decision on the legality of artificial insemination by an appellate court."[30]

Statutes

A survey of physicians who practiced AID, published in the *New England Journal of Medicine* in 1979, showed deficiencies in the application of AID. An editorial appearing with the article concluded that it was time for legislators to "declare the legitimacy of the children, and protect the liability of all directly involved."[31] At that time, only six states had specifically legalized AID.[32] Today 24 states have AID laws on their books. For the most part these laws establish rights and are positive in tone.[33]

Some states, including California, Colorado, Minnesota, Montana, Nevada, Wisconsin, and Wyoming, have adopted Section 5 of the Uniform Parentage Act. This stipulates that if the husband and wife sign a written consent form for AID, the husband is, for legal purposes, the same as a natural father. This confers rights on the husband. Section 5 also protects the donor by stating he is not the natural father. Wisconsin's law is even more explicit on this point; it states that the donor "bears no liability for the support of the child."[34] It then makes clear that the donor "has no parental *rights* with regard to the child."[35]

State laws also establish the child's legitimacy and in this sense protect the offspring of AID. The laws do this either by stating the child is legitimate or by stating that the husband is the natural father, which has the same effect. Oregon is the only state requiring that the donor not knowingly have "any disease or defect . . . to be transmissible by genes" or a venereal disease. By so doing it protects the prospective parents and the child. Oregon is also the only state to authorize AID for unmarried women; hence, it is the only state to address the question of right of access regardless of marital status.

Several states require that AID be performed only by a licensed physician and provide for records to be kept, sealed and left unopened except under court order. Presumably, files will not be opened for specious reasons or in a way that will intrude on the donor's anonymity.

Table 1. State Laws on Artificial Insemination by Donor*

Licensed physician required
 Alaska, California, Colorado, Connecticut, Georgia, Minnesota, Montana, Nevada, New York (refers to "authorized persons"), Oklahoma, Oregon, Washington, Wisconsin, Wyoming.

Consent of husband required
 Arkansas, Louisiana, Maryland, Michigan, Tennessee, Texas.

Written consent of husband and wife required
 Alaska, California, Colorado, Connecticut, Florida, Georgia, Kansas, Minnesota, Montana, Nevada, New York, North Carolina, Oklahoma, Oregon, Washington, Wisconsin, Wyoming.

Husband's consent presumed
 Arkansas, Maryland.

Records kept and sealed
 California, Colorado, Connecticut, Kansas, Minnesota, Montana, Nevada, Oklahoma, Oregon, Washington, Wisconsin, Wyoming.

Criteria for donor established
 Oregon.

*Child of AID is legitimate***
 Alaska, Arkansas, Connecticut, Florida, Georgia, Kansas, Maryland, Michigan, New York, North Carolina, Oklahoma, Tennessee, Texas.

*Husband is treated as the natural father***
 California, Colorado, Louisiana (the husband cannot disavow paternity if he consented to AID), Minnesota, Montana, Nevada, Oregon, Washington, Wisconsin, Wyoming.

Specifies that donor is not the father
California, Colorado, Minnesota, Montana, Nevada, Texas, Washington ("unless the donor and the woman agree in writing that said donor shall be the father"), Wisconsin, Wyoming.

Specifies that donor has no rights or obligations
Connecticut (neither the donor nor his relatives can inherit from the child; the donor has no right or interest in the child), Oregon, Wisconsin.

Authorizes AID for unmarried women
Georgia (the statute refers to artificial insemination on "any female human being" but elsewhere requires written consent of husband and wife), Oregon.

*The Virginia statute was unavailable at the time of this writing.

**These have the same effect, which is to recognize the child's legitimacy, but they do this through different means. One grants legitimacy directly to the child; the other grants the child legitimacy through the husband by declaring him to be the natural father.

The following list of statutes was obtained from Andrews (1984a):300–301:
Alaska Stat. s.24.20.045 (Supp. 1982); Ark.Stat.Ann. s.61-141 (1971); Cal. Civ. Code s.7005 (West Supp. 1983); Colo. Rev. Sta. s.19-6-106 (1978); Conn. Gen. Stat. ss.45-69f to -69n (1981); Fla. Stat. Ann. s.742.11 (West Supp. (1983); Ga. Code Ann. ss.74-101.1,-9904 (1982); Kan. Stat. Ann. ss.23-128 to 130 (1981); La. Civ. Code Ann. art. 188 (West Supp. 1983); Md. Est. & Trusts Code Ann. s.1-206(b) (1974); Mich. Comp. laws Ann. s.333.2824 (1980); and s.700.111 (1980); Minn. Stat. Ann. s.257.56; Mont. Rev. Code Ann. s.40-6-106 (1981); Nev. Rev. Stat. s.126.061 (1979); N.Y. Dom. Rel. Law s.73 (McKinney 1977); N.C. Gen. Stat. s.49A-1 (1976); Okla. Stat. Ann. tit. 10, ss.551-553 (West Supp. 1982-1983); Or. Rev. Stat. ss.109.239, et seq. (1981); Tenn. Code Ann. s.53-446 (Supp. 1981); Tex. Fam. Code Ann. s.12.03 (Vernon 1975); Va. Code s.64.1-7.1 (1980); Wash. Rev. Code Ann. s.26.26.050 (West Supp. 1983-1984); Wis. Stat Ann. s.767.47 (9) (West 1981), s.891.40 (West Supp. 1982-1983); Wyo. Stat. s.14-2-103 (1978).

In summary, nearly one-half of the states provide a congenial context for AID by declaring the AID child to be the legitimate offspring of a consenting husband and wife. Most of the state laws go no further than this, however. Oregon, with a law that requires genetic screening and details the donor's lack of rights and obligations vis-a-vis the child, is the exception. Its law addresses the interests of multiple parties—the parents, child, donor, and physician. Fully half of the states are silent on the issue of AID. A dearth of policy surely makes some physicians wary of performing AID and couples hesitant to seek it. Silence detracts from access to AID and leaves infertile couples with fewer options.

Voluntary Guidelines

Voluntary guidelines drawn up by medical groups have done more than public policy to define the rights and responsibilities of AID participants. Two of the more important, those proposed by the American Fertility Society (AFS) and the American Association of Tissue Banks (AATB), were issued following the publication of the 1979 survey in the *New England Journal of Medicine*. They demonstrate the willingness of the medical profession to police itself, especially when doing so may forestall government regulation. The AATB, for example, notes that government policy is desirable at times but should be minimal in order to "protect but not stifle scientific and clinical development." It would welcome federal policy mandating the screening of donor sperm for transmissible diseases.[36] It recognizes that without policy, "[i]ncidents of diseases caused by insemination of donor sperm could do damage to both the public and the future of human semen cryobanking."

The Ad Hoc Committee on Artificial Insemination of the AFS issued its report in November, 1980, establishing guidelines for donor selection, recipient selection, and techniques for freezing semen.[37] The report also proposed model legislation and developed a sample agreement of understanding to be signed by parties to AID. Among other things, the report recommends that AID be performed only by a licensed physician,[38] donors be screened for genetic illness, and the donor sign a consent form. It also absolves the donor of any "rights in or liability to" the child conceived through the donation of his sperm. The report outlines the physician's obligations and clears the practitioner of liability if the recipient does not disclose her marital status or if there are pregnancy complications, defects in the child, or sexually transmitted diseases in the recipient. It also declares nonliability for wrongful birth actions, status as an accessory to adultery, and child support.

One section grants the child legitimate status and specifies that the child "shall have all the rights of a child conceived by natural means using the spouse's sperm, including but not limited to the rights of inheritance and support." It explicitly states the child is not the donor's child and that AID with the spouse's consent is not an act of adultery by the mother.

The AATB guidelines are detailed and quite long.[39] They provide for rigorous screening of donors for personality, physical characteristics, and occupational, historical or other factors that may pose a risk of defect in the infant.[40] The standards are so stringent that they give credence to the oft-made observation that the child of AID is more protected than the average child of a natural union where the father is not screened at all. The AATB warns its members to police themselves so that self-regulation will stave off government regulation. Although the guidelines themselves do not define the rights of parties, they do communicate the message that families have the right to a healthy child. Standardization, the AATB states, protects "the recipient, the progeny and the family unit."

Physicians adhere to voluntary guidelines in varying degrees. Some private physicians act in the virtual absence of guidelines; others follow rather rigid rules. For example, Chicago's cryobank, the Cryo Lab Facility (one of sixteen sperm cryobanks in the United States), screens for a long list of problems, among them Tay-Sachs, sickle-cell anemia, hepatitis, and syphilis; takes an oral three-generation medical history; and limits the number of pregnancies per donor to five.[41] The University of North Carolina at Chapel Hill screens its donors two times a year for gonococcus.[42] It also conducts a lengthy genetic screening and in August, 1983, began to forbid homosexuals from donating, a move that raises the question of whether men can be turned away solely because of their sexual orientation.

In summary, voluntary practices do more than statutes or court decisions to protect individual interests. The screening recommendations evince a concern for quality that is important for individual rights. Although not explicitly stated, the message of these recommendations is that prospective parents have an interest in a healthy child and the offspring of AID have an interest in being born healthy. The provisions relating to record keeping and secrecy recognize and codify the interest of the donor. Overall, the guidelines address all facets of AID, including donor screening, donor consent, recipient consent, and sperm preservation techniques. They recognize the interests of multiple parties—donor, recipient, child, and practitioner—and attempt to achieve these interests in a positive, nonpunitive sense. The key weaknesses are promulgation and enforcement. Inasmuch as these are only voluntary recommendations, peer sanctions are the only grounds for enforcement. At the least, they help establish a standard that can be used by policy-makers considering future legislation.

Summary

Artificial insemination by donor was introduced in the U.S. in the midst of hostile assumptions that AID was adulterous and produced an illegitimate child. Today, some 40 years later, AID is practiced amid an increasingly hospitable terrain characterized by statutes in 24 states that define, in varying degrees, the rights and responsibilities of interested parties. The most detailed law is that of Oregon, which defines AID, provides for AID for single women, calls for the screening of the donor, and spells out the rights and obligations of the child and donor. New laws appear to have been prompted by voluntary guidelines within the medical profession. This suggests that self-regulation can substitute for official regulation or can set a standard for the content of public policy.

Existing AID policy recognizes groups with claimed rights, including the donor, recipient couple, legal father, and child. It recognizes various dimensions of these rights, such as the donor's right to privacy, the couple's right to a legitimate family unit, and the child's right to legitimacy. To this extent it expands individual rights. AID was at first a unidimensional issue revolving around the legitimacy of the child. With application and litigation has come a subdivision of the issue so that today AID is increasingly an individualized matter. The shift from simple generalizations to more complex realities promotes the habit of attending to individual interests that is a hallmark of civil liberties.

A number of questions remain that are likely to be litigated and/or legislated in the future and will continue to direct attention to individual rights. Questions about the rights of donors have heretofore focused on the need for anonymity, for example, but other issues remain. May a potential donor turned away for sexual orientation claim discrimination and thus raise the issue of a right to donate? Will donors one day claim an interest in finding their offspring, much as women who once gave up infants for adoption try to find them years later? Does the donor have the right to stipulate who receives his sperm?

Another issue that has already risen is the right of the AID child to have access to files to find out the identity of the donor who is his or her biological father.[43] The measures doctors have taken in the past to protect the donor's anonymity make such a quest often impossible. New laws that require record-keeping in state departments of health will change this, however, and it is likely that court orders will be sought to discover the donor's identity. Here a balance must be drawn between the rights of the donor and the rights of the offspring.

The policy on AID implicitly recognizes new dimensions on the right to bodily privacy. It recognizes the right to choose *to* conceive, which is a corollary of the right *not to* conceive that was given constitutional basis in the Supreme Court decisions of *Griswold v. Connecticut*, 381 U.S. 479 (1965) and *Eisenstadt v. Baird*, 405 U.S. 438 (1972), yet it does not explicitly make this part of policy. Thus, the right to conceive is still less established than the right not to conceive. Reproductive rights will be expanded when the right to conceive is granted full legal or constitutional status.

If it errs in either direction, the state errs on the side of under-, not over-regulation. It is clear that AID is not used by an authoritarian state to foist a laboratory technique on an unwitting public along the lines of Huxley's *Brave New World*. On the contrary, AID remains inaccessible to some couples as a result of ambiguous policy that makes physicians wary of using donated sperm. Alternative conception is an individual option, not a government protocol. The real issue is whether there is a right *to* AID, not a freedom from it.

In Vitro Fertilization

The first human infant to have been fertilized *in vitro*, Louise Brown, was born in 1978 in England. Since then over 400 *in vitro* babies have been born around the world. Nearly 100 of these have been born in the U.S. *In vitro* fertilization is used primarily for women with blocked or missing Fallopian tubes that prevent ova from traveling down the tubes for fertilization.[44] In 1982 only ten programs operated in the U.S. By 1984 the number had grown to

64. One physician opined that IVF centers will be "coming out of the woodwork in the next few years."[45]

The birth of Louise Brown and subsequent babies created an intense reaction, both positive and negative. On the one hand, the public looked with satisfaction at pictures of an attractive infant girl born after conception in a glass dish. Infertile women looked with interest on IVF's possibilities, and researchers applauded a technique that furthered the benevolent aim of creating life.

On the other hand, IVF unleashed a spate of moral and ethical debates. Detractors claimed that IVF manipulated nature and was not natural.[46] They feared that it would lead to frightening things, such as the loss of family,[47] commercial sales of human eggs and embryos,[48] cloning,[49] animal-human hybrids, and extracorporeal gestation.[50] Finally, they condemned what they saw as experimentation with human embryos.[51]

The first indication of official reaction to IVF came before the birth of Louise Brown but after English researchers began experimenting with IVF. Dr. Pierre Soupart of Vanderbilt University requested $375,000 from the National Institutes of Health for a three-year study of IVF's safety.[52] In response, NIH officials asked the Ethics Advisory Board (EAB) of the then Department of Health, Education, and Welfare to determine if experimentation with embryos were ethical. The board members, appointed in 1977, issued a generally positive report in 1979 concluding that federal support "would be acceptable from an ethical standpoint."[53] The EAB noted that "the human embryo is entitled to profound respect" but it concluded that embryos do not enjoy "the full legal and moral rights attributed to persons."[54] Moreover, it took note of the high rate of embryo loss in nature. Most embryos, unbeknownst to the male and female couple, are silently sloughed out of the body. Of all eggs fertilized in a living human female, only 37 percent go on to become babies. The other 63 percent are lost, often as nature's way of ridding itself of defective embryos.[55]

With this in mind, and also with the idea that IVF's purpose was to create life, the EAB concluded that embryo loss is ethically acceptable in order to help couples conceive, provided that: the research followed guidelines in the Code of Federal Regulations about experimentation with humans, was designed primarily to establish IVF safety, was begun only after all parties were informed about the research, and did not experiment upon embryos beyond fourteen days.[56] The board recognized that an "opportunity for abuse" existed but felt that this did not justify broadly forbidding all IVF research.[57]

Despite the positive recommendations, the government turned down Soupart's proposal and has declined to fund IVF research in the years since. This decision has made IVF an oddity within the medical field in that the clinical application of IVF on infertile couples has preceded scientific experimentation. This makes infertile couples, upon whom an incompletely studied technology is applied, unwitting, albeit eager, experimental subjects. It is not farfetched to presume that the IVF success rate, still "depressingly low,"[58] would be more impressive had IVF been buttressed by experimentation in controlled scientific conditions. Absent governmental funding, however, such experimentation is unlikely to take place. The government's funding refusal has had other impacts as well. The ambiguity of IVF's status inhibits doctors in some states from practicing IVF. This puts an added burden on infertile couples who must travel to another state to have access to the technique. The experimental status of IVF also deters insurance companies from reimbursing users fully for their expenses.[59]

The federal government's reluctance to fund IVF is done not so much from intransigence but from moral and ethical hesitations over the status of the embryo. To this extent, it represents a concern for individual rights—those of the embryo—which is commendable in a nation with a history of respect for civil rights. Yet it also represents a misplaced absolutism that focuses almost solely on the embryo's interests. A more judicious concern for individual rights would weigh the embryo's interests in relation to those of other parties, such as the interests of the prospective parents in conception. The funding refusal gives the embryo the absolute right not to be experimented upon. The issue is still unidimensional and will continue to be that way until further litigation and policy unfold the multidimensional nature of the situation.

Judicial Decisions

Two judicial decisions support IVF in principle. The first, a case that stayed at the trial court level, dates to 1973, when Doris and John Del Zio of Florida became the first American couple to try

IVF.[60] Mrs. Del Zio had a laparoscopy at New York's Columbia/Presbyterian Hospital in which an egg was retrieved. The Chairman of the Department of Obstetrics and Gynecology, apparently fearful of the legal repercussions of this untested technique, refused to allow the procedure to go on, and, the story goes, opened the container that held the egg. Her physical status prevented Mrs. Del Zio from having another laparoscopy. The couple filed suit in 1974. Four years later, shortly after the birth of the world's first IVF baby, a trial court awarded $50,000 to Mrs. Del Zio for mental anguish. The case established no legal precedent although it did, in the words of one observer, point to a couple's "right to collect damages when someone tries to thwart their *in vitro* fertilization."[61]

The second IVF case arose as a result of an Illinois law stating that any person who united ovum and sperm outside the human body was "deemed to have the care and custody" of the child.[62] This effectively chilled IVF in Illinois, mainly because it was unclear when the physician's custody ended. One state representative in legislative debate asked if, for example, a doctor or nurse who assisted in *in vitro* fertilization could "be somehow called upon years later to pay for an appendectomy for [the resulting] child." The bill's sponsor said "yes."[63]

In response to this law, an Illinois couple who wanted to try IVF filed a class action suit along with their physician and the American Civil Liberties Union of Illinois on behalf of other infertile couples who could be helped by IVF.[64] The Attorney General of Illinois and the State's Attorney of Cook County wrote an opinion stating that physicians were within the law if they refrained from "willfully endangering or injuring the embryo." The destruction of an embryo would be, under the law, the same as a legal abortion.

This opinion established a parallel between the embryo and the fetus by noting that inasmuch as abortions are legal, it would make little sense to consider the destruction of an embryo, which is considerably less developed than a fetus, not to be legal. The case also pointed to the right of an embryo not to be experimented upon in a way that would willfully injure it. The decision was enough to encourage Illinois physicians to go ahead with IVF with the idea that they would transfer all embryos to avoid custodial ambiguities. Still, as representatives in the Illinois legislature themselves note, "a legal cloud exists over . . . *in vitro* fertilization" in the state.[65]

Of perhaps more importance as a policy guide in the judicial arena are the U.S. Supreme Court decisions dealing with reproductive freedom. Although they do not relate directly to *in vitro* fertilization, they do establish the rights of individuals to make decisions about whether to bear or beget a child. These decisions establish a couple's constitutional right to decide not to conceive a child (*Griswold v. Connecticut,* 381 U.S. 479 [1965]) or not to bear one (*Roe v. Wade,* 410 U.S. 113 [1973]). *In vitro* fertilization raises issues about a couple's right to decide *to* conceive a child. The precedent arising from the Court's reproductive privacy cases led the EAB authors to warn that "where reproductive decisions are concerned, it is important to guard against unwarranted governmental intrusion into personal and marital privacy."[66] In addition, as one author notes,"[t]here is no question that a married couple has a right to determine whether and when to bear a child through intercourse."[67] It seems reasonable to presume the couple has the same right to decide whether and when to conceive a child through artificially aided techniques.

Statutes

The EAB report recommended that "model or uniform laws . . . be developed to define the rights and responsibilities of all parties involved in [*in vitro* fertilization]."[68] States have not implemented this recommendation, although a number of laws do cover IVF issues. Three types of laws relate to IVF: federal laws regulating human experimentation, laws limiting fetal research, and laws limiting research on embryos. The first type encompasses federal policy stipulating that medical institutions receiving federal funds have Institutional Review Boards to review research involving human subjects.[69] The second type includes state laws limiting research on fetuses that are about to be aborted or that have been aborted.[70] A list of these states is included in Table 2. The variety of terms is confusing; it is not clear whether a "live premature child," "any unborn or aborted child," and "fetuses" include embryos fertilized *in vitro*. Although the intent of the framers of these statutes was to limit research on aborted or about-to-be-aborted fetuses, courts in each state could conceivably extend the words of the laws to include embryos.

The third type of law, statutes covering embryos, has been enacted in several states. Once again the terminology varies. The states variously refer to an "embryo," "a human conceptus," and "the product of conception," and limit research on this entity. Only two states mention *in vitro* fertilization by name. The laws forbid experimentation on embryos altogether or forbid it without the mother's consent. Some states allow experimentation in order to diagnose a disease of the mother or to preserve the mother's or embryo's health. Most of the laws also forbid the sale, transfer, or distribution of embryos or fetuses for improper uses. This addresses the fear that eggs or embryos will be sold to infertile couples or research firms. A similar fear in Britain has been addressed by the proposal that Parliament forbid cloning, cultivation of embryos beyond early stages, transfer of embryos used for research, the sale or export of embryos, and breeding of embryos for research purposes.[71]

Pennsylvania is the only state to go beyond the question of experimentation in IVF. It requires that records be kept of the names, locations and sponsors of IVF. It also asks practitioners to keep records of the number of eggs fertilized, destroyed, and implanted during the *in vitro* process.

In summary, statutes on IVF are inchoate. Most of the states are silent on the issue. The states with policy focus on experimentation, which is far different from establishing guidelines that define the rights and responsibilities of the involved parties. Pennsylvania is the only state that sets parameters for the process of IVF itself and it does this only cursorily. Guidelines are still needed in all states to protect the interests of parties in IVF. It would be reasonable, for example, to set minimum qualifications for IVF practitioners and programs, as AID laws limit the practice to licensed physicians. It would also be expedient to require record-keeping, provided the laws also protect physicians from liability for admitting embryos are destroyed. Records would protect the interests of prospective parents by giving them data with which to compare and contrast success rates for various facilities; minimum qualifications would protect the parents as consumers of IVF. Either addition to the laws would diversify policy beyond the now single-minded concern for the embryo.[72]

Voluntary Guidelines

In February, 1984, the official journal of the American Fertility Society, *Fertility and Sterility*, published an "Ethical Statement on *In*

Vitro Fertilization"[73] and "Minimal Standards for Programs of *In Vitro* Fertilization."[74] The Ethical Statement, representing the consensus of a special ethics committee set up within the AFS, opined that concepti are the property of the people who donated their eggs and sperm for fertilization. The "owners" may donate the concepti to other couples or they may offer them for examination providing certain limits are respected. Concepti may be examined for only 14 days after insemination and must be disposed of after that time. Any cryopreservation of the concepti must be done only for "the reproductive life of the female donor." The statement went on to conclude that IVF in general is ethical, as is the donation of sperm and oocytes. The statement, especially with its fourteen day limit, reflects the conclusion reached five years earlier in the report of HEW's Ethics Advisory Board.[75]

The matter of oocyte donation anticipates issues that will be raised in embryo transfer. The ethical statement makes the question of donation an essentially private matter between couples and their physicians. It also brings sperm, eggs, and embryos to the same level. Although all are microscopic collections of cells of similar physiological significance, different public auras have been attached to them. Sperm are treated as disposable. Eggs, only recently released from their internal homes for viewing by outsiders, have a positive mystique attached to them. Hence the question of egg donation raises more concern than sperm donation. Human embryos, too, have been only recently available for other humans to view. They, too, have a mysterious aura attached to them even though, technically, they are simply "collections of cells, and not . . . fetuses."[76]

The "Minimal Standards for Programs of *In Vitro* Fertilization" recommends that confidential records be kept of the steps of *in vitro* fertilization, including the number of eggs recovered, fertilized, cleaved, and transferred; and the number of pregnancies and births. It also recommends that summaries of the statistics be made available to the public. It mirrors the Pennsylvania law, which also calls for record-keeping.

The AFS has now set up a committee, composed of American IVF pioneers, informally titled the "Special Interest Group in *In Vitro* Fertilization," to look into, among other things, certification of *in vitro* programs.[77] The minimal requirements for AFS approval will presumably include a requirement for staffing. As one physician has suggested, minimum credentials for certification might include on each IVF team a supervising reproductive endocrinologist, a cell biologist experienced in handling human tissues, including embryos; an expert in semenology; a steroid biochemist; a person trained in ultrasonography, and an infertility surgeon.[78] *In vitro* physicians agree that the laboratory work is extremely important in IVF and that everything, from the closing of doors to the choice of pipettes, is under scrutiny as a possible variable affecting the fertilization of the egg and the development of the embryo.[79] The possibility that new IVF programs will be started without proper laboratory staffing is of concern to physicians at established IVF centers.

Voluntary guidelines can arguably forestall or replace government regulation. They can also set a standard that will direct the content of that regulation if it does occur. Inasmuch as there is no central clearinghouse for IVF researchers,[80] it is unclear how many physicians receive standards such as those published in *Fertility and Sterility* and follow them thereafter. Moreover, existing legal ambiguities work against open reporting of results. Physicians who publish the results of their programs, including information on the number of embryos not transferred, put themselves at risk. This helps explain why a national or international registry of results has thus far proved elusive.

Another form of self-regulation comes from guidelines formulated within each hospital where *in vitro* fertilization is performed. Vanderbilt University Medical Center, for example, has an ethicist on staff who has helped formulate internal guidelines. Hospitals receiving federal funds have institutional review boards that watch over experimental procedures. Other hospitals have detailed consent forms that inform prospective couples of the risks of IVF.[81] In the absence of detailed public policy, patients themselves must bear part of the responsibility for selecting a center that conforms with acceptable criteria. Dr. Joseph Schulman of the *in vitro* program at George Washington University recommends that couples ask whether the IVF program they have chosen conforms to the AFS standards.[82] Dr. Jan Friberg of Mount Sinai Hospital Medical Center in Chicago suggests that prospective patients ask if the hospital has an institutional review board.[83] Other physicians suggest that patients select a medical center connected with an academic setting.

In summary, guidelines developed with the private sector do more than public policy in addressing problematic issues, such as the ownership of the concepti, the length of time a conceptus may be frozen, and the length of time a conceptus may be kept alive without being frozen. They give credence to the observation of Dr. Howard Jones, founder of the nation's first IVF center in Norfolk, Virginia, that "[m]edicine in general has done very well in this matter by regulating itself."[84] The guidelines are pragmatic rather than speculative; they are limited to existing problems and do not anticipate future problems such as cloning and commercialism. As Jones says, "it is only logical that a discussion of the ethics of *in vitro* fertilization be confined to a discussion of the ethics of *in vitro* fertilization."[85]

The medical profession shows some uncertainty over the degree of regulation desired. On the one hand, physicians are not wont to invite government participation in medical decisions. On the other hand, as one doctor puts it, "once *in vitro* fertilization starts to be regulated, it will also be funded."[86] There is also the fear, expressed by Dr. Alan De Cherney of Yale University, that if no one else takes the initiative to manage and oversee *in vitro* fertilization, the physicians will be mired in administrative duties that will push them further from the art of IVF medicine and toward the technocracy of it.[87] De Cherney fears IVF centers "managed by administrator-businessmen and white-frocked *technodocs*." Paradoxically, he goes on, "constraint may ultimately provide greater freedom." By developing its own guidelines before governmental regulations become established, the medical profession increases the odds that regulation, once it develops, will follow the direction set within the medical community.

Table 2. State Laws Relating to In Vitro Fertilization

Mentions in vitro fertilization by name
New Mexico (defined as "any fertilization of human ova which occurs outside the body of a female"), Pennsylvania (defined as the "purposeful fertilization of a human ovum outside the body of a living human female").

Forbids nontherapeutic experimentation on . . .
Arizona (embryo)

California ("aborted product of human conception other than fetal remains")

Illinois (fetus or unborn child defined as "a human being from fertilization until birth")

Indiana (aborted fetus)

Kentucky (live or viable aborted child)

Louisiana (human embryo or fetus)

Maine (live human fetus, where any "live born" is the "product of conception after complete expulsion from its mother, irrespective of the duration of pregnancy" [this excludes embryos conceived in vitro but would cover embryo transfer])

Massachusetts (live human fetus)

Michigan (live human embryo)

Minnesota (living human conceptus, where a conceptus is defined as "any human organism, conceived either in the human body or produced in an artificial environment other than the human body, from fertilization through the first 265 days thereafter")

Missouri (fetus or child aborted alive)

Montana (live premature child)

Nebraska (live or viable aborted child)

New Mexico (product of conception from the time of conception)

North Dakota (fetus, which includes an embryo)

Ohio (the product of human conception)

Oklahoma (child or unborn child resulting from an abortion)

Pennsylvania (any unborn or aborted child where unborn child is a "human being from fertilization until birth")

Rhode Island (fetus, which includes "an embryo or neonate")

South Dakota (fetuses)

Tennessee (aborted fetus)

Utah (live or unborn child)

Wyoming (live or viable aborted child)

Allows diagnostic procedures to preserve health of fetus or embryo

Arizona, Massachusetts, Michigan, Minnesota, Missouri, Nebraska, New Mexico, North Dakota, Oklahoma, Rhode Island, Utah

Allows experimentation on dead fetus with mother's consent

Illinois, Massachusetts, Michigan, North Dakota, Pennsylvania, Rhode Island, South Dakota, Tennessee

The following list of statutes was obtained from Andrews (1984a:297-298):

Ariz. Rev. Stat. Ann. s.3602302 (Supp. 1982-1983); Cal. Health & Safety Code s.25956 (West Supp. 1983); Ill. Ann. Stat. ch. 38 s.81-26,-32,-32.1 (Smith-Hurd Supp. 1983–1984); Ind. Code s.35-1-58.5-6 (1979); Ky. Rev. Stat. Ann. s.436.026 (1975); La. Rev. Stat. Ann. s.14:87.2 (West 1974); Me. Rev. Stat. Ann. tit. 22 s.1593 (West 1980); Mass. Ann. Laws ch.112s.12J (Michie/Law Co-op Supp. 1982); Mich. Comp. Laws Ann. ss.333.2685-.2692 (West 1980); Minn. Stat. Ann. s.145.421-.422 (West Supp. 1982); Mo. Ann. Stat. s.188.037 (Vernon Supp. 1983); Mont. Code Ann. s.50-20-108 (3) (1981); Neb. Rev. Stat. s.28-342, 28-346 (1979); N.M. Stat.

Ann. s.24-9A-1 et seq. (1981); N. D. Cent. Codes .14-02.2-01 to -02 (Allen Smith 1981); Ohio Rev. Code Ann. s.2919.14 (Baldwin 1982); Okla. Stat. Ann. tit. 63 s.1-735 (West Supp. 1982-1983); Pa. Stat. Ann. tit. 18 s.3216 (Purdon Supp. 1983–1984); R. I. Gen. Laws s.11-54-2 (Supp. 1982); S. D. Comp. Laws Ann. s.34-23A-17 (1977); Tenn. Code Ann. s.39-4-208); Utah Code Ann. s.76-7-310 (Allen Smith 1978); Wyo. Stat. 35-0-113 (1977).

Summary

In vitro fertilization started off with a groundswell of ethical and moral charges and countercharges. Great excitement accompanied the birth of the world's first IVF baby; at the same time, ethicists issued alarm calls. Forgotten in all this was the infertile couple. Their right to conceive has been largely overlooked in the furor over experimentation. Most attention has been drawn to the embryo.

In vitro fertilization policy identifies the interests of a new group—the embryo. The EAB report stated that "the human embryo is entitled to profound respect," but went on to note that "this respect does not necessarily encompass the full legal and moral rights attributed to persons."[88] It concluded that some embryo loss for the purpose of helping infertile couples conceive is "acceptable from an ethical standpoint, within the limits established in the report." Thus, in balancing the interests of the embryo and the interests of the infertile couple, the board ultimately weighted the couple's interests more heavily. Despite this conclusion, state statutes appear to weigh the embryo's interests more carefully than those of the prospective parents. The statutes focus on limiting experimentation on embryos. Apart from those states that allow fetal or embryo experimentation to diagnose remedial action for the mother, the interests of the adults who have given their eggs or sperm are not mentioned. Statutory law promotes the rights of the embryo. It forbids nontherapeutic experimentation not intended to preserve the embryo's life or health. This establishes the embryo's right not to be examined for reasons other than to preserve its life or health and it grants to the embryo a certain autonomy. Thus far, only nonauthoritative bodies, such as the EAB and the American Fertility Society, address the rights of the prospective parents.

In vitro fertilization policy, as AID policy, shows that a Brave New World of government-foisted techniques is not in sight. Instead, the federal government, by not funding IVF research, and state governments, by protecting embryos, make access to IVF difficult.

No authoritative policy has recognized a right of infertile couples to conceive that parallels the right of a fertile couple not to conceive. *In vitro* policy is still a largely unidimensional body of law that focuses on the rights of the embryo. To this extent the law promotes interests of one group (embryos) at the expense of those of another (parents). However, just as AID policy eventually became more multidimensional as it focused on issues other than the child's legitimacy, so too will IVF policy, with time, litigation, and prompting from the private sector, take on an increasingly complex tone recognizing the interests of varied participants.

Conclusion

Alternative conception is the creation of the human conceptus in the absence of sexual intercourse. It is done either in a hospital, as in the case of *in vitro* fertilization or embryo transfer, or in a physician's office, as in the case of artificial insemination. A third party applies the technique; other parties may or may not contribute ova and sperm. Alternative conception is used by couples who are either infertile or who wish not to pass genetic defects to their offspring.

Artificial insemination, *in vitro* fertilization, and embryo transfer have enough in common to warrant joint study as the technology of alternative conception. This technology is based on a simple principle: after sperm is obtained, it may be used to fertilize a human ovum by inserting it directly into the uterus (fertilization *in vivo*) or by uniting sperm and ovum in a glass dish (fertilization *in vitro*). Variations of this technique exist and are especially numerous if donor tissues are used. The offspring may be partly, wholly, or not at all related genetically to the legal parents. The freezing of embryos, first practiced in Australia and only recently begun in the United States, opens up further possibilities.

Once the technology of alternative conception is identified, the next step is to study the law that is a corollary of it. "It is as it should be," Oliver Wendell Holmes once said, "that the law is always behind the times."[89] True to form, the policy on alternative conception is incomplete and tentative. A policy is emerging, however, and it is the purpose of this paper to identify its rudiments, as measured by judicial, legislative, and medical reaction to AID and IVF.

At the very least, the paper revealed the feasibility of studying the policy of alternative conception as an entity.

Artificial insemination and *in vitro* fertilization, although different techniques, raise similar policy concerns. In varying degrees, each suggests the need for policy relating to, for example, the freezing and storage of sperm, ova, and embryos; ownership of donated tissues; legality of selecting only certain "types" of people for receipt of the tissues; buying and selling of tissues; rights of access of all people to the tissues; and disposal of sperm, ova, and embryos. To accept alternative conception as an area of policy study is to suggest research ideas relating to three basic areas of policy research: history, process, and impact.

This paper draws several conclusions about the nature of alternative conception policy:

1. As it originally evolved, the policy of alternative conception was largely unidimensional, focusing on the legitimacy of the child in AID and the rights of the embryo in IVF. It demonstrated a concern for those entities that emerged from the technology, and not for the users of it.

2. The policy of alternative conception has become increasingly multidimensional as litigation has increased. The legal arena gives users of the techniques (prospective parents and practitioners) the opportunity to raise public claims.

3. State statutes have speeded policy multidimensionality more than have federal regulations. Even though state statutes appear to lack uniformity, they address a range of issues that prompt policy makers to consider a variety of individual interests. State experimentation reveals the complexity of this issue. It plays its traditional role in providing a testing ground for policy before the federal government puts a uniform cast on that policy.

4. Within the inchoate nature of the evolving policy, voluntary guidelines developed by private medical groups have encouraged a concern for the multidimensional nature of the issue. The practitioners of a technique in this case have demonstrated a greater appreciation of the rights and responsibilities of multiple parties than have public decision-makers. This points to the possible role private interest groups play in protecting individual rights when complex technologies are at stake. Their incentive is to forestall government regulation or to provide a model for regulation if it appears to be inevitable.

5. With litigation and legislation has come an appreciation of the relativity of each right claimed in alternative conception. The more parties that are uncovered and the more rights that are claimed, the greater the relativity of each claimed interest. The process is additive; the need to balance conflicting rights encourages yet more litigation and legislation.

In short, alternative conception techniques have expanded individual rights by directing attention to these rights, stimulating new groups of litigants to come forth with asserted claims, and, generally, encouraging a habit of looking at the implications of the technologies on individual rights. The technology of alternative conception is Janus-like in the literature. It is seen on the one hand as a last hope for infertile couples. It is seen on the other hand as a weapon associated with negative and frightful images. It is the stuff of negative utopias such as those fictionalized by Huxley and Orwell. In the wrong hands, writers assume, technology turns into a brutal instrument capable of quashing the very people who brought it about.

Artificial insemination and *in vitro* fertilization, as reproductive technologies of the twentieth century, show that technology in fact is less harmful than technology in fiction. It is, in fact, helpful. One key is the individualized, decentralized nature of the political system, which divides issues into concrete, justiciable matters that are dealt with in an incremental, relatively dispassionate manner. The judicial arena, for example, is "essentially backwards-looking."[90] It does not prevent abuses but instead "vindicate[s] the rights of plaintiffs who have suffered abuse."[91] The propensity of judges to react rather than initiate helps mitigate the speculative nature of the ills of alternative conception that are debated in the popular press.

Aldous Huxley spurs the imagination; empirical inquiry fosters realism. An inquiry into existing policy reveals that new techniques have created a receptive, not authoritarian, climate for individual rights. The growth of parties and rights has focused new attention on and sensitivity to individual rights. The technology of alternative conception offers couples a choice. As one physician notes, "people are afraid of new techniques and think they are being victimized."[92] What they do not realize, he continues, "is that nothing is done without the person's permission." The policy of alternative conception sets the framework, creating a sensitivity to the interests of varied parties. The actual decisions are made against this backdrop by the users themselves. The technique and its policy maximize individual choice.

Notes

I wish to acknowledge the help provided by the Council of Faculty Research, Eastern Illinois University, that made much of the research for this paper possible. I also wish to thank the staff at the Center for Fertility and Reproductive Research at Vanderbilt University Medical Center, particularly Dr. Anne Colston Wentz, Dr. Bobby Webster, Ms. Carol Dalglish, Ms. Catherine Garner, Dr. B. Jane Rogers, and Dr. Richard M. Zaner; Dr. Jan Friberg of Mount Sinai Hospital Medical Center, Chicago; and Dr. Edward Marut of Michael Reese Hospital, Chicago.

1. See *infra*, p. 2.

2. See *infra*, p. 9 and note 58.

3. Here a surrogate mother is artificially inseminated with the sperm of the father-to-be. If a conception takes place, five days later the embryo is removed from the surrogate and transferred to the wife. If the embryo attaches itself to the placenta, a pregnancy occurs and approximately 36 weeks later the wife will have the child. Embryo transfer is used when the woman has a normal uterus and is capable of carrying a child but does not produce normal ova. It is estimated that this condition afflicts up to 50,000 American women. At present, two infants have been born as a result of embryo transfer.

For the techniques of embryo transfer, see Harris Brotman, "Human Embryo Transplants," *The New York Times Magazine*, Jan. 8, 1984, pp. 42–49; John E. Buster, *et al.*, "Non-Surgical Transfer of an In-Vivo Fertilised Donated Ovum to an Infertility Patient," 8328 *Lancet* 816 (April 9, 1983); Maria Bustillo, *et al.*, "Delivery of a Healthy Infant Following Nonsurgical Ovum Transfer," Letter to Editor, 251 *Journal of the American Medical Association* 889 (Feb. 17, 1984); D. Franklin, "Embryo Transfer: It's a Boy," 125 *Science News* 85 (Feb. 11, 1984); Gary D. Hodgen, "Surrogate Embryo Transfer Combined with Estrogen-Progesterone Therapy in Monkeys" 250 *Journal of the American Medical Association* 2167 (Oct. 28, 1983); and J. A. Treichel, "Embryo Transfers Achieved in Humans," 124 *Science News* 69 (July 30, 1983). For a discussion of the problems and promises of embryo transfer, see Howard W. Jones, Jr., "Variations on a Theme," 250 *Journal of the American Medical Association* 2182 (Oct. 28, 1983); and LeRoy Walters, "Ethical Aspects of Surrogate Embryo Transfer." 250 *Journal of the American Medical Association* 2183 (Oct. 28, 1983).

4. Already one Australian infant has been born after having been

frozen for four months, thawed, and transferred to the uterus of its mother. See "Pregnancy with Frozen Embryos is Successful," *New York Times*, May 24, 1983, p. 19.

5. It is estimated that in 1976 10 percent of all married couples trying to conceive were infertile. By 1984 15 percent were infertile. Lori B. Andrews, *New Conceptions: A Consumer's Guide to the Newest Infertility Treatments* (New York: St. Martin's Press, 1984), p. 2. Couples are said to be infertile if they have tried unsuccessfully to conceive for one year or longer or if the female member of the pair is unable to carry a pregnancy to term. Written information from Center for Fertility and Reproductive Research, Department of Obstetrics and Gynecology, Vanderbilt University Medical Center, Nashville, Tennessee. One of every six American couples of childbearing age (15 percent) is infertile according to this definition. Forty percent of infertility problems are traceable to the male, 40 percent to the female, 20 percent to the couple together, and 10 percent have no known cause. "What You Should Know about Infertility," 15 *Contemporary OB/GYN* 101 (Feb., 1980). The incidence of infertility is rising, in part, because women are waiting past their fertility peak to conceive, pelvic inflammatory disease is increasing in frequency, birth control methods are used that, when stopped, decrease fertility, and environmental factors are causing a decline in the male sperm count. Andrews, p. 10.

6. See *supra* note 5.

7. A Harris survey in 1978 of American women showed that most favored IVF although they wanted it barred until its safety was demonstrated. A Gallup poll of men and women showed that 75 percent of those who understood IVF favored it. Ethics Advisory Board, Department of Health, Education, and Welfare, *Report and Conclusions: HEW Support of Research Involving Human In Vitro Fertilization and Embryo Transfer*, May 4, 1979 (Washington, D.C.: U.S. Government Printing Office, 1979), p. 88. [Hereinafter cited as EAB Report.]

8. As Dr. Bobby Webster of Vanderbilt University's Center for Fertility and Reproductive Research put it, "With knowledge comes power, the ability to conquer, and the chance to give hope where there once was not hope." Personal interview. May 24, 1984.

9. For example, R.G. Edwards, "Factors Influencing the Success of in Vitro Fertilization for Alleviating Human Infertility," 1 *Journal of in Vitro Fertilization and Embryo Transfer* 3, 14 (March, 1984), describes some of the new opportunities for research now open as a result of IVF. Generally, this includes the opportunity to study "aspects of human reproductive physiology, embryology, and pregnancy which were otherwise inaccessible or unapproachable."

10. The Vatican newspaper, for example, condemned the use of a frozen embryo to obtain a pregnancy because the sperm used to fertilize the egg came from masturbation, which is a "deviation" in the eyes of the Catholic Church. "Vatican Condemns Birth From a Frozen Embryo," *New York Times*, April 18, 1984, p. 5. Since masturbation is used to obtain sperm for

AID, IVF, and ET, it can be asssumed the official position of the Catholic Church condemns these as well.

11. Jeremy Rifkin, for example, President of the Foundation for Economic Trends, has gone to court challenging the right of Fertility and Genetics Research, Inc., to patent a catheter used in embryo transfer. He claims that the technique "reduces the process of human reproduction to a commercialized product to be bought and sold in the marketplace." Sandra Blakeslee, "Birth Results from Transferred Embryo," *New York Times*, Feb. 4, 1984, p. 6.

12. Richard M. Zaner, "A Criticism of Moral Conservatism's View of In Vitro Fertilization and Embryo Transfer," 27 *Perspectives in Biology and Medicine* 200, 203 (Winter, 1984).

13. Its first recorded use on an animal was in 1784 and on a human in 1790. Jeffrey M. Shaman, "Legal Aspects of Artificial Insemination," 18 *Journal of Family Law* 331, 331 n.1 (1979–1980).

14. Artificial insemination with the husband's sperm is performed when the husband and wife cannot copulate due to obesity, illness, or impotence, or in an effort to bypass the cervix when the wife has what is known as hostile cervical mucus. It is also done with frozen sperm if the husband is away for long periods of time or will be undergoing chemotherapy or a vasectomy. Written information from The New York Fertility Research Foundation, Inc.

15. "Artificial Insemination: A Booklet for Physicians," p. 9. Distributed by the American Fertility Society.

16. *Mother Earth News* 79 (Nov.–Dec. 1981).

17. Today 31.4 percent of physicians surveyed who perform AID use frozen sperm. Martin Curie-Cohen, *et al.*, "Current Practice of Artificial Insemination by Donor in the United States," 300 *New England Journal of Medicine* 585, 587 (Mar. 15, 1979).

18. Quoted in Andrews, *supra* note 5.

19. Quoted in Illinois Legislative Council, Research Memorandum File 9-302, "Artificial Insemination and Surrogate Mother Agreements: Legal Concerns," Nov. 1, 1982, p. 3.

20. William J. Curran and E. Donald Shapiro, *Law, Medicine, and Forensic Science* (3rd ed. Boston: Little, Brown and Company, 1982), p. 932.

21. One survey showed that 32 percent of the physicians responding used multiple donors in the same cycle. Curie-Cohen, *supra* note 17. As one New York City doctor said in justifying the mixing of two donors per cycle, "I never really know for sure who is the father." Telephone interview, March 5, 1984. Name available upon request.

22. S. J. Behrman, "Artificial Insemination and Public Policy," 300 *New England Journal of Medicine* 619, 620 (March 15, 1979).

23. Curie-Cohen, *supra* note 17, p. 589.

24. *Id.*, 587. In some cases, the record keeping is coded by the physician and decipherable only to him or her. The physician quoted in *supra* note 21 goes to great lengths to keep these records confidential. He keeps them at

home and notes that his wife's instructions are to destroy them upon his death. He calls himself a "compulsive record-keeper in every other respect." The need for hidden records makes him "uncomfortable" but he values the importance of anonymity.

25. The survey showed, among other things, that few physicians screened for genetic illnesses of the donor. Only one percent of the doctors tested for Tay-Sachs disease, a fatal inherited illness, and only 26 percent tested for a variety of other genetic disorders. Curie-Cohen, *supra* note 17, p.585. See also Behrman, *supra* note 22, p.619. Almost all of the physicians, 96 percent, however, took an oral history of the genetic defects of the donor and asked donors to fill out a checklist of family diseases. Curie-Cohen, p. 586.

26. For a discussion of court cases dealing with artificial insemination, see Curran and Shapiro, *supra* note 20, pp.931–935. See also *C.M. v. C.C.*, 152 N.J.Super. 160, 377 A.2d 821 (1977).

27. This is mitigated by the fact that in California the person who attends a live birth simply records that fact and "makes no judgment regarding the paternity of the child." The birth certificate is directed more to establishing citizenship than to revealing paternity. Clarification of paternity is not necessary. "Artificial Insemination," *supra* note 15, p. 5.

28. For an example of a case that does address the donor's interests, see *C.M. v. C.C.*, 152 N.J.Super. 160, 377 A.2d 821 (1977). This case was different from most because the mother knew the donor. Here the donor, C.M., willingly gave his sperm to C.C., a single woman, who inseminated herself with it. After the child was born, C.M. sought visitation privileges over the objection of C.C. The court granted to C.M. the privileges as well as the responsibilities of fatherhood. These privileges included visitation rights and an acknowledgement that C.M. was, under the law, the same as the natural father.

29. A lingering question is the right of single women to secure access to AID. Andrews, *supra* note 5, p. 195, reports that a single woman sued the Wayne State University AID clinic for refusing her access to AID. The dispute was resolved in her favor out of court.

30. The case of *People v. Sorenson* was handed down by an appellate court, but it did not fully legitimize AID.

31. Behrman, *supra* note 22, p. 620.

32. *Id.*

33. A number of states clarified existing ambiguous laws to allow a consenting husband to be the presumed father of an AID child. One researcher found that 10 of 17 states polled had clarified their laws in this way. Illinois Legislative Council, *supra* note 19, p. 5.

34. Oregon also absolves the donor of obligations.

35. Emphasis added. Oregon and Connecticut also sever the donor's rights vis-a-vis the child. Connecticut, for example, states that neither the donor nor his relatives may inherit from the child who dies intestate.

36. American Association of Tissue Banks, Newsletter, Nov. 1980, Vol. 4, p. 38.

37. The American Fertility Society, *Report of the Ad Hoc Committee on Artificial Insemination*. Distributed by the American Fertility Society, Birmingham, Alabama, 1980.

38. It calls for criminal penalties if anyone other than a health practitioner performs AID.

39. AATB Newsletter *supra note* 36.

40. They look for a genetic history that puts the donor "at risk of more than one percent for producing a child with a birth defect and/or a genetic disease."

41. Dr. Alfred Morris, Cryo Lab Facility, Chicago. Telephone interview, March 5, 1984. Limiting the number of pregnancies is more important in a small than a large community where involuntary inbreeding might be more likely to occur. It has been estimated that one could expect only one unwitting marriage of half-siblings in a century. Curie-Cohen, *supra note* 17, p. 589.

42. Written information on AID from the University of North Carolina-Chapel Hill, Chapel Hill, North Carolina. For a report of the University of North Carolina's screening program, see M. Chrystie Timmons, *et al.*, "Genetic Screening of Donors for Artificial Insemination," 35 *Fertility and Sterility* 451 (April, 1981).

43. Suzanne Rubin, 32, is a California woman trying to find her AID father. She wants to secure paternity support and to confront the man for having donated his sperm. She claims the physician erred in helping her mother conceive because her mother was, at the time, emotionally unstable. The claim that a physician should screen potential mothers must be balanced against another claimed right, that of all couples to secure access to AID. Rubin's quest is described in Walter S. Feldman, "Artificial Insemination: The Rights of the Child," 10 *Legal Aspects of Medical Practice* 7 (Dec., 1982).

44. It is used to a lesser extent when a woman's cervix is such that sperm cannot penetrate, the male sperm count is low, and no identifiable source of infertility is present. Jones, *supra note* 3, p. 2182. Alan Trounson, an IVF pioneer in Australia, estimates that over 80 percent of normally infertile couples can be helped by IVF. Cited in R. G. Edwards and Jean M. Purdy, *Human Conception In Vitro* (London: Academic Press, 1982), p. 334.

45. Dr. Florence Haseltine of Yale University, quoted in Gina Kolata, "In Vitro Fertilization Goes Commercial," 221 *Science* 1160 (Sept. 16, 1983).

46. In vitro supporters respond that IVF is no more unnatural than a caesarean birth or the use of an incubator to keep alive premature infants. See Andrews, *supra* note 5, p. 141. Says the founder of the nation's first IVF program in Norfolk, Virginia, "every request of a physician to diagnose and treat disease is a request to manipulate nature." *Id.*

47. See, for example, Linda Piedra, Letter to the Editor, *New York Times Magazine*, Feb. 19, 1984, p. 94, responding to an article on ovum transfer: "Taking into account the failure of many modern marriages, it might be possible for these children to have genetic parents and birth parents and divorced parents and stepparents, and ultimately the feeling of having no

parents at all." In contrast, H. W. Jones, Jr., "The Ethics of In-vitro Fertilization—1981," in Edwards and Purdy, *supra* note 44, p. 355, notes that "the process of in-vitro fertilization demands sacrifice on the part of both husband and wife beyond anything required for normal procreation." He notes that this kind of sacrifice is indicative of a stable couple "willing to go the last mile" to overcome infertility.

48. This fear has been voiced by Leon Kass, among others. See Andrews, *supra* note 5, pp. 143–144. One Midwest neonatal specialist called the news that the first embryo transfer baby was born "scary." He envisioned the repercussions and television commercials in 20 years: "Genes—guaranteed or your money back" or "Embryo banks—dark-haired children $25,000, blondes $20,000, foreigners $5,000." Personal interview, February 2, 1984. Name available upon request.

49. Cloning has so far been achieved only for insects and amphibians. Seymour Lederberg, "Law and Cloning—The State as Regulator of Gene Function," in Aubrey Milunsky and George P. Annas, eds., *Genetics and the Law* (New York: Plenum Press, 1976), p. 378. In 1966 Oxford researchers produced frogs from the intestinal cells of tadpoles. George P. Smith, II, *Genetics, Ethics and the Law* (Gaithersburg, MD: Associated Faculty Press, Inc., 1981), p. 105. In cloning, researchers destroy the nucleus of a donor egg cell, insert the nucleus from any body cell of the animal, fertilize the two in a petri dish, and implant the egg so it will gestate. Smith, p. 105. In response to the claim that IVF will lead to cloning, the EAB Report, *supra* note 7, p. 102, noted that legislation can prevent abuses but it "is neither justified nor wise" to forbid IVF research because of this "uncertain or remote risk."

50. EAB Report, *supra* note 7, p. 51.

51. For a comprehensive review of the ethical dimensions of IVF in the literature, see LeRoy Walters, "Human In Vitro Fertilization: A Review of the Ethical Literature," 9 *The Hastings Center Report* 23 (August, 1979). Legal issues are well covered in Dennis M. Flannery, *et al.*, "Test Tube Babies: Legal Issues Raised by *In Vitro* Fertilization," 67 *Georgetown Law Journal* 1295 (1979).

In response to the claim of experimentation, it is pointed out that embryonic loss in nature is great. When fertilization occurs in nature, 18 percent of the embryos are lost during the first week of pregnancy and 32 percent more are lost during the second week. As it turns out, in nature only 37 percent of embryos go on to become babies. The rest are expelled. EAB Report, *supra* note 7, p. 1. The embryo loss in IVF is greater than under natural conditions, to be sure, but physicians see embryo loss as one of the costs of IVF. Clifford Grobstein, Michael Flower, and John Mendeloff, "External Human Fertilization: An Evaluation of Policy," 222 *Science* 127, 128 (Oct. 14, 1983). Inasmuch as IVF's success rate is growing and may even exceed that of nature (John F. Kevin, *et al.*, "Incidence of Multiple Pregnancy After In-Vitro Fertilisation and Embryo Transfer," 8349 *Lancet* 537, 539 [Sept. 3, 1983]), the embryo loss will become less of an issue as time goes by.

52. The facts are from Andrews, *supra* note 5, p. 145.
53. EAB Report, *supra* note 7, p. 103.
54. *Id.*, p. 101.
55. See *supra* note 51.
56. EAB Report, *supra* note 7, pp. 106–107.
57. *Id.*, p. 102. It noted that individual abuses could be prevented through legislation or "good judgment." Zaner, *supra* note 12, p. 208, makes the interesting observation that those who would bar all IVF because of possible later abuses "distrust" individuals because they assume these individuals "are not able to resist the temptation to continue each step down the slippery slope all the way to the bottom."
58. R. G. Edwards and P. C. Steptoe, "Current Status of In-Vitro Fertilisation and Implantation of Human Embryos," No. 8362 *Lancet* 1265 (Dec. 3, 1983). The success rate varies from center to center and according to the way "success" is measured. In vitro fertilization involves a series of steps: (1) an egg(s) is retrieved in a surgical operation known as a laparoscopy, (2) eggs are fertilized with the husband's sperm, (3) fertilized eggs cleave into 2-, 4-, or 8-celled concepti, (4) embryo(s) are transferred to the uterus in a simple procedure, (5) embryos implant to produce a pregnancy, and (6) the pregnancy is ongoing and leads to the birth of an infant. The success rate for the first four steps is high but it drops dramatically at the stage of implantation. Success rates are higher if a center defines them as the number of births per transfer. They are lower if defined as the number of births per laparoscopy. To give an example, 343 patients began hormonal stimulation at Yale University School of Medicine between June 1982 and early 1984. A sizable number of the patients failed to stimulate, so these patients did not continue the treatment. Others underwent laparoscopies in which no eggs were retrieved. For still others, eggs did not fertilize. In the end, embryos were transferred in 140 patients. Twenty-six became pregnant and 10 gave birth. Telephone conversation with Fanny Nero, Coordinator of In Vitro Fertilization Program, Women's Center Infertility Clinic, Yale University School of Medicine, Feb. 28, 1984. Thus, the success rate, as defined by the number of births per transfer, is 7 percent. It would be lower if defined as the number of births per laparoscopy. It seems to be the case that a program's success rate increases after the first six months of operation. The pioneering Bourne Hall Clinic, Cambridge University, reported a 16.5 percent pregnant rate per transfer for the first part of its operation, for example, and now reports a 30 percent pregnancy rate. Edwards, *supra* note 9, p. 3. Recent data presented at The Third World Congress of In Vitro Fertilization and Embryo Transfer in Helsinki, May, 1984, reveal that for 58 of the world's 193 in vitro centers that responded to a survey, 7733 transfers were performed and 512 babies were eventually born. Dr. Anne Colston Wentz, Department of Obstetrics and Gynecology, Vanderbilt University Medical Center. Personal interview, May 23, 1984.
59. The direct costs of a single in vitro attempt can be $3000 to $4000. If hospitals itemize expenses, insurance companies will pay for certain por-

tions of the expenses, such as the anesthesiologist's fee. Couples must absorb part of these costs in addition to the indirect costs of travel to the medical center, hotel bills, and salary lost from taking time off from work. Since the odds are only one in five or less for each attempt, a couple may multiply these expenses three or more times and still not have a pregnancy to show for it.

60. This account is from Andrews, *supra* note 5, p. 155.

61. *Id.*

62. *Ill. Rev. Stat.*, Ch. 38 s. 81-26 (1983).

63. Representative Greiman recounting the question and answer in a debate taking place in the Illinois Assembly on May 27, 1983. State of Illinois, 83rd Gen. Assem., House of Representatives, Transcription Debate, HB 671, p. 147.

64. Andrews, *supra* note 5, p. 152.

65. Representative Greiman, Transcription Debate, *supra* note 63, p. 148.

66. EAB Report, *supra* note 7, p. 102.

67. Andrews, *supra* note 5, p. 154.

68. EAB Report, *supra* note 7, p. 104.

69. *Id.*, p. 107.

70. Andrews, *supra* note 5, pp. 148–149.

71. Diana Brahams, "In Vitro Fertilisation and Related Research: Why Parliament Must Legislate," 8352 *Lancet* 726, 729 (Sept. 24, 1983).

72. It is not at all clear that concerns over spare embryos are in the embryo's best interest. Physicians now feel pressure to transfer all embryos to the uterus. Studies show, however, that the chances of embryo implantation are greatest when one to four embryos are transferred. Dr. Anne Colston Wentz, *supra* note 58, reporting on data gathered in England and Australia. In over 30 percent of cases, surgeons retrieve five or more eggs. Alexander Lopata, "Concepts in Human In Vitro Fertilization and Embryo Transfer," 40 *Fertility and Sterility* 289, 299 (Sept. 1983). This gives physicians and patients a choice of discarding (or in the future freezing) one or more embryos so that the remaining embryos would have a greater chance of survival.

73. "Ethical Statement on In Vitro Fertilization," 41 *Fertility and Sterility* 12 (Jan. 1984).

74. "Minimal Standards for Programs of In Vitro Fertilization," 41 *Fertility and Sterility* 13 (Jan. 1984).

75. EAB Report, *supra* note 7, pp. 106–107.

76. Edwards and Purdy, *supra* note 44, p. 364.

77. Dr. Anne Colston Wentz, *supra* note 58. The by-laws were drafted at the Third World Congress of In Vitro Fertilization and Embryo Transfer held May, 1984, in Helsinki.

78. Dr. Bobby Webster, Department of Obstetrics and Gynecology, Vanderbilt University Medical Center. Personal interview, May 24, 1984.

79. See, for example, Dr. Bobby Webster, *id.*; and Dr. Edward Marut, Director, In Vitro Fertilization Program, Michael Reese Hospital, Chicago. Personal interview, March 29, 1984.

80. Joel Brinkley, "Uncertain Present for In Vitro Fertilization," *New York Times*, Feb. 5, 1984, p. 20E.

81. Mount Sinai Hospital Medical Center, Chicago, asks patients to sign a form holding personnel at the hospital harmless against any claim that they have custody of a child resulting from in vitro fertilization. The consent form at Vanderbilt Unviersity Medical Center is four pages long and covers such contingencies as accidental loss of embryos, mental distress, and discomfort associated with hormonal medication.

82. Brinkley, *supra* note 80.

83. Dr. Jan Friberg, Director, Reproductive Endocrinology/Infertility, Department of Obstetrics and Gynecology, Mount Sinai Hospital Medical Center of Chicago. Personal interview, March 28, 1984.

84. Brinkley, *supra* note 80.

85. Cited in Edwards and Purdy, *supra* note 44.

86. Dr. Jan Friberg, *supra* note 83. Leon Kass, cited in EAB Report, *supra* note 7, p. 53, observes: "As he who pays the piper calls the tune, Federal support would make easy the Federal regulation and supervision of this research."

87. Alan H. DeCherney, "Doctored Babies," 40 *Fertility and Sterility* 724 (Dec. 1983).

88. EAB Report, *supra* note 7, p. 101.

89. Quoted in Benno C. Schmidt, Jr., "Pluralistic Programming and Regulation of Mass Communications Media," in Glen O. Robinson, ed., *Communications for Tomorrow: Policy Perspectives for the 1980's* (New York: Praeger Publishers, 1978), p. 224.

90. Harold P. Green, "The Fetus and the Law," in Milunsky and Annas, *supra* note 49, p. 24.

91. *Id*.

92. Dr. John Credico, Obstetrician/Gynecologist. Personal interview, March 3, 1984.

2

Human Embryos and Research

The View from Britain

The Warnock Commission

We now turn to the issues arising from the possible use of human embryos for *scientific research*. The question before the Inquiry was whether such research should be allowed. To answer this we found it necessary to look at the very earliest stages of human embryonic development, described in the following paragraphs.

Early Human Development

At fertilization the egg and sperm unite to become a single cell. The nucleus of this cell contains the chromosomes derived from both parents. This single cell is totipotential, as from it develop all the different types of tissue and organs that make up the human body,

---

The "Report of the Committee of Inquiry into Human Fertilization and Embryology" (popularly known as the Warnock Commission Report) was presented to the British Parliament in July 1984 by the Secretary of State for Social Services on behalf of the Department of Health and Social Security. The sixteen member committee, chaired by Dame Mary Warnock, DBE, had been established by Parliament in July 1982 and charged with "examining the social, ethical and legal implications of recent, and potential developments in the field of human assisted reproduction." (p. iv) The recommendations of the Report were not binding, and several members of the Committee attached "Expressions of Dissent" to the majority report on matters of a) "surrogacy" and b and c) "use of human embryos in research".

© 1984, London: Her Majesty's Stationery Office.

47

as well as the tissues that become the placenta and fetal membranes during intra-uterine development. *In vivo*, fertilization takes place in the upper portion of the fallopian tube and the fertilized egg then passes down the fallopian tube into the cavity of the uterus over a period of four to five days. At first, when it reaches the cavity of the uterus, it remains free-floating until it begins to attach to the uterine wall at the start of implantation. This is considered to begin on the sixth day following fertilization. During implantation, which occurs over a period of six to seven days, the embryo enters the endometrium, the lining of the uterus; at the eleventh to thirteenth day after fertilization, implantation is complete.

While the fertilized egg is still in the upper portion of the fallopian tube, it begins to divide into first two, then four, then eight, then sixteen smaller cells, and so on by a process called cleavage. At the start of cleavage, in a two or four-cell embryo, each cell retains its totipotential capacity. Thus if separation occurs at the two-cell stage, each may develop to form a separate embryo. Such a separation could lead to identical twins.

When sixteen or more cells have resulted from cleavage, the cells hang together in a loosely packed configuration, similar to that of a blackberry, called a morula. The morula stage is reached at about the same time as the embryo *in vivo* reaches the uterine cavity. At about the same time a fluid-filled space begins to form in an eccentric position within the substance of the morula. Once this accumulation of fluid has occurred the embryo is described as a blastocyst. Within the blastocyst a thicker section of the cyst wall becomes identifiable as the inner cell mass; it is within the inner cell mass that the embryo proper, eventually to become the fetus, develops. The remaining cells of the thin walled portion of the blastocyst develop to become part of the placenta and fetal membranes. At about the time that the blastocyst begins to implant, a second fluid-filled space, the amniotic cavity, also appears within the inner cell mass. Between the two cystic spaces within the blastocyst, a plate of cells is formed. This is described as the embryonic disc; within it the first recognizable features of the embryo proper will appear.

The first of these features is the primitive streak, which appears as a heaping-up of cells at one end of the embryonic disc on the fourteenth or fifteenth day after fertilization. Two primitive streaks may form in a single embryonic disc. This is the latest stage at which identical twins can occur. The primitive streak is the first of several identifiable features which develop in and from the embryonic disc during the succeeding days, a period of very rapid change in the embryonic configuration. By the seventeenth day the neural groove appears and by the twenty-second to twenty-third day this has developed to become the neural folds, which in turn start to fuse and form the recognizable antecedent of the spinal cord.

Once fertilization has occurred, the subsequent developmental processes follow one another in a systematic and structured order, leading in turn through cleavage, to the morula, the blastocyst, development of the embryonic disc, and then to identifiable features within the embryonic disc such as the primitive streak, neural folds and neural tube. Until the blastocyst stage has been reached the embryo *in vivo* is unattached, floating first in the fallopian tube and then in the uterine cavity. From the sixth to the twelfth or thirteenth day internal development proceeds within the blastocyst while during the same period implantation is taking place. Both the internal and external processes of development are crucial to the future of the embryo. If the inner cell mass does not form within the blastocyst there is no further embryonic development; while if implantation does not occur the blastocyst is lost at or before the next menstrual period.

Identical developmental processes are followed by embryos fertilized *in vitro*. In these, following fertilization, the first cleavage divisions will occur before the embryo is transferred back to the uterus. Thereafter, where implantation takes place, the developmental process will be identical for both *in vitro* and *in vivo* embryos, but there is a very high wastage rate for both as a result of their frequent failure to implant.

The Starting Point for Discussion

It was the development of IVF that, for the first time, gave rise to the possibility that human embryos might be brought into existence which might have no chance to implant because they were not transferred to a uterus and hence no chance to be born as human beings. This inevitably led to an examination of the moral rights of the embryo.

Some people hold that if an embryo is human and alive, it follows that it should not be deprived of a chance for development, and therefore it should not be used for research. They would give moral approval to IVF if, and only if, each embryo produced were to be transferred to a uterus. Others, while in no way denying that human embryos are alive (and they would concede that eggs and sperm are also alive), hold that embryos are not yet human persons and that if it could be decided when an embryo becomes a person, it could also be decided when it might, or might not, be permissible for research to be undertaken. Although the questions of when life or personhood begin appear to be questions of fact susceptible of straightforward answers, we hold that the answers to such questions in fact are complex amalgams of factual and moral judgements. Instead of trying to answer these questions directly we have therefore gone straight to the question of *how it is right to treat the human embryo*. We have considered what status ought to be accorded to the human embryo, and the answer we give must necessarily be in terms of ethical or moral principles.

Defining the Limits of Research

We have so far simply spoken of research and given little indication of the scope of this term. We believe that a broad division into two categories can be made. The first, which we term pure research, is aimed at increasing and developing knowledge of the very early stages of the human embryo; the second, applied research, is research with direct diagnostic or therapeutic aims for the human embryo, or for the alleviation of infertility in general. Research aimed at improving IVF techniques would come into this second category. We exclude from the concept of research what we have called new and untried treatment, undertaken during the attempt to alleviate the infertility of a particular patient. We recognize that these distinctions are not absolute. The categories may often overlap, but we feel that they have a certain validity.

Arguments Against the Use of Human Embryos

It is obvious that the central objection to the use of human embryos as research subjects is a fundamental objection, based on moral principles. Put simply, the main argument is that the use of human embryos for research is morally wrong because of the very fact that they are human, and much of the evidence submitted to us strongly supports this. The human embryo is seen as having the same status as a child or an adult, by virtue of its potential for human life. The right to life is held to be the fundamental human right, and the taking of human life on this view is always abhorrent. To take the life of the innocent is an especial moral outrage. The first consequence of this line of argument is that, since an embryo used as a research subject would have no prospect of fulfilling its potential for life, such research should not be permitted.

Everyone agrees that it is completely unacceptable to make use of a child or an adult as the subject of a research procedure which may cause harm or death. For people who hold the views outlined above, research on embryos would fall under the same principle. They proceed to argue that since it is unethical to carry out any research, harmful or otherwise, on humans without first obtaining their informed consent, it must be equally unacceptable to carry out research on a human embryo, which by its very nature, cannot give consent.

In addition to the arguments outlined above, and well represented in the evidence, many people feel an instinctive opposition to research which they see as tampering with the creation of human life. There is widely felt concern at the possibility of unscrupulous scientists meddling with the process of reproduction in order to create hybrids, or to indulge theories of selective breeding and eugenic selection.

Those who are firmly opposed to research on human embryos recognize that a ban on their use may reduce the volume not only of pure research but also research in potentially beneficial areas, such as the detection and prevention of inherited disorders, or the alleviation of infertility, and that in some areas such a ban would halt research completely. However they argue that the moral principle outweighs any such possible benefits.

Arguments For the Use of Human Embryos

The evidence showed that the views of those who support the use of human embryos as research subjects cover a wide range. At one end is the proposition that it is only to *human persons* that respect must be accorded. A human embryo cannot be thought of as a person, or even as a potential person. It is simply a collection of cells which, unless it implants in a human uterine environment, has no potential for development. There is no reason therefore to accord these cells any protected status. If useful results can be obtained from research on embryos, then such research should be permitted. We found that the more generally held position, however, is that though the human embryo is entitled to some added measure of respect beyond that accorded to other animal subjects, that respect cannot be absolute, and may be weighed against the benefits arising from research. Although many research studies in embryology and developmental biology can be carried out on animal subjects, and it is possible in many cases to extrapolate these results and findings to man, in certain situations there is no substitute for the use of human embryos. This particularly applies to the study of disorders occurring only in humans, such as Down's syndrome, or for research into the processes of human fertilization, or perhaps into the specific effect of drugs or toxic substances on human tissue.

The Legal Position

We examined the current position of the *in vivo* embryo in law. The human embryo *per se* has no legal status. It is not, under law in the United Kingdom, accorded the same status as a child or an adult, and the law does not treat the human embryo as having a right to life. However, there are certain statutory provisions that give some level of protection in various respects. The effect of the Offences Against the Person Act 1861, together with the Abortion Act 1967 (in Scotland the common law as amended by the Abortion Act 1967), is such that abortion is a criminal offense save in the circumstances provided for by the legislation. The Infant Life Preservation Act 1929 (which does not apply in Scotland) has as its purpose the protection of the life of a child capable of being born alive. Under civil law in England and Wales the Congenital Disabilities (Civil Liability) Act 1976 allows, in limited circumstances, damages to be recovered where an embryo or fetus has been injured *in utero* through the negligence of some third person. It is thus accorded a kind of retrospective status where it is born deformed or damaged as a result of injury. This act does not apply in Scotland or Northern

Ireland. The legal position at common law is thought to be similar in Scotland, although the law has yet to be tested. Thus, at present the law provides a measure of protection for the embryo *in vivo*. The remainder of this chapter deals exclusively with the *in vitro* embryo.

Although, therefore, the law provides a measure of protection for the human embryo *in vivo* it is clear that the human embryo under our definition of the term is not, under the present law in the United Kingdom, accorded the same status as a living child or an adult, nor do we necessarily wish it to be accorded that same status. Nevertheless we were agreed that the embryo of the human species ought to have a special status and that no one should undertake research on human embryos the purposes of which could be achieved by the use of other animals or in some other way. The status of the embryo is a matter of fundamental principle which should be enshrined in legislation. **We recommend that the embryo of the human species should be afforded some protection in law.** We examine below what that protection should be.

That protection should exist does not entail that this protection may not be waived in certain specific circumstances. Having examined the evidence presented to us about the types of research which might be carried out on human embryos produced *in vitro*, the majority of us[1] hold that such research should not be totally prohibited. We do not want to see a situation in which human embryos are frivolously or unnecessarily used in research but we are bound to take account of the fact that the advances in the treatment of infertility, which we have discussed in the earlier part of this report, could not have taken place without such research; and that continued research is essential, if advances in treatment and medical knowledge are to continue. A majority of us therefore agreed that research on human embryos should continue. Nevertheless, because of the special status that we accord to the human embryo, such research must be subject to stringent controls and monitoring. Moreover, we would not want any handling or transportation of human embryos *in vitro* to fall outside these controls. **We recommend that research conducted on human *in vitro* embryos and the handling of such embryos should be permitted only under license. We recommend that any unauthorized use of an *in*** *vitro* embryo would in itself constitute a criminal offence.[2] We see these controls as essential to safeguard the public interest and to allay widespread anxiety.

Time Limit on Keeping Embryos Alive *In Vitro*

The statutory body which we propose should issue licenses for research will have as one its main functions the regulation of research. First it will have to be assured that no other research material is available for the particular project in mind, and second, it will have to limit the length of time for which an embryo can be kept alive *in vitro*. While, as we have seen, the timing of the different stages of development is critical, once the process has begun, there is no particular part of the developmental process that is more important than another; all are part of a continuous process, and unless each stage takes place normally, at the correct time, and in the correct sequence, further development will cease. Thus biologically there is no single identifiable stage in the development of the embryo beyond which the *in vitro* embryo should not be kept alive. However we agreed that this was an area in which some precise decision must be taken, in order to allay public anxiety.

The evidence showed a wide range of opinion on this question. One argument put forward may be termed the strictly utilitarian view. This suggests that the ethics of experiments on embryos must be determined by the balance of benefit over harm, or pleasure over pain. Therefore, as long as the embryo is incapable of feeling pain, it is argued that its treatment does not weigh in the balance. According to this argument the time limit for *in vitro* development, and for research on the embryo, could be set either when the first beginnings of the central nervous system can be identified, or when functional activity first occurs. If the former is chosen, this would imply a limit of twenty-two or twenty-three days after fertilization, when the neural tube begins to close. As to the latter in the present state of knowledge the onset of central nervous system functional activity could not be used to define accurately the limit to research, because the timing is not known; however, it is generally thought to be considerably later in pregnancy. With either limit, proponents suggests subtracting a few days in order that there would be no possibility of the embryo feeling pain.

The Royal College of Obstetricians and Gynaecologists suggested that embryos should not be allowed to develop *in vitro* beyond a limit of seventeen days, as this is the point at which early neural development begins. The British Medical Association favored a limit of fourteen days and a number of groups, including the Medical Research Council and the Royal College of Physicians suggested that the limit should be at the end of the implantation stage. Again, some groups submitting evidence suggested that no embryo which had gone beyond the beginning of the implantation stage should be used for research.

The Inquiry's View

As we have seen, the objection to using human embryos in research is that each one is a potential human being. One reference point in the development of the human individual is the formation of the primitive streak. Most authorities put this at about fifteen days after fertilization. This marks the beginning of individual development of the embryo. Taking such a time limit is consonant with the views of those who favor the end of the implantation stage as a limit. We have therefore regarded an earlier date than this as a desirable end-point for research. **We accordingly recommend that no live human embryo derived from *in vitro* fertilization, whether frozen or unfrozen, may be kept alive, if not transferred to a woman, beyond fourteen days after fertilization, nor may it be used as a research subject beyond fourteen days after fertilization. This fourteen day period does not include any time during which the embryo may have been frozen. We further recommend that it shall be a criminal offense to handle or to use as a research subject any live human embryo derived from *in vitro* fertilization beyond that limit. We recommend that no embryo which has been used for research should be transferred to a woman.**

A further question on which the licensing body will have to be satisfied is the origin of the embryos to be used. There is a number of possible sources of human embryos for research use. First, current IVF procedures often result in the production of a number of "spare" embryos that will not be transferred to a woman and these, if they are not needed for treatment purposes, could be used as research subjects. Second, clearly it is also possible to produce embryos *in vitro*, using donated eggs and semen, with the sole intention of using them for research. Third, a possible source would be embryos which happened to be produced during the course of research concentrating on, for example the fertilization capacity of human eggs or semen, but where the primary aim of that research is not to bring embryos into existence.

We are satisfied that "spare" embryos may be used as subjects for research; **and we recommend accordingly a need to obtain *consent* to the method of use or disposal of spare embryos. We recommend that as a matter of good practice no research should be carried out on a spare embryo without the informed consent of the couple for whom that embryo was generated, whenever this is possible.**

The problem discussed in the following paragraphs was a very difficult one for the Inquiry to resolve and members gave it a great deal of thought over an extended period. Some members, although they agree that research on spare embryos may legitimately be undertaken, see a clear moral distinction between the research use of embryos available by chance, which were not needed for the purposes of treatment, and on the other hand the generation of embryos brought into being for the purposes of research alone and where there is no question of their being transferred to a woman. And this includes embryos which come into existence as a by-product of research on fertilization. These members argue that it cannot be consonant with the special status that the Inquiry as a whole has agreed should be afforded to the human embryo, to cause it to exist, yet to allow it no possibility of implantation. Similarly others argue that it is fertilization itself that is unique and it ought not to be undertaken when there is no chance whatever that the potential for human development will be fulfilled.

All members who are opposed to the deliberate generation of embryos for research accept that this might slow down the pace of research and that not every kind of research could be carried out using only embryos which were adventitiously available. Despite the fact that the research in question would be mainly for the alleviation of infertility and the prevention of hereditary disease, they adhere to the view that, whatever the handicap to scientific progress, it would be morally wrong to bring human embryos into being solely for the purpose of research.

There is a further argument that if it is once thought permissible to allow embryos to come into being with the sole intention that they be used for research, this would open the way for an ever-increasing use of human embryos for routine and less valid research, whatever may have been the original intention of regulation. Once a foot is set on the "slippery slope" of deliberate creation of embryos, no end can be set to the dangers. Nevertheless, the argument runs, research on embryos may be justified, provided that the embryos used as subjects of research were brought into being, not primarily for research, but in order to alleviate a particular case of infertility. This argument in part rests on the doctrine known to philosophers as "double effect": an act which would be wrong if chosen for its own sake may be justified if it occurs as a by-product of some other, well-intentioned act. According to this view, therefore, there would be no general acceptance of research on embryos, but acceptance only in the limited circumstance of the existence of "spare" embryos. Those who hold this view would argue that it would be preferable on moral grounds that there should be no research on embryos rather than research regardless of the circumstances in which the embryos were brought into being.

Other members did not make the same distinction between spare and deliberately generated embryos. They argue that if research on human embryos is to be permitted at all, it makes no difference whether these embryos happen to be available or were brought into existence for the sake of research. In neither case would these embryos have a potential for life, because in neither case were they to be transferred to a uterus. Further, in both cases, research would be subject to the limitations outlined above and the moral status of the embryo would be the same, and subject to the same fourteen day limitation.

Members who hold this view give a great deal of weight to the consideration that to prohibit the generation of embryos specifically for research would severely curtail the range and scientific validity of research on human embryos, and in some fields would effectively preclude it entirely. In addition, even if some gametes were donated for research purposes, it would not be possible to undertake any research on the process of fertilization itself using human eggs and sperm since this process would necessarily result in some cases in the generation of an embryo. Research on the fertilization of eggs stored by freezing is essential if there is ever to be the possibility that frozen eggs may be used in infertility treatment; and the use of frozen eggs, if the technique could be developed, would raise fewer ethical problems than the freezing of embryos. A further argument for the generation of embryos for research is that as the techniques of freezing become more successful there would be fewer spare embryos available for research. For couples would probably prefer to freeze any embryos which could not be used immediately in an IVF treatment for use either if the initial embryo transfer were unsuccessful, or for a subsequent pregnancy. Moreover it is argued that spare embryos are not necessarily ideal material for research. Inevitably and quite rightly, those embryos that are developing best are replaced in the mother, and the "spares" tend to be less good. This could well affect the findings of any research project.

Members of the Inquiry who subscribed to the view that research on spare embryos should be permitted were nevertheless divided on the question whether research should be permitted on embryos brought into existence specifically for that purpose or coming into existence as a result of other research. However, we are nevertheless agreed that the issue is of such importance that it should be controlled by legislation, and not left to the discretion of the licensing body. Despite our division on this point, a majority of us **recommend that the legislation should provide that research may be carried out on any embryo resulting from *in vitro* fertilization, whatever its provenance, up to the end of the fourteenth day after fertilization, but subject to all other restrictions as may be imposed by the licensing body.**

Expression of Dissent: The Use of Human Embryos in Research

We have signed the main report subject to our reservations the reasons for which are set out below on the recommendation on page 58, from which we dissent. We agree with our colleagues that the embryo of the human species has a special status but differ from them as to what this implies.

When Does Life Begin?

Public concern about the embryo which led to the establishment of this Inquiry is often expressed in the form of the question, "When does life begin?" This cannot be answered in a simple fashion. An ovum is a living cell as is a spermatozoon; both can be properly described as alive. The cluster of cells which is the embryo is likewise alive. But this is not what people are really asking. Their real question is "When does the human person come into existence?" This cannot be answered in a simple fashion either. The beginning of a person is not a question of fact but of decision made in the light of moral principles. The question must therefore be refined still further. It thus becomes "At what stage of development should the status of a person be accorded to an embryo of the human species?" Different people answer this question in different ways. Some say at fertilization, others at implantation, yet others at a still later stage of development. Scientific observation and philosophical and theological reflection can illuminate the question but they cannot answer it.

The Special Status of the Embryo

The special status of the human embryo and the protection to be afforded to it by law do not in our view depend upon the decision as to when it becomes a person. Clearly, once that status has been accorded all moral principles and legal enactments which relate to persons will apply. But before that point has been reached the embryo has a special status because of its potential for development to a stage at which everyone would accord it the status of a human person. It is in our view wrong to create something with the potential for becoming a human person and then deliberately to destroy it.

We therefore recommend that nothing should be done that would reduce the chance of successful implantation of the embryo.

It may be argued that the ovum and sperm also have the potential for becoming a human person and yet their loss at menstruation and ejaculation or by experimentation is accepted. It is true that the ovum and sperm are genetically unique but neither alone, even in the most favorable environment, will develop into a human person. They do not have this potential. The embryo, on the other hand, given the appropriate environment, will develop to the stage at which there would be general agreement that the status of a person be accorded to it. It must therefore be given special protection so that this potential can normally be fulfilled.

Experimentation

We would therefore support the creation of embryos with a view to their ultimate implantation in the uterus. The number created should be the optimum judged clinically to be necessary to secure implantation. More embryos should not be implanted than is clinically judged to be optimum solely because they have been created as this would both diminish the chance of their survival and expose the mother to the danger of multiple pregnancy. In the event of there being more embryos than is judged right to implant at any one time the remainder should either be frozen with a view to implantation at a later date or allowed to die. They should not be used for experimentation. Still less should embryos be deliberately created for the purpose of experimentation.

We therefore recommend that experimentation on the human embryo is not permitted.

Progress in Treatment of Infertility

A ban on experimentation will not halt progress in the treatment of infertility. Progress can still be made by animal and other experimentation and by the constant endeavour to improve the treatment procedure. Comparison with heart-transplantation makes this clear. Initial attempts were uniformly unsuccessful. Each attempt was however undertaken, with the hope of success; at no stage was a transplant undertaken with the intention the patient should not survive in order to gain knowledge as to how to improve the procedure. Continued therapeutic efforts backed by animal and other research have produced steadily improving results. Likewise embryos should not be created with a view to their destruction in order to improve the results from *in vitro* fertilization.

Infertility can be a heavy burden for an individual couple; it is right that efforts should be made to alleviate it. This does not however justify the use of any possible means. The advance of scientific knowledge is likewise of great value but again does not justify the use of any means. Because embryos have the potential to become human persons neither the relief of infertility nor the advance of knowledge justifies their deliberate destruction.

Consequences of Permitting Any Experimentation

The ethical status of a procedure is determined by an analysis of the procedure itself. But when questions of public policy arise it is necessary also to look beyond the procedure to possible consequences. The proposal that the creation of embryos for research should be banned but that experiments on embryos created to relieve infertility which are no longer required for that purpose—so called "spare" embryos—be permitted, comes into this category. In our view experiments on "spare embryos" are wrong. But even if they were deemed right, the consequences of permitting them would be unacceptable. There would be a strong temptation for doctors to harvest more embryos than strictly required for the immediate therapeutic purpose in order to provide "spare embryos." "Spare" would become a euphemism.

Moreover as the number provided by this means would not meet the large demand foreseen by our colleagues the pressure for permission to create embryos specifically for research would grow. Likewise, limitations on the time and type of research would be eroded. Already voices are being raised for research to be permitted to a point beyond the fourteenth day after fertilization recommended by this Inquiry. Similarly, if the use of embryos for testing of drugs, albeit under exceptional circumstances were to be permitted, it would be difficult to maintain the limitation. Large numbers of new drugs are developed every year, many of which might be suitable for use by pregnant women. If a few were to be tested on embryos the demand for more to be screened in this way would inevitably grow. We conclude that experimentation on embryos is not only unethical in principle but that the consequences of granting even limited permission for experimentation would be such as to lead inevitably to extensive use of embryos for this purpose.

We therefore recommend that the embryo of the human species be afforded special protection in law.

In order to achieve this legislation should be introduced to the effect that the unauthorized handling of a human embryo constitutes a criminal offense. Authorized handling should be under the control of a statutory licensing body which should have power to grant permission for the handling of embryos created with a view to implantation.

Notes

1. *Aborted embryos* The focus of this chapter is on the very early human embryo. Almost all of these embryos will result from *in vitro* fertilization,

although some might be obtained from uterine lavage. We are conscious, however, that there are other whole live embryos and fetuses of greater gestational age, which may become available for research following termination of pregnancy. We recognise that both abortion and the Code of Practice contained in the report on "The Use of Fetuses and Fetal Material for Research" (The Peel Report) HMSO 1972 are very much outside our terms of reference. Nevertheless it seems to us totally illogical to propose stringent legislative controls on the use of very early human embryos for research, while there is a less formal mechanism governing the research use of whole live embryos and fetuses of more advanced gestation. Although we understand that these mechanisms have worked well, we consider there is a case for bringing any research that makes use of whole live aborted embryos or fetuses—whether obtained from *in vitro* fertilization, uterine lavage, or termination of pregnancy—within the sort of legislation framework proposed in this report. We suggest that this be given urgent consideration.

3

Differential Treatment of Men and Women by Artificial Reproduction Statutes

Jack F. Williams

[The Constitution] is made for people of fundamentally differing views, and the accident of our finding certain opinions natural and familiar or novel and even shocking ought not to conclude our judgment upon the question whether statutes embodying them conflict with the Constitution of the United States.
                    —*Lochner v. New York*, 198 U.S. 45, 76 (1905)
                                        (Holmes, J. dissenting)

Introduction

For the law to remain relevant it must progress as society progresses. Advances in science and technology must be followed by advances in the law. This essay will focus on two particular advances in science and technology—artificial insemination by donor and surrogate motherhood—and the laws relevant to these two methods of artificial reproduction. Specifically, the essay will discuss the differential treatment of infertile men and women by artificial reproduction statutes.

As will be noted, most jurisdictions have enacted statutes providing that children born by the AID process be deemed legitimate and establishing that the husband[1] of the natural mother of the AID child be deemed the natural and legal father. However, no

---

Jack F. Williams serves as a law clerk to the Honorable William J. Holloway Jr., Chief Judge, U.S. Court of Appeals for the Tenth Circuit. This article first appeared in the Tulsa Law Journal, 1986.

such statutes exist for surrogate motherhood arrangements. Therefore, a child born from a surrogate motherhood arrangement will be born illegitimate absent a saving statute;[2] the wife of the natural father must adopt the child to be deemed the legal mother.[3]

The essay will first explore the typical AID and surrogate motherhood procedures. To understand fully their legal implications one must become familiar with the medical techniques and procedures used. Second, the essay will discuss the differences in the law's treatment of the two artificial reproduction procedures. Finally, the differences in treatment will be analyzed with an eye toward possible constitutional violations due to the unequal treatment of infertile men and women.

Artificial Reproductive Methods

Artificial Insemination by Donor

Medical Process

Today, artificial insemination is a widely accepted nonexperimental procedure. The process generally entails the introduction of male sperm into a female patient with a needleless hypodermic syringe.[4] Presently, three approaches to artificial insemination exist. First, when insemination is accomplished with the husband's sperm, the procedure is identified as Artificial Insemination Homologous (AIH).[5] Second, when insemination is accomplished with a donor's sperm, the procedure is labeled Artificial Insemination Heterologous (AID).[6] Third, when insemination is accomplished with a mixture of the husband's sperm and a donor's sperm, the procedure is called Confused Artificial Insemination (CAI).[7] With all three procedures, fertilization occurs inside the mother's body and not in the laboratory. This essay will concern itself with AID, for this particular procedure presents the legal issues most analogous to those generated by surrogate motherhood.

AID technology has been progressing rapidly since the first reported case in America in 1884.[8] Even before this incident, however, artificial insemination in farm animals was a growing practice. Presently, through modern cryogenic capabilities, semen can be frozen and stored for future use in sperm banks.[9] Some banks operate as commercial enterprises with little or no licensing requirements. Donor[10] selection is also largely unregulated. Many studies have shown that the recordkeeping with regard to donors is minimal.[11]

Only four people are directly concerned in the AID process—the mother, her husband, the donor, and, in most cases, the physician.[12] The husband is the only participant not playing an active role in the process. The AID child is not considered a participant, but is rather the product of the process.

Legal Treatment of AID

Among the legal issues[13] considered by courts in cases involving AID are adultery, the legal status of the child, and the parental status of the parties involved (donor, husband, and wife). Historically, AID has been viewed as an undesirable method of procreation. In 1945, a commission appointed by the Archbishop of Canterbury strongly criticized AID and recommended that it be made a criminal offense.[14] In a report published in 1960, the United Kingdom Feversham Committee also concluded that AID was an undesirable practice.[15]

AID was first considered by a North American court in 1921 in *Orford v. Orford*.[16] In *Orford*, the Supreme Court of Ontario expressed the view in dictum that a wife's submission to AID without her husband's consent would constitute adultery. The court stated that the essence of the offense of adultery was not so much the joinder of sexual organs as it was "the voluntary surrender . . . of the reproductive powers or faculties" by the wife to someone other than her husband.[17] A broader conclusion was reached by an Illinois trial court in 1954, which held that a child conceived by AID with or without the husband's consent constituted adultery and that the child so conceived would be illegitimate.[18] Not until the opinion of Lord Wheatley in a 1958 Scottish Court of Sessions case was AID viewed as not adulterous. Lord Wheatley stated that "[u]nilateral adultery is possible, as in the case of a married man who ravishes a woman not his wife, but self-adultery is a concept as yet unknown to the law."[19] Noting that adultery is concerned with the means and not the end result, the court held that AID even without the husband's consent was not equivalent to the physical contact proscribed by adultery. In *People v. Sorensen*,[20] the California Supreme Court, in confirming a conviction under a criminal nonsupport statute, also concluded that AID was not adultery.[21] The *Sorensen* approach is the modern view in the United States.

At common law, the AID child would have been illegitimate absent a contrary statutory or common law presumption[22] or a saving statute.[23] *Gursky v. Gursky*[24] is a case in point. In *Gursky,* the New York Supreme Court viewed the AID child as illegitimate and noted that AID did not adhere to and satisfy the requirements of the state adoption statute.[25] Presently, many states provide by statute that an AID child shall have the same status as a naturally conceived child so long as both husband and wife consented to the procedure.[26] These statutes generally classify the husband as the child's natural father,[27] although such a result is a medical impossibility.

People v. Sorensen,[28] the case espousing the modern views on AID and adultery, is also the leading case as to the issue of paternity. In *Sorensen,* the California Supreme Court held that a husband who consented to AID was the child's lawful father and was to be registered as such on the birth certificate even if sterile.[29] Furthermore, in *In re Adoption of Anonymous,*[30] a husband who had consented to AID was deemed a parent whose consent was needed to allow the wife's new husband to adopt the AID child.[31] As previously noted, the modern trend is for a jurisdiction to have an AID statute making the husband who consents to AID the natural father of the child.[32]

Thus, in summary, absent a saving statute, a presumption of legitimacy, or an AID statute, an AID child is born illegitimate. However, the trend is to provide by statute that an AID child be deemed legitimate and that the husband of the mother be deemed the natural father of the child without resort to an adoption procedure.

Surrogate Motherhood

Medical Process

Surrogate motherhood is a generic term which can refer to several techniques, including one in which gestation takes place in a womb other than that of the egg donor. This technique may be used when pregnancy would be hazardous, impossible, or undesirable.[33] A woman in this situation could have ova removed from her body, fertilized *in vitro*,[34] and then implanted into the womb of a surrogate mother who would carry the baby to term.[35] However, the popular version of surrogate motherhood occurs when a woman conceives a child by AID, carries the baby to term, and relinquishes it to the sperm donor after birth in accordance with a preconception agreement. In most cases, the sperm donor's wife will adopt the child. In this latter scenario, surrogate motherhood has been regarded as the "female counterpart to AID."[36] As with AID, this version of surrogate motherhood is largely technologically independent.

The surrogate motherhood agreement is primarily a relationship based on contract principles.[37] The surrogate contracts to conceive the child of the husband by means of artificial insemination in return for expenses and, usually, a fee. Thus, the surrogate motherhood agreement requires the making of personal choices and commitments months in advance of performance.[38]

Four people are directly concerned in the surrogate motherhood process—the father, his wife, the surrogate mother, and, in most cases, the physician.[39] The wife is generally the only participant not playing an active role in the process.[40] Like the AID child, the surrogate motherhood child is not considered a participant, but is rather the product of the process.

Legal Treatment of Surrogate Motherhood

As previously stated, the surrogate motherhood arrangement is based on contract principles. However, several legal obstacles to surrogate motherhood agreements exist. In at least twenty-four states, paying a mother to give up a child for adoption is unlawful.[41] For example, in *Doe v. Attorney General*,[42] the Michigan Court of Appeals held that the Michigan "baby brokering" law[43] prohibited payment to a surrogate mother in connection with an adoption. The court held that a couple's fundamental right to make procreative decisions encompassed the right to bear a child with the aid of a third party—the surrogate.[44] However, the court held that this constitutional right did not give the surrogate the right to bear a child for pay or to use the adoption laws to transfer the child to the contracting couple.[45] On the other hand, in *Surrogate Parenting Associates, Inc. v. Commonwealth ex rel. Armstrong*,[46] the Kentucky Supreme Court found fundamental differences between the surrogate parenting procedure and the buying and selling of children. These differences included the "central fact [that] in the surrogate parenting procedure . . . the agreement to bear the child is entered into *before* conception" and the surrogate's primary motivation for agreeing to the procedure is not to relieve herself of the burden of childrearing, but to help a couple have a biologically related child.[47] The *Surrogate Parenting* rationale appears to be the more compelling, as a surrogate motherhood arrangement is not what the legislatures had in mind when they enacted the baby selling laws. Furthermore, if one is to assume, as the Michigan Court of Appeals has, that the right to procreative decisions encompasses the right to bear a child with the aid of a surrogate, then it would seem only logical that the surrogate be paid for the services she performs. Any other result is not only detrimental to the collaborative right of procreation, but also ill-fated because it will force surrogate arrangements into hiding. Although the surrogate will appear to provide her services altruistically, financial arrangements will be made under the table.

Yet another obstacle to surrogate motherhood is the AID statutes. These statutes specifically provide that a sperm donor is not the legal father of a child conceived by the artificial insemination of a woman not his wife.[48] This obstacle, however, is mere fantasy. The purposes of AID statutes are to make the AID child legitimate[49] and to make the consenting husband of the mother the child's natural father.[50] AID statutes were not passed to regulate situations in which the sperm donor was known and did indeed wish to be the legal father.[51]

In *Syrkowski v. Appleyard,*[52] the Michigan Court of Appeals strictly applied the state's paternity act to deny an attempt by a husband sperm donor to use a custody proceeding to validate a surrogate arrangement.[53] The court stated:

> We view the surrogate mother arrangements with caution as we approach an unexplored area in the law which, without a doubt, can have a profound effect on the lives of our people. The courts should not be called upon to enlarge the scope of The Paternity Act to encompass circumstances never contemplated thereby. Studied legislation is needed before surrogate arrangements are recognized as proposed under the facts submitted herein.[54]

The Michigan Supreme Court later reversed the court of appeals, stating that the trial court had jurisdiction under the state's paternity act to allow the plaintiff Syrkowski to prove paternity.[55] It may be an overstatement to conclude that *Syrkowski* itself legalizes surrogate motherhood; however, the trend is undeniably toward making surrogate motherhood arrangements legal and viable exercises of the right of procreation. Presently, twenty-one jurisdictions are considering surrogate motherhood legislation.[56] Of these jurisdictions, only four are considering prohibiting the surrogate process.[57]

Thus, in summary, assuming that surrogate motherhood is lawful, a child born from this process may nevertheless be deemed illegitimate absent a surrogate motherhood statute[58] or saving statute. Furthermore, the wife of the father is not deemed the natural parent of the child as is her male AID counterpart. Instead, for her to obtain the rights and responsibilities of a natural parent, she must adopt the child of her husband.[59]

Equal Protection Analysis Under the Fourteenth Amendment

Sex-based Classifications

The fourteenth amendment to the United States Constitution states, in part:

> No State shall make or enforce any law which shall abridge the privileges or immunities of citizens of the United States; nor shall any State deprive any person of life, liberty, or property, without due process of law; *nor deny to any person within its jurisdiction the equal protection of the laws.*[60]

What this passage means has been and will always be the subject of great debate. Most commentators are in agreement, however, that the purpose of the equal protection clause is to protect those people excluded from the political process or, as has more recently been the case, to protect those rights viewed as fundamental in our society.[61]

An argument can be advanced that AID statutes violate the equal protection clause because they allow infertile men to exercise their right of procreation with the aid of a third party donor while not encompassing the right of infertile women to exercise their right of procreation with the aid of a third party surrogate. Although it must be recognized that the state has particularly broad powers regarding the rights and status of parents and children, the power of the state is necessarily subject to the demands of the equal protection clause.[62]

In analyzing whether AID statutes violate the Constitution, one must first determine the proper standard for reviewing the classification created by these statutes. Since *Craig v. Boren*,[63] the standard for review has been settled, at least in theory. "To withstand constitutional challenge, previous cases establish that *classifications by gender* must serve important governmental objectives and must be substantially related to achievement of those objectives."[64] This standard of review, however, presupposes that the court has found a gender-based classification. Such an observation begs the question. What is a gender-based classification? Section 5 of the Uniform Parentage Act[65] (U.P.A.) provides:

(a) If, under the supervision of a licensed physician and with the consent of her husband, a wife is inseminated artificially with semen donated by a man not her husband, *the husband is treated in law as if he were the natural father of a child thereby conceived*. The husband's consent must be in writing and signed by him and his wife. The physician shall certify their signatures and the date of the insemination, and file the husband's consent with the [State Department of Health], where it shall be kept confidential and in a sealed file. However, the physician's failure to do so does not affect the father and child relationship. All papers and records pertaining to the insemination, whether part of the permanent record of a court or a file held by the supervising physician or elsewhere, are subject to inspection only upon an order of the court for good cause shown.

(b) The donor of semen provided to a licensed physician for use in artificial insemination of a married woman other than the donor's wife is treated in law as if he were not the natural father of a child thereby conceived.[66]

Section 5 has had a great influence on subsequent AID statutes in the United States. It will serve, therefore, as a useful statutory model in our equal protection analysis. Section 5 confers a benefit to infertile married men. That is, a married man who consents to have his wife artificially inseminated by a donor will, upon the birth of a child, be "treated in law as if he were the natural father."[67] Again, is this a gender-based classification?

The answer to this pivotal question might appear quite simple to novices in the constitutional field; a gender-based classification is one that is based on men and women and the differences between them. To those commentators well-versed in the law, however, the answer is not so simple. At least since *Geduldig v. Aiello*[68] and *Personnel Administrator v. Feeney*,[69] the answer, although fundamental, has often proved mysterious. A statute that discriminates on its face between men and women is gender-based.[70] However, under *Aiello*, a statute that discriminates between pregnant and non-pregnant persons is not a gender-based classification.[71] This is true even though to date only women can become pregnant, and, therefore, only women can be harmed by pregnancy. Thus, a characteristic as closely associated with gender as pregnancy is not the basis of a gender-based classification. The conclusion that pregnancy-based classifications are not in themselves gender-based may suggest an exceedingly formalistic view. This, nevertheless, is the view of a majority of the Supreme Court.

The pivotal question then becomes whether AID statutes more closely resemble *Craig*-type or *Aiello*-type statutes. A few examples may help to shed light on this issue. In *Aiello*, we know that the difference between pregnant and non-pregnant persons is not gender-based. But what if the Court were confronted with a medical disability plan that differentiated between vasectomies and hysterectomies or between male and female breast cancer? In these examples we have something more than an *Aiello*-type classification because the distinctions are gender-based. So, too, is the distinction drawn by AID statutes. AID statutes confer a benefit to infertile men in the form of an irrebuttable presumption. Men who consent to the AID process are treated as the legal parent of the child. This is so even though the child could not possibly be the offspring of the infertile man. Thus, AID statutes create a legal fiction which benefits infertile married men and permits them to exercise their fundamental right of procreation. No such benefit is conferred upon infertile married women.

Assuming that AID statutes as written fall under the *Craig* classification, they cannot be saved merely because an infertile woman may take steps to adopt the child and, thus, attain the rights conferred by the AID statutes to infertile men. The argument goes on to say that if a woman fails to take advantage of the procedures available, she should not be heard to complain of the discriminatory impact of AID statutes. But this type of argument was expressly rejected in *Kirchberg v. Feenstra*.[72] In *Kirchberg*, the Supreme Court invalidated a statute that gave a husband, as head and master of property jointly owned with his wife, the unilateral right to dispose of the property without his spouse's consent. The state's view was that the statutory scheme was not unconstitutional because it provided a procedure whereby the wife could have made a "declaration by authentic act" and stopped the disposition of the property.[73] The additional procedure also required that the declaration be filed in the mortgage and conveyance records of the parish in which the property was located.[74] The Court stated that "the 'absence of an insurmountable barrier' will not redeem an otherwise unconstitutionally discriminatory law."[75] The rationale in *Kirchberg* is compelling. AID statutes confer certain rights upon infertile men and, by implication, withhold those same rights from infertile women. Infertile women could obtain the same rights given to infertile men automatically by statute, by engaging in the additional procedure of adoption. Certainly, in many cases adoption is not an insurmountable barrier.[76] However, under *Kirchberg*, the goal need not be unattainable.

One may advance the argument that whatever the impact, without discriminatory legislative motives, AID statutes should be declared constitutional.[77] This would be the case had we been confronted with a gender-neutral statute as in *Feeney*, but as previously noted, AID statutes are not and cannot be construed as gender-neutral. Infertile men and women are similarly situated. Neither can exercise their right of procreation without the aid of a third party semen donor or surrogate. Only infertile men, however, are entitled to the special rights afforded by AID statutes.[78]

A finding that AID statutes are unconstitutional because they violate the equal protection clause is supported by the traditional Tussman-tenBroek equal protection model.[79] Under the Tussman-tenBroek model, one must look beyond the classification to the purpose of the law in question.[80] The purpose of AID statutes is the achievement of some positive public good. Specifically, AID statutes provide a means whereby a couple who cannot conceive a child can, in fact, have a child with the aid of a donor. This child will be deemed legitimate and the husband treated as the natural father. Tussman and tenBroek speak of the relation of the classification to the purpose of the law as the relation of the "trait" to the "mischief."[81] In our case, the trait is all males who are married and infertile or who carry a hereditary disease. The mischief is to help infertile couples have a child part "theirs" whose legal parents are the mother (wife) and her husband (father).

The usual equal protection problem concerns the relation of two classes to one another.[82] The first class consists of all individuals possessing the defining trait[83]—in this case, all married men who are infertile or who have a hereditary disease. The second class consists of all individuals tainted by the mischief at which the law aims[84]—in this case, all married men and women who are infertile or who carry hereditary diseases, who want a child of "their" own who is deemed legitimate, and who want to be treated as the natural parents. The first class is defined by the legislative classification drawn by AID statutes, while the second class consists of those individuals similarly situated with respect to the purposes of the AID statues.

Tussman and tenBroek then talk of five possible relationships between the trait and the mischief.[85] Relationship three is applicable to our case; that is, the AID statues are underinclusive. All who are included in the class are tainted with the mischief, but others who are tainted are not included within the classification. Therefore, a prima facie violation of the equal protection clause has been shown.[86] The question then becomes to what degree a legislature should be permitted to generalize or to deal with portions of a problem at a time and thus to fall short of perfect congruence. Whatever that exact figure may be, a fifty percent congruency is too inexact. The fact that over fifty percent of all infertility is traceable to the woman becomes paramount.[87] Thus, sex is not a sufficiently accurate proxy for infertility. Granted, legislatures are not required to meet perfect congruency; however, when the classification is sex-based, such a great amount of incongruency is intolerable. Furthermore, "[l]egislative classifications which distribute benefits and burdens on the basis of gender carry the inherent risk of reinforcing stereotypes about the 'proper place' of women and their need for special protection."[88]

This result is highlighted by the use of a technique articulated in *Orr v. Orr.*[89] In *Orr,* the Supreme Court directly analogized race discrimination to sex discrimination. "There is no question but that Mr. Orr bears a burden he would not bear were he female. The *issue is highlighted, although not altered,* by transposing it to the sphere of race."[90] An artificial reproduction statute providing that infertile white men would be treated as the natural father of a child while denying the same benefit to infertile black men would be clearly unconstitutional. The result should be no less in this case. It is important to note that even under the traditional Tussman-ten-Broek equal protection model, the classification would be unconstitutional. Thus, a fortiori, the classification would be unconstitutional under most of the more liberal feminist equality models.[91]

Application of the Middle Tier Approach

After the case has been made that AID statutes discriminate against infertile women,[92] the burden is on the party seeking to uphold the AID statute (in this case, the state) to advance an "exceedingly persuasive justification for the challenged classification."[93] The governmental interests in enacting AID statutes are to preserve marriage between an infertile couple,[94] to codify certain common law presumptions,[95] to provide for the legitimacy of AID children,[96] to avoid transmission of genetic disease,[97] and to promote collaborative procreation.[98] The fundamental question is whether these reasons convert into important governmental objectives and whether the AID statute is substantially related to the achievement of these objectives.[99] It is important to note that the test is phrased in the conjunctive; therefore, both conditions must be met.

Do the proffered governmental reasons convert into important governmental objectives? Certainly all five reasons are legitimate. The latter three may also be important. Certainly the right to procreate is not only important, but also compelling.[100] Therefore, at least some of the reasons for AID statutes may be said at first glance to convert into important governmental objectives.

Are the AID statutes substantially related to the achievement of the proffered governmental objectives?[101] The only logical and rational answer is no. The AID statutes are grossly underinclusive. If the proffered reasons for the statutes are important, and we have assumed they are, then denying their special rights to couples who cannot procreate due to the woman's infertility frustrates those purposes.[102] Presently, in the United States, one in six people is affected by infertility.[103] More than one-half of these infertilities are traceable to the woman.[104] Therefore, not encompassing women in AID-like statutes and, thus requiring them to adopt a child conceived through a surrogate arrangement frustrates the articulated purposes of the AID statutes.[105]

It goes without saying that laws may classify even though classification is in a real sense inequality. The Constitution has never required that things different in fact be treated in law as though they were the same. Abstract symmetry is not demanded by the Constitution.[106]

Are infertile men and women similarly situated in exercising their right of procreation through the aid of a third party? In essence, the question may be whether surrogate motherhood is the female counterpart to AID. Cutting through the factual distinctions, the answer by necessity must be yes, at least until the development of the artificial womb.[107] This is so because the focus must be on the right of procreation and not on surrogate motherhood as the remedy or means by which the right may be exercised.

This is not to say, however, that AID and surrogate motherhood may not be differentiated. For example, the identity of the surrogate in a surrogate motherhood arrangement is known, while in the typical AID case the donor is anonymous.[108] Although these differences are important, they are not compelling enough to restrict the rights of infertile women. "Though the historical subjection of women was premised on biological differences, the present institutions and customs which rest on that subjection cannot be justified by reference to the 'nature of things.' "[110] These factual differences, however, go to the remedy or means by which a woman exercises her right of procreation. As to the right itself, men and women are similarly situated.[111]

Many criticisms have been leveled against the concept and practice of surrogate motherhood. Among these criticisms are (1) the physical harm to the couple or surrogate; (2) the possible mental and physical harm to the child; (3) the "commercialization" of procreation (e.g., "rent a womb"); and (4) the fear that surrogate motherhood will confuse family lineage and blur the meaning of the traditional family.[112] These criticisms, however, are not insur-mountable. First, any harm to the couple or donor can be lessened by requiring a licensed medical practitioner to perform the medical procedures needed for surrogate motherhood. States could also require greater information and counselling for the parties about the process.[113] Some of these services are already provided for in the AID process. Second, increased mental and physical harm to the child from surrogate motherhood vis-à-vis AID is not substanti-ated by the evidence.[114] Furthermore, experimentation with em-bryos not implanted is already unlawful in many states.[115] Third, there is no evidence that surrogate motherhood will increase the commercialization of procreation any more than AID.[116] Any ad-vertisement of surrogate services would be subject to state regula-tion. Fourth, there has also been no evidence that surrogate motherhood vis-à-vis AID will confuse family lineage or blur the meaning of the traditional family.[117] The American view is that the family has the right to decide when and how to increase its mem-bership.[118]

It is important to note that most of the criticisms against surro-gate motherhood were previously advanced against another form of artificial reproduction—AID.[119] Thus, no valid reasons exist against providing infertile women the same rights as infertile men. "[A] legal distinction based on the natural lottery of physical equip-ment is not reasonable."[120] Moreover, perceived immorality alone is not sufficient to justify limiting the reproductive rights of others without a showing of tangible harm to some legitimate state inter-est.[121]

Equal Protection Right of Procreation

The differential treatment of infertile men and women by artificial reproduction statutes has been framed up to this point in terms of equality. As Professor Peter Westen has shown, however, a claim of equality always masks a claim of substantive right.[122] Here, the substantive right is the right of procreation.

The roots of the right of procreation can be found in *Skinner v. Oklahoma.*[123] In *Skinner,* the Supreme Court stated that marriage and procreation are among "the basic civil rights of man."[124] How-ever, in *Skinner* and in more recent cases dealing with procreation, the opinions presuppose that procreation will take place within a marriage or a traditional family[125] and assume that the conception and bearing of children was natural.[126] Whether these precedents will apply to the surrogate motherhood relationship would be conjecture at this point.

The right to procreate was given a shot in the arm by *Roe v. Wade*[127] and its progeny. Whether the right of privacy will protect an infertile woman's right to procreate with the aid of a surrogate is debatable. As Professor Robertson has eloquently stated, "[f]reedom to have sex without reproduction does not guarantee freedom to have reproduction without sex. Full procreative freedom would include both the freedom *not* to reproduce and the freedom *to* reproduce when, with whom, and by what means one chooses."[128] However, it is difficult to envision today's Supreme Court expanding *Roe* to include the affirmative right to procreate.

The importance of the right of procreation is not necessarily founded upon the concept of an equal protection fundamental right,[129] but that the right of procreation is impinged by artificial reproduction statutes which classify on the basis of sex. Therefore, impingement on the right of procreation solidifies the view that contemporary artificial reproduction statutes are unconstitutional, for they not only frustrate the right, but also classify on the basis of sex.

Constitutional Remedy

After a court declares a statutory scheme unconstitutional, it must fashion an appropriate remedy. Basically, a court may fashion three types of remedies for the violation.

The first remedy for the court is to refuse to enforce the unconstitutional statute.[130] Such a remedy would not be appropriate in this case for two related reasons. Technically, the typical case in which a court should refuse to enforce a statute is when the statute affirmatively restricts the rights of a particular class.[131] The AID statutes are not within such a class of statutes. Instead, they were passed for some public good (i.e., to legitimize AID children and to treat the husband of the mother as the natural father). Pragmatically, refusing to enforce AID statutes helps no one and hinders the fundamental right of procreation. To deny to infertile men that which has been denied to infertile women is like throwing the baby out with the bath water. Such a result would be ludicrous.

The second remedy for the court is that espoused by Professor Ely for statutes struck down due to gender-based classifications. Ely writes that a court should render unconstitutional a statute which discriminates on the basis of sex, and, if the statute were to be reenacted by the legislature, the court should uphold it.[132] Ely rests this novel approach on the observation that many, if not most, laws that discriminate on the basis of sex were initially passed before women's suffrage.[133] or at least before women were a political force.[134] Ely points out that women in America are not discrete nor insular nor even a minority.[135] This is a pivotal fact in Ely's view of equal protection analysis. Without a finding that the group discriminated against is a discrete and insular minority, Ely finds no reason for the court to aggressively scrutinize legislation affecting it.[136] Although logical, Ely's remedy is nevertheless overly simplistic when viewed in light of the current political process. No doubt women are a political force to be reckoned with at the national level. However, their national force has not been converted into any real grass roots force at the state level.[137] AID statutes are state statutes passed by state legislatures, and state legislatures are typically male dominated.[138] Ely's remedy gives the ultimate power back to those who abused it in the first instance. Such a result cannot help but conjure up images of the proverbial fox guarding the chicken coop; at best, the chickens are left with an uneasy feeling.

The third remedy for the court is to judicially refashion the right at issue. A similar process is often undertaken to keep from declaring a law unconstitutional. A typical example is to read the term "man" to include "woman."[139] Essentially, the court would take notice of the purposes of the AID statute and extend its benefits to the class discriminated against (i.e., infertile women, their husbands, and any children born of surrogate motherhood arrangements). Such a result would not only promote the purposes of the AID statutes, but also promote those purposes more perfectly. One adverse to what has been labeled substantive due process or, more cynically, super-legislating, may cry foul to such a remedy. After all, the result would make surrogate motherhood or something akin to it lawful, a decision the legislature should make. Furthermore, such a remedy is quite similar to the remedy ordered by the Supreme Court in *Roe v. Wade* and would be subject to all the criticism mounted against *Roe*. These fears, however, are unfounded. We are concerned with an equal protection case and not a substantive due process case. We are not directly concerned with the nebulous right of privacy, but a classification based on sex. We are also not dealing with the creation of a "new" right as in *Roe*, but with a right already expressed by legislatures and conferred to infertile men. Finally, conferring this right to infertile women is not comparable to the step taken by the Supreme Court in *Roe*. Extending a right previously denied to a class on account of sex should never be viewed as a quantum leap.[140]

Conclusion

Advances in science and technology now permit an infertile woman to exercise her right of procreation through the aid of a surrogate. However, the offspring born of a surrogate arrangement is technically illegitimate, and the woman must adopt the child to obtain the rights of a natural parent. No such obstacles are present when an infertile man exercises his right of procreation through the aid of a semen donor. To the contrary, AID statutes affirmatively remove these obstacles, but only for infertile men. As previously noted, the classification drawn by these artificial reproduction statutes is unconstitutional because it violates the equal protection clause. The only appropriate remedy is to extend the benefit conferred by AID statutes to infertile women. This may be a de facto call for recognition of surrogate motherhood, but it is a de facto call required by the Constitution. Any other conclusion would relegate women to second class citizenship. Any other result would hamper the exercise of a right as fundamental as any—the right to procreate.

Notes

1. The term "mother" and "father" contain within them assumptions that most of us take for granted. Thus, use of the term "husband" rather than "father" reflects the lack of a word to describe adequately the difference in the roles of these two men in the artificial reproduction scenario.

2. For a typical saving statute, see D.C. Code Ann. Sections 16-908 (1981). This section states that "(a) child born in wedlock or born out of wedlock is the legitimate child of its father and mother and is the legitimate relative of its father's and mother's relatives by blood or adoption." Id.

3. In this sense, adoption may be viewed as a "burden" placed upon the wife of the natural father.

4. See The Boston Women's Health Book Collective, "The New Our Bodies, Ourselves" 318 (1984): Palm & Hirsh, Legal Implications of Artificial Conception, 1982 *Med. Trial Tech*, Q. 404, 406; Wadlington, Artificial Conception: The Challenge for Family Law, 69 Va. L. Rev. 465, 468 (1983).

5. AIH may be used when normal copulation fails because of various medical problems. See Carson & Batzer, Homologous Artificial Insemination, 26 *J. Reproductive Med.* 231 (1981).

6. AID, at least to married couples, is presumed not to be the first alternative. AID, however, may be used either if the husband is sterile or fears transmitting genetic disease. See. W. Finegold, "Artificial Insemination" 18 (2d ed. 1976); Palm & Hirsh, supra note 4, at 407.

7. CAI is often cynically referred to as the "French firing squad technique." One justification for CAI contemplates a possible psychological benefit to a sterile husband who might rationalize that he has fathered the child conceived by his wife. Wadlington, *supra* note 4, at 469. One author suggests, however, that this structural fantasy exposes those men who would be poor AID candidates. A. Guttmacher, W. Best & F. Jaffe, Birth Control and Love: The Complete Guide to Contraception and Fertility, 279–80 (2d rev. ed. 1969).

8. R. Snowden & G. D. Mitchell, The Artificial Family, 13 (1981).

9. For an interesting review of sperm banking in the U.S., see Human Artificial Insemination and Semen Preservation (G. David & W. Price ed. 1980).

10. "It has long been known that the term 'donor' is a euphemism and that, in fact 'donors' receive standard payments for 'donations' in various localities." Wadlington, *supra* note 4, at 471. For an interesting profile of a sperm donor, see Yagoda, "Daddy?" *Campus Voice*, Feb.–Mar. 1985, at 46.

11. See Curie-Coehn, Luttrell & Shapiro, "Current Practice of Artificial Insemination by Donor in the United States" 300 *New Eng. J. Med.* 585 (1979).

12. Although a physician is not necessary to artificially impregnate a woman, many statutes require that a physician perform the artificial insemination. See Ga. Code Ann. § 74-101.1(a) (Supp. 1985).

13. Of course, AID generates more than legal issues. There are ethical and religious issues which are as compelling as their legal counterparts. Many ethicists have stated their profound aversion to artificial manipulation of a natural process so closely tied to the mystery of life. See generally P. Ramsey, Fabricated Man: The Ethics of Genetic Control (1970). Both the Roman Catholic and Orthodox Jewish teachings consider AID adultery. The Boston Women's Health Book Collective, *supra*, note 4, at 319.

14. R. Snowden & G. D. Mitchell, *supra* note 8, at 15.

15. *Id.*

16. 58 D.L.R. 251 (Ont. 1921).

17. *Id.* at 258.

18. *Doornbos v. Doornbos*, 23 U.S.L.W. 2308 (Super. Ct., Cook County,

Ill., 1954), *aff'd,* 139 N.E. 2d 844 (1956). The court, however, found no difficulty with AIH from a legal point of view.

19. *MacLennan v. MacLennan,* 1958 Sess. Cas. 105, 114.

20. 68 Cal. 2d 280, 437 P.2d 495, 66 Cal. Rptr. 7 (1968) (en banc).

21. The court dismissed the idea that the doctor or donor and the wife commit adultery through the artificial insemination process, stating: "Since the doctor may be a woman, or the husband himself may administer the insemination by a syringe, this is patently absurd; to consider it an act of adultery with the donor, who at the time of insemination may be a thousand miles away or may even be dead, is equally absurd." *Id.* at __, 437 P.2d at 501, 66 Cal. Rptr. at 13.

22. For a typical presumption of legitimacy applicable to a child born during wedlock, see *Kusior v. Silver,* 54 Cal. 2d 603, 354 P.2d 657, 7 Cal. Rptr. 129 (1960) (en banc).

23. See *supra* note 2 for an example of a saving statute.

24. 39 Misc. 2d 1083, 242 N.Y.S.2d 406 (Sup. Ct. 1963).

25. See *Strnad v. Strnad,* 190 Misc. 786, 78 N.Y.S.2d 390 (Sup. Ct. 1948). In *Strnad,* the court stated that an AID child had been potentially adopted or semi-adopted by a husband consenting to artificial insemination, even though adoption has always been statutory. *Id.* at __, 78 N.Y.S.2d at 391–92.

26. See, e.g., Conn. Gen. Stat. Ann. §§ 45-69f to 69n (West 1981); Ga. Code Ann. § 74-101.1 (Supp. 1985); Kan. Stat. Ann. §§ 23-128 to 129 (1981); N.C. Gen. Stat. § 49A-1 (1984); Okla. Stat. tit. 10, §§ 551-553 (1981).

27. See e.g., Cal. Civ. Code § 7005 (West 1983); Ga. Code Ann. § 74-101.1 (Supp. 1985); La. Civ. Code Ann. art. 188 (West Supp. 1985); Or. Rev. Stat. § 109.243 (1983).

28. 68 Cal. 2d at 280, 437 P.2d at 495, 66 Cal. Rptr. at 7.

29. *Id.* at __ 437 P.2d at 500, 66 Cal. Rptr. at 12.

30. 74 Misc. 2d 99, 345 N.Y.S.2d 430 (Sur. Ct. 1973).

31. *Id.* at __, 345 N.Y.S.2d at 435-36.

32. There has also been considerable debate among commentators about the potential rights and responsibilities of donors. In C.M. v. C.C., 152 N.J. Super. 160, 377 A.2d 821 (Juv. & Dom. Rel. Ct. 1977), a New Jersey court granted a semen donor visitation rights to a child conceived by an unmarried woman impregnated by his sperm. In that case, the donor and the woman knew each other. Section 5 of the Uniform Parentage Act explicitly provides that a donor of semen will not be regarded as the legal father of the child. Unif. Parentage Act § 5(b), 9A U.L.A. 592–93 (1979). For an interesting discussion of when it may be in the best interests of an AID child to learn of the donor's identity, see Smith, "The Razor's Edge of Human Bonding: Artificial Fathers and Surrogate Mothers," 5 *W. New Eng. L. Rev.* 639, 648 (1983).

33. A woman who would use this type of surrogate motherhood arrangement is typically one who is fertile but has a heart condition, partial paralysis, or a history of miscarriages, or who cannot interrupt a career for pregnancy. Palm & Hirsh, *supra* note 4, at 414.

34. Unlike AID, *in vitro* fertilization (IVF) is technologically dependent. IVF requires extraction of a ripe egg from an ovary, fertilization in a glass dish, and implantation back into the womb. The Boston Women's Health Book Collective, *supra* note 4, at 320.

35. There are several documented reasons given for becoming a surrogate mother. The first is that acting as a surrogate satisfies some sentimental or maternal instinct. The other reasons are based on altruism, financial need, and a fascination with pregnancy. Smith, *supra* note 32, at 649–50.

36. *Id.* at 649.

37. See Note, "Surrogate Motherhood: Contractual Issues and Remedies Under Legislative Proposals," 23 *Washburn L.J.* 601, 602 (1984).

38. See Comment, "Surrogate Mother Agreements: Contemporary Legal Aspects of a Biblical Notion," 16 U. Rich. L. Rev. 467, 469 (1982).

39. See *supra* note 12.

40. Of course, this is not true when the wife's egg is transplanted into the womb of a surrogate.

41. Andrews, "The Stork Market: The Law of the New Reproduction Technologies," *A.B.A. J.*, Aug. 1984, at 50, 52. The typical fee for surrogate services is $10,000 plus all medical, legal, and insurance costs. Gelman & Shapiro, "Infertility: Babies by Contract," *Newsweek*, Nov. 4, 1985, at 74. A couple can expect to pay $25,000 to $30,000 overall. *Id.* at 75.

42. 106 Mich. App. 169, 307 N.W.2d 438 (1981).

43. Mich. Comp. Laws Ann. § 710.54 (West Supp. 1985).

44. 106 Mich. App. at 173, 307 N.W.2d at 441.

45. *Id.*

46. No. 85-SC-421-DG (Ky. Feb. 6, 1986). The action arose when the state attempted to revoke petitioner's corporate charter for abuse and misuse of corporate powers. *Id.* at 1. The state alleged that petitioner's surrogate parenting procedures violated state laws prohibiting the sale of babies. *Id.* at 1–2.

47. *Id.* at 5–6 (emphasis in original).

48. See *supra* notes 26–27.

49. See Comment, *supra* note 38, at 472.

50. See Andrews, *supra* note 41, at 53.

51. Cf. *C.M. v. C.C.*, 152 N.J. Super. 160, 377 A.2d 821 (Juv. & Dom. Rel. Ct. 1977) (court granted sperm donor whose identity was known to unwed mother visitation rights to AID child).

52. 122 Mich. App. 506, 333 N.W.2d 90 (1983).

53. *Id.* at 509, 333 N.W.2d at 91.

54. *Id.* at 515, 333 N.W.2d at 94 (footnote omitted).

55. *Syrkowski v. Appleyard*, 420 Mich. 367, 362 N.W.2d 211 (1985).

56. 11 Fam. L. Rep. (BNA) 3001, 3003 (Jan. 29, 1985).

57. *Id.* at 3003. One commentator has expressed the view that surrogate motherhood violates the thirteenth amendment prohibition against slavery—sale of one person by another. Holder, "Surrogate Motherhood: Babies for Fun and Profit," *Case & Com.*, Mar.–Apr. 1985, at 3, 9. This view, I believe, shows a fundamental lack of understanding of surrogate motherhood.

58. For example, Maryland House of Delegates Bill No. 1552, proposed during the 1985 session, would have provided that all children born by the surrogate motherhood process are legitimate. H.D. 1552, 1985 Md. Leg.

59. Technically, the wife could use a streamlined procedure for a step-parent adoption in a jurisdiction that recognizes such a procedure. See Andrews, *supra* note 41, at 5?

60. U.S. Const. amend. XIV, § 1 (emphasis added).

61. See generally J. Ely, Democracy and Distrust: A Theory of Judicial Review (1980).

62. See e.g., *Caban v. Muhammed*, 441 U.S. 380 (1979) (Court struck down on equal protection grounds a New York statute allowing unwed mother, but not unwed father, to block adoption of child by withholding consent).

63. 429 U.S. 190 (1976).

64. *Id.* at 197 (emphasis added); see also *Califano v. Webster*, 430 U.S. 313, 316–17 (1977) (applying the *Craig* standard to challenged provisions of Social Security Act).

65. 9A U.I.A. 592–93 (1979). The U.P.A. was approved by the National Conference of Commissioners on Uniform State Laws in 1973 and by the A.B.A. House of Delegates in 1974.

66. *Id.* (emphasis added).

67. *Id.* § 5(a). Section 5 also confers benefits on the wife of the infertile man because she can exercise her right of procreation and on the AID child who will be presumed legitimate.

68. 417 U.S. 484 (1974). *Aiello* involved a state statute establishing a disability insurance system for private employees. Plaintiffs challenged the statute as underinclusive on equal protection grounds for its failure to insure the risk of disability from a normal pregnancy. The Supreme Court upheld the statute. *Id.* at 494.

69. 442 U.S. 256 (1979). In *Feeney*, plaintiff challenged a state hiring and promotion statute favoring veterans for civil service positions. Although the statute operated "overwhelmingly to the advantage of males," the Court upheld the statute against an equal protection challenge. *Id.* at 259.

70. See *Craig*, 429 U.S. at 197; *Reed v. Reed*, 404 U.S. 71, 76–77 (1971). But see *Kahn v. Shevin*, 416 U.S. 351, 352 (1974) (upholding a Florida statute providing for a property tax exemption for widows).

71. 417 U.S. at 496 n.20; see also *Feeney*, 442 U.S. at 275 (classification was one of veteran and non-veteran).

72. 450 U.S. 455, 461 (1981).

73. *Id.* at 460–61.

74. *Id.* at 460 n.8.

75. *Id.* at 461 (citations omitted).

76. This is not the case with an unmarried woman or a woman engaged in a lesbian relationship. Moreover, couples seeking surrogates have usually exhausted the possibility of adoption. See *Gelman & Shapiro, supra* note 41, at 74.

77. Accord *Feeney*, 442 U.S. at 272.

78. It is relevant to note that the first AID statute was passed in the early

1960's when women were not a politically active group. In terms of reproduction, women have been the victims of discrimination as far back as the Old Testament. See L. Gordon, Woman's Body, Woman's Right: A Social History of Birth Control in America, 1–46 (1976). American women began their quest for reproductive freedom with the birth control movement of the mid-nineteenth century. See Robertson, "Procreative Liberty and the Control of Conception, Pregnancy, and Childbirth," 69 Va. L. Rev. 405, 405(1983). For an interesting discussion of the background of birth control in the United States, see L. Gordon, supra. The law's response to the childbearing issue marks a pivotal point in the emergence of women as first class citizens. Scales, "Towards a Feminist Jurisprudence," 56 Ind. L.J. 375, 376 (1981). Yet, as Professor Ely notes, "exaggerated stereotyping . . . has long been rampant throughout the male population and consequently in our almost exclusively male legislatures in particular." J. Ely, supra note 61, at 164. "Absent a strong demonstration of mitigating factors, therefore, we would have to treat gender-based classifications that act to the disadvantage of women as suspicious." Id.

79. Tussman & tenBroek "The Equal Protection of the Laws," 37 Calif. L. Rev. 341 (1949).

80. Id. at 346.

81. Id.

82. Id. at 347.

83. Id.

84. Id.

85. Id. Tussman and tenBroek use Venn diagrams to demonstrate ideal limits of reasonableness, unreasonableness, underinclusiveness, overinclusiveness, and both over- and underinclusiveness. Id.

86. Id. at 348.

87. Textbook of Medicine, 1780 (P. Beeson & W. McDermott 14th ed. 1975). This source attributes 40% of all infertility to men and 70% to women. (A total in excess of 100% indicates multiple causes infertility.) Id.; see also Palm & Hirsh, supra note 4, at 404.

88. Orr v. Orr, 440 U.S. 268, 283 (1979) (citation omitted).

89. Id. at 268. Appellant, ordered to pay alimony to his wife upon divorce, challenged on equal protection grounds Alabama statutes that could require husbands, but not wives, to pay alimony. Id. at 271.

90. Id. at 273 (emphasis added); see also Scales, supra note 78, at 393.

91. See Scales, supra note 78, at 434–35. The author recognizes that in utero pregnancy is a difference between the sexes that cannot be ignored. But this does not negate gender-neutral childrearing or parenting concepts. Under the author's "incorporationist approach," the classification drawn by AID statutes would be unconstitutional. Id. at 435.

92. AID statutes also discriminate against the husband of an infertile woman and against any child born by the surrogate motherhood process. Accord Califano v. Goldfarb, 430 U.S. 199 (1977) (plaintiff was a man complaining of discrimination against his deceased wife).

93. Kirchberg v. Feenstra, 450 U.S. 455, 461 (1981); see also Wengler v.

Druggists Mutual Ins. Co., 446 U.S. 142, 151 (1980) (state's justification for unequal treatment of men and women under Missouri workers' compensation laws was insufficient to support the statutory advantage).

94. See R. Snowden & G.D. Mitchell, *supra* note 8, at 75.

95. The typical presumption relevant here is the Lord Mansfield presumption that a child born during wedlock is the natural child of his mother and her husband. See Andrews, *supra* note 41, at 53. Such a presumption is in effect in at least 18 states. *Id.*

96. This is unequivocally one of the major thrusts of the AID statutes. Note, "Artificial Insemination and Surrogate Motherhood—A Nursery Full of Unresolved Questions," 17 *Willamette L. Rev.* 913, 924–25 (1981). Legitimacy is always in the best interest of the child, and the best interest of the child is a compelling state interest. See Graham, "Surrogate Gestation and the Protection of Choice, 22 *Santa Clara L. Rev.* 291, 304 (1982).

97. See Palm & Hirsh, *supra* note 4, at 407.

98. Through collaborative conception one can exercise the right of procreation. Robertson, *supra* note 78, at 423. For an excellent discussion on the constitutional right of procreation, see *id.* at 414–20.

99. *Craig v. Boren*, 429 U.S. 190, 197 (1976); see also *Califano v. Webster,* 430 U.S. 313, 316–17 (1977).

100. See *Skinner v. Oklahoma* 316 U.S. 535, 541 (1942); Robertson, *supra* note 78, at 414–20.

101. See *supra* notes 94–98 and accompanying text.

102. When viewed in this light, the AID statutory scheme seems more ludicrous than it is in fact. There is no question, however, that the contemporary policy completely frustrates an infertile woman's right of procreation.

103. Andrews, *supra* note 41, at 50.

104. See *supra* note 87.

105. "If childrearing were the sole reason for procreation, adoption might well serve the procreative needs of infertile persons. The urge to procreate, however, usually involves a desire to transmit one's own genetic heritage to the child and to participate in gestation and parturition." Robertson, *supra* note 78, at 423 (footnote omitted). An adoption proceeding in his context appears absurd. Furthermore, there is the existence of a birth certificate and other records declaring the adoption of the child. See R. Snowden & G.D. Mitchell, *supra* note 8, at 18.

106. *Skinner,* 316 U.S. at 540.

107. "The [surrogate] process is not biologically different from the reverse situation where the husband is infertile and the wife conceives by artificial insemination." Surrogate Parenting Associates, Inc. v. Commonwealth *ex rel.* Armstrong, No. 85-SC-421-DG, slip op. at 7 (Ky. Feb. 6, 1986).

108. Smith, *supra* note 32, at 654.

109. *Id.*

110. Scales, *supra* note 78, at 425.

111. The right/remedy (method) dichotomy is not novel. Merely because men and women are not similarly situated as to the remedy does

not, of itself, impact adversely on the right when men and women are similarly situated. Cf. *Parham v. Hughes*, 441 U.S. 347, 362 (1979) (White, J., dissenting).

112. Robertson, *supra* note 78, at 424–25.

113. *Id.* at 433–34. By requiring greater screening for surrogate motherhood and not for AID, a state may generate more equal protection concerns. The Constitution may require that AID donors be screened as well. Many would agree with this proposition, but it may not be constitutionally mandated. As to the remedy or means by which men and women exercise their right to procreate, they are not similarly situated. This fact will not, however, work to deny the right altogether. Cf. *Roe v. Wade*, 410 U.S. 113 (1973) (a state may regulate the right to terminate a pregnancy, but cannot deny such a right).

114. Robertson, *supra* note 78, at 434.

115. Andrews, *supra* note 41, at 51–52.

116. See Graham, *supra* note 96, at 304–05.

117. Robertson, *supra* note 78, at 425; see also Kass, "Making Babies Revisited," 54 *Pub. Interest* 32 (1979); Kass, "Making Babies—the New Biology and the "Old" Morality," 26 *Pub. Interest* 18 (1972).

118. Robertson, *supra* note 78, at 435.

119. See R. Snowden & G.D. Mitchell, *supra* note 8, at 117, 121, 127.

120. Robertson, *supra* note 78, at 428 (footnote omitted).

121. See *Poe v. Ullman*, 367 U.S. 497, 545–46 (1961) (Harlan, J., dissenting).

122. Westen, "The Empty Idea of Equality," 95 *Harv. L. Rev.* 537 (1982).

123. 316 U.S. 535 (1942).

124. *Id.* at 541.

125. See *Griswold v. Connecticut*, 381 U.S. 479 (1965).

126. See *Cleveland Bd. of Educ. v. LaFleur*, 414 U.S. 632 (1974); *Eisenstadt v. Baird*, 405 U.S. 438 (1972); *Stanley v. Illinois*, 405 U.S. 645 (1972).

127. 410 U.S. 113 (1973).

128. Robertson, *supra* note 78, at 406 (emphasis in original).

129. Only a few rights have been classified as fundamental equal protection rights. Among them are voting rights, e.g., *Kramer v. Union Free School Dist. No. 15*, 395 U.S. 621 (1969); *Cipriano v. City of Houma*, 395 U.S. 701 (1969); *Harper v. Virginia Bd. of Elections*, 383 U.S. 663 (1966); *Carrington v. Rash*, 380 U.S. 89 (1965); *Reynolds v. Sims*, 377 U.S. 533 (1964); certain criminal procedural rights, e.g., *Douglas v. California* 372 U.S. 353 (1963); *Griffin v. Illinois*, 351 U.S. 12 (1956); the right of interstate travel e.g., *Shapiro v. Thompson*, 394 U.S. 618 (1969); *United States v. Guest*, 383 U.S. 745 (1966); and possibly the right to privacy concerning decisions of intimacy and procreation, e.g., *Whalen v. Roe*, 429 U.S. 589 (1977); *Skinner v. Oklahoma*, 316 U.S. 535 (1942).

130. See *Marbury v. Madison*, 5 U.S. (1 Cranch) 137, 177–80 (1803); cf. *Norton v. Shelby County*, 118 U.S. 425, 442 (1886) ("An unconstitutional act is not a law . . . it is . . . as inoperative as though it had never been passed.").

131. See *Craig v. Boren*, 429 U.S. 190 (1976).

132. J. Ely, *supra* note 61, at 169–70.

133. The nineteenth amendment became effective in 1920. Therefore, laws passed before 1920 would fall into this class. AID statutes, as previously noted, were first passed in 1964 (Georgia) and, thus, would not fall within the class.

134. Professor Ely does not point to any specific date when women became a political force in the United States.

135. J. Ely, *supra* note 61, at 164.

136. *Id.*

137. Although this statement is illogical on its face, it is nevertheless true. In this regard, the women's movement is much like the labor movement, which also historically has had greater power on the national rather than the state level.

138. In state legislatures, maleness is the norm. Presently, 83% of all state legislators are men.

139. This is often the tack used by courts when confronted with a criminal statute that contains the term "man." But see *Michael M. v. Superior Court*, 450 U.S. 464 (1981) (statutory rape law protecting females under 18 survived equal protection challenge of male charged with its violation).

140. See Robertson, *supra* note 78, at 429.

4

The Dilemma of Surrogate Parenthood

John J. Mandler

People who want to participate in surrogate parenthood arrangements[1] often find themselves in complex and frustrating legal situations.[2] Despite the increasing popularity and availability of these arrangements,[3] no state legislature has passed a comprehensive statute to regulate them.[4] The few courts that have considered these arrangements have done little to help formulate a rational and consistent policy.[5] With no law to guide their actions, the participants subject themselves, their counsel, and their physicians to significant risks.[6]

Surrogate parenthood requires extensive planning. Those who want to take advantage of it often seek the advice of a physician or attorney, who has experience with either surrogate parenthood arrangements or family and domestic relations law.[7] Some of these people may seek assistance from one of the specialized surrogate parenthood clinics or centers that have opened in the past few years.[8] After the physician, attorney, or clinic counselor determines that the individuals are suitable candidates for surrogate parenthood,[9] and after the individuals have paid the (usually non-refundable) initial fee,[10] they must find a woman who will agree to conceive and bear the child. Typically, surrogate parenthood clinics have information about fertile women interested in serving as surrogate mothers or a system for locating such women. This process may require the parents to study the biographies of poten-

---

John J. Mandler is an attorney practicing in Washington, D.C. This article first appeared in the Georgetown Law Journal, 1985.

tial surrogates and negotiate with candidates, or to publicize their situation in the hope of finding a woman willing to conceive and bear a child for them.[11]

Once the particular surrogate becomes involved, the parties must negotiate the terms of the arrangement. The arrangement may involve a formal written agreement covering all issues that may arise during the course of the insemination and pregnancy. The final terms are affected by the laws of the states where the surrogate will give birth and where the prospective parents will live. Under current law, most terms of a surrogate agreement are not legally enforceable, but the document may serve as a "gentleman's agreement" which shapes the conduct of the parties.[12]

Analysis of some actual situations illustrates the legal oblivion in which participants in surrogate parenthood arrangements exist. The Stiver-Malahoff case is one dramatic example. In early 1982, Judy Stiver, a married woman from Lansing, Michigan, entered into a formal written agreement with Alexander Malahoff, an accountant from New York City who was unable to have children naturally with his wife. Stiver agreed to be inseminated artificially with Malahoff's semen and to conceive and bear his child.[13] As part of the arrangement, Mrs. Stiver agreed to forego sexual intercourse with her husband Ray for a period of time to ensure that any child she might conceive would be a result of the artificial insemination.[14] In January 1983, she gave birth to a boy; she and Malahoff believed he was Malahoff's son.[15]

The baby boy was born with microcephaly, an abnormally small head, which threatened to leave him severely retarded.[16] Later, he developed a staph infection that further endangered his life.[17] When Malahoff refused to allow medical treatment of the infection, the baby's doctors received a court order mandating it.[18] Malahoff then began to question whether he was the child's biological father and decided that he did not want the impaired child.[19] Mrs. Stiver and her husband argued that the child was not theirs either, and that, under the agreement, Malahoff was responsible for the baby's care and custody.[20]

Blood tests involving the child (whom Malahoff's attorney identified as "Baby Doe,"[21] a name usually reserved for a child of unknown or confidential origins), Malahoff, and Mr. Stiver were administered. The results, announced to the participants on the

Donahue television program,[22] indicated that Malahoff could not be the boy's father and that Ray Stiver was the probable father.[23] Later, Ray Stiver revealed that he had fathered a microcephalic child in a previous marriage.[24] That child was mentally retarded and died in early childhood.[25]

Eventually, the unwanted baby boy went to live with his natural parents, the Stivers,[26] while Malahoff was left to contemplate his options, which included another attempt at surrogate parenthood.[27] This unsettling resolution raises some of the critical legal questions surrounding surrogate parenthood arrangements: how the contracts can be enforced, how a state can protect its interest in the arrangements, and how disputes among the parties to surrogate parenthood arrangements can be resolved.

In his book *The Surrogate Mother,*[28] Noel Keane relates many situations with results even more disturbing than those of the Stiver-Malahoff affair.[29] Particularly germane to this discussion is the story of Bill and Bridget,[30] an infertile couple, and Diane, the surrogate with whom they contracted to bear Bill's child. Diane had agreed to conceive through artificial insemination by donor (AID), using Bill's semen, and to bear the child in exchange for payment of her pregnancy-related expenses.[31] She agreed to forgo a fee for carrying and delivering the child because Tennessee, the state in which she resided and would have the baby, has a law forbidding payment of money in connection with the adoption of a child or the termination of parental rights.[32]

During her pregnancy, Diane repeatedly demanded that Bill and Bridget pay not only her medical expenses, but also expenses relating to her drug and alcohol addictions, which were unknown to Bill and Bridget when they entered into the surrogate parenthood arrangement.[33] In addition, while pregnant with Bill's baby, Diane lived with a series of lesbian lovers under circumstances that threatened both her physical health and mental stability.[34] The child, a boy, was born with fetal alcohol syndrome and had to be detoxified at birth.[35]

Diane continued to demand more money of Bill and Bridget after the child's birth. When Tennessee child welfare authorities tried to deprive her of custody of her other child on grounds of unfitness, she fled to Florida.[36] Because Diane could not be found, Bill and Bridget's legal adoption of the boy was threatened.[37] Tennessee law complicated matters further: Bill's name could not appear on the boy's birth certificate because Diane, as the natural mother, was the baby's only legally recognized parent.[38] The child lived with Bill (his natural father) and Bridget, who had only Diane's temporary permission to keep him, and was abandoned for all intents and purposes by Diane, his natural mother.[39]

Keane tells another story about a couple named Lorelei and John.[40] Lorelei, a transsexual, could not bear children, and so the couple entered into a surrogate parenthood arrangement with Rita.[41] Rita agreed to conceive John's child through AID with John's semen and to bear the child in exchange for payment of her expenses.[42] When Rita learned that some surrogates were receiving compensation above payment of pregnancy-related expenses, she demanded $7500 to fulfill her part of their agreement.[43] She threatened to abort the child or to keep it after birth.[44] Eventually she refused to surrender custody of the child.[45] Later, in order to preserve Lorelei's anonymity, Lorelei and John settled—unfavorably for them—a lawsuit they had brought to obtain custody of the child.[46] The suit was refiled after the story was reported in the national media.[47]

These unfortunate stories are not told in order to suggest that only unstable and desperate people try to create families through surrogate parenthood arrangements. Instead, they are included to highlight the potential legal and emotional complications that confront those who choose surrogate parenthood. Parties to a surrogate parenthood arrangement face a legal frontier, where courts tread reluctantly and haphazardly and legislatures act tentatively.[48] The participants in such arrangements, as well as their counsel and physicians, are expanding the possibilities of parenthood,[49] and, in the process, are creating legal dilemmas that require definite answers.[50]

This essay tries to fill the void in surrogate parenthood law. First, the essay will discuss two specific areas of law that might limit or otherwise affect surrogate parenthood arrangements and will try to resolve any uncertainties these areas of the law create.[51] Then it will consider the proper theoretical framework for regulation of surrogate parenthood arrangements, assuming the propriety of such arrangements.

Discovering the Legal Obstacles to Surrogate Parenthood Arrangements [¹]

Complications among the parties do not pose the only obstacles to surrogate parenthood arrangements; the law may also interfere. Before it considers the theory for regulating surrogate parenthood arrangements, this essay will identify these legal obstacles to surrogate parenthood. [52]

Babyselling and Adoption

The first potential obstacle concerns the relationship between surrogate parenthood and state laws regulating adoption and termination of parental rights. The law of almost every state prohibits the payment of any consideration in connection with the adoption of a child or the termination of parental rights, a practice commonly referred to as "babyselling." [53] Critics of surrogate parenthood have pointed to the facial similarities between babyselling and surrogate parenthood arrangements involving compensation of the surrogate. [54] In 1981, Steven L. Beshear, the Attorney General of Kentucky, compared compensation of surrogates to babyselling, writing that any contractual element of a surrogate parenthood arrangement would be unenforceable as a violation of both the public policy against babyselling and the Kentucky statute prohibiting payment of consideration in connection with an adoption. [55] William J. Brown, the Attorney General of Ohio, also has written that compensation of a surrogate would violate Ohio law forbidding payment to secure an adoption. [56]

The few court decisions concerning surrogate parenthood have generally accepted the babyselling analogy. [57] The court in *Beshear v. Surrogate Parenthood Associates, Inc.*, however, looked beyond the similarity between babyselling and surrogate parenthood to find that the two practices are essentially different. It wondered, "[H]ow can a father be characterized as either adopting or buying his own child?" [58]

Although they generally recognize that many state officials will continue to view surrogate parenthood as a violation of the laws against babyselling, [59] commentators tend to reject the babyselling analogy. [60] Focusing on a series of cases that held the laws against babyselling inapplicable in family adoption situations, these commentators emphasize that the biological relationship between the natural father and the child distinguishes surrogate parenthood arrangements from situations that the laws against babyselling were designed to control.

In *Reimche v. First National Bank of Nevada*,[61] for example, the Ninth Circuit upheld an agreement giving custody of a child born to an unmarried couple to the child's father, in exchange for his promise to support the child and provide for the child's mother in his will. The court sustained the mother's right to sue the deceased father's estate for specific performance of the promise, reversing a lower court ruling that the agreement was void as against public policy.[62] The decision emphasized three factors: The mother had no motive of pecuniary gain, she did not initiate the agreement, and the agreement was in the child's best interests.[63] The court said specifically that fears of "bartering and child selling" are not present in arrangements that involve a child's parents and/or close family members.[64] Similarly, in *In re Estate of Shirk*,[65] the court decided that laws against babyselling and the making of contracts relating to adoptions would not apply to a situation in which a woman took custody of her daughter's child, in exchange for a promise to leave the daughter one-third of her estate.[66] The court in *Clark v. Clark*,[67] relying on an earlier Pennsylvania decision, *Enders v. Enders*,[68] held that when an agreement providing for payment in connection with an adoption was made in a family situation and was in the child's best interests, the contract was not against public policy and should be allowed to stand.[69] *Clark* upheld a contract between a divorced couple which provided that the husband's father would have custody of their child in return for the grandfather's support of the child's mother for life.[70]

Commentators who discuss these cases argue that adoption and antibabyselling laws are designed to regulate situations in which strangers to a child and its mother seek to adopt the child and the child's conception and birth are not purposeful, at least insofar as the adoptive parents are concerned.[71] The surrogate parenthood arrangement is different because the natural father is not a stranger[72] and because the child's birth is purposeful and designed to secure for the natural father a biologically related child.[73]

Another adoption-related issue must also be considered. No

state law now permits a prospective parent to consent to the adoption of his or her child, or to the termination of his or her parental rights and responsibilities, before the child's birth. This legal doctrine does not affect surrogate parenthood arrangements, however, because it addresses circumstances not present in the surrogate parenthood context. In the usual voluntary termination of parental rights and responsibilities scenario, a pregnant woman decides to surrender her child for adoption by unrelated parties. Often the woman is unmarried or under some other social or economic pressure that makes her vulnerable to exploitation and impairs her judgment. In such situations, the law imposes a mandatory waiting period so that the woman is as free as possible from the stress caused by her pregnancy.

In a surrogate parenthood arrangement, these conditions do not exist. The surrogate's pregnancy is purposeful and planned. She negotiates the surrogate parenthood contract with the natural father, and only when she is satisfied with it does she undergo insemination. She is under no time constraints because she can negotiate for as long as she feels is necessary before accepting the contract and agreeing to the requirement that she terminate her parental rights to the child. She generally makes a decision only after her careful consideration of all aspects of the arrangement in consultation with legal, medical, and psychological/psychiatric counsel. In short, traditional legal thinking about termination of parental rights and responsibilities does not apply to surrogate parenthood arrangements. Thus, the laws that reflect this thinking should have no effect on such arrangements.

Artificial Insemination and Legal Paternity

Another set of laws that may affect surrogate parenthood arrangements are laws regulating paternity and determinations of paternity.[74] Some of these laws were prompted by the development of artificial insemination (AI) and the use of AID by married couples who could not conceive children naturally because of the husband's infertility (or the couple's unwillingness to use the husband's sperm because of his history of genetic disorders). In AID, the identity of the biological father usually is not known to the couple, and the man supplies his semen with no intention of asserting any parental rights toward the child to be conceived or assuming any responsibility for the child.[75]

Statutes regulating artificial insemination generally contain a presumption in favor of the paternity of the natural mother's husband, which may or may not be rebuttable. The Uniform Parentage Act (UPA)[76] is the basis for many such state statutes regulating AID. Under the UPA, the husband of a married woman is presumed to be her child's father if the child is born during the marriage or within 300 days of a divorce of separation.[77] As long as the wife receives AID through a licensed physician and the husband has consented to the procedure, the husband is treated by law as the child's natural father.[78] Failure to file the proper documentation does not affect the child's status.[79] The semen donor is not regarded as the child's natural father.[80] While the UPA allows any "interested party" to bring an action to determine paternity,[81] only the child, the natural mother, or the man presumed to be the natural father under the UPA qualifies to bring an action to declare or deny the existence of a parent-child relationship.[82]

These provisions affect surrogate parenthood arrangements because they deprive the natural father of standing to establish his paternity if the surrogate is married when she conceives the natural father's child. This deprivation is especially troublesome in light of the tendency of some physicians and attorneys to favor as surrogates married women who have previously given birth.[83] Because of these complications, Keane does not like to use married surrogates.[84] A law regulating surrogate parenthood must still resolve the paternity problems that result from applying current paternity laws to surrogate parenthood arrangements.

Some commentators have suggested that surrogate parenthood is the biological counterpart of AID and that the surrogate's role is equivalent to that of the AID semen donor.[85] This similarity between surrogate parenthood and AID has led the commentators to two principal conclusions: first, that the law controlling AID should provide a basis for regulating surrogate parenthood arrangements[86] and second, that statutory distinctions between allowing payment to semen donors for the semen used in AID and allowing payment to surrogates for their services may be an unconstitutional denial of equal protection.[87]

Other commentators do not accept the analogy to AID law. Krimmel, for example, argues that surrogate parenthood is more "dramatic" than AID because the surrogate's role entails more personal involvement than does the semen donor's role in AID.[88] One student commentator argues that surrogate parenthood and AID are completely different because they are designed to deal with different problems.[89]

A more obvious equivalent to AID now exists in the form of "prenatal adoption" or "embryo transfer," a practice that entails transferral (before implantation occurs) of a fertilized ovum from the uterus of one woman to the uterus of another woman, who will give birth to and raise the child. This method is a clear counterpart to AID.[90] The roles of the ovum donor and the semen donor are comparable because their limited involvement is completed at the earliest stage of pregnancy, before either has an opportunity to form any lasting attachment to the developing child. Unlike the surrogate who carries the developing child through nine months of pregnancy, neither the semen donor nor the ovum donor participates in this critical bonding process. Thus, because of the fundamental dissimilarity between AID and surrogate parenthood, which is highlighted by the close analogy between AID and embryo transfer, AID law should not serve as a legal framework for regulating surrogate parenthood arrangements.

Regulating Surrogate Parenthood Arrangements

Those who advocate banning surrogate parenthood arrangements, particularly state legislators who want to criminalize them,[91] must reconcile their arguments with the growing body of law recognizing a broad right to privacy and reproductive freedom.[92] A line of cases that extends as far back as *Skinner v. Oklahoma*[93] has brought under the Constitution's implied protection a number of personal privacy activities relating to the bearing and begetting of children, including the right to be free from both forced sterilization[94] and government interference in the use of contraceptive devices,[95] and the right to obtain an abortion.[96] Another line of cases has recognized an only slightly less expansive personal freedom within the context of marital and family relationships. These decisions establish that people are reasonably free to marry[97] and to govern their family lives without unnecessary state interference.[98]

Both lines of cases are grounded in a generalized constitutional right of privacy that courts have found to be implied in various constitutional provisions.[99] Some courts have said, however, that the right to privacy is limited.[100] In addition, some commentators have indicated that the right to privacy is not broad enough to shield surrogate parenthood arrangements from state intervention.[101] On the other hand, other commentators argue that a state ban on surrogate parenthood would restrict too closely the right to privacy by curtailing reproductive freedom.[102]

John Robertson believes that the logical implication of the abortion and contraception cases such as *Griswold*, *Eisenstadt*, *Roe*, and *Carey* is that the right to privacy protects the ability of persons to participate in surrogate parenthood arrangements, at least when the persons seeking to have a child using a surrogate's services are a married couple.[103] Noel Keane contends that any regulation of surrogate parenthood that would exclude the only means that some people have to procreate would be an unconstitutional burden on the privacy right of married couples (and possibly single people) to make intimate family decisions such as whether and how to have a child.[104] He argues further that surrogate parenthood arrangements among consenting adults are valid exercises of personal liberty with which the state cannot interfere on purely "moralistic" grounds (such as a preference for natural conception and pregnancy).[105]

These commentators conclude that the constitutionally proper approach for states to take to surrogate parenthood is to enact legislation that would provide reasonable regulation of such arrangements.[106] Such regulation should not unduly restrict the rights of people to participate in surrogate parenthood arrangements,[107] but should protect the children so conceived[108] and the people vulnerable to exploitation.[109] The regulation also should relieve the state of the responsibility for and the costs of caring for impaired children born of surrogate parenthood arrangements.[110]

The right of privacy has been greatly expanded by the courts since its earliest articulations.[111] Although the right is well entrenched, it is not unlimited.[112]

Yet, some state courts have used the right to privacy to sanction the termination of life-supporting medical treatment,[113] which goes far beyond the scope of the privacy right in its earliest formulations.[114] Surrogate parenthood, on the other hand, falls close to the original parameters of the privacy right because it is an attempt, usually by married couples, to structure a family, an activity similar to those given constitutional protection in cases such as *Meyer* and *Pierce*.[115] Courts must overcome their reluctance to address the issue of surrogate parenthood and must acknowledge that the right to privacy and reproductive freedom protects such arrangements, at least when infertile married couples enter into them in the hope of creating a family.[116] Legislatures must recognize that outright bans on surrogate parenthood arrangements may not be constitutional and must therefore create an orderly system for ensuring that surrogate parenthood arrangements serve socially beneficial purposes.[117]

Notes

1. The usual procedure in surrogate parenthood arrangements is for a couple who cannot have children naturally to arrange to have a fertile woman conceive a child through artificial insemination with the husband's semen. The fertile woman then bears the child. Keane, *Legal Problems of Surrogate Motherhood*, 1980 S. Ill. U.L.J. 147, 147–48. (In some cases, the couple wants to isolate the wife's genetic component because she carries a genetic disease; the couple wants children biologically related only to the husband.) As part of the agreement, the surrogate agrees to terminate her parental rights to the child and to consent to the child's adoption by the married couple or by the wife alone (when the natural or biological father is unable to assert his paternity). *Id.* The infertile couple then raises the child as its own natural child. *Id. See generally* the discussion of surrogate parenthood in Andrews, *The Stork Market: The Law of the New Reproduction Technologies*, 70 A.B.A. J. 50 (1984) [hereinafter cited as Andrews, *Stork Market*].

Walter Wadlington describes the surrogate mother and, indirectly, the surrogate parenthood arrangement, as follows:

While the term "surrogate mother" can refer to a number of different situations, including that in which gestation takes place in a womb other than that of the egg donor, it is widely used today in the United States to describe the woman who conceives a child by AID [artificial insemination by donor], carries it to term, and then relinquishes it to the sperm donor in accord with a contract executed before the child's conception. Ordinarily the surrogate mother in such a scenario receives a fee or honorarium from the sperm donor, who also pays for all the expenses of the procedure. There can be many variations of such a contract, but they center on a promise that the [surrogate] will relinquish the child to the biological father immediately after birth, renouncing all rights to the child and consenting to adoption if this is deemed necessary.

W. Wadlington, Cases and Other Materials on Domestic Relations 443 (1984).

The term *surrogate parenthood arrangement* refers to the relationship among the surrogate, the man whose semen is used to impregnate the surrogate (defined as the *natural father*), the natural father's wife (if he is married), and the surrogate's husband (if she is married). The term encompasses more than the actual written agreement (defined as the *surrogate parenthood contract*), which includes only the formal terms upon which the parties have agreed.

2. *See, e.g.,* Commonwealth *ex rel.* Beshear v. Surrogate Parenting Assocs., No. 81-CI-429 (Franklin Cir. Ct., Ky. Oct. 26, 1983) (state statutes regulating adoption and termination of parental rights not applicable to rights of surrogate parents); Keane, *supra* note 1, at 147 (parties to surrogate parenthood arrangements act without certainty of legal consequences; traditional legal doctrines and concepts insufficient); Note, *Surrogate Mothers: The Legal Issues,* 7 Am. J. L. & Med. 323, 345 (1981) (surrogate parenthood legislation necessary to protect against "misplaced assumptions and liabilities" of parties to surrogate parenthood arrangements) [hereinafter cited as Note, *Surrogate Mothers*].

3. *See generally Bill Seeks to Clarify Limbo of Surrogate Births,* Wash. Post, Mar. 19, 1984, at B1, col. 5 [hereinafter cited as *Bill*]; Brozan, *Surrogate Mothers: Problems and Goals,* N.Y. Times, Feb. 27, 1984, at C12, col. 2; Marcus, *The Baby Maker,* National L.J., Aug. 25, 1980, at 1, col. 2.

4. *See infra* note 48 (discussing state legislative action concerning surrogate parenthood).

5. In the only surrogate parenthood case that a state court of highest authority had decided, the Supreme Court of Michigan held that the local trial court has jurisdiction under Michigan's paternity statute to determine who is the biological father of a child born under a surrogate parenthood arrangement, even if the surrogate is married. Syrkowski v. Appleyard, No. 751,057, slip op. at 4–6 (Mich. Jan. 17, 1985) (per curiam). In *Syrkowski*, the plaintiff natural father filed a friendly suit against the surrogate seeking a court order declaring that, under the terms of the state paternity statute, he was the legal father of the child. *Id.* at 1–2. The Michigan Attorney

General intervened, arguing that other Michigan statutes create a presumption that a child born to a married woman is the legal child of her husband. *Id.* at 3. Both the trial court and the intermediate level appellate court decided that the state paternity statute could not apply to surrogate parenthood arrangements. *Id.* at 3-4. The Supreme Court reversed, finding that the lower courts' interpretation of the paternity statute was concerned solely with the provision of financial support for children born out of wedlock. *Id.* at 4-6. The Supreme Court was careful to note that all its determination required was the issuance of a filiation order recognizing "something that no one seriously disputes, viz., that [Syrkowski] is the biological father of [the child]." *Id.* at 4. The court specifically refused to give any guidance as to the natural father's other rights and available remedies. *Id.*

In Doe v. Kelley, 106 Mich. App. 169, 307 N.W.2d 438 (1981), *cert. denied,* 459 U.S. 1183 (1983), Noel Keane and his co-counsel argued that the right to privacy and reproductive freedom gives constitutional protection to a person's decision to enter into a surrogate parenthood arrangement. 106 Mich. App. at 172-73, 307 N.W.2d at 440-41. The court did not accept the argument completely and said that though such a right may protect the parties' ability to enter into and carry forth the arrangement, it does not bar the state from regulating (or prohibiting) the payment of compensation for surrogate services in such an arrangement. 106 Mich. App. at 173-74, 307 N.W.2d at 441.

In *In re* Baby Girl, No. 83AD (Jefferson Cir. Ct., Ky. Mar. 8, 1983), the court held that the Kentucky statute regulating termination of parental rights could not apply to surrogate parenthood arrangements. Slip op. at 2, 4-5. In Commonwealth *ex rel.* Beshear v. Surrogate Parenting Assocs., Inc., No. 81-CI-429 (Franklin Cir. Ct., Ky. Oct. 26, 1983), the court held that surrogate parenthood arrangements are outside the scope of Kentucky laws regulating termination of parental rights and adoption and that the statutes prohibiting payment or collection of fees to procure a child for adoption do not apply to surrogate parenthood because of the child's biological relationship to the natural father. Slip op. at 2-4. The court specifically stated that a man cannot adopt his own child; hence, adoption laws cannot apply to surrogate parenthood arrangements. Slip op. at 3.

The District of Columbia Superior Court, Family Division, found that it could not dispense with the provisions of the local adoption statute in the context of a stepparent adoption resulting from a surrogate parenthood arrangement. *In re* Petition of R.K.S. for Adoption, Daily Wash. L. Rptr., June 6, 1984, at 1117, col. 3 (D.C. Super. Ct., Fam. Div. Apr. 13, 1984). In *R.K.S.,* the court was concerned about both the novelty of surrogate parenthood arrangements and the fact that the surrogate was living with her husband at the time of the arrangement. *Id.* at 1117, 1120. The court emphasized that District of Columbia law provides a rebuttable presumption that the child of a married woman is the legal child of her husband, and that the parties had not proven conclusively that the petitioner for adoption was the child's biological father. *Id.* at 1120. The court believed that it should investigate the facts behind the stepparent adoption, including the background of the participants. *Id.* The *R.K.S.* court paid scant attention to the planning that went into the formation of the surrogate parenthood arrangement and (like most of the courts that have considered surrogate parenthood arrangements) discounted the importance of the participants' expectations.

Generally, courts have been very reluctant to deal with surrogate parenthood arrangements. The few decisions dealing with surrogate parenthood have been inconsistent and unnecessarily narrow. Only a comprehensive statute will provide guidance to those who seek to use surrogate parenthood arrangements in order to create families and to overcome the obstacles that nature has put in the way of their desire to be parents.

6. *See infra* notes 22 to 27 and accompanying text (discussing outcome of Stiver-Malahoff situation, especially multimillion-dollar lawsuit pending between Malahoff, the Stivers, and other parties); *infra* notes 29 to 47 and accompanying text (discussing two situations in which married couples participating in surrogate parenthood prevented from obtaining complete legal satisfaction by absence of relevant law).

7. *See generally* N. Keane & D. Breo, The Surrogate Mother (1981).

8. *See generally* Brozan, *supra* note 3; N. Keane & D. Breo, *supra* note 7; Bill, *supra* note 3.

9. Because such counselors exercise professional judgment in screening candidates for parenthood, not everyone who wants to participate in surrogate arrangements are accepted as clients. Keane relates the story of Olive May and Adam, a couple he found unfit to be parents because of her age (she was at least sixty years old) and his bizarre behavior. N. Keane & D. Breo, *supra* note 7, at 139–40.

10. *See id.* at 144 (agreement Keane signs with potential natural father requires $2000 payment and release of attorney from liability).

11. *See generally id.*

12. Brophy, *A Surrogate Mother Contract to Bear a Child,* 20 J. Fam. L. 263, 264–65 (1982).

13. Transcript of Donahue television interview, No. 02023 (Feb. 2, 1983) [hereinafter cited as Donahue transcript].

14. *Id.*

15. *Id.*

16. *Id.;* Wash. Post, Jan. 21, 1983, at A11, col. 3.

17. Wash. Post, Jan. 21, 1983, at A11, col. 3

18. *Id. But see* Donahue transcript, *supra* note 13 (Malahoff disputes that he refused to consent to medical care for child). At the same time, Mrs. Stiver said that she felt no maternal bond to the child. Andrews, *Stork Market, supra* note 1, at 56.

19. Donahue transcript, *supra* note 13.

20. *Id.*

21. *Id.*

22. *Id. See* Andrews, *Stork Market, supra* note 1, at 56 (quoting George

Annas, who said situation made soap operas pale in comparison). For critical analyses of the publicity surrounding the Donahue interview, see McCrory, *Curb Lurid Donahue Shows: Adopt a Baby,* Wash. Post, Feb. 6, 1983, at B2, col. 1 (criticizing publicity surrounding Stiver-Malahoff situation as invasion of privacy; calling for ban on surrogate parenthood arrangements); Raspberry, *Layaway Baby,* Wash. Post Feb. 4, 1983, at A17, col. 4 (criticizing actions of Malahoff and Stiver and manner in which situation publicized).

23. Wash. Post, Feb. 3, 1983, at A8, col. 1.

24. Donahue transcript, *supra* note 13.

25. *Id.*

26. *Id.* (detailing Stivers' plans to raise baby as their own).

27. Donahue transcript, *supra* note 13 For details of the lawsuit that Malahoff filed against the Stivers, and of their counterclaims and third-party claims, see Andrews, *Stork Market, supra* note 1, at 56.

28. N. Keane & D. Breo, *supra* note 7. Keane has received national attention for his legal representation of, and public advocacy for, those who seek to participate in surrogate parenthood arrangements. He is generally recognized for his expertise and broad practical experience in the field of surrogate parenthood. *See generally* Marcus, *supra* note 3. William Pierce describes Keane as the person "largely responsible for the emergence of surrogate-parenting enterprises as a legal issue. . . . Keane is clearly the best-known advocate of surrogate parenting enterprises in the United States." Pierce, *Survey of State Activity Regarding Surrogate Motherhood,* 11 *Fam. L. Rep.* (BNA) No. 12, at 3001 (Jan. 29, 1985).

29. *See generally* N. Keane & D. Breo, *supra* note 7.

30. Keane uses pseudonyms for most of the clients about whom he writes in order to protect their privacy. *Id.* at 11.

31. *Id.* at 102–03.

32. Tenn. Code Ann. § 36-1-135 (1984). It is the payment of money for a person's consent to an adoption or termination of parental rights that is commonly labelled "babyselling." N. Keane & D. Breo, *supra* note 7, at 18, 112. *See also infra* note 53 (discussing statutes precluding payment for adoption).

33. N. Keane & D. Breo, *supra* note 7, at 103–07, 109–10, 128–32.

34. *Id.* at 107–08. For example, Diane began to have her labor contractions in the midst of a struggle between her present and former lovers. The former lover created such havoc in the hospital waiting room that Bill and Bridget could not assist Diane in the birth. *Id.*

35. *Id.* at 108; Andrews, *Stork Market, supra* note 1, at 56.

36. N. Keane & D. Breo, *supra note* 7, at 109–11, 128.

37. *Id.* at 110–12, 127–32.

38. Tenn. Code Ann. § 68-3-305 (1984). N. Keane & D. Breo, *supra* note 7, at 111. The Tennessee statute does not allow an unmarried woman to name a putative father on her child's birth certificate. *Id.*

39. N. Keane & D. Breo, *supra* note 7, at 100–12.

40. These are the names that Keane uses for the married couple. *Id.* at

157. Their real names are Bjorna and James Noyes. N.Y. Times, June 6, 1981, at A19, col. 6.

41. N. Keane & D. Breo, *supra* note 7, at 150, 162–67. Keane refers to her as "Rita.' *Id*. at 168. "Rita" actually goes by two names, either Nisa Bhimani or Denise Lucy Thrane. N.Y. Times, June 6, 1981, at A19, col. 6.

42. N. Keane & D. Breo, *supra* note 7, at 168–69, 197–98.

43. *Id*. at 201–04.

44. *Id*. at 198, 202.

45. *Id*. at 208–09.

46. *Id*.; N.Y. Times, June 6, 1981, at A19, col. 6.

47. N. Keane & D. Breo, *supra* note 7, at 209.

48. Although a number of state legislatures have considered the issue, no state has legalized surrogate parenthood arrangements or declared them illegal. Pierce, *supra* note 28, at 3003. The Michigan legislature has considered a surrogate parenthood bill. Detroit News, Feb. 9, 1983, at C-10, col. 2. The bill was approved in committee, but ultimately was rejected by the state House of Representatives. Detroit News, Oct. 19, 1983, at A-3, col. 5. The sponsor, state Representative Richard Fitzpatrick, has been seeking enactment of a surrogate parenthood act since 1981. Office of Rep. Richard Fitzpatrick, Press Release on Bill to Regulate Surrogate Parenting (Feb. 8, 1983) (copy on file at *Georgetown Law Journal*). The Committee on the Judiciary of the California Assembly considered a surrogate parenthood act but the proposal was not enacted. Nat'l L.J., July 12, 1982, at 5, col. 1. Some testimony before the California committee was later published as commentary on the surrogate parenthood phenomenon. Krimmel, *The Case Against Surrogate Parenting*, Hastings Center Rep., Oct. 1983, at 35 (opposing surrogate parenthood in all forms). Even earlier, Alaska had briefly considered a surrogate parenthood bill. Nat'l L.J., July 12, 1982, at 5, col. 1.

William Pierce reports the following legislative activity relating to surrogate parenthood as of early 1985: About 20 states and the District of Columbia have considered or are considering surrogate parenthood in some way but no state has legalized or prohibited surrogate parenthood arrangements. In 15 states (Alaska, California, Connecticut, Hawaii, Illinois, Kansas, Maryland, Massachusetts, Minnesota, New Jersey, New York, Oregon, Rhode Island, South Carolina, and Virginia), the legislative activity has focused on allowing surrogate parenthood arrangements. In four jurisdictions (Alabama, the District of Columbia, Kentucky, and Oklahoma) the focus is on prohibiting surrogate parenthood arrangements. In Michigan there is support for proposals on both sides of the issue. Pierce, *supra* note 28, at 3003. In recent months, the District of Columbia has considered legislation somewhat favorable to surrogate parenthood arrangements. Keen, *Councilman Ray Proffers "Baby" Bill*, Wash. Blade, Mar. 1, 1985, at 5, col. 2.

49. Surrogate parenthood is only one of a series of new reproductive technologies that are now available. They are detailed more completely in Wadlington, *Artificial Conception: The Challenge for Family Law*, 69 Va. L. Rev. 465 (1983). For a less technical discussion, see Andrews, *Stork Market, supra*

note 1; Andrews, *Brave New Baby,* Student Lawyer, Dec. 1983, at 25 [hereinafter cited as Andrews, *Brave New Baby*]. Among these new techniques are *in vitro* fertilization and embryo transfer. For a more complete discussion of these new reproductive technologies and of the impact of a surrogate parenthood statute on them, see *infra* Part V.

50. Among the most critical questions raised by surrogate parenthood are the following:

1. Who may participate?
2. How may the suitability of individual participants be determined?
3. What type of acts should fall within the scope of any proposed regulation?
4. What type of medical supervision should be required?
5. What are the rights and obligations of the surrogate during pregnancy?
6. What are the rights and obligations of the natural father (and his spouse, if he is married) during pregnancy?
7. What are the rights and obligations of the respective parties after live birth?
8. What are the rights and obligations of the respective parties after miscarriage or stillbirth?
9. What compensation may the surrogate receive?
10. What is the legal status of the child at birth?
11. What steps must the surrogate take to surrender her rights as parent?
12. What steps must the natural father take to assert his rights as parent?
13. What steps must the natural father's spouse take to gain or assert parental rights?
14. What procedures must the surrogate follow if she decides to keep the child?
15. What are the rights and obligations of the natural father if the surrogate decides to keep the child?

51. This note does not offer a detailed discussion of all the legal obstacles that may hinder surrogate parenthood, because numerous commentators have more than adequately presented these issues. For a full and balanced discussion, see generally Brophy, *supra* note 12; Coleman, *Surrogate Motherhood: Analysis of the Problems and Suggestions for Solutions,* 50 Tenn. L. Rev. 71 (1982); Handel & Sherwyn, *Surrogate Parenting,* Trial, Apr. 1982, at 57; Keane, *supra* note 1; Rushevsky, *Legal Recognition of Surrogate Gestation,* 7 Women's Rts. L. Rptr. 107 (1982); Note, *Surrogate Mothers, supra* note 2; Comment, *Contracts to Bear a Child,* 66 Calif. L. Rev. 611 (1978) [hereinafter cited as Comment, *Contracts*]; Comment, *Parenthood by Proxy: Legal Implications of Surrogate Parenting,* 67 Iowa L. Rev. 385 (1982) [hereinafter cited as Comment, *Parenthood by Proxy*]; Comment, *The Surrogate Child: Legal Issues and Implications for the Future,* 7 J. Juv. L. 80 (1983) [hereinafter cited as Comment, *Surrogate Child*]; Note, *In Defense of Surrogate Parenting: A Critical Analysis of the Recent Kentucky Experience,* 69 Ky L.J. 877 (1981) [hereinafter cited as Note, *Kentucky Experience*]; Comment, *Surrogate Mother Agreements; Contemporary Legal Aspects of a Biblical Notion,* 16 U. Rich. L. Rev. 467 (1982)

[hereinafter cited as Comment, *Contemporary Legal Aspects*]; Note, *Surrogate Motherhood: Contractual Issues and Remedies under Legislative Proposals*, 23 Washburn, L.J. 601 (1984) [hereinafter cited as Note, *Contractual Issues and Remedies*]; Comment, *Surrogate Motherhood: A Nursery Full of Unresolved Problems*, 17 Willamette L.J. 913 (1981).

52. Before one can construct a meaningful statute to provide guidance to participants in surrogate parenthood arrangements, one must consider the impact of such threshold issues as the laws prohibiting babyselling, regulating adoption, and providing for legal paternity, as well as the constitutionality of outright bans on surrogate parenthood arrangements and the proper degree of state regulation. There are other questions, generally considered as issues of family law, that concern surrogate parenthood and deserve brief mention. One student commentator has discussed the possibility that laws against fetal experimentation enacted in many states may present an obstacle to surrogate parenthood arrangements. Note, *Surrogate Mothers, supra* note 2, at 328. The student determined that these laws do not apply to surrogate parenthood arrangements because they are designed to protect the life and health of a fetus. *Id.* Surrogate parenthood arrangements do not pose a threat to the health of a fetus and therefore do not fit the statutory purpose. *Id.* A well-drafted statute should also address each subsidiary legal or policy issue in a well-reasoned manner. A criticism of current statutory proposals is that they lack "reason." Pierce, *supra* note 28, at 3004 (best of existing bills falls far short of basic requirement of "statutory sense").

53. Keane's review of state adoption laws indicated that, in 1980, payment of any compensation beyond expenses in connection with an adoption was illegal in 41 states. N. Keane & D. Breo, *supra* note 7, at 273. At least 24 states have enacted statutes that make illegal the payment of any fees (except certain enumerated legal and medical expenses) in connection with an adoption. *See* Ala. Code § 26-10-8 (1975); Ariz. Rev. Stat. Ann. § 8-126(c) (1974); Cal. Penal Code § 273(a) (West Supp. 1983); Colo. Rev. Stat. § 19-4-115 (1978); Del. Code Ann. tit. 13, § 928 (1981); Fla. Stat. Ann. § 63.212 (West Supp. 1985); Ga. Code Ann. § 19-8-19 (1982); Idaho Code § 18-1511 (1979); Ill. Ann. Stat. ch. 40 §§ 1526, 1701–1703 (Smith-Hurd 1980); Ind. Code Ann. § 35-46-1-9 (Burns Supp. 1984); Iowa Code Ann. § 600.9 (West 1981); Ky. Rev. Stat. § 199.590(2) (1982); Md. Ann. Code art. 16, § 83 (1981); Mass. Gen. Laws Ann. ch. 210, § 11A (West Supp. 1984); Mich. Comp. Laws Ann. § 710.54 (West Supp. 1983–1984); Nev. Rev. Stat. § 127-290 (1983); N.J. Stat. Ann. § 9:3-54 (West Supp. 1984); N.Y. Soc. Serv. Law § 374(6) (McKinney 1983); N.C. Gen. Stat. § 48-37 (1984); Ohio Rev. Code Ann. § 3107.01(a) (Page 1982); S.D. Codified Laws Ann. § 25-6-4.2 (1984); Tenn. Code Ann. § 36-1-135 (1984); Utah Code Ann. § 76-7-203 (1978); Wis. Stat. Ann. § 946.716 (West 1982).

In some states, however, adoptive parents need not account for amounts paid in connection with a stepparent adoption; this provides a way for an unmarried surrogate to receive compensation beyond payment of expenses. *See* Ariz. Rev. Stat. Ann. § 8-126(a) (1974); Cal. Penal Code

§ 273(a) (West 1974); Fla. Stat. Ann. § 63.212 (West Supp. 1985); Ill. Rev. Stat. ch. 40, §§ 1702–1704 (1981): Ill. Ann. Stat. ch. 40 §§ 1702–1704 (Smith-Hurd 1980); Iowa Code Ann. § 600.9 (West 1981); N.J. Stat. Ann. § 9:3-54 (West Supp. 1984); Wis. Stat. Ann. § 946.716 (West 1982).

A stepparent adoption, which in a surrogate parenthood arrangement would involve the child's adoption by the natural father's spouse, can take place only when the natural father can place his name on the birth certificate. N. Keane & D. Breo, *supra* note 7, at 273–74.

54. This analysis usually refers only to surrogate parenthood arrangements that involve compensating the surrogate beyond payment of her medical and related expenses. It is fairly well established that paying reasonable medical expenses does not violate state laws against babyselling. *See* Doe v. Kelley, 106 Mich. App. at 173–74, 307 N.W.2d at 441 (1981) (no direct statutory bar to surrogate parenthood arrangements providing for no compensatory payment to surrogate); Letter from James H. Lincoln, Executive Judge, Juvenile Division, Wayne County Probate Court, to Margaret Pfieffer (Mar. 2, 1977), *reprinted in* N. Keane & D. Breo, *supra* note 7, at 334–35 (paying pregnancy-related medical, legal, and transportation expenses legal and customary in adoption cases) [hereinafter cited as Letter from Judge Lincoln].

55. Op. Ky. Att'y Gen., No. 81-18 (Jan. 26, 1981). For detailed analysis and criticism of this opinion, see Note, *Kentucky Experience, supra* note 51.

56. Op. Ohio Att'y Gen., No. 83-001 (Jan. 3, 1983).

57. For example, see the result in Doe v. Kelley, 106 Mich. App. 169, 307 N.W.2d 438 (1981), discussed more completely *supra*, at note 2.

58. No. 81-CI-429, slip op. at 3 (Franklin Cir. Ct., Ky. Oct. 26, 1983).

59. *See, e.g.*, Note, *Surrogate Mothers, supra* note 3, at 327 (babyselling analysis provides available means to block surrogate parenthood arrangements); Comment, *Contracts, supra* note 51, at 613 (courts likely to see surrogate parenthood as raising same problems as babyselling); Comment, *Contemporary Legal Aspects, supra* note 51, at 478 (babyselling analogy will be used, but is not proper).

60. *See, e.g.*, Coleman, *supra* note 51, at 79, 108–09 (paying surrogate no threat to "family" or child; social and economic pressures present in babyselling not present in surrogate parenthood); Keane, *supra* note 1, at 155–57 (surrogate agreeing to provide services, not forced relinquishment of her child); Rushevsky, *supra* note 51, at 116–17, 130 (mother under no economic pressure to sell child, as natural father obliged to provide child support); Comment, *Contemporary Legal Aspects, supra* note 51, at 478–79 (unlike babyselling, no black-market profiteering involved in surrogate parenthood arrangements).

61. 512 F.2d 187 (9th Cir. 1975).

62. *Id.* at 187–90.

63. *Id.*

64. *Id.* at 190.

65. 186 Kan. 311, 350 P.2d 1 (1960).

66. 186 Kan. at 316–18, 350 P.2d 7–8, 12.

67. 122 Md. 114, 89 A. 405 (1913).

68. 164 Pa. 266, 30 A. 129 (1894).

69. 122 Md. at 119–20, 89 A. at 407–08.

70. 122 Md. at 116–17, 89 A. at 406.

71. The laws against babyselling are designed to combat pressures placed on a pregnant woman to put her child up for adoption. For more complete discussion of this point, see the commentary cited in note 51, *supra*. *See also* Keane, *supra* note 1, at 155 (natural father party to surrogate parenthood arrangement, thus no "sale" of unrelated baby). Analogous to this point, however, is the belief of some commentators that surrogate parenthood might lead to the exploitation of economically deprived women. *See* Blakely, *Surrogate Mothers: For Whom Are They Working?*, Ms., Mar. 1983, at 18, 20 (surrogate parenthood arrangements victimize surrogates economically and place them under social pressure); Krimmel, *supra* note 48, at 38 (economic pressures may force poor women to become surrogates in order to support themselves and families); American College of Obstetricians and Gynecologists, Ethical Issues in Surrogate Motherhood, Press Release and Guidelines (May 10, 1983) (physicians must guard against potential exploitation of economically disadvantaged women) [hereinafter cited as ACOG Press Release and Guidelines].

72. *See* Commonwealth *ex rel.* Beshear v. Surrogate Parenting Assocs., Inc., No. 81-CI-429, slip op. at 3 (child born of surrogate parenthood arrangement father's child through biological ties).

73. *See, e.g.*, Coleman, *supra* note 51, at 108–09 (surrogate parenthood arrangement made before child conceived; adults involved make free choice); Comment, *Contemporary Legal Aspects*, *supra* note 51, at 478–79 (surrogate parenthood arrangements planned and deliberate; no duress, hurried decision making, or bidding involved).

74. *See* Alaska Stat. § 25.20.045 (Supp. 1982); Ark. Stat. Ann. § 61-141 (1971); Cal. Civ. Code § 7005 (West Supp. 1983); Colo. Rev. Stat. § 19-6-106 (1978); Conn. Gen. Stat. §§ 45-69f to -69n (1981); Fla. Stat. Ann. § 742.11 (West Supp. 1983); Ga. Code Ann. §§ 74-101.1, 74-9904 (1982); Ill. Ann. Stat. ch. 40, §§ 1451–1453 (Smith-Hurd 1983); Kan. Stat. Ann. §§ 23-128 to -130 (1981); La. Civ. Code Ann. art. 188 (West Supp. 1983); Md. Est. & Trusts Code Ann. § 1-206(b) (1974) and Md. Ann. Code art. 20, § 212 and art. 43, § 556E (1980); Mich. Comp. Laws Ann. §§ 333.2824, 700.111 (1980); Minn. Stat. Ann. § 257.56 (West 1982); Mont. Code Ann. § 40-6-106 (1981); Nev. Rev. Stat. § 126-061 (1979); N.Y. Dom. Rel. Law § 73 (McKinney 1977); N.C. Gen. Stat. § 49A-1 (1976); Okla. Stat. Ann. tit. 10, §§ 551–553 (West Supp. 1982–1983); Or. Rev. Stat. §§ 109.239, .243, .247, 677.355, .360, .365, .370 (1981); Tenn. Code Ann. § 53-446 (Supp. 1981); Tex. Fam. Code Ann. § 12.03 (Vernon 1975); Va. Code § 64.1–7.1 (1980); Wash. Rev. Code Ann. § 26.26.050 (West Supp. 1983–1984); Wis. Stat. Ann. § 767.47(9) (West 1981), § 891.40 (West Supp. 1982–1983); Wyo. Stat. § 14-2-103 (1978).

75. Wadlington, *supra* note 49, at 468–73.

76. Unif. Parentage Act, 9A U.L.A. 587 (1973).

77. *Id.* § 4(a)(1).

78. *Id.* § 5(a).

79. *Id.*

80. *Id.* § 5(b).

81. *Id.* § 6(b).

82. *Id.* § 6(a).

83. *See generally* Bumiller, *Mothers for Others,* Wash. Post, Mar. 9, 1983 at B1, col. 3.

84. N. Keane & D. Breo, *supra* note 7, at 287.

85. *See Coleman, supra* note 51, at 81–82 (surrogate parenthood biological counterpart of AID); Comment, *Parenthood by Proxy, supra* note 51, at 386 & n.10 (same).

86. *See* Robertson, *Surrogate Mothers: Not So Novel After All,* Hastings Center Rep., Oct. 1983, at 28 (surrogate parenthood, like AID, form of collaborative reproduction and legal issues basically same).

87. *See* Coleman, *supra* note 51, at 81–82 (failure to allow payment of surrogate while allowing payment of semen donor may be violation of equal protection).

88. Krimmel, *supra* note 48, at 36. Although Krimmel does not accept the analogy between AID and surrogate parenthood, he says that the two practices present the same ethical dilemma. *Id.* at 36.

89. Comment, *Contemporary Legal Aspects, supra* note 51, at 473–74.

90. In embryo transfer, an ovum donor is impregnated through AID using the sperm of the partner of a woman who either cannot conceive a child or must isolate her genetic component because she carries a genetic disease. Once the ovum is fertilized, the physician performing the transfer waits 48 to 72 hours before transferring the embryo—long enough for several cell divisions to occur, but not for the embryo to implant in the ovum donor's uterine wall. Using a long, wide tube, the physician then gently washes out the ovum donor's uterus, picks up the embryo in the tube, and transfers it to the uterus of the sperm donor's partner (who will be referred to here as the "gestating mother"). Her uterus has been made ready for implantation either naturally (by using an ovum donor with a matching menstrual cycle) or chemically (by treatment with hormones). Once implantation occurs, the gestating mother carries the developing child through a normal pregnancy and gives birth as if she had conceived the child naturally. *See generally* Bustillo et al., *Nonsurgical Ovum Transfer as a Treatment in Infertile Women: Preliminary Experience,* 251 J. A.M.A. 1171 (1984); *"Prenatal Adoption" Is the Objective of New Technique,* N.Y. Times, June 14, 1983, at C1, col. 4.

The steps of embryo transfer can also be reversed. A woman who can conceive but cannot hold a pregnancy will arrange to transfer a naturally fertilized ovum to another woman (who will be referred to here as the "gestating surrogate"). The gestating surrogate will carry the developing child through the normal gestation period, will give birth as if she had conceived the child, and then will surrender her parental rights and responsibilities to the child in favor of the biological mother and father. This form of embryo transfer (which will be referred to here as "reverse embryo transfer") is closely akin to surrogate parenthood.

91. The goal of statutes such as those recently considered in Alabama,

the District of Columbia, Kentucky, Michigan, and Oklahoma is to make surrogate parenthood illegal. *See supra* note 48. *See also* Keen, *supra* note 48 (discussing District of Columbia statute); *see generally* Pierce, *supra* note 28.

92. *See, e.g.,* Carey v. Population Servs. Int'l, 431 U.S. 678 (1977) (state law limiting minors' access to contraceptives violates privacy right); Roe v. Wade, 410 U.S. 113 (1973) (privacy right protects woman's decision to abort; late in pregnancy, right limited by compelling state interest in maternal and fetal health); Eisenstadt v. Baird, 405 U.S. 438 (1972) (state law restricting use of contraceptives outside of marriage violation of privacy right); Griswold v. Connecticut, 381 U.S. 479 (1965) (state law prohibiting use of contraceptives within marriage violation of privacy right); Skinner v. Oklahoma, 316 U.S. 535 (1942) (procreation fundamental interest and basic civil right; state cannot deny equal protection of that right). The Supreme Court has described this right to privacy or reproductive freedom in the following manner: "The decision whether or not to bear or beget a child is at the very heart of [a] cluster of constitutionally protected choices." *Carey,* 431 U.S. at 685. The choices protected encompass a range of family-related matters, including marriage, procreation, and child rearing. *Id.* at 684–85. What *Carey* makes clear is that the Constitution protects the freedom of the *decision*. The Court said that a state cannot regulate behavior in a manner so intrusive that individual decisions are burdened. *Id.* at 687. The abortion funding cases also support this point. *See* Harris v. McRae, 448 U.S. 297, 312, 317–18 (1980) (*Roe* and its progeny protect right to choose to abort but not do not grant entitlement to abortion funding); Maher v. Roe, 432 U.S. 464, 471–74 (1977) (same).

93. 316 U.S. 535 (1942).

94. *Id.* The *Skinner* Court overturned a state statute allowing sterilization of all persons convicted two or more times of felonies involving moral turpitude. *Id.* at 536. A wide variety of felonies were seen to involve moral turpitude, while certain others, which provided for equal penalties, were not. *Id.* at 537–39. The Court found that the power to procreate is a "basic liberty" and a "basic civil right" and that the state violated the constitutional guarantee of equal protection to all in the exercise of any fundamental right. *Id.* at 541.

95. Carey v. Population Servs. Int'l, 431 U.S. 678 (1977); Eisenstadt v. Baird, 405 U.S. 438 (1972); Griswold v. Connecticut, 381 U.S. 479 (1965).

96. Roe v. Wade, 410 U.S. 113 (1973).

97. *See* Loving v. Virginia, 388 U.S. 1 (1967) (striking down state antimiscegenation statute that forbade whites from marrying nonwhites but allowed all other races to intermarry). *But cf.* Doe v. Commonwealth's Attorney, 425 U.S. 901 (1976) (mem.), *aff'g* 403 F. Supp. 1199 (E.D. Va. 1975) (statute criminalizing sodomy between consenting adults of same sex not violative of privacy right because not considered intrusion into marriage, home, or family life).

98. *See* Pierce v. Society of Sisters, 268 U.S. 510 (1925) (parents free to choose private schooling for their children; children under authority of those who nurture them); Meyer v. Nebraska, 262 U.S. 390 (1923) (parents have right to choose education for their children, including education in

foreign language; liberty involves right to make home and raise children). *But see* Prince v. Massachusetts, 321 U.S. 158 (1944) (parents may not place their children in position of risk or in psychological or physical danger).

99. The Supreme Court has not been precise in detailing where the right to privacy has its fundamental roots. In *Griswold*, the majority said that the first, third, fourth, fifth, and ninth amendments guarantee the right to privacy. 381 U.S. at 484–85. Justice Goldberg in his concurrence said that the right is grounded in the ninth amendment, 381 U.S. at 486–87 (Goldberg J., concurring), and that the right, at least in marital situations, deserved constitutional protection. *Id.* at 495–97 (Goldberg, J., concurring). In *Roe v. Wade*, the Court found the right rooted in the fourteenth amendment's "concept of personal liberty." 410 U.S. at 153. The lower court had based its finding on the ninth amendment. *Id.*

100. *See* Roe v. Wade, 410 U.S. 113, 153–54 (1973) (right to privacy not absolute; state may regulate abortion to further compelling interests); *cf.* Doe v. Kelley, 106 Mich. App. 169, 173–74, 307 N.W. 2d 438, 441 (1981) (right to privacy not broad enough to prohibit state application of anti-babyselling statute to surrogate parenthood arrangement).

101. *See* Rushevsky, *supra* note 51, at 113 (limitations on privacy right make application of right to surrogate parenthood doubtful); Comment, *Contemporary Legal Aspects, supra* note 51, at 481 (validity of applying right of procreative freedom to surrogate parenthood doubtful; couple obtains child but does not procreate).

102. *See* Coleman, *supra* note 51, at 82 (fundamental right to procreate and raise family may include right to participate in surrogate parenthood arrangements); Robertson, *supra* note 86, at 32 (logical implication of abortion and contraception cases is that privacy right covers surrogate parenthood, at least in marriage); *see also* Keane, *supra* note 1, at 165 (ban on surrogate parenthood unconstitutional; denies to some their only means to procreate); Note, *Kentucky Experience, supra* note 51, at 930 (outright ban on surrogate parenthood unconstitutional; regulation only valid if achieved by least burdensome means).

103. Robertson, *supra* note 86, at 32.

104. Keane, *supra* note 1, at 165.

105. *Id.* at 166.

106. *See, e.g.,* Robertson *supra* note 86, at 33 (permissible and reasonable for state to set minimum standards for surrogate parenthood arrangements); Rushevsky, *supra* note 51, at 142 (carefully drawn statute providing for minimal regulation proper); Note, *Kentucky Experience, supra* note 51, at 926–27 (narrowly drawn statute regulating surrogate parenthood shifts state-individual balance in favor of state).

107. A statute unduly restricting surrogate parenthood might not be constitutional. *See* Keane, *supra* note 1, at 165 (states may not impose regulations making infertile couple's use of surrogate parenthood arrangements illegal); Note, *Kentucky Experience, supra* note 51, at 930 (least burdensome regulations proper to meet legitimate state interests; overly restrictive regulations improper).

108. *See* Coleman, *supra* note 51, at 79–80 (primary state interest is in

child to be conceived); Note, *Kentucky Experience, supra* note 51, at 930 (regulation must be designed to protect child to be conceived). Krimmel, in response to this concern, argues that surrogate parenthood is inherently dangerous for the child so conceived. Krimmel, *supra* note 48, at 37–38. He warns that the use of surrogate parenthood could lead to eugenic practices, exacerbate tensions in both the surrogate's and the natural father's families, and create gaps in the child's genetic history. *Id.*

109. *Cf.* ACOG Press Release and Guidelines, *supra* note 71 (advising physicians to protect against exploitation of surrogates).

110. In the Stiver-Malahoff situation, discussed *supra* at notes 13 to 27 and accompanying text, Malahoff had decided that if the child were his, he would ask the Michigan Department of Social Services to assume responsibility for the child. Donahue transcript, *supra* note 13. States can and should take measures to recover expenses related to the care of children born of surrogate parenthood arrangements gone awry. *See infra* text accompanying note 137 (discussing provision in proposed bill to protect state from expenses).

111. In its earliest formulation, the right to privacy was used to protect the family structure. *See* Pierce v. Society of Sisters, 268 U.S. 510 (1925) (family has right to be free from all but most necessary state interference); Meyer v. Nebraska, 262 U.S. 390 (1923) (same). As the Supreme Court has recently reinterpreted the right, it protects against nearly all state sanctioned restrictions on an individual's procreative freedom. The most striking examples of this trend are Bellotti v. Baird, 443 U.S. 622 (1979), in which the Supreme Court struck down a Massachusetts statute requiring consent of a parent or a juvenile court judge before a minor child could obtain an abortion, and Planned Parenthood of Cent. Mo. v. Danforth, 428 U.S. 52 (1976), in which the Supreme Court struck down parts of a Missouri statute that required, among other things, a husband's consent before his wife could obtain an abortion. The family unit no longer seems central to the privacy right. *See* Carey v. Population Servs. Int'l, 431 U.S. 678, 687 (1977) (state cannot unduly burden *individual* procreative decisions). *But see* H.L. v. Matheson, 450 U.S. 398 (1981) (upholding Utah statute construed as requiring parental notification before minor child's abortion).

The Supreme Court has recognized that some limitations on the right to privacy are proper when the limitations are related to legitimate state interests. *See* City of Akron v. Akron Center for Reproductive Health, 462 U.S. 416, 427–31 (abortion right limited by compelling state interests in protecting potential human life and preserving maternal health) (citing Roe v. Wade, 410 U.S. 113, 154, 162 (1973)); Prince v. Massachusetts, 321 U.S. 158, 169–70 (1944) (parental freedom does not allow parents to place children at risk; parents may not "make martyrs of their children"). Such regulations may not overly burden access to a protected activity. *Compare* Bellotti v. Baird, 443 U.S. 622 (1979) (overturning statute requiring parental consent for minor's abortion where withholding consent amounted to veto) *with* H.L. v. Matheson, 450 U.S. 398 (1981) (upholding more limited statute requiring parental notification of minor child's abortion when possible).

This discussion does not consider the use of the right to privacy in criminal cases, in which the courts have discussed a suspect's right to be "left alone" in the absence of probable cause or reasonable suspicion.

112. The federal courts have indicated a willingness to restrict the right of privacy. In 1983, the Supreme Court reaffirmed *Roe* in a trio of abortion cases: City of Akron v. Akron Center for Reproductive Health, 462 U.S. 416 (1983); Planned Parenthood Ass'n of Kansas City, Mo., Inc. v. Ashcroft, 462 U.S. 476 (1983); Simopolous v. Virginia, 462 U.S. 506 (1983). Justice O'Connor's dissenting opinion in *City of Akron* signals a new willingness on the part of the more conservative justices to readdress the privacy issues presented in *Roe* and its progeny. *See* 462 U.S. at 452 (O'Connor, J., with White & Rehnquist, JJ., dissenting) (state's compelling interests in maternal health and potential human life present throughout pregnancy including first trimester); *see also supra* note 111 (discussing limitations on right to privacy related to legitimate state interests).

The United States Court of Appeals for the District of Columbia Circuit recently held that the right to privacy is not broad enough to encompass a general protection of consenting adults to engage in homosexual conduct. Dronenburg v. Zech, 741 F.2d 1388, 1391–92 (D.C. Cir. 1984). The *Dronenburg* court gave the right to privacy a narrow reading, limiting the right to circumstances similar to those before the Supreme Court in the abortion and contraception cases (*Griswold, Loving, Eisenstadt, Roe,* and *Carey). Id.* at 1395–96.

While these opinions do not directly implicate a person's ability to participate in surrogate parenthood arrangements, they signal a possible reluctance on the part of the federal courts to provide protection for such activity. *But see infra* note 115 and accompanying text (discussing close relationship between surrogate parenthood and family governance cases such as *Meyer* and *Pierce*).

Interestingly, because the *Dronenburg* court placed so much emphasis on the fact that homosexual activity does not fit into the procreative freedom rationale that it found in the Supreme Court's line of privacy cases, it might view surrogate parenthood arrangements more generously.

113. John A. Kennedy Mem. Hosp. v. Bludworth, 452 So. 2d 921 (Fla 1984); *In re* Quinlan, 70 N.J. 10, 355 A.2d 647 (1976).

114. The cases vindicating such individual "liberties" as the right to terminate life-supporting medical treatment seem far afield from the basic rights, discussed more completely in note 111, *supra,* that form the core of the right to privacy.

115. Surrogate parenthood, in most instances, is an attempt by an infertile married couple to bear a child biologically related to the father. Robertson, *supra* note 86, at 29. The attempt involves an aspect of the marital relationship that the right to privacy has protected since its earliest articulations: raising children. Surrogate parenthood is generally nothing more than an attempt by couples who cannot bear children by ordinary means to share in that experience. Keane, *supra* note 1, at 155–56.

116. Several commentators would limit access to surrogate parenthood relationships to married couples, though often these suggestions do not

rest on constitutional grounds. *See* Comment, *Parenthood by Proxy, supra* note 51, at 388 (societal reasons favoring surrogate parenthood extend only to "nuclear family"; such limitation may be unconstitutional); *Surrogate Mothers, supra* note 2, at 346–57 & n.124 (surrogate parenthood only allowable for necessity; only married couples given full measure of *Griswold/ Eisenstadt/Carey* privacy protection); *cf.* Keane, *supra* note 1, at 165 (infertile couples must have access to only means of implementing right to bear child).

117. *See* Robertson, *supra* note 86, at 34 (regulating process of forming surrogate parenthood arrangement can ensure that process is done well).

5

Surrogate Parenting:
The British View
The Warnock Commission

What is Surrogacy?

Surrogacy is the practice whereby one woman carries a child for another with the intention that the child should be handed over after birth. The use of artificial insemination and the recent development of *in vitro* fertilization have eliminated the necessity for sexual intercourse in order to establish a surrogate pregnancy. Surrogacy can take a number of forms. The commissioning mother may be the genetic mother, in that she provides the egg, or she may make no contribution to the establishment of the pregnancy. The genetic father may be the husband of the commissioning mother, or of the carrying mother; or he may be an anonymous donor. There are thus many possible combinations of persons who are relevant to the child's conception, birth, and early environment. Of these various forms perhaps the most likely are surrogacy involving artificial insemination, where the carrying mother is the genetic mother inseminated with semen from the male partner of the commissioning couple, and surrogacy using *in vitro* fertilization where both egg and semen come from the commissioning couple, and the resultant embryo is transferred to and implants in the carrying mother.

There are certain circumstances in which surrogacy would be an option for the alleviation of infertility. Examples are where a woman has a severe pelvic disease which cannot be remedied

---

This is an excerpt from the British "Report of the Committee of Inquiry into Human Fertilization and Embryology" (The Warnock Commission), 1984.

© 1984, London: Her Majesty's Stationery Office.

surgically, or has no uterus. The practice might also be used to help those women who have suffered repeated miscarriages. There are also perhaps circumstances where the genetic mother, although not infertile, could benefit from the pregnancy being carried by another woman. An example is where the genetic mother is fit to care for a child after it is born, but suffers from a condition making pregnancy medically undesirable.

If surrogacy takes place it generally involves some payment to the carrying mother. Payment may vary between reimbursement of expenses, and a substantial fee. There may, however, be some instances where no money is involved, for example, where one sister carries the pregnancy for another.

The Present Position

There is at present no provision for a surrogacy service within the National Health Service. Private agencies exist in certain other countries and in the United Kingdom one agency is said to have started to operate. The practice is not in itself unlawful. None of the parties to a surrogacy arrangement, including any agency operating on a commercial basis, contravenes existing criminal law, unless the terms of the agreement contravene the provisions of adoption law, which prohibit payments in connection with adoption (Section 50 of the Adoption Act 1958).

Any surrogacy arrangement would necessarily involve some form of agreement between the parties concerned, however informal. Although it may be assumed that in the majority of cases the agreement would be kept and the matter never brought before a court, it is likely that grave difficulties of enforcement would ensue in the event of a dispute over such an agreement. There is little doubt that the courts would treat most, if not all, surrogacy agreements as contrary to public policy and therefore unenforceable. Where one party broke the agreement the other party could not expect to invoke the court's assistance. Thus, if the carrying mother changed her mind and decided she wished to keep the child it is most unlikely that a court would order her, because she had previously agreed to do so, to hand over the child against her will. Nor in such a case would a court order the surrogate mother to repay any fee paid to her under the terms of the agreement.

The courts do, however, have jurisdiction over children which is quite separate from and independent of the law of contract. Where a court has to consider the future of a child born following a surrogacy agreement, it must do so in accordance with the child's best interests in all the circumstances of the case, and not according to the terms of any agreement between the various adults. The child's interests being the first and paramount consideration, it seems likely that only in very exceptional circumstances would a court direct a surrogate mother to hand over the child to the commissioning couple. The present state of the law makes any surrogacy agreement a risky undertaking for those involved.

Many unforeseen events may occur between the moment of entering into the surrogacy agreement and the time for handing over the child, and these may alter the whole picture. Apart from the most obvious one of the surrogate mother changing her mind, it may, for example, be discovered that the child is handicapped or the commissioning mother may die or become disabled.

Embryo transfer makes possible for the first time a situation where the carrying mother is not the genetic mother. Where there has been a donation of egg or embryo to the carrying mother we have recommended that the woman who gives birth should, for all purposes in law, be regarded as the mother. The position following surrogacy is far less straightforward. It is not difficult to envisage circumstances where serious arguments could develop as to whether the genetic mother or the carrying mother ought in truth to be regarded as the mother of the child. The resolution of this issue could be of great importance in questions such as inheritance, citizenship, or a claim for wrongful death.

The Father's Position

We have also considered the case of the commissioning father. In most cases the genetic father will be the husband of the commissioning mother. As regards enforcing any surrogacy agreement to which he is party, the commissioning father faces the difficulties described above. He may also be vulnerable to a claim by the carrying mother for an affiliation order if she keeps the child and the court might or might not make such an order according to the facts of the particular case. Unless he is married to the carrying mother he will, in the eyes of the law, be treated as an "unmarried" father with all the consequences that ordinarily flow from that.

Arguments Against Surrogacy

There are strongly held objections to the concept of surrogacy, and it seems from the evidence submitted to us that the weight of public opinion is against the practice. The objections turn essentially on the view that to introduce a third party into the process of procreation which should be confined to the loving partnership between two people, is an attack on the value of the marital relationship. Further, the intrusion is worse than in the case of AID, since the contribution of the carrying mother is greater, more intimate and personal, than the contribution of a semen donor. It is also argued that it is inconsistent with human dignity that a woman should use her uterus for financial profit and treat it as an incubator for someone else's child. The objection is not diminished, indeed it is strengthened, where the woman entered an agreement to conceive a child, with the sole purpose of handing the child over to the commissioning couple after birth.

Again, it is argued that the relationship between mother and child is itself distorted by surrogacy. For in such an arrangement a woman deliberately allows herself to become pregnant with the intention of giving up the child to which she will give birth, and this is the wrong way to approach pregnancy. It is also potentially damaging to the child, whose bonds with the carrying mother, regardless of genetic connections, are held to be strong, and whose welfare must be considered to be of paramount importance. Further it is felt that a surrogacy agreement is degrading to the child who is to be the outcome of it, since, for all practical purposes, the child will have been bought for money.

It is also argued that since there are some risks attached to pregnancy, no woman ought to be asked to undertake pregnancy for another, in order to earn money. Nor, it is argued, should a woman be forced by legal sanctions to part with a child, to which she has recently given birth, against her will.

Arguments For Surrogacy

If infertility is a condition which should, where possible, be remedied, it is argued that surrogacy must not be ruled out, since it offers to some couples their only chance of having a child genetically related to one or both of them. In particular, it may well be the only way that the husband of an infertile woman can have a child. Moreover, the bearing of a child for another can be seen, not as an undertaking that trivializes or commercializes pregnancy, but, on the contrary, as a deliberate and thoughtful act of generosity on the part of one woman to another. If there are risks attached to pregnancy, then the generosity is all the greater.

There is no reason, it is argued, to suppose that carrying mothers will enter into agreements lightly, and they have a perfect right to enter into such agreements if they so wish, just as they have a right to use their own bodies in other ways, according to their own decision. Where agreements are genuinely voluntary, there can be no question of exploitation, nor does the fact that surrogates will be paid for their pregnancy of itself entail exploitation of either party to the agreement.

As for intrusion into the marriage relationship, it is argued that those who feel strongly about this need not seek such treatment, but they should not seek to prevent others from having access to it.

On the question of bonding, it is argued that as very little is actually known about the extent to which bonding occurs when the child is *in utero*, no great claims should be made in this respect. In any case the breaking of such bonds, even if less than ideal, is not held to be an overriding argument against placing a child for adoption, where the mother wants this.

The Inquiry's View

The question of surrogacy presented us with some of the most difficult problems we encountered. The evidence submitted to us contained a range of strongly held views and this was reflected in our own views. The moral and social objections to surrogacy have weighed heavily with us. In the first place we are all agreed that surrogacy for convenience alone, that is, where a woman is physically capable of bearing a child but does not wish to undergo pregnancy, is totally ethically unacceptable. Even in compelling medical circumstances the danger of exploitation of one human being by another appears to the majority of us far to outweigh the potential benefits, in almost every case. That people should treat others as a means to their own ends, however desirable the consequences, must always be liable to moral objection. Such treatment of one person by another becomes positively exploitative when financial interests are involved. It is therefore with the commercial exploitation of surrogacy that we have been primarily, but by no means exclusively, concerned.

We have considered whether the criminal law should have any part to play in the control of surrogacy and have concluded that it should. We recognise that there is a serious risk of commercial exploitation of surrogacy and that this would be difficult to prevent without the assistance of the criminal law. We have considered whether a limited, non-profit making surrogacy service, subject to licensing and inspection, could have any useful part to play but the majority agreed that the existence of such a service would in itself encourage the growth of surrogacy. **We recommend that legislation be introduced to render criminal the creation or the operation in the United Kingdom of agencies whose purposes include the recruitment of women for surrogate pregnancy or making arrangements for individuals or couples who wish to utilize the services of a carrying mother; such legislation should be wide enough to include both profit and non-profit making organizations. We further recommend that the legislation be sufficiently wide to render criminally liable the actions of professionals and others who knowingly assist in the establishment of a surrogate pregnancy.**

We do not envisage that this legislation would render private persons entering into surrogacy arrangements liable to criminal prosecution, as we are anxious to avoid children being born to mothers subject to the taint of criminality. We nonetheless recognize that there will continue to be privately arranged surrogacy agreements. While we consider that most, if not all, surrogacy arrangements would be legally unenforceable in any of their terms, we feel that the position should be put beyond any possible doubt in law. **We recommend that it be provided by statute that all surrogacy agreements are illegal contracts and therefore unenforceable in the courts.**

We are conscious that surrogacy like egg and embryo donation may raise the question as to whether the genetic or the carrying mother is the true mother. Our recommendations elsewhere cover cases where eggs or embryos have been donated. There remains however the possible case where the egg or embryo has not been donated but has been provided by the commissioning mother or parents with the intention that they should bring up the resultant child. If our recommendation is accepted, such cases are unlikely to occur because of the probability that the practitioner administering the treatment would be committing an offense. However, for the avoidance of doubt, we consider that the legislation should be sufficiently widely drawn to cover any such case. If experience shows that this gives rise to an injustice for children who live with their genetic mother rather than the mother who bore them then in our view the remedy is to make the adoption laws more flexible so as to enable the genetic mother to adopt.

Expression of Dissent: Surrogacy

In the following paragraphs we express dissent from some of the views of the Inquiry on the question of surrogacy. There are, we hold, rare occasions when surrogacy could be beneficial to couples as a last resort. On those occasions gynecologists should not be denied the option of suggesting surrogacy to their patients. In the best interests of all concerned, however, and particularly in the best interests of the child that may ensue, we think that stringent care and control is necessary. We recommend that the licensing authority proposed by the Inquiry should include surrogacy within its terms of reference, and that any non-profit agency that wished to assist in making surrogacy arrangements would have to be licensed by the authority.

We wish to make it clear that we share many concerns with our colleagues. The practice of surrogacy could lead to serious problems, and we do not wish to deny these problems. Equally we regard it as of immense importance that people considering getting involved in surrogacy, in whatever way, should be fully aware of the complications that could ensue.

Even in our disagreement there is much common ground. We go along entirely with our colleagues in our disapproval of surrogacy for convenience. We also agree that the criminal law should be brought in to prevent the operation of profit making agencies in this field, although our reasons for this are somewhat different from those of our colleagues. In our view the question of exploitation of the surrogate mother, or the treating of her as a means to other people's ends, is not as clear cut a moral issue as our colleagues assert. On the other hand we hold firmly that the very difficult personal, legal, and social issues raised by surrogacy lie close to those raised in adoption and fostering and hence that there should be no place for commercial operations just as there is no place for commercial adopting agencies.

Our disagreement with our colleagues becomes most marked in the discussion of the use of criminal law to resist surrogacy. Whatever we as an Inquiry may recommend, the demand for surrogacy in one form or another will continue, and possibly even grow. Some of this demand might well be frivolous or misplaced, but there are undoubtedly couples who, for medical reasons, will seek surrogacy as a last resort. Our colleagues, by their recommendation would prevent gynecologists from offering any form of assistance to such couples to achieve a surrogate pregnancy. As a consequence couples may give up any hope of a child, may take further risks such as of more miscarriages, or may decide to venture into some sort of "do-it-yourself" arrangement. The latter possibility—that couples are driven into making their own arrangements—is particularly unsatisfactory. These arrangements would be unsupported by medical and counseling services and would lack the anonymity that the Inquiry has recommended to protect all parties in infertility treatments from legal and emotional complications.

Having considered the risks on both sides of a finely balanced argument we have come to the conclusion that it would be a mistake to close the door completely on surrogacy being offered as a treatment for childlessness. We are concerned, however, about the way in which it might be offered. We believe that the proposed licensing authority should include surrogacy within its remit. The authority would have the power to license an agency or agencies to make arrangements for surrogacy. These arrangements would include the matching of commissioning parents with surrogate mothers, and the provision of adequate counseling to ensure that the legal and personal complications of surrogacy were fully understood. The only agencies which could be licensed would be those in which child-caring skills were well represented and in which there was no commercial motive. Thus adoption and fostering agencies or some new agency, similarly staffed and run, could be appropriate candidates for licensing. We are not suggesting that the licensing authority establish an agency, only if one is proposed it be empowered to consider its application. Access to a licensed agency could only be by referral from a consultant gynecologist.

The presence of a licensed agency should not in our opinion render illegal any surrogacy arrangements that did not use the agency, as it would clearly be undesirable that a child's conception and birth should have any taint of illegality attached to it. On the other hand anyone (including a medical practitioner) who made surrogacy arrangements for a couple and who was not licensed to do so would be committing an offense, regardless of whether they were acting for profit.

We recognize the difficulties in the way of the commissioning couple acquiring parental status. We believe that if steps are taken to regularize surrogacy through licensing, some form of adoption procedure must be open to couples. Under present law money may not change hands in the process of adoption. Nevertheless, most surrogate mothers would expect payment for their services. In our opinion payments to a surrogate mother should not be a barrier to the child being adopted by the commissioning couple.

If our proposals are accepted, we believe that it would be inappropriate for steps to be taken to provide that all surrogacy agreements are illegal contracts. For the time being the courts should be free to consider individual cases on their own merits if they so choose.

We do not believe that public opinion is yet fully formed on the question of surrogacy, which has burst into prominence only in the last year or so. Thus we think it is too early to take a final decision one way or the other. We wish to have the opportunity in the next few years to see what the demand is, whether an agency is prepared to come forward to satisfy it, and whether the consequences are generally acceptable or not. We simply ask that the door be left slightly ajar so that surrogacy can be more effectively assessed.

[*Editor's Note:* In 1985, a British court, confronting the issue for the first time, upheld a surrogacy agreement and awarded custody of the child to the commissioning couple. In the United States, in 1987, a New Jersey appeals court ruled against the surrogate mother, Mary Beth Whitehead, and awarded custody of "Baby M" to the child's natural father, Dr. William Stern.]

6

Prenatal Injury:
Emerging Causes of Action Against Parents

Robert H. Blank

In the past several decades, major changes have occurred in the body of case law surrounding the processes of birth and pregnancy. Preconception, conception, and prenatal legal actions are commonplace in part due to alterations in social values regarding birth and pregnancy. Major causes of the growing legal attention to these subjects are the recent advances in medical science which have brought about significant changes to the physiological aspects of the birth process and altered perceptions of it. "In short, the advances in medical science have reshaped the way American society thinks about birth."[1]

Along with the altered values and the advances in medical science, many legal controversies have arisen regarding prenatal and even preconception injuries. The growing number of these birth and pregnancy cases are causing judicial considerations of many new and novel causes of action. According to Lambert this cluster of topics surrounding prenatal injury "presents a series of anguished questions, inevitably enmeshing the torts watcher in what Darwin called 'the web of life.'"[2] Terms like "wrongful pregnancy," "wrongful life," and "wrongful birth" are quickly emerging, resulting in substantial questioning of previous legal and policy assumptions. It is not surprising that there is wide divergence in the reaction of the courts to these cases, both in recognizing a cause of action and determining the appropriate amount of damages, if any,

---

Robert H. Blank is an associate professor of political science at Northern Illinois University.

to be awarded—the law in this area is far from being settled; it is just beginning to develop. This paper attempts to review systematically court action in the area of prenatal injury particularly as it leads to a cause of action against the parents.

Framing a Cause of Action for Prenatal Injury

The child's right to recover from a third party for prenatal injuries, though largely unquestioned today, is a very recent judicial development. Prior to 1946, the courts largely accepted the precedence of *Dietrich v. Inhabitants of Northampton*[3] where the Massachusetts Supreme Court disallowed recovery for negligently inflicted prenatal injuries in a wrongful death action of a child that did not survive its premature birth. In arriving at its decision, the *Dietrich* court relied on the lack of precedent and upon the concept that the fetus was part of the mother and not a separate entity. Subsequently, in *Allaire v. St. Luke's Hospital*[4] the Illinois Supreme Court in following *Dietrich* held that an action for injuries could not be maintained by a plaintiff who at the time of injury was a prenatal infant with no separate legal existence.

As medical science learned more about prenatal development, the *Dietrich* rule was attacked for its illogical legal bases and for its inconsistency with biological knowledge. The fact that the unborn child's property and contract rights were legally protected under common law while its personal rights were not was criticized as illogical. Also, it was argued that at least after viability, when the child is capable of maintaining independent life, it is a separate entity and not simply an appendage of its mother. Another objection to this cause of action, that proof of causation is more difficult in prenatal injury cases, was weakened as medical knowledge about the causes of congenital damage expanded.

As a result of these increasingly vocal attacks on *Dietrich*, in *Bonbrest v. Kotz*,[5] the court established a new trend in recognizing for the first time a common law right of action for prenatal injuries. The court held that a child was permitted to recover for injuries suffered before birth, provided that the fetus was viable at the time of the injury and subsequently born alive. The *Bonbrest* court reasoned that once the child demonstrated that it was capable of surviving outside the mother's womb, the argument that the fetus had no independent existence was inapplicable. It argued that if such an action was denied, there would be a wrong for which there was no remedy.

After *Bonbrest*, the right to recover for injuries sustained *in utero* gained rapid and widespread acceptance. For instance, in *Woods v. Lancet*[6] the court concluded that "To hold, as a matter of law, that no viable fetus has any separate existence which the law will recognize is for the law to deny a simple and easily demonstrable fact. This child, when injured, was in fact, alive and capable of being delivered and of remaining alive, separate from its mother." Likewise the *Smith v. Brennan*[7] majority said:

> regardless of analogies to other areas of law, justice requires that the *principle be recognized that a child has a legal right to begin life with a sound mind and body.* If the wrongful conduct of another interferes with that right, and it can be established by competent proof that there is a causal connection between the wrongful interference and the harm suffered by the child when born, damages for such harm should be recoverable by the child.

According to Prosser,[8] the trend toward allowing recovery after the abandonment of *Dietrich* was "the most spectacular abrupt reversal of a well-settled rule in the whole history of the law of torts." Today, all states recognize a cause for action by a subsequently born child against a third party for prenatal injury.

Despite the consensus of the courts to recognize a cause of action for prenatal injury, many inconsistencies remain. One of the most critical differences focuses on whether a fetus must reach a certain stage of development at the time of injury before there can be a settlement. Other crucial distinctions center on the scope of liability, the standards of causation required, and whether or not the injured child must be born alive. Before examining the various types of prenatal actions, the difficult issue of viability will be discussed.

The Viability Rule for Prenatal Torts

Although there is a clear case law trend in favor of allowing a claim for prenatal injury regardless of the stage of gestation during which the injury occurred, there is far from unanimity in the courts on the question of viability. the viability rule developed originally as a means of distinguishing cases from *Dietrich* which assumed that the fetus was part of the mother. In *Bonbrest*, the court refuted *Dietrich* by concluding that a viable fetus could sustain life independent of the mother and was, therefore, a distinct legal entity. Courts relying on *Bonbrest* thus often limited the authority of their decisions to suits involving injuries incurred after viability. For instance in *Albala v. City of New York*,[9] the New York Court of Appeals upheld the viability requirement when it refused recovery for injuries suffered by a previable fetus. A primary rationale used by many courts sustaining the viability rule is that proving causation is difficult when the injury occurs in the previable stages of fetal development.

Increasing numbers of courts, however, have either expressly renounced the viability rule or ignored it. The Georgia Supreme Court[10] held that viability was not the deciding factor in a prenatal personal injuries action and that recovery for any injury suffered after the point of conception should be permitted. Another state court,[11] held that the fetus "from the time of conception becomes a separate organism and remains so. . . ." According to the court in *Smith v. Brennan*,[12] "Whether viable or not at the time of injury, the child sustains the same harm after birth, and therefore should be given the same opportunity for redress." In *Sylvia v. Gobeille*[13] a Rhode Island court stated: "We are unable logically to conclude that a claim for injury inflicted prior to viability is any less meritorious than one sustained after."

The trend toward abolition of the viability rule is a just one because the harm sustained by the child may be the same whether the injury occurred before or after viability.

> Once the child is born alive, it is a separate human being deserving of compensation, regardless of whether it was a separate legal entity at the time the injury was originally inflicted. At birth, and throughout its life, the child exhibits the injury which was caused by the prior negligent act.[14]

A California court recently agreed with this reasoning and concluded that birth is the condition precedent that establishes the beginning of the child's rights.[15] A tort action may be maintained if the child is born alive—whether the injury occurred before viability or after is immaterial once birth takes place. Injuries inflicted in the first trimester are likely to produce the most severe congenital deformities. Thus, the viability rule precludes many of the most meritorious claims. The presumption here is that the fetus from the time of conception becomes a separate organism and remains so throughout its existence.

Another reason for rejecting viability as a pivotal point in defining the legal rights of the fetus is its arbitrariness.[16] As neonatal intensive care technology improves, viability, or that point at which the fetus can survive outside the mother's uterus, will be pushed back earlier in gestation. Also, there remains considerable disagreement as to which of many criteria, including fetal age and weight, is most adequate in determining viability, and over the preciseness of any such measures. Moreover, the viability rule is difficult to apply because it is an indeterminate concept that depends on the individual development of a specific fetus, the health of the mother, the quality of neonatal care available, the competency of the attending physician and a host of other factors. As a result, there is no way of determining whether or not a particular fetus was viable at the time of injury, unless it was immediately born.[17] Insofar as viability is usually impossible to ascertain, the theory is impractical as a measure of liability and ought to be abolished as a criterion.[18]

In a further extension of this logic, some courts recognize a cause of action for personal injuries that occur prior to conception. In *Renslow v. Mennonite Hospital*,[19] a physician was held liable for injuries suffered by an infant girl as a result of a blood transfusion to the mother that occurred nine years before the child's birth. These "preconception torts" arise when a negligent act has been committed against a person not yet conceived but whose eventual existence is foreseeable.

Wrongful Death of The Unborn

Under common law the death of a person may not be compensated by civil court. In order to alleviate the harsh common law rule of no liability for the death of a person, wrongful death statutes in all jurisdictions are designed to fill the void and provide compensation to survivors. There are, however, many problems in bringing wrongful death actions for the death of an unborn child. First, the provisions of the statutes themselves vary considerably across the states. Moreover, variation in judicial construction and interpretation of the statutes is even greater. Therefore, it is not surprising that the courts remain divided concerning whether or not a fetus may be the subject of a wrongful death action and, if so, under what conditions. Despite these inconsistencies, there are clear patterns that indicate a growing acceptance of a cause of action.

In addition to the difficulties raised by variation in the statutes and their interpretation, requirements for the existence of a cause of action in wrongful death also make application to the unborn problematic. Typical requirements of the statutes include: (1) the existence of a "person" who has died; (2) the death of the person of injuries resulting from a wrongful act, neglect or default that would have conferred a cause of action upon the person who has died, had that person survived; and (3) the act, neglect or default that caused the fetal injury must have been performed by another. Although the third requisite is generally amenable to proof, especially in light of advances in medicine, the first two are not. Critical remaining issues are (1) whether a fetus which is never born alive is a person within the meaning of the statute and (2) whether the plaintiff can prove that the injury caused the unborn child's death.

Causation

In considering actions for wrongful death of a fetus, early courts concluded that the action should be dismissed because of the difficulty of demonstrating causation of prenatal injury and the possibility of fictitious claims. These objections have been undercut to a great degree by advances in medical science.[20] Proof of the cause of an unborn child's death can be made by expert testimony as in other wrongful death torts.[21] Various diagnostic techniques such as ultrasound can be used to establish trauma or injury to the fetus immediately after an accident. Furthermore, advances in pathology provide more objective data for evaluating causation of an unborn's death.

In addition to the availability of more precise medical evidence of causation, courts increasingly have rejected the arguments of denying cause on the basis of the difficulty of proving causation or of the possibility of fictitious claims. The court in *Woods v. Lancet*,[22] concluded that difficulty in proving legal and factual causation should not affect substantive rights. Another court stated that proof is no more problematic in a prenatal injury case than in any other personal injury case.[23]

Is the Unborn a Person?

The major remaining basis of the inconsistency of establishing a cause of action for wrongful death of the unborn is the question of whether or not a fetus is a person under the appropriate statutes and if so at what point in gestation?[24] This issue is crucial because if the fetus is defined as a person, the action will be recognized; if not, the action will be dismissed. Ordinarily, the courts focus on three elements to determine if a fetus is a person. First, they examine the legislative intent in the enacting statute. If a fetus is not specifically included in the statute, the court can either extend by implication a cause of action for the fetus[25] or defer to the legislature to make explicit their intention to include the unborn as a person.[26]

In situations where the statutes are not explicit, the courts are attentive to the legal status of unborns traditionally enjoyed in the state in other types of action. Finally, they will consider community knowledge and attitudes about the unborn.[27] Here again the role of medicine is critical in shifting the balance toward recognizing a cause of action for the unborn. Social recognition of the fetus as a person has been heightened by a variety of techniques that allow visualization of the fetus early in gestation and by the emergence of fetal surgery and therapy.[28] According to Scofield, "parental concern with the unborn has increased with advances in medical science, and this reality supports inclusion of the unborn within the meaning of death statutes."[29]

As a result of amended wrongful death statutes that facilitate inclusion of the unborn, as well as the other social/legal forces noted above, a majority of jurisdictions now allow a cause for action for the death of an unborn. However, as stated earlier, there is a significant variation in the criteria used to qualify a fetus for legal status, primarily focusing on viability and whether or not the fetus was live-born, if even for a few minutes. In some cases it has been held that a fetus, regardless of viability at the time of injury, is a person for purposes of the wrongful death statute. In *Presley v. Newport Hospital*,[30] for instance, the court held that the fetus, whether viable or previable, is a person within the meaning of the Rhode Island statute. Similarly, the Supreme Court of Louisiana affirmed an award under the wrongful death statute for the death in a car crash of a fetus in the sixth month.[31]

Contrarily, other courts have held that a fetus is a person under a wrongful death statute only if it is viable at the time of the injury.[32] In *Green v. Smith*[33] for example, the court drew a clear distinction between the common law cause of action on behalf of an infant for injuries suffered prior to viability and a statutory cause of action for destruction of a fetus not yet viable. The loss incurred by a live-born child burdened with defects resulting from a prenatal injury is the same whether the injury is suffered prior to or after viability. However, the wrongful death statute provides for the recovery of the death of a "person" and the court found no basis on which to hold that one can cause the death of a fetus not yet viable.

Finally, to cover all possible combinations, some courts have concluded that a fetus, whether viable or previable, is not a person under the wrongful death statute and, therefore, its beneficiaries have no cause of action to seek recovery for the loss. For instance, the Pennsylvania Supreme Court denied recovery under the wrongful death statute for death resulting from an injury to a fetus in the eighth month of pregnancy.[34] In *Justus v. Atchison*[35] the court stated that if the legislature meant the fetus to be a person under the wrongful death statute, it would determine "to confer legal personality on unborn fetuses." Likewise, a Tennessee court[36] concluded that it was not appropriate or necessary to judicially determine when life begins because the creation of a wrongful death statute is properly the business of the legislative branch of government. Expansion of benefits to include viable fetus, fetus, and/or embryo is within its exclusive province.

Of those jurisdictions which recognize any cause of action for a fetus under wrongful death, virtually all have abandoned the live-birth requirement. Most courts allow an action when a fetus is prenatally injured, is subsequently stillborn, and its representative attempts to recover for wrongful death. The Vermont Supreme Court held that a viable fetus, subsequently stillborn, is a person under the Vermont wrongful death statute.[37] In agreement, the Missouri Supreme Court held that parents may maintain a wrongful death claim for their stillborn fetus.[38] The court agreed with the plaintiffs that there is "no substantial reason why a tortfeasor who causes prenatal death should be treated more favorably than one who causes prenatal injury." Similarly, the *Danos* court stated that it was illogical for the cause of action to depend on whether the child was stillborn or lived outside the womb for a few minutes. Rejecting a cause of action for the fetus's wrongful death would simply serve to benefit the person causing the injury. In *Eich v. Town of Gulf Shores*,[39] the court stated that logic, fairness, and justice compel recognition of an action for prenatal injuries causing death before birth. These courts agree that the live-birth requisite is logically indefensible in that one who injures a fetus later born alive only enough to cause damages must pay for his actions while one who injures a fetus severely enough to kill it does not. This would serve only to reward the tortfeasor for his severity in inflicting the injury. According to Winborne,[40] "it would be bizarre to hold that the greater the harm inflicted the better the opportunity for exoneration of the defendant."

Despite these criticisms of the live-birth requirement and the trend toward its rejection in wrongful death actions, a few courts remain adamant in its use. Some courts have argued that lines must be drawn and that requiring a live birth has an advantage of establishing to a legal certainty that there was a living person.[41] From the moment of conception onward there must be some cut-off point and to place this at the moment of live birth provides some degree of certainty to an otherwise speculative situation. Whatever the persuasiveness of these arguments, the *Justus* court held that a rejection of a wrongful death action for the death of a stillborn fetus is not illogical, nor is non-recovery contrary to public policy because it provides an incentive for tortfeasors to refrain from efforts to save their victim's lives. In *Lacesse v. McDonough*,[42] a Massachusetts Court stated that "if the fetus is not born alive, it is not such a person and will not suffer injury."

Damages

Another area of incongruous judicial decision-making in prenatal wrongful death actions centers on recovery of damages. Although many courts are willing to recognize a cause of action, the extent of damages is difficult to prove. Damages in a wrongful death settlement are intended to benefit survivors and compensate them for their loss. In addition to determining what constitutes a fair award, the courts have to deal with how to differentiate between the losses of fetuses at different stages in gestation. Is the emotional distress resulting from the death of a liveborn greater than that of a stillborn? Of an embryo?

Although the court in *Evans v. Olson*[43] held that there is no more speculation as to the probability of pecuniary loss with a stillborn than a child, other courts have held that damages associated with the loss of services and support is not recoverable because there are no competent evidences to the child's capabilities and potentialities.[44] For the unborn, none of the usual criteria such as mental capacity, personality traits, and training are present. In 1983, an Illinois appellate court[45] affirmed a jury verdict of $125,000 in a wrongful death action involving an unborn child. Although the court admitted the difficulty of providing adequate evidence for determining pecuniary loss, it noted that the Illinois wrongful death statute provides for pecuniary compensation to the next of kin. While the appeals court said it would have awarded a substantially reduced sum, it found the question properly that of the jury and let it stand.

In *Danos v. St. Pierre*,[46] the Supreme Court of Louisiana posited that in awarding damages in prenatal wrongful death cases, the trial judge may look at a number of factors for determining the extent of damages suffered by the parents. These factors include: (1) the stage of pregnancy at which death occurs, (2) the number of children the couple has, (3) the probability of the pregnancy going to full term, (4) whether the mother used artificial means to induce pregnancy, (5) prenatal care of the unborn child, and (6) prenatal preparation for the forthcoming child such as house additions and baby furniture. Inherent in this approach is a dependency on the emotional ties between the mother and her unborn child. As noted earlier, new techniques which allow visualization of the fetus early in pregnancy such as ultrasound and fetoscopy along with amniocentesis, which identifies fetal sex, are strengthening the emotional bonds as well as the social recognition of the fetus as a person. Women who have undergone prenatal diagnosis often refer to the fetus as a baby and name it after knowing its sex. The court in *Johnson v. Superior Court*[47] concluded that the mother forms a sufficiently close relationship with her fetus during pregnancy that its death will foreseeably cause her severe emotional distress. When the death results from medical malpractice or other negligence rather than natural and unavoidable causes, the loss is all the more poignant and should be legally redressable. Trends in prenatal diagnosis and monitoring are certain to enhance the measure of damages for emotional distress.

Prenatal Injury Actions

An unborn child can be injured though not killed through the tortious act of another person during the child's gestation. Although inconsistencies exist in case law as to viability, proof of causation and so forth, a consensus now exists in all 50 states that there is a right of a child to bring common law action for injuries suffered before birth. This unanimity has been achieved in a short span in part because new medical knowledge of the deleterious effects of particular action on the unborn permitted causation susceptible to legal proof.

As in all tort action, the plaintiff must prove existence of a legal duty on the part of the defendant to conform to a specific standard of conduct for the protection of the plaintiff against unreasonable risk of injury as well as a breach of that duty by the defendant. For the breach to occur, there must be actual misfeasance—the defendant must be found to have been affirmatively negligent. Moreover, it must be proven that damage was suffered by the plaintiff and that the proximate cause of the damage was the negligence of the defendant. Legal causation may be established even though the biological processes which bring the injury about are not precisely understood. Legal cause does not need to be the sole or even predominant cause of the injury. It is only required that the defendant's conduct must be a substantial or material factor in bringing about the injury—but for the defendant's negligent conduct the injury would have not occurred.

Tort actions predicated on prenatal injury have arisen from various factual settings including automobile accidents and medical malpractice. To date, most prenatal injury suits have been brought against third parties, particularly physicians and other health providers who allegedly failed to exercise the proper standard of care and through their negligence caused damage. Once the fetus is recognized as a legal entity separate from the mother, torts for prenatal injury become identical in principle to other malpractice suits. Given the growing state of medical knowledge about fetal development and the expanding array of diagnostic techniques, torts for prenatal injury have become a common medical malpractice suit.

A recent case, however, demonstrates the unique nature of many emerging causes of action in this area. In *Payton v. Abbott Labs*,[48] a class action suit brought by approximately 4,000 women exposed to the drug diethylstilbestrol (DES), the women are suing because their mothers ingested DES while pregnant and transmitted the drug to them *in utero*. As a result, they are now at increased risk for a rare type of genital cancer as well as abnormalities of the reproductive organs. The defendants were pharmaceutical companies (Abbott, Eli Lilly, Merck, Rexall, Squibb and Sons, and Upjohn) all of which manufactured and marketed DES as a miscarriage preventative between 1945 and 1976. The plaintiffs contended that the defendants were negligent in marketing DES and that they should be compensated for the higher risk of cancer and other abnormalities incurred. To confuse the situation even more, most of the plaintiffs were unable to identify the specific manufacturer of the DES ingested by their mothers.

Based on precedents treating *in utero* injury resulting from ingestion of a drug by the mother, the court held that the plaintiffs could maintain a cause of action. The *Payton* court rejected the defendants' arguments that recovery should be denied because of the difficulty of proving causation and because of the risk of fictitious claims. The difficulties of proof or the possibility of false claims could not bar action by plaintiffs with medically demonstratable injuries. They only would have to satisfy the normal requirements of any tort action.

Although *Payton* was rendered in response to a certified question by the federal court as to whether there is a cause of action in Massachusetts for those injured by a drug prior to birth, the precedental force is expected to be substantial. According to Seksay, the prenatal injury holding in *Payton* results in a potential increase in liability for anyone who negligently supplies a pregnant woman with drugs or medication.[49] Under *Payton*, Massachusetts courts, in accord with the courts and legislatures of other jurisdictions, are gradually extending legal rights to the unborn.

Criminal Law and the Unborn

Another area of law which demonstrates an inconsistent and at times incoherent view of the status of the unborn is criminal law, particularly homicide and child abuse. For purposes of criminal law, the fetus generally has not been recognized as a "person" or "human being." Under common law, the unborn fetus was not considered a person to whom the law of homicide applied. In some jurisdictions no penalties were imposed for homicide unless the victim had been born. For instance in *People v. Greer*,[50] an Illinois court ruled that causing the death of a fetus is not murder unless the fetus is born alive and subsequently dies of the injuries inflicted. Similarly, a New Jersey court[51] ruled that fetuses were victims of murder only because they were born alive and then died, while *People v. Guthrie*[52] dismissed a charge of negligent homicide where the victim was a fetus "ready for birth."

One response to the failure of common law to provide redress for the killing of a fetus was for state legislatures to explicitly define it in the penal codes. The Iowa Code (§707.7, West 1979) for instance defines feticide as the intentional termination of a human pregnancy after the second trimester, while the New York Penal Law (§125.00) defines homicide as including the death of an unborn child of more than 24 weeks. The California Penal Code (§187, West Suppl. 1982) was amended in 1976 to define murder as "the unlawful killing of a human being, or a fetus, with malice aforethought." The California legislature amended the code in response to a ruling by the California Supreme Court[53] that a viable fetus, stillborn as the direct result of an assault, had not become a person at the time of viability for purposes of the state's murder statute, which referred only to the killing of a "human being." As the California Supreme Court noted in a later case,[54] the legislature included the fetus by creating a new category of murder, not by redefining the term "human life" to include the fetus. In *People v. Apodoca*[55] a California appeals court affirmed a conviction for second-degree murder of a 22 to 24 week old fetus in a case where the defendant repeatedly struck a pregnant woman with the intent to kill the unborn fetus.

Despite the increased tendency of courts and legislatures to provide some criminal protection of the unborn, the courts continue to define such protections narrowly. According to Parness[56] one reason for this hesitancy may lie in their misunderstanding of *Roe v. Wade*. In *People v. Smith*[57] a California appellate court affirmed the dismissal of a homicide charge against a man who allegedly murdered a previable human fetus even though the criminal statute had been amended to include a fetus. The court based its decision on the *Roe* court's handling of viability:

> The underlying rationale of *Wade*, therefore, is that until viability is reached, human life in the legal sense has not come into existence. Implicit in *Wade* is the conclusion that as a matter of constitutional law the destruction of a non-viable fetus is not the taking of human life. It follows that such destruction cannot constitute murder or other form of homicide, whether committed by a mother, a father (as here), or a third person.[58]

According to Parness, the California court clearly misread *Roe*.[59] In *Roe*, the Supreme Court held only that a previable fetus was not a "person" enjoying Fourteenth Amendment protection and specifically refused to resolve the difficult question of when life begins. In actuality, the Court noted that while fetuses are treated differently under the law than living persons, the unborn have been accorded certain legal rights.

Other state supreme courts have shown a similar reluctance to extend legal protection to the unborn, despite clear statutory intent. For example, the Supreme Court of Louisiana[60] sustained a motion to void an indictment of a defendant for the murder of a fertilized, implanted fetus in spite of the criminal homicide statute that specified that the term "person" included a human being from the moment of fertilization and implantation.[61] Despite legislative action to reverse the common law definition of homicide in Louisiana the court precluded the unborn from full legal protection. At most, the perpetrators of such action are subject to prosecution under lesser offenses such as assault and battery of the pregnant woman. According to Parness and Pritchard,[62] "Notwithstanding the Supreme Court's recognition that legal protection of children may sometimes cover the unborn, relatively few states have enacted criminal laws protecting the unborn." Although a viable fetus likely may be a victim of homicide in many states, it is unlikely that previable fetuses will be considered such.

Another set of criminal codes relevant to the unborn are the child abuse laws. Here the guidelines are even less developed and more fragmented. In *Reyes v. Superior Court*,[63] a California appeals court found that the felony child-endangering statute was not violated by the continued use of heroin by the mother during the last two months of pregnancy, despite warnings from a public health nurse, which led to the heroin addiction of twin boys. Conversely, in *In re Baby X*[64] a Michigan appellate court upheld the conviction for child abuse of a woman who gave birth to a child addicted to heroin.

Torts For Wrongful Life

A related but more recent variety of prenatal torts, which Capron[65] terms "by far the most unusual and troublesome set of liability issues emerging from the intersection of law and human genetics," is the tort for wrongful life. A tort for wrongful life is a suit brought on behalf of an affected infant, most commonly against a physician or other health professional who, it is alleged, negligently failed to inform the parents of the possibility of their producing a severely defective child, thereby preventing a parental choice to avoid conception or birth of the child. The unique aspect of such suits is the assumption that a life has evolved which should not have. If not for some negligence of the defendant, the child plaintiff would never have been born. Although the term "wrongful life" has been applied to a variety of situations, including those where parents are suing for damages to the child, it is more precise to limit wrongful life action to that brought solely by the affected *child*. Most recent suits for wrongful life have been brought on behalf of children with severe mental or physical defects asking for monetary damages awarded on the basis of their very existence, as compared to a state of nonexistence. Wrongful life suits differ from traditional negligence actions in that the harm here is in being born even though compensation ultimately is asked in the form of monetary damages.

> What the infant plaintiff alleges is that the breach of duty led approximately to his birth—the maturing of the harm—and, thus, he is forced to endure life with defects which he would not be forced to do but for the defendant's breach of duty.[66]

Legal questions surrounding wrongful life action, therefore, center on whether the defendant has a legally cognizable duty to the infant plaintiff even though the plaintiff was not born or in some cases even conceived at the time of the defendant's allegedly negligent act. There is considerable disagreement over whether or not the plaintiff is harmed by the defendant's negligence and if so, how damages can be measured. A question that the courts traditionally have been unwilling to face is whether or not the infant plaintiff is damaged by being born with defects when the only alternative is nonexistence. The plaintiff here must successfully argue that he would have been better off had he never been born. On public policy grounds, which have been interpreted by many legal observers as always favoring life over nonexistence, most courts have asserted that the plaintiff cannot be harmed by his birth.

Despite continued debate over the concepts of duty, harm, and proximate cause, recent court decisions indicate that the courts now might be willing to accept such cases of action. Additionally, many legal observers have come out in support of such action. Rogers argues that recognition of wrongful life claims promotes societal interest in genetic counseling and prenatal testing, deters medical malpractice, and at least partially redresses a clear and undeniable wrong.[67] In agreeing with an earlier article that "the awarding of monetary damages is an appropriate remedy for the wrongful life plaintiff," Kashi argues that while the child's life is not "wrongful," neither is it as it should be.[68] He states that the rejection of causes of action for wrongful life represent "a clear case of meritorious cause of action being denied because of its ill-chosen label."

Although Capron appears cautious in his view of torts for wrongful life, he supports an intermediate position—permitting recovery of some damages in severe cases but rejecting compensation of a defective child for the full amount by which his life differs from "normal life."[69] Contrarily, Trotzig rejects the notion of damages in such cases and states that it is absurd that "anyone, no matter how deformed, should be compensated for having to be alive."[70] Tedeschi, too, doubts whether logically or legally there can be such a thing as a "damage of being born" since the plaintiff would not exist if the claimed negligent act had not occurred.[71] He argues that claims for wrongful life are "doomed to failure" since the element of damage is missing if no difference can be drawn between the results of the act and its absence: "By his cause of action, the plaintiff cuts from under him the ground upon which he needs to rely in order to prove his damage."

Legal Precedents and Trends

Prior to the late 1970s, the courts unanimously refused to recognize the possibility of a cause of action for wrongful life. In 1967, the New Jersey Supreme Court declared[72] that the preciousness of human life, no matter how burdened, outweighs the need for recovery by the infant. To award damages to the affected child would be counter to public policy which views the right to life as inalienable in our society. Similarly, the *Dumer v. St. Michael's* court[73] dismissed a suit filed for wrongful life, but found that the parents had a cause, thus producing a clear legal distinction between torts for wrongful life and torts for wrongful birth, giving legal cognizance to the latter.

During the late 1970's the courts, while continuing to reject a wrongful life cause of action, began to make subtle distinctions that shifted toward recognition of legally cognizable harm to the child. Moreover, a number of trial courts ruled in favor of the plaintiffs and increasingly strong dissents on the higher courts acknowledged causes of action for wrongful life. According to Cohen,[74] *Park v. Chessin*[75] "marked the first step toward judicial acceptance of the theory of 'wrongful life.'" The suit was brought on the child's behalf for conscious pain and suffering resulting from the specialist's advice to the parents to have another child although they had already had one child die from polycystic kidney disease.[76] Although later overruled, an intermediate appellate court held that *both* the parents and the child had a cause of action and declared that "decisional law must keep pace with expanding technological, economic and social change."[77] For the first time, a cause of action was stated for the child, because "once having been born alive . . . said child comes within the 'orbit of the danger' for which the defendants could be liable."

This recognition of a legally cognizable action for wrongful life, however, was shortlived, or at least sidetracked. The *Park* decision was reviewed by the New York Court of Appeals as a companion case in *Becker v. Schwartz*[78] and overruled. Although the parents in both cases were allowed to recover their pecuniary loss, the court refused to permit recovery for emotional or psychiatric damages, arguing that this would "inevitably lead to drawing of artificial and arbitrary boundaries" as well as offend public policy. The infant plaintiffs in both *Park* and *Becker* were barred from recovery of any damages because of the inability of the law to make a comparison between life with handicaps and no life at all. The court specifically refused to accept the idea that a child may legally expect a life free from deformity and in direct reference to the lower court decision stated: "there is no precedent for recognition . . . of 'the fundamental right of a child to be born as a whole, functional human being . . .' "

Although it is yet too early to predict that future wrongful life decisions will recognize a cause of action for the affected child, a distinct trend continues in that direction. *Curlender v. Bio-Science Laboratories*,[79] in which a California appeals court agreed that a Tay-Sachs infant was entitled to seek recovery for alleged wrongful life, represents a step toward that end. The court concluded that the breach of duty of the laboratory was the proximate cause of an injury cognizable at law—the birth of the plaintiff with such defects. The court dismissed without discussion the central rationale for barring recovery in previous wrongful life cases since *Gleitman*—the value of nonexistence versus life with handicap—and focused attention instead on the resulting condition of the child.

> The reality of the "wrongful-life" concept is that such plaintiff both exists and suffers, due to the negligence of others. It is neither necessary nor just to retreat into meditation on the mysteries of life. We need not be concerned with the fact that had defendants not been negligent, the plaintiff might not have come into existence at all. The certainty of genetic impairment is no longer a mystery. In addition a reverent appreciation of life compels recognition that plaintiff, however impaired she may be, has come into existence as a living person with certain rights.[80]

In *Curlender* the court argued that perceptive analysis of the wrongful life concept requires recognition of the great distinctions in the conditions of the particular plaintiffs as well as the changing policy context. The court noted the "progression in our law" toward allowing recovery in such cases as well as the "gradual retreat" from use of "impossibility of measuring damages" as the sole ground for barring recovery by infants. The dramatic increase in genetic knowledge and the skills needed to avoid genetic disease is also introduced as a mitigating factor. Finally, the court cited the persistence of wrongful life litigation, despite the "cool reception" from the courts as evidence of the "serious nature of the wrong" and an "understanding that the law reflects, perhaps later than sooner, basic changes in the way society views such matters." In reversing the superior court's dismissal of this tort, the appeals court stated: "We see no reason in public policy or legal analysis for exempting from liability for punitive damages a defendant who is sued for committing a 'wrongful life' tort."[81]

In *Procanik v. Cillo*[82] the New Jersey Supreme Court ruled that a congenitally defective child may maintain an action to recover at least the extraordinary medical expenses he will incur over a lifetime, though it refused to allow recovery of general damages for emotional distress or "diminished childhood." Moreover, in January 1983, a unanimous decision of the Supreme Court of Washington State in *Harbeson v. Parke-Davis*[83] strongly approved the principle of wrongful life as well as wrongful birth. The court found that the parents have a right to prevent the birth of a defective child and that health care providers have a duty to impart to the parents material information about the likelihood of birth defects in their future children. The child born with such defects has a right to bring a wrongful life action against the health provider. According to the court, it would be illogical to permit only parents, not the child, to recover for the cost of the child's own medical care. The child's need for medical care and other special costs related to his or her defect will not disappear when the child attains majority. The burden of these costs should fall not on the parents or the state, but on the party whose negligence was the proximate cause of the child's need for extraordinary care. The child should be able to collect a lifetime of medical and educational costs or any other costs of the deformity, according to the court. However, following the reasoning of the California Supreme Court[84] the Washington court denied the child recovery for general damages such as pain and suffering.

Other recent decisions recognizing a cause of action for wrongful life against third parties are *Call v. Kerzirian*[85] and *Graham v. Pima City*.[86] In *Call*, a California appeals court ruled that damages for extraordinary expenses for specialized teaching and training and special equipment that an unhealthy infant will need because of her defect are recoverable. In *Graham*, the Pima City Superior Court approved a settlement of $380,000 for a wrongful life action. Conversely in *Di Natale v. Lieberman*[87] a Florida court ruled that a child born with physical or mental defects does not have a cause of action against any party on account of his or her having been born. In *Strohmaier v. Associates in Obstetrics and Gynecology*[88] the Michigan Appeals Court denied a cause of action for wrongful life because of the difficulty in assessing damages for being born, while in *Dorlin v. Providence Hosp.*[89] and *Nelson v. Krusen*[90] a child's claim for wrongful life was rejected because the assessment of damages would be too speculative. The judicial landscape, then, continues to be divergent.

Consequences of Wrongful Life

The literature is replete with references to the dangerous consequences of recognizing a cause of action for wrongful life. Oftquoted is the statement that the "legal implications of such a tort are vast; the social impact could be staggering."[91] Some observers predict a "flood of litigation" and multimillion dollar settlements imposing an "intolerable burden" on the medical community, escalating maternity costs, and reducing services in some cases. Chapman notes a fear that "Down's Syndrome children from all over could come into court and sue with such an action recognized."[92] Others dispute these claims and argue that relatively few children would be able to assert reasonably that they would have been better off not being born. Those commentators in favor of awarding damages usually emphasize traditional tort functions of justice to the harmed, deterrence, and punishment.

If responses to other malpractice actions can be taken as examples, it appears reasonable to assume that many physicians and health professionals will react to torts for wrongful life by practicing defensively. Although this is a desired goal of torts when it results in better care, wrongful life situations do present a unique dilemma because the response is reflected in heightened use of amniocentesis and abortion. As a result, judicial recognition of wrongful life actions might "induce physicians to abort all borderline fetuses," including those whose karyotypes or biomedical patterns are ambiguous or those whose prenatal diagnoses reveal minimal genetic defects.[93] Furthermore, physicians might be less prone to use heroic neonatal intensive care to save severely premature infants, for fear of later being sued for keeping them alive with damages. It is likely that a mentality could develop that assumes that the most effective protection from wrongful life torts is to ensure that such infants are not born.

More crucial, however, is the potential impact of acceptance of the concept of wrongful life on perceptions by the public of those persons born with genetic or other congenital defects. Sorenson contends that the amount of prejudice now directed toward mentally and physically disabled persons is already "generally more than that expressed toward various minority groups."[94] If the courts recognize wrongful life, it is probable that these attitudes will be accentuated and social intolerance for the disabled will increase since, it might be presumed, they should not have been born. It might also be feasible under such conditions for society to sue parents for the costs of maintaining such children in public institutions, although this would require substantial value alterations in the United States. The danger of establishing arbitrary categories of individuals "rightfully" born and "wrongfully" born is obvious. "A cogent policy justification for the continued dismissal of "wrongful life actions," according to Friedman, "is the possible societal acceptance of the belief that if the life of a genetically defective being is wrongful, then only his death can be 'rightful.' "[95] Ironically, what is viewed as "protecting the rights" of the plaintiff in a particular case might result in degrading the rights of those affected by genetic disease as a group.

Parental Liability for Prenatal Injury

The high incidence of congenital defects caused by the fetal environment has given rise to increased concern for the rights of the unborn child to be born free from avoidable prenatal injury. It is clear from the discussion of trends in tort law that the fetus is being accorded an expanding protection of civil law against injury caused by third parties. Although these trends conflict with some aspects of the *Roe* decision, ironically the legalization of abortion aroused concern for the unborn child and has facilitated this pattern. As noted earlier, new technical innovations and knowledge of fetal development have helped clarify the deleterious effects of certain environmental influences and reinforced the acceptance of prenatal torts.

These general trends toward recognition of a legal status for the unborn have substantial consequences for redefining the legal context of maternal responsibility toward the fetus. Because the immediate cause of most prenatal injuries is the disruption of the intrauterine environment and the parents, primarily the mother, largely control that environment, it is logical that attention be placed on those factors over which they influence control. Many actions of the mother might cause harm to the fetus, either through ignorance or with knowledge of the potential dangers.[96] Not surprisingly, there is a clear trend toward recognition of causes of action against parents by children injured prenatally. Obviously, this trend produces a conflict between the child's right to be born free from parentally-induced prenatal injury and the parental right of autonomy. By holding a woman liable to her infant for negligent care of her body during pregnancy, the woman's freedom to control her body is violated. Contrarily, because of the consequential role she plays in the development of the fetus and its total dependence on her, it might be argued that once she decides to bear a child she has a duty to restrict her freedom.

Two basic legal developments have been especially critical in this emergence of parental responsibility. The first is simply the expanding sphere of liability for prenatal injury which logically leads to those individuals most likely to cause injury, the parents. The second legal development is the abrogation of the intrafamily immunity doctrine, which traditionally protected the parents from liability. The former trend was discussed above while the latter is briefly examined here.

Parent-Child Immunity Doctrine

Until recently, the parent-child (or intrafamily) immunity doctrine barred any tort action brought by a child against his or her parent. This doctrine was first enunciated in *Hewlett v. George*[97] where the court reasoned that an action by a child against his parents would disrupt peace in the family and was against public policy. According to Simon, the immunity rule was not predicated upon a lack of duty of reasonable care owed the child by the parent, but solely on the child's procedural disability to sue.[98] The parent avoids liability on the theory that the child's right to recovery should be sacrificed for the public good. For nearly a century, this doctrine, itself based on no precedential authority, prevented unemancipated minor children from taking legal action against their parents.

In recent decades, however, the immunity rule has come under heavy criticism and its validity has been challenged by many courts. The traditional arguments in favor of denying tort action by children against parents—that it would destroy family harmony,[99] disturb parental discipline and control,[100] undermine the welfare by weakening the family unit[101] and result in fraud and collusion against insurance companies—have gradually been dismissed by the courts either through the granting of a widening series of exceptions or by judicial abrogation of the doctrine entirely.

Abandonment of the parental relationship,[102] emancipation of the child,[103] injury in the course of a business activity[104] and intentional or reckless injury of the child by the parent[105] have all been accepted by courts as exceptions to the immunity doctrine. The common denominator underlying these exceptions is that the rule of immunity is applied only where clear reasons for the rule are present. Although the parents should be immune for liability in torts committed in their parental status, courts have allowed action in those cases not arising directly out of the parent-child relationship or where the parent has relinquished his or her status as parent.

Courts in other jurisdictions have gone beyond this reasoning and abrogated entirely the parent-child immunity doctrine. Since 1963 when the Wisconsin Supreme Court threw out the immunity rule,[106] an increasing number of states have abandoned support of the rule and allowed tort actions of children against parents.[107] In *Plumley v. Klein*[108] for example, the court held that parent tort immunity should be overruled and that a child may maintain a lawsuit against his or her parent for injury suffered as a result of ordinary negligence of the parent. The court noted, however, that exceptions exist if the alleged negligent act involves the exercise of reasonable parental authority over the child. As noted earlier, public expectation of what is reasonable or responsible parental action are likely to change in light of knowledge provided by medical science and the available technologies.

At this point, over 30 states have abrogated the immunity doctrine. In the remainder, exceptions to the rule are freely granted such that it seems unlikely that prenatal injury torts against parents would be summarily dismissed. The courts generally agree that the child's personal rights are more worthy than property or contract rights which are already protected.[109] Also, it is argued that society's best interests dictate that those individuals who are tortiously injured be compensated for their injury so that they do not become wards of the state.[110] Finally, the courts see little family tranquility protected in denying a tort action solely on the basis of the immunity rule.[111] According to the court in *Sorenson v. Sorenson*,[112] it is the injury itself, not the lawsuit, that disrupts harmonious family relations. The child's relationship to the tortfeasor should not result in denial of recovery for a wrong to his person.[113]

Some jurisdictions continue to make distinctions between situations directly involving parental discretion over the control of the minor child and other negligent acts by a parent. In *Silesky v. Kelman*[114] for example, the court abrogated parental immunity except where the alleged negligent act involves the exercise of reasonable parental authority or discretion with respect for providing necessities for the child. One method which has been viewed favorably by several courts is the use of a "reasonable parent standard" to determine when parental conduct is actionable. According to Atchison,[115] such a standard strikes a balance between the child's right to recover for a tortiously inflicted injury and the parents' need to discipline and to use authority, judgment, and discretion in raising the child.

The clear trend of many state courts to disregard the parent-child immunity rule logically opens the way for expanding prenatal injury causes of action to include suits of children against parents for negligence in the prenatal period. Along with the rapidly advancing state of medical knowledge in fetal development and the growing medical evidence of the deleterious effects of maternal behavior on the fetus, there is a heightened recognition of parental liability for negligent injury to minor children by the courts. This is reinforced by the universally recognized liability of third parties for prenatal injury. Based on these factors, an action by a child against its parents for negligent injury suffered prior to birth seems increasingly likely and logically consistent. Although no court has yet awarded damages for such an action, several recent court decisions demonstrate its imminence.

Court Reference to Parental Liability

Recently, the Michigan Court of Appeals recognized the possibility of maternal liability for prenatal conduct.[116] The court upheld the right of a child allegedly injured prenatally to present testimony concerning his mother's negligence in failing to take a pregnancy test when her symptoms suggested pregnancy and her failure to inform the physician who diagnosed pregnancy that she was taking tetracycline, a drug that might be contraindicated for pregnant women. Noting that the Michigan Supreme Court had determined that a child could bring suit for prenatal injury and that the immunity doctrine had been discarded, the *Grodin* court ruled and the injured child's mother would "bear the same liability as a third person for injurious, negligent conduct that interfered with the child's 'legal right to begin life with a sound mind and body.' "

The key question in *Grodin* was whether or not parental immunity should insulate the mother (and her homeowners' policy) from liability where the alleged negligent act involves an exercise of "reasonable parental discretion" in medical decision-making. According to the court, a woman's decision to continue taking drugs during pregnancy is an exercise of her parental discretion. The crucial point is whether the decision reached by the woman in a particular case is a "reasonable exercise of parental discretion."

Similarly, in *Payton v. Abbott Labs,*[117] the court's decision in favor of a cause of action for an infant injured prenatally against anyone who negligently supplies a pregnant woman with drugs leaves the door open for a child to sue family members for injuries resulting from the improper administration of a drug to its mother during gestation. The *Payton* opinion patently approves of recovery for any prenatal injury if the harm can be demonstrated by medical evidence and proven in court. Under this ruling, it is clear that the child of a woman addicted to drugs may be able to bring an action to recover for injuries caused by the mother's addiction.

The increased probability of tort action against parents is also reflected in current trends in criminal cases. A Michigan court convicted a heroin addict of child abuse when she gave birth to an addicted baby.[118] In the only appellate case to address this issue, a California appeals court reversed a conviction of an addict who gave birth to a child congenitally addicted to heroin on the ground that the California criminal code for child abuse was not intended to include the unborn.[119] According to Robertson,

> This interpretation of that statute is erroneous, for it overlooks the fact that the abused child here is not the fetus, but the child who has been born and is suffering from injuries occurring before its birth. There is nothing in the history or wording of the statute that requires the abusive conduct to occur after birth, as long as the child who suffers from the prenatal injuries is born before the action is brought. Indeed, to limit the statute to postnatal actions would be inconsistent with California homicide law, which imposes liability for prenatal actions that cause death postnatally.[120]

It is clear that courts in many states will soon be faced with criminal law cases involving the actions of pregnant women. It seems equally likely that some women will be convicted for injuring their fetuses at the same time that they are guaranteed abortions through the second trimester by *Roe v. Wade*.

Wrongful Life Action Against Parents

One extension of the concept of wrongful life that promises a severe impact on social values and on notions of responsibility is a damage claim brought against the parents charging their liability for their own child's birth under handicap. For instance, what liability do parents have if, given accurate advice from the physician regarding the risk of genetic disease, they disregard it and either (1) fail to undergo amniocentesis or (2) refuse to abort the abnormal fetus, resulting in a child with a genetic disorder? If a claim for damages against a physician can stand, cannot a suit against the parents also succeed? While some observers[121] conclude that torts for wrongful life against parents will fail, others[122] are less certain. Until now in cases of genetic disease, one has been able to argue that the parents could not be held accountable for circumstances beyond their control and that the child's handicap is simply an unfortunate fate. However, there is evidence that, given the state of human genetic technology, the legal climate might be fluctuating toward sympathy for the affected child. Capron suggests that the acceptance of such torts or similar actions by other "agencies of social control" might lead to "unprecedented eugenic totalitarianism."[123]

Despite suggestions that torts for wrongful life against parents by genetically affected children are improbable as well as undesirable, the thrust of the progression of decisions summarized here illustrates that the courts are, indeed, moving in that direction. The majority in *Curlender* argued that fears over the determination that infants have rights cognizable at law would open the way for such a plaintiff to bring suit against its own parents for allowing it to be born are "groundless." It goes on to note, however, that *if* the parents make a conscious choice to proceed with the pregnancy despite full knowledge that a seriously impaired infant will be born, "we see no sound public policy which should protect those parents from being answerable for the pain, suffering and misery which they have wrought upon their offspring." Whether or not Annas[124] is correct in believing that the California case is "against the weight of judicial authority," there appears to be a growing concern for the rights of the affected children.

At least partly in response to *Curlender,* the California legislature passed and the governor signed a bill that provides that no cause of action arises against a parent of a child based upon the claim that the child should not have been conceived or, if conceived, should not have been allowed to have been born alive. No such action has been taken in any other state and it is unclear whether courts presented with the appropriate facts would hold parents civilly liable for not aborting their child.[125]

Shaw agrees with the principle implied by *Curlender.* Women who are informed that their fetus is defective should incur a "conditional prospective liability" for negligent acts toward their fetus if they fail to utilize their constitutional right to abort. She would permit children harmed by the behavior of their mother during pregnancy to sue their mothers:

> Withholding of necessary prenatal care, improper nutrition, exposure to mutagens and teratogens, or even exposure to the mother's defective intrauterine environment caused by her genotype, as in maternal PKU, could all result in an injured infant who might claim that his right to be born physically and mentally sound had been invaded.[126]

151

Contrarily, Annas argues that while this position might be a logical extension of permitting the child a cause of action on its own behalf, there are policy objections which focus on protecting the unborn child.[127] Rejecting the notion that there is a "right to be born both physically and mentally sound" he contends that such a "right" could easily turn into a "duty on the part of potential parents . . . to make sure no defective, or 'abnormal' children are born." Similarly, Dinsdale concludes that in cases where parents consciously choose to give birth despite risks of impairment to the child,

> constitutional considerations preventing state intrusion upon parental rights of privacy, free exercise of religion, and family autonomy should prevail. In light of the inherently undefinable and, at least at the present time, only reluctantly recognized right of a child to be born unimpaired, more established parental rights necessitate that the decision to deem nonlife more valuable than life be left to the parent rather than to a jury after the fact. Even if a state were willing to assume responsibility for making this judgment in lieu of the parent, the state would find itself on an anfractuous drawing. Recognition of the child versus parent wrongful life cause of action would be only the beginning of more difficult and inappropriate incursion into the realm of childbirth and pregnancy, a realm which should best be governed by the parents.[128]

Cohen contends that because of strong public policy considerations, the acceptance of wrongful life is not likely to lead to the "acceptance of intrafamily wrongful life actions."[129] Since liability in an intrafamily wrongful life action would turn on the moral question of whether the parents should have had the child, it should be beyond the scope of judicial review. Given the constitutional guarantee of the right of privacy parents have, not only to choose not to have a child *(Roe v. Wade)*, but also to be free to choose to give birth to a child *(Eisenstadt v. Baird)* "a child should not be able to sue his parents for making such a choice."[130] This choice represents a moral question on the part of the parents, not a legal one, and should not give rise to a cause of action by a deformed child against his parents.

Despite these disclaimers, what are the implications if litigation by an infant plaintiff (most likely initiated by counsel representing his/her rights) is successful and he is awarded damages from the parents from birth with specific disabilities because the parents' "irresponsible" action had contributed to the disability? If the parents give birth to a fetus known to be defective, part of the parents' responsibility might be perceived as compensating the resulting child, even though the plaintiff would not exist if the parents made the opposite decision. One result would be that parental responsibility might evolve into a legal duty to refrain from having children under a variety of circumstances or to abort all defective fetuses. Although many observers view this possibility with repugnance, Shaw envisions beneficial results in this redefinition of parental responsibility:

> If the freedom to choose whether or not to have a child is limited by the threat of civil liability for having a child who is genetically defective, our posterity will be the beneficiaries. We will have decided that there is no "absolute right to reproduce" and that instead it is a "limited privilege" to contribute one's genetic heritage to future generations.[131]

Implications of Parental Liability

What might appear to be a just and humane means of compensating children for damages suffered in specific cases, however, might serve to redefine parental responsibility in procreation more generally. Torts for wrongful life have strong potential to encourage or coerce parents to reexamine value systems that assume the child to have limited rights vis-à-vis the parents. In addition to the individualist premise that each person has the "right" to be born free of defects to the maximum extent possible, such torts also include a societal dimension relating to responsibilities toward future generations. Both of these aspects might conflict directly with and limit the parents' procreation prerogative. The eugenic implications of such lawsuits appear to be unplanned and simply a byproduct of the set of individual suits, but encouragement of such action by society might reflect an underlying predisposition to control procreation decisions and consciously limit parental discretion.

Although the courts until now have been unwilling to award damages based on "unavertable genetic diseases," the context is being altered substantially by broadened availability and knowledge of ever more sophisticated prenatal diagnostic and screening techniques. If the parents consciously reject prenatal diagnosis in a clear case of risk, refuse to participate in available carrier screening programs, or do not allow their newborn to be tested for PKU and other metabolic disorders, and a handicapped child results directly from their action or lack of action, the child appears to have reasonably strong cause of action once the wrongful life concept is accepted. Although the disability might not directly result from parental negligence, the parents' failure to take prudent action to avoid such a result might be persuasive evidence against them.

Obviously, the merits of any case revolve around the certainty that such a disability could have been avoided through actions of the parents. As the state of human reproductive technology and knowledge of the fetal environment advances to provide effective means of alleviating fetal disorders, parents might be expected to bear legal as well as moral responsibility for their actions in accepting or rejecting available technologies. In the absence of more direct compulsory eugenic legislation, torts for wrongful life, for prenatal injury, and wrongful death might serve as means by which society defines "responsible" and "irresponsible" procreation decisions. Courts' recognition of the rights of progeny to sue for damages from their parents represents a strong, though indirect, pressure on parents predisposed against human genetic intervention technologies to utilize them. By allowing compensation to affected children through such torts, society, as reflected through its courts, puts its mark of disapproval on such parental actions.

The challenges these trends in tort law raise for the rights of women to privacy and autonomy in childbearing are consequential. As noted earlier, it is the mother who has a direct influence over the health of the fetus. Maternal behavior and conditions during gestation are receiving heightened scrutiny by the courts. As medical evidence demonstrates the deleterious effects on the fetus of maternal malnutrition, smoking, alcohol and drug use, sexually transmitted infections and so forth, the courts are likely to recognize a more rigid standard of care and find women legally responsible for lifestyle decisions that harm the fetus. In their willingness to accept a wide array of causes of action for prenatal injury and to place responsibility (blame) for such injury on the mother, the courts are, perhaps unintentionally, contributing to the constriction of women's procreative rights, particularly to choices made during pregnancy. As such, these decisions raise considerable social policy issues concerning sexual equality.

Notes

1. Winborne, *Handling Pregnancy and Birth Cases.* New York: McGraw Hill, 1983.
2. Lambert, "Law in the Future: Tort Law 2003." *Trial* 19 (1983), p.65.
3. 138 Mass. 14 (1884).
4. 184 Ill. 359, 56 N.E. 638 (1900).
5. 65 F. Supp. 138 (D.D.C. 1946).
6. 303 N.Y. 349, 102 N.E. 2d 691 (1951).
7. 31 N.J. 353, 157 A. 2d 497 (1960).
8. Prosser, *Handbook of the Law of Torts* 4th ed. 1971.
9. 78 A.D. 2nd 389, 434 N.Y.S. 2d 400 (1981), Also see *Evans v. Olson,* 550 P.2d 924 (Ok. 1976).
10. *Hornbuckle v. Plantation Pipe Line Co.,* 212 Ga. 504, 93 S.E. 2d 727 (1956).
11. *Bennett v. Hymers,* 101 N.H. 483, 147 A. 2d 108 (1958).
12. Supra, note 7, at 504.
13. 101 R.I. 76, 220 A. 2d 222 (1966).
14. Simon, "Parental Liability for Prenatal Injury." *Col. J. Law Soc. Rel.* 14 (1978), p.55.
15. *Wilson v. Kaiser Foundation Hosps.,* 141 Ca. A. 3d 891, 190 Cal. Rptr. 649 (1983).
16. The medical parameters of viability are in a constant state of change because of the emergence of neonatal technologies to save earlier term premature infants.
17. Simon, supra note 14, p. 56.
18. Lambert, supra note 2, p. 65, favors discarding the dependence on the concept of viability on these grounds.
19. 67 Ill. 2d 348, 367 N.E. 2d 1250 (1977). Also, *Turpin v. Sortini* 31 Cal. 3d 220 (1982) and *Harbeson v. Parke Davis* 98 Wash. 2d 460, 656 P. 2d 483 (1983).
20. Blank, *Redefining Human Life: Reproductive Technologies and Social Policy.* Boulder: Westview, 1984.
21. *Eich v. Town of Gulf Shores,* 300 So. 2d 354 (Ala. 1974).
22. Supra note 6.
23. Supra note 7.
24. A related question is whether or not the fetus must be live-born before action is involved.
25. *Group Health Association v. Blumenthal,* 295 Md. 104, 453 A. 2d 1198 (1983).

26. *Justus v. Atchison*, 19 Cal. 3d 564, 565 P. 2d. 122 (1977) and *Egbert v. Wenzl*, 199 Neb. 573, 260 N.W. 2d 480 (1977).

27. Kader, "The Law of Tortious Prenatal Death Since *Roe v. Wade.*" *Mo. Law Rev.* 45 (1980), p. 653.

28. See Blank, supra note 20, pp. 124ff.

29. Scofield, "Recovery for Tortious Death of The Unborn." *So. Car. Law Rev.* 33 (1982), p. 803.

30. 365 A. 2d 748 (R.I. 1976).

31. *Danos v. St. Pierre*, 402 So. 2d 633 (La. 1981). A concurring opinion stated that the word person should include an unborn child from the moment of fertilization and implantation. Also, *O'Grady v. Brown*, 645 S.W. 2d. 904 (Mo. 1983).

32. In *Shirley v. Bacon*, 267 S.E. 2d 809 (1980) a Georgia Court ruled that wrongful death action was contingent on the fetus being "quick" at the time of its death.

33. 71 Ill. 2d. 501, 377 N.E. 2d. 37 (1978). Similar decisions were rendered in *Salazar v. St. Vincent Hosp.* (1980) and *Wallace v. Wallace*, 421 A. 2d. 134 (1980).

34. *Scott v. Kopp*, 494 Pa. 487, 431 A. 2d. 959 (1981). Similar findings that a wrongful death action cannot be maintained for the death of a viable fetus have been given in New York (*Albala*, 1981), California (*Wilson*, 1983), Iowa (*Dunn v. Rose Way*, 1983), and Florida (*Duncan v. Flynn*, 1978).

35. Supra note 26.

36. *Hamby v. McDaniel* (1977).

37. *Vaillancourt v. Medical Center Hosp. of Vermont*, 425 A 2d. 92 (1980).

38. *O'Grady v. Brown*, 645 S.W. 2d. 904 (1983).

39. Supra note 21. Also see *Volk v. Baldazo*, 103 Id. 570, 651 P. 2d. 11 (1982).

40. Supra note 1, p. 357.

41. Supra note 34.

42. 279 N.E. 2d. 339 (Mass. 1972) at 173.

43. 550 P. 2d. 924 (Ok. 1976).

44. *Miller v. Highlands Ins. Co.*, 336 So. 2d. 636 (Fla. 1976). The *Miller* court did, however, hold recoverable medical and funeral expenses.

45. *Jones v. Karraker*, 109 Ill. A. 2d. 363, affd. 10 FLR 1043 (1983).

46. 402 So. 2d. 633 (La. 1981).

47. 123 Ca. A. 3d. 1002, 177 Cal Rptr. 63 (1981).

48. 83 F.R.D. 382 (D. Mass. 1974).

49. Seksay, "Tort Law—Begetting a Cause of Action for Those Injured by a Drug Prior to Birth." *Suffolk U. Law Rev.* 17 (1983), p. 266.

50. 79 Ill. 2d. 103, 402 N.E. 2d. 203 (1980).

51. *State v. Anderson*, 343 A. 2d 505 (1975).

52. 97 Mich. App. 226, 293 N.W. 2d. 775 (1980).

53. *Keeler v. Superior Court*, 470 P. 2d. 617, 87 Cal. Rptr. 481 (1970).

54. Supra note 26.

55. 76 Cal. App. 3d. 479, 142 Cal. Rptr. 830 (1978).

56. Parness, "The Duty to Prevent Handicaps; Laws Promoting the

Prevention of Handicaps to Newborns." *W. New Eng. Law Rev.* 5 (1983), P. 444.

57. *People v. Smith* (1976).

58. Ibid. at 757.

59. Supra note 56, p. 445

60. *State v. Brown,* 378 So. 2d 916 (La. 1979).

61. *La. Rev. Stat. Ann.* § 1412 (7).

62. Parness and Pritchard, "To Be or Not to Be: Protecting the Unborn's Potentiality of Life." *Univ. Cinn. Law Rev.* 51 (1982), p. 270.

63. *Reyes v. Superior Court,* 75 Cal. App. 3d. 214, 141 Cal Rpt.

64. 97 Mich. App. 111 (1980).

65. Capron, "Tort Liability in Genetic Counseling." *Col. Law Rev.* 79, (1979), p. 681.

66. Note, "A Cause of Action for 'Wrongful Life.'" *Minn. Law Rev.* 55 (1970), p. 67.

67. Rogers, "Wrongful Life and Wrongful Birth: Medical Malpractice in Genetic Counseling and Prenatal Testing." *So. Car. Law Rev.* 33 (1982?), p. 757.

68. Kashi, "The Case of the Unwanted Blessing: Wrongful Life." *Univ. of Miami Law Rev.* 31 (1977), p. 1432. Cohen '*Park v. Chessin:* The Continuing Judicial Development of the Theory of Wrongful Life.'" *Am J. Law and Med.* 4 (1978), p. 214, agrees, contending that courts have the capacity to adjudicate wrongful life suits. He and others have proposed methods of measuring damages in such suits.

69. Supra note 65.

70. Trotzig, "The Defective Child and the Actions for Wrongful Birth." *Fam. Law Quart.* 14 (1980), p.32.

71. Tedeschi, "On Tort Liability for 'Wrongful Life.'" *Israel Law Rev.* 1 (1966).

72. *Gleitman v. Cosgrove,* 49 N.J. 22, 227 A. 2d. 689 (1967).

73. 69 Wis. 2d. 766, 233 N.W. 2d. 372 (1975).

74. Supra note 68, p. 217.

75. 60 App. Div. 2d. 80 400 N.Y.S. 2d. 110 (1977), mod. N.Y.L.J. (1978).

76. According to Perkoff, "Renal Diseases" in *Genetic Disorders of Man,* p. 443, this is a fatal hereditary disease of such nature that there exists a "substantial probability" that any future baby of the same parents will be born with it.

77. *Park* at 112.

78. 46 N.Y. 2d. 895, 413 N.Y.S. 2d. 895, 386 N.E. 2d. 807 (1978).

79. 165 Cal. Rptr. 477 (1980).

80. *Ibid.* at 488.

81. *Ibid.* at 490. In *Schroeder v. Perkel,* 87 N.J. 53 (1981), the court agreed with *Curlender* and allowed an infant plaintiff born with cystic fibrosis to collect for his "wrongful," "diminished" life.

82. N.J. Sup. Ct. No. A-89 (1984).

83. 98 Wash. 2d 460, 656 P. 2d 483 (1983).

84. *Turpin v. Sortini,* 31 Cal. 3d 220 (1982).

85. 135 Ca. A. 3d 189, 185 Cal. Rptr. 103 (1982).

86. Pima Cty Super. Ct., No. 190297 (January 1983).

87. 409 So. 2d 512 (Fla. 1982).

88. 122 Mich. App. 116, 332 N.W. 2d 432 (1982).

89. 118 Mich. App. 831, 325 N.W. 2d 600 (1982).

90. 635 S.W. 2d 582 (Tex. 1982).

91. *Zepada v. Zepada,* 41 Ill. App. 2d 240, 190 N.E. 2d. 849 (1968).

92. Chapman, "What are Your Odds in the Prenatal Gamble." *Leg. Asp. of Med. Prac.* 31 (1979), p.34.

93. Friedman, "Legal Implications of Amniocentesis." *U. Penn. Law Rev.* 123 (1974), P. 154.

94. Sorenson, "Some Social and Psychologic Issues in Genetic Screening," in Bergsma, ed. *Ethical, Social and Legal Dimensions of Screening for Human Genetic Disease.* New York: Stratton, 1974, p. 172.

95. Supra note 93, p. 154.

96. These include alcohol consumption, drug abuse, cigarette smoking, malnutrition, venereal disease and exposure to chemicals and radiation.

97. 68 Miss. 703, 9 So. 885 (1891). This precedent held even in cases of intentional and malicious injury to the child by the parents. For example, see *Roller v. Roller,* 37 Wash. 242 (1905).

98. Supra note 14, p. 61.

99. *Dunlap v. Dunlap,* 84 N.H. 352 (1930).

100. *Brennecke v. Brennecke,* 336 S.W. 2d 68 (1960).

101. *Tucker v. Tucker,* 395 P. 2d. 67 (1964).

102. Supra note 99.

103. *Logan v. Reeves,* 209 Tenn. 631, 354 S.W. 2d 789 (1962).

104. *Trevarton v. Trevarton,* 151 Colo. 418, 378 P. 2d 640 (1963).

105. *Teramano v. Teramano,* 216 N.E. 2d 375 (1966).

106. *Goller v. White,* 122 N.W. 2d 193 (1963).

107. *Ard v. Ard,* 414 So. 2d 1066 (1982).

108. 388 Minn. 1, 199 N.W. 2d 169 (1972).

109. *Hebel v. Hebel,* 435 P. 2d 8 (1967).

110. *Streenz v. Streenz,* 471 P. 2d 282 (1970).

111. *Peterson v. Honolulu,* 262 P. 2d 1007 (1969).

112. 330 N.E. 2d 907 (1975).

113. *Briere v. Briere,* 107 N.H. 432, 224 A. 2d 588 (1966).

114. 161 N.W. 2d 631 (1975).

115. Atchison, *"Ard v. Ard:* Limiting the Parent-Child Immunity Doctrine." *U. Pitt. Law Rev.* 44 (1983), P. 1003.

116. *Grodin v. Grodin,* 102 Mich. App. 396, 301 N.W. 2d 869 (1980).

117. 83 F.R.D. 382 (D. Mass, 1974).

118. *In re Baby X,* 97 Mich. App. III (1980).

119. *Reyes v. Superior Court,* 75 Cal. App. 3d 214, 141 Cal. Rptr. 912 (1977).

120. Robertson, "Procreative Liberty and Control of Conception, Pregnancy and Childbirth." *Va. Law Rev.* 69 (1983), p. 439.

121. Supra, note 65.

122. Shaw, "Genetically Defective Children: Emerging Legal Considerations." *Am. J. Law and Med.* 3 (1978).

123. Capron, "The Wrong of 'Wrongful Life,' " in Milunsky and Annas, eds., *Genetics and the Law II*. New York: Plenum, 1980.

124. Annas, "Righting the Wrong of 'Wrongful Life.' " *Hastings Center Report* 11 (1981), p. 8.

125. Doudera, "Fetal Rights? It Depends." *Trial* 18 (1982), pp. 38–44.

126. Shaw, "Preconception and Prenatal Torts," in Milunsky and Annas, eds., supra note 123, p. 229.

127. Supra note 124, p. 9.

128. Dinsdale, "Child v. Parent: A Viable New Tort of Wrongful Life?" *Ariz. Law Rev.* 24 (1982), pp. 419–420.

129. Cohen, Supra note 68, p. 231.

130. *Ibid.*

131. Shaw, supra note 122, p. 340.

7

Reproductive Technology and the Procreation Rights of the Unmarried

Harvard Law Review

Recent advances in the technology of reproduction have made nonmarital procreation a feasible alternative to "natural" procreation within marriage. Such techniques as artificial insemination,[1] *in vitro* fertilization,[2] embryo transfer,[3] and surrogate mothering[4] have increased the options available to an individual who wishes to create a family in which, by design, she or he will be the sole rearing parent.[5] Yet courts' and legislatures' historical disapproval of procreation outside marriage[6] suggests that they are likely to restrict unmarried persons' access to the new reproductive technology.[7]

This essay argues that legislatures and courts cannot constitutionally prevent unmarried persons from procreating by means of reproductive technology. Part I considers the ways in which legislatures, courts, and doctors restrict access to existing nontraditional methods of reproduction. Part II argues that the due process clauses of the fifth and fourteenth amendments encompass a right to procreate. Part III examines whether this right extends to unmarried as well as married persons and concludes that barring unmarried persons' access to reproductive technology violates equal protection. Part IV advocates the adoption of regulations on the use of such technology that would be narrowly tailored to advance

---

This article first appeared as an Editorial Note in the Harvard Law Review, 1985.

legitimate state interests without depriving unmarried persons of their right to procreate.

The Current Legal Status of Reproductive Technology

Artificial Insemination

Only about ten percent of the doctors who perform artificial inseminations are willing to do so for unmarried women.[8] The unwillingness of many of the remaining ninety percent probably stems from personal philosophies or religious beliefs.[9] Although such private biases are beyond the reach of constitutional challenge, the doctors' reluctance may be induced or reinforced by state laws that lead them to believe artificial insemination is legal only when performed for married women.[10] Twenty-five states have statutes dealing with artificial insemination,[11] yet the vast majority of these statutes operate only to legitimize children conceived by a married woman inseminated with the sperm of a donor who is not her husband.[12] These laws largely ignore the prospect that unmarried women will also seek access to the procedure,[13] although at least 1500 such women are artificially inseminated annually.[14] The meaning of these statutory omissions—whether they should be construed to prohibit or tacitly to allow unmarried women to be artificially inseminated—is currently far from clear,[15] and the ambiguity undoubtedly discourages many physicians from performing the procedure.[16]

In Vitro Fertilization and Embryo Transfer

Only two states—Illinois and Pennsylvania—have passed legislation that directly regulates either *in vitro* fertilization or embryo transfer.[17] The Pennsylvania statute simply requires "persons conducting, or experimenting in, *in vitro* fertilization" to file regular reports on such information as the personnel employed and the number of fertilization efforts performed; the only penalty prescribed is a fine for failure to submit the reports.[18] By contrast, the Illinois statute defines the early-stage embryo resulting from a successful fertilization attempt as a "human being" and makes the "person who intentionally causes the fertilization" responsible for "care and custody" of the embryo;[19] a physician who "endanger[s]" the "life or health" of an embryo is subject to criminal prosecution.[20] The attorney general of Illinois stated in 1982 that *in vitro* fertilization would not be prosecuted under the statute,[21] but he did not address the legality of embryo freezing, a technique used to increase the success rate of *in vitro* fertilization. Consequently, doctors and prospective recipients remain uncertain whether the Illinois statute prohibits the performance of *in vitro* fertilization.[22]

Several states that lack statutes explicitly regulating *in vitro* fertilization and embryo transfer have enacted laws that restrict or prohibit experimentation on, or the sale or donation of, embryos and fetuses.[23] A number of state legislatures drafted these fetal protection laws in response to the 1973 decision in which the Supreme Court recognized a constitutional right to procure an abortion in certain circumstances.[24] Because these statutes have not been amended to address recent advances in reproductive technology, it remains unclear whether they apply to the new techniques and whether they discourage doctors from performing such services.[25]

Surrogate Mothering

To date, only a few state courts and state attorneys general have considered the legal implications of surrogate mothering. Perhaps because there are no state statutes addressing this issue directly, the courts that have dealt with surrogate mothering contracts have applied existing paternity acts[26] or adoption statutes, which typically prohibit prospective parents from paying for adoptions.[27] Most of these courts have held the contracts void—the result recommended by those attorneys general who have addressed the issue—although several different reasons have been offered: that such contracts constitute illegal private adoption arrangements,[28] that they improperly separate a child from his or her natural mother,[29] and that they are contrary to public policy.[30] Despite this generally unsympathetic legal treatment, however, the business of surrogate mothering is on the rise.[31] This trend has led several state legislatures to consider bills that would explicitly prohibit the practice.[32]

Substantive Due Process and the Right to Procreate

No court thus far has ruled on whether the Constitution grants anyone—either married or unmarried—a right of access to reproductive technology.[33] If the Supreme Court were to deem pro-creation a fundamental right protected by the due process clause, however, a flat prohibition on the use of such technology would violate the constitutional rights of persons seeking to procreate.[34] Although it is unclear whether statutes currently regulating re-productive technology amount to bans of this kind, the recognition of a right to procreate would prevent such measures from depriv-ing unmarried persons of access to the new technology.

The Supreme Court has considered questions relating to procrea-tion in comparatively few cases. These cases have clustered around three issues: state-ordered sterilization, contraception, and abor-tion. Although the cases address specific aspects of the procreation process, they can best be explained as stages in the elaboration of a more general right that guarantees the individual a substantial measure of control over all aspects of procreation.

The Supreme Court has decided only two cases on the legality of state-mandated sterilization. In 1927, the Court concluded in *Buck v. Bell*[35] that the sterilization of imbeciles without their consent violated neither due process nor equal protection.[36] *Buck*, however, is now widely regarded as an aberration, largely the product of a misguided, pseudoscientific eugenics fad.[37] *Skinner v. Oklahoma*[38] commands greater respect. In *Skinner*, an equal protection case decided in 1942, the Court invoked strict scrutiny to invalidate a criminal statute that ordered sterilization as the punishment for repeated felony convictions but that exempted certain "white col-lar" crimes such as embezzlement.[39] In addition to considering the equal protection issue, the Court emphasized the importance of procreation to the individual and to society.

Writing for the Court, Justice Douglas termed the right to have offspring "a sensitive and important area of human rights. . . . a right which is basic to the perpetuation of a race."[40] Justice Douglas did not at first appear to limit his defense to the rights of married persons. Later in the opinion, however, he wrote: "We are dealing here with legislation which involves one of the basic civil rights of man. Marriage and procreation are fundamental to the very exis-tence and survival of the race. . . . [The person sterilized by the state] is forever deprived of a basic liberty."[41] From this passage, one could argue that Justice Douglas meant to protect procreation only within marriage. But this view seems ill-founded. Sterilization does not deprive a person of the right to marry; yet if sterilized, one *is* deprived of the ability to have genetic offspring. Thus, the "basic liberty" at stake in *Skinner* seems to be tied to procreation itself—to the ability to contribute one's own genetic material to future generations. Because this ability is unaffected by the individual's marital status, that status seems irrelevant to the Court's solicitude for procreation.

Yet the claim that *Skinner* refers only to procreation within marriage appears to gain support from *Griswold v. Connecticut*.[42] In *Griswold*, the Court held that Connecticut's ban on the use of contraceptives violated the right of *marital* privacy.[43] In subsequent cases, however, the Supreme Court made clear that the right to avoid procreation by using contraceptives is grounded on *individual* liberty and that marital privacy is only one aspect of that liberty. *Eisenstadt v. Baird*[44] specifically extended the *Griswold* reasoning to the unmarried:

> It is true that in *Griswold* the right of privacy. . . . inhered in the marital relationship. Yet the marital couple is not an independent entity with a mind and heart of its own, but an association of two individuals each with a separate intellectual and emotional makeup. If the right of privacy means anything, it is the right of the *individual*, married or single, to be free from unwarranted governmental intrusion into matters so fundamentally affecting a person as the decision whether to bear or beget a child.[45]

Eisenstadt thus supports the view that the individual's right to substantial control over decisions about procreation flows not from the marital relationship, but from each individual's interest in autonomy. This view finds further support in the Court's cases discussing the right to terminate pregnancy. *Roe v. Wade*[46] emphasized the intimate relationship between procreation and the constitutional right of privacy.[47] And just as *Eisenstadt*, a contraception case, established that this privacy interest belongs to all individuals regardless of their marital status, abortion cases following *Roe* have made it clear that the abortion right may be exercised by a woman irrespective of her marital status.[48]

When considered as a whole, the Supreme Court's decisions dealing with various aspects of the reproductive process reveal a common premise: decisions about procreation are protected by the individual's constitutional right of privacy.[49] If the Court were expressly to recognize a procreation right of such broad scope, states would bear a very heavy burden in attempting to justify restrictions on access to the new reproductive technology. The degree to which specific reproductive techniques could legitimately be regulated would depend on the particular countervailing state interests asserted.[50]

It might be argued, however, that the Supreme Court has not embraced so broad a right and that unmarried persons' rights to prevent and terminate pregnancy do not imply the affirmative right to procreate. This argument would presume that the Court's decisions have sprung not from a concern for individual rights but rather from a desire to decrease the incidence of nonmarital procreation.[51] Indeed, according to this view, an extension of substantive due process to nonmarital procreation would be irrational. But to reason in this way is to ignore the Court's consistent reliance on expansive notions of individual privacy and autonomy in explaining its decisions in this area.[52] Such a constricted reading of the cases therefore seems untenable.[53]

Unmarried Persons, Equal Protection, and Reproductive Technology

The Supreme Court has clearly guaranteed, at least for married persons, the fundamental right to procreate.[54] Thus, before a state can selectively restrict the exercise of that right, it must show that its reasons for treating certain persons differently from others comport with equal protection doctrine. If a state permits married persons to procreate by means of reproductive technology, its denial of identical access to unmarried persons might violate unmarried persons' constitutional right to equal protection of the laws.

The Legitimacy of Marital Classifications

Although the Supreme Court has recognized a state interest "in protecting 'legitimate family relationships,' . . . and [in] the regulation and protection of the family unit,"[55] it has never clearly defined what the family unit is. Traditionally, marriage has served as a convenient dividing line between those relationships the state protects and those it does not. The law has assumed that an individual who chooses to marry deserves favorable treatment, regardless of whether the individual's reasons for making that choice would meet with society's approval.[56] Society's attitudes toward unmarried persons have long been negative; these attitudes have been based on the sorts of archaic stereotypes[57] that the Court has disallowed as grounds for legislative classifications.[58] Moreover, the Court has questioned the validity of classifications that, in defining the family, emphasize formal structures rather than the underlying values furthered by the institution.[59] If unmarried as well as married persons are able to inculcate those values in their families, restrictions on nonmarital procreation would serve only to maintain superficial structures and stereotypes at the expense of fundamental social goals.

A state's authority to prevent individuals from entering into a certain kind of relationship—for example, a nonmarital family— should ultimately be determined by "where the relationship's objective characteristics locate it on a spectrum from the most intimate to the most attenuated of personal attachments."[60] The reasons for having a child—to love and be loved by that child, to educate and convey personal ideals and values, to contribute a part of oneself to future generations—do not turn on marital status. Similarly, both marital and nonmarital families can foster the familial values the Constitution seeks to protect.[61] Moreover, unmarried persons who procreate by means of reproductive technology possess certain "objective characteristics"—blood relationship with their children,[62] parental duty to support those children,[63] parental intention to form a family[64]—that should locate their families at the intimate end of the relationship "spectrum." Finally, in the contexts of contraception[65] and child rearing,[66] the Supreme Court has invalidated legal presumptions favoring married over unmarried persons. These factors suggest that courts should recognize unmarried persons and their children as legitimate families, and should subject classifications drawing distinctions between marital and nonmarital families to heightened scrutiny.[67]

State Interests and the Requirement of Narrowly Tailored Regulation

In order to demonstrate an interest sufficiently compelling to override unmarried persons' procreation rights, or to justify disparate treatment based on marital status, a state should have to allege differences between married and unmarried persons—actual differences, not distinctions based on stereotypical assumptions—and show that allowing unmarried persons to parent would have identifiable and significant negative results. In other words, the state should have to demonstrate that its interest is either compelling or substantial—depending on whether a classification triggers strict or intermediate scrutiny—*and* that the classification is neither over- nor underinclusive. The two justifications most likely to be advanced for denying unmarried persons access to reproductive technology are the state's interest in public morals and its interest in health and safety.[68] Although these interests are significant, they do not justify barring unmarried persons access to reproductive technology, for any such ban would sweep too broadly in certain respects and not broadly enough in others.

The Interest in Public Morals

Because the new reproductive techniques achieve procreation without coitus, certain moral concerns that might justify prohibiting fornication—interests in preventing extramarital sex[69] or preventing teenage pregnancy[70]—are not present. A total ban on access would do nothing to further these interests. A state might contend, however, that expanding procreative alternatives for unmarried persons would threaten the fundamental status of marriage and the traditional family unit. The state might argue, for example, that the existence of families created with the aid of reproductive technology would disrupt "traditional" family values by discouraging individuals who want to have children from getting married.

This argument fails for at least two reasons. First, as this essay has argued, recognizing and protecting only marital families despite the existence of other family forms that can adequately foster society's values is an unwarranted elevation of form over substance.[71] Second, there is little reason to expect that individuals who favor traditional marriage would suddenly change their beliefs; the individuals most likely to seek access to the techniques are those who desire to have their own genetic offspring yet are either unable or unwilling to marry.[72] Therefore, any statute that sought to protect traditional marriage by withholding reproductive technology from unmarried persons would be fatally overinclusive.[73] For these reasons, the state's interest in public morals would not justify such a statute.

Health and Safety Interests

If a particular reproductive procedure were found to pose a substantial health risk to either children or parents, the state could probably restrict the technique.[74] To date, however, reproductive technology appears to have raised no such problems. Certain procedures—such as artificial insemination and surrogate mothering—are virtually identical to "natural" procreation and thus involve no greater danger of physical injury to either children or parents.[75] In addition, a major federal study of *in vitro* fertilization and embryo transfer found that the health threat to children conceived by those methods is insufficient to justify banning the procedures.[76] The study also suggested that the techniques probably present no greater risk to parents than does natural procreation.[77]

A more serious concern is that children born to unmarried persons by means of noncoital reproduction will be psychologically damaged or socially stigmatized, and that the state must therefore disallow such reproduction in order to protect children. This reasoning rests on two assumptions: that children might be harmed by learning of their nonnatural origins, and that children might be harmed by having only a single parent.

Considered alone, the first assumption, even if true, would suggest that a ban on unmarried persons' access to reproductive technology would be underinclusive, since such a concern would also logically apply when children are born into a *marital* family by artificial means.[78] In addition, there is no reason to suppose that children would suffer any greater harm from learning that their births were technologically aided than from learning that they were adopted. In both situations, children might experience a longing to discover their identities, to seek out their unknown biological parents—although in the case of reproductive technology, there would usually be only one unknown parent rather than two. In addition, children conceived through reproductive technology would have the reassurance that their births were not accidental, but were the determined efforts of individuals dedicated to the idea of having a family.

The second assumption, that children raised by one parent[79] rather than two are disadvantaged emotionally, apparently derives more from social bias than from well-grounded psychological theory.[80] Further, because state legislatures have permitted single persons to adopt children,[81] denying such persons the right to become parents by other means seems inconsistent. The analogy to adoption is imperfect: whereas a state might believe that children are better off with one parent than with none at all, and might therefore permit adoption by unmarried persons, it might not wish to facilitate the conception of children intended in advance to be raised by only one parent. Nonetheless, the adoption analogy does suggest that states believe children will not be irreparably or even seriously harmed by having only a single parent. Taken together, these factors suggest that these two assumptions are insufficient to warrant a ban on the use of reproductive technology by unmarried persons.

A state might also consider prohibiting surrogate mothering out of concern for surrogates' psychological well-being, in view of the trauma that some surrogate mothers have experienced upon having to give up their children.[82] It seems doubtful, however, that *all* surrogates run an equally high risk of psychological harm; thus, a blanket ban would seem unnecessary to further the state's legitimate health interest.[83] In addition, there is a narrower, less intrusive means of accommodating the state's interest; requiring preliminary psychological screening of women who wish to be surrogates.[84] The availability of this less intrusive means should lead courts using even an intermediate level of scrutiny to invalidate absolute bans on surrogate mothering.

Conclusion

The recent monumental advances in the field of reproductive technology have raised a host of legal issues. One of the many changes brought about by the new technology is the increased feasibility of nonmarital parenthood. Yet much of the existing legislation that addresses issues of procreation and parenting is either silent or vague on whether unmarried persons may employ these procedures.

A wide variety of human interests and needs might motivate an unmarried person to seek to procreate with the aid of reproductive technology—interests and needs that extend far beyond the traditional use of such technology to aid infertile couples. *All* persons, married and unmarried, may benefit from raising families. Unmarried persons, when given the opportunity to parent, are likely to provide their children with as much love and care as married parents do. If reproductive technology makes it possible for the unmarried person to have her or his own child, it is discriminatory and socially unwise to deny that person the right to procreate simply because she or he "may be unable to find a suitable spouse, be unwilling to marry, or object to heterosexual intercourse."[85]

State-created barriers to unmarried persons' access to reproductive technology raise the question whether there is a constitutional right to procreate. Although the Supreme Court has yet to address the issue directly, a sensitive reading of the Court's decisions in relevant areas suggests that it has implicitly recognized such a right. Given the right's existence, individuals may not be arbitrarily deprived of the ability to exercise it through the use of reproductive technology. To be sure, certain state interests warrant careful consideration, yet these interests can be reconciled with unmarried persons' procreation rights by means of legislation that grants access to reproductive technology regardless of marital status and that also mandates careful monitoring to prevent abuses.

The new reproductive technology, by expanding procreative alternatives for both married and unmarried persons, demands that we reexamine our assumptions about what constitutes a family and who is entitled to the law's protection. In responding to the legal challenges posed by the new technology, courts and legislatures should recognize that individuals who do not fit within traditional narrow definitions of family can and should be allowed to foster society's most cherished values through procreation and child rearing.

Notes

1. The most common form of this treatment is heterologous artificial insemination, or AID (artificial insemination, donor). In AID, a woman is impregnated by injection into her vagina or uterus of the sperm of a man not her husband. *See* Blakiston's Gould Medical Dictionary 123 (4th ed.

1979); Wadlington, *Artificial Conception: The Challenge for Family Law,* 69 Va. L. Rev. 465, 468 (1983). *See generally* W. Finegold, Artificial Insemination (2d ed. 1976) (comprehensive reference work on artificial insemination). Each year, as many as 20,000 women are artificially inseminated in the United States. *See* Andrews, *The Stork Market: The Law of the New Reproductive Technologies,* A.B.A. J., Aug. 1984, at 50.

2. *In vitro* (literally, "in glass") fertilization has enabled women with blocked or damaged fallopian tubes to conceive or bear children in at least 700 cases to date. *See* Wallis, *The New Origins of Life,* Time, Sept. 10, 1984, at 46. In *in vitro* fertilization, mature ova are surgically removed from a woman and placed in a laboratory medium together with male sperm. After fertilization and several cell divisions, the early-stage embryo is implanted in the uterus of either the ovum donor or another woman. *See* Wadlington, *supra* note 1, at 473–74; N.Y. Times, Jan. 13, 1984, at A10, col. 6. *See generally* C. Grobstein, From Chance to Purpose: An Appraisal of External Human Fertilization (1981) (discussing *in vitro* fertilization and its ethical implications).

3. Embryo transfer allows an infertile woman to bear her husband's genetic child. An "ovum donor" is artificially inseminated; after approximately five days, the developing embryo is flushed from the donor's uterus and implanted in the uterus of the woman who will carry the child. Two births achieved through embryo transfer in early 1984 focused attention on the procedure and led commentators to predict its future popularity. *See* Brotman, *Human Embryo Transplants,* N.Y. Times, Jan. 8, 1984, § 6 (Magazine), at 42. *See generally* C. Grobstein, *supra* note 2 (discussing embryo transfer procedure and its ethical implications).

4. Surrogate mothers are artificially inseminated with an unrelated donor's sperm. Surrogate mothering differs from artificial insemination in that the surrogate signs a contract obliging her to yield the child to the sperm donor and is paid for her services. *See* Wadlington, *supra* note 1, at 475. *See generally* N. Keane & D. Breo, The Surrogate Mother (1981) (comprehensive treatment of surrogate mothering).

5. The law has already recognized at least one type of family arrangement created by a single parent: all states currently permit an unmarried person to adopt. *See* Kritchevsky, *The Unmarried Woman's Right to Artificial Insemination: A Call for an Expanded Definition of Family,* 4 Harv. Women's L.J. 1, 31 & n.151 (1981). One obvious difference between families created by adoption and those created with the aid of reproductive technology is that, in the latter, offspring will usually be the biological children of the parent.

6. Statutes criminalizing fornication, which are still on the books in many states despite their nonenforcement, *see, e.g.,* Mass. Gen. Laws Ann. ch. 272, § 18 (West 1970), theoretically restrict procreation outside marriage. Harsh laws respecting illegitimacy—which precluded nonmarital children from suing their natural parents for support or from inheriting by intestate succession—were also probably intended in part to discourage nonmarital sexual activity. *See* C. Foote, R. Levy & F. Sander, Cases and Materials on Family Law 626–36 (1976).

This legal disapproval has recently begun to ease: some fornication statutes have been held to be unconstitutional invasions of privacy, *see,* e.g., State v. Saunders, 75 N.J. 200, 381 A.2d 333(1977); the Supreme Court has invalidated some of the legal sanctions imposed on illegitimate children, *see* Mills v. Habluetzel, 456 U.S. 91 (1982); Gomez v. Perez, 409 U.S. 535 (1973); Levy v. Louisiana, 391 U.S. 68 (1968); and unmarried fathers' parental rights have been expanded, *see,* e.g., Caban v. Mohammed, 441 U.S. 380 (1979) (granting unmarried fathers some power to block the adoption of their children by others); Stanley v. Illinois, 405 U.S. 645 (1972) (rejecting state's conclusive presumption that unmarried fathers are unfit parents). *But see* Lehr v. Roberton, 103 S. Ct. 1985 (1983) (allowing unmarried father's parental rights to be terminated without notice).

7. Legislative and judicial restrictions on the use of such technology may extend to married persons as well. For example, many states have laws that may limit or prohibit anyone's use of *in vitro* fertilization or embryo transfer. *See infra* pp. 672–73. Similarly, several courts have invalidated surrogate mothering contracts entered into by married couples. *See infra* pp. 673–74 & notes 28–30. If, as this chapter asserts, the procreation right belongs to unmarried and married persons alike, some of the arguments suggested here for challenging restrictions on unmarried persons' access to reproductive technology could also be used by married persons.

8. *See* Curie-Cohen, Luttrell & Shapiro, *Current Practice of Artificial Insemination by Donor in the United States,* 300 New Eng. J. Med. 585 (1979).

9. Unmarried women step outside the bounds of traditional behavior merely by seeking artificial insemination; yet many of those who seek access to the procedure—lesbian couples, for example—are even further from the social mainstream. *See* Donovan, *The Uniform Parentage Act and Nonmarital Motherhood-by-Choice,* 11 N.Y.U. Rev. L. & Soc. Change 193, 195–96 (1983).

10. See Kritchevsky, *supra* note 5, at 3; Robertson, *Procreative Liberty and the Control of Conception, Pregnancy, and Childbirth,* 69 Va. L. Rev. 405, 419 n.36 (1983); Dullea, *Artificial Insemination of Single Women Poses Difficult Questions,* N.Y. Times, Mar. 9, 1979, at A18, col. 1.

11. *See, e.g.,* Fla. Stat. Ann. § 742.11 (West Suppl. 1983); Tex Fam. Code Ann. § 12.03 (Vernon 1975). *See generally* Andrews, *supra* note 1, at 54–55 (listing states regulating reproductive technology).

12. Most of these statutes follow a model similar to § 5 of the Uniform Parentage Act, 9A U.L.A. 587, 592 (1979). Because a child conceived through the AID process, *see supra* note 1, is not the biological offspring of the mother's husband, the Act's drafters thought it necessary to grant a presumption of legitimacy to all such children born without a marriage. *See* Unif. Parentage Act § 5, 9A U.L.A. 587, 592 (1979).

13. The notable exception is Oregon's statute, which expressly allows both married and unmarried women to use AID. *See* Or. Rev. Stat. § 677.365 (1983).

Courts might invalidate a law that fails to address the issue of unmarried women's access to artificial insemination on the ground that the law's vagueness chills physicians' willingness to perform the procedure by creating a threat of prosecution. *Cf.* Colautti v. Franklin, 439 U.S. 379, 396 (1979) (abortion); Smith v. Hartigan, 556 F. Supp. 157, 162 & n.10 (N.D. Ill. 1983) (*in vitro* fertilization).

14. *See* Donovan, *supra* note 9, at 195.

15. At least one commentator, however, has read the current laws not to preclude access to artificial insemination. *See* Kritchevsky, *supra* note 5, at 18–23.

16. Doctors' refusal to artificially inseminate unmarried women does not bar all access to the procedure, but rather encourages laypersons to perform the procedure without medical supervision. The simplicity of artificial insemination enables women who are turned away by clinics to inseminate themselves, *see* C.M. v. C.C., 152 N.J. Super. 160, 377 A.2d 821 (1977), thereby depriving the state of the opportunity to screen donors for genetic defects or infectious diseases. *See generally* Curie-Cohen, Luttrell & Shapiro, *supra* note 8, at 585–87 (describing screening procedures). In addition, whereas the sperm donor for a clinical insemination is usually anonymous, *see* Annas, *Fathers Anonymous: Beyond the Best Interests of the Sperm Donor,* 14 Fam. L.Q. 1, 10 (1980), the donor in a do-it-yourself insemination is likely to be known to the recipient. This can result in bitter and complicated custody disputes, especially in those states that have not adopted legislation clarifying the rights and duties of the various parties to artificial insemination. *See* C.M. v. C.C., 152 N.J. Super. 160, 377 A.2d 821 (1977).

17. *See* Ill. Rev. Stat. ch. 38 § 81-26(7) (West 1983); Pa. Cons. Stat. Ann. tit. 18 § 3213(e) (Purdon 1983).

18. *See* Pa. Cons. Stat. Ann. tit. 18, § 3213(e) (Purdon 1983).

19. *See* Ill. Rev. Stat. ch. 38, § 81-26(7) (West 1983).

20. *See id.* ch. 23 ¶¶ 2354–2355.

21. The attorney general's statement came only after a married couple and their doctor filed a class action claiming that the statute prohibited responsible physicians from performing *in vitro* fertilization. *See* Smith v. Hartigan, 556 F. Supp. 157, 162–63 (N.D. Ill. 1983).

22. Because of the relatively low rate of success in implanting embryos, *see* Brotman, *supra* note 3, at 46, doctors administer hormones to induce superovulation, then remove and fertilize several ova at a time. All but one embryo (which is implanted) are frozen to await a future need, although they may become unnecessary if the initial attempt at fertilization is successful. In the only judicial opinion addressing this issue, the district court left unclear whether disposing of frozen embryos would lead to prosecution under the Illinois statute. *See Smith,* 556 F. Supp. at 163; *supra* p. 672 & notes 19–21. The plaintiffs in *Smith* filed an amended complaint on February 17, 1983, requesting clarification of the legality of freezing embryos; the district court expects to hear argument on this question in early 1985.

23. *See, e.g.,* Mass. Gen. Laws Ann. ch. 112, § 12J (West 1983) (restricting research on fetuses); Mich. Comp. Laws § 333. 2690 (1979) (prohibiting the donation or sale of a fetus or embryo for experimentation); Andrews,

supra note 1, at 50–52 (noting that it is unclear whether such statutes entail an absolute ban on *in vitro* fertilization and embryo transfer). *See generally id.* at 54–55 (listing state statutes regulating reproductive technology).

It is odd that these statutes, which were drafted out of concern for maintaining respect for human life, might be applied to prohibit procedures that are used to bring about pregnancy. But the laws might be invoked in an effort to protect surplus frozen embryos, *see supra* note 22, the legal status of which remains uncertain. *See Troubling Test-Tube Legacy,* Newsweek, July 2, 1984, at 54; N.Y. Times, June 18, 1984, at B10, col. 5

24. Roe v. Wade, 410 U.S. 113 (1973); *see* L. Andrews, New Conceptions: A Consumer's Guide to the Newest Infertility Treatments, Including in Vitro Fertilization, Artificial Insemination, and Surrogate Motherhood 148–49 (1984).

25. Existing legislation applies to married and unmarried persons alike, thus potentially prohibiting access to the procedures altogether.

Despite the absence of legislation that clearly regulates the procedures, *in vitro* fertilization and embryo transfer clinics apparently do not extend their services to unmarried persons, *see* L. Andrews, *supra* note 24, at 123; Robertson, *supra* note 10, at 420 n.36, probably because most doctors prefer not to aid unmarried persons in procreating, *see supra* pp. 670–71. In addition, doctors concerned about the legality of providing *in vitro* fertilization and embryo transfer to unmarried persons are likely to rely, in the absence of substantive regulation, on the legal judgments set forth in a study compiled by the former Department of Health, Education, and Welfare, the only government study of the techniques. *See* Protection of Human Subjects—HEW Support of Human in Vitro Fertilization and Embryo Transfer: Report of the Ethics Advisory Board, 44 Fed. Reg. 35,033 (June 18, 1979) [hereinafter cited as "E.A.B. Report"]. The study stated that the Constitution probably grants only married couples a right of access to those procedures, *see id.* at 35,048, 35,051; it recommended that unmarried persons be denied access to the new procedures, and suggested federal funding of fertilization programs for "infertile couples." *See, e.g., id.* at 35,056. After only minimal consideration of unmarried persons in its section on constitutional issues, *see id.* at 35,048–49, the report found research on *in vitro* fertilization acceptable only if such research were "attempted with gametes obtained from lawfully married couples" and if embryos were "transferred back to the wife whose ova were used for fertilization," *id.* at 35,057. Doctors who rely on the study will undoubtedly refuse unmarried persons access to *in vitro* fertilization and embryo transfer.

In actuality, however, the study has no binding force. Because Congress has never approved funding for the new technology, *see* Lorio, *In Vitro Fertilization and Embryo Transfer: Fertile Areas for Litigation,* 35 Sw. L.J. 973, 978 (1982), the Department of Health and Human Services (formerly Health, Education, and Welfare) cannot impose conditions on clinics performing the techniques.

26. *See* Syrkowski v. Appleyard, No. 71057 (Mich. Jan. 17, 1985).

27. *See*, e.g., Mich. Comp. Laws § 710.54(1) (1979) ("[Except with court approval,] a person shall not offer, give, or receive any money or other consideration or thing of value in connection with [an adoption or related practices].").

One court has denied that adoption statutes may be used to regulate surrogate mothering. The court maintained that a natural father cannot properly be characterized as either a buyer or an adoptive father of his own child. *See* Kentucky v. Surrogate Parenting Assocs., 10 Fam. L. Rep. (BNA), 1105, 1106 (Ky. Cir. Ct. Oct. 26, 1983), *appeal docketed*, No. 84-CA-136-I (Ky. Ct. App. Mar. 28, 1984).

28. *See In re* Baby Girl, 9 Fam. L. Rep. (BNA), 2348 (Ky. Cir. Ct. 1983) (holding transfer of child from surrogate to alleged father invalid because placement was done privately, without permission of the state); Doe v. Kelley, 6 Fam. L. Rep. (BNA) 3011, 3013–14 (Mich. Cir. Ct. 1980), *aff'd*, 106 Mich. App. 169, 173–74, 307 N.W.2d 438, 441 (1981), *cert. denied*, 103 S. Ct. 843 (1983).

29. *See* Op. Ohio Att'y Gen. No. 83-001 (Jan. 3, 1983) (available on LEXIS, States Library, OhioAG file). The assumption that the surrogate is a child's "natural" parent may be based largely on the fact that the child carried by the surrogate is her genetic child. But the use of *in vitro* fertilization would make such a definition less axiomatic. If a donor's sperm fertilized a donated ovum *in vitro* and the resulting embryo were implanted in a surrogate's womb, the surrogate would have only a gestational relation to the resulting child. It is entirely nuclear how courts would resolve conflicting claims for a child born in such a manner. *See generally* Wadlington, *supra* note I, at 486–97 (positing possible legal relationships resulting from use of various procreative techniques). The process described is more expensive and complicated than "traditional" surrogate mothering is, *see supra* note 4, but it has at least two advantages: it would allow women to have their own genetic children without undergoing pregnancy; and it might circumvent the legal reasoning currently employed to invalidate surrogate arrangements, by making unclear whether a surrogate is a child's "natural" mother.

30. *See* Op. Ky Att'y Gen. No. 81-18, 7 Fam. L. Rep. (BNA) 2246, 2247 (1981).

31. *See, e.g.*, Brozan, *Surrogate Mothers: Problems and Goals*, N.Y. Times, Feb. 27, 1984, at C12, col. 2 (describing the opening in New York City of an infertility center to match couples with potential surrogates).

32. *See, e.g.*, *To Be Born, to Die*, A.B.A. J., Feb. 1984, at 27, 28 (discussing proposed Michigan statute that would outlaw surrogate mothering contracts).

33. One federal court has heard such a theory argued, but left the issue unresolved. *See* Smith v. Hartigan, 556 F. Supp. 157, 160–64 (N.D. Ill. 1983).

34. The privacy right is said to be found in the "penumbras" of various parts of the Bill of Rights. *See* Griswold v. Connecticut, 381 U.S. 479, 484–85 (1965); L. Tribe, American Constitutional Law § 15-3, at 893 (1978). State action that implicates that right infringes on individuals' "liberty," which is

protected by the due process clauses of the fifth and fourteenth amendments. *See id.*

35. 274 U.S. 200 (1927).

36. *See id.* at 207–08.

37. *See* Cynkar, Buck v. Bell: *"Felt Necessities" v. Fundamental Values?*, 81 Colum. L. Rev. 1418 (1981). Most scholars agree that the case would be overturned if presented to the Supreme Court today. *See* Burgdorf & Burgdorf, *The Wicked Witch Is Almost Dead*: Buck v. Bell *and the Sterilization of Handicapped Persons,* 50 Temp. L.Q. 995, 1011, 1023 (1977); Cynkar, *supra,* at 1456; Murdock, *Sterilization of the Retarded: A Problem or a Solution?,* 62 Calif. L. Rev. 917, 921 (1974).

The only rationale that might justify the *Buck* result today is that incompetents may lack the full capacity for individual choice. *See In re Grady,* 85 N.J. 235, 265, 426 A.2d 467, 482–83 (1981). Thus, some incompetents, like children, might not be entitled to full control over their procreative decisions. *See infra* note 48. But children are deprived of procreative autonomy only until they reach adulthood; sterilization is permanent.

38. 316 U.S. 535 (1942).

39. *See id.* at 541.

40. *Id.* at 536.

41. *Id.* at 541.

42. 381 U.S. 479 (1965).

43. *See id.* at 485–86.

44. 405 U.S. 438 (1972) (plurality opinion).

45. *Id.* at 453. Although *Eisenstadt* was a plurality opinion, its specific language referring to *individual* freedom from governmental intrusion into procreative choices was quoted with approval by the majority in Carey v. Population Servs. Int'l, 431 U.S. 678, 685 (1977). *See also id.* at 687 ("Read in light of its progeny, the teaching of *Griswold* is that the Constitution protects individual decisions in matters of childbearing from unjustified intrusion by the State").

46. 410 U.S. 113 (1973). *Roe's* discussion of the aspects of life protected by the privacy right has been incorporated into later cases. *See, e.g., Carey,* 431 U.S. at 685.

47. *See Roe,* 410 U.S. at 152–54.

48. *See* Planned Parenthood Ass'n v. Danforth, 428 U.S. 52 (1976). Some limitations on the privacy right are still considered valid. *Cf.* H.L. v. Matheson, 450 U.S. 398 (1981) (upholding constitutionality of state statute requiring doctors to give notice to parents of minors seeking abortions); Bellotti v. Baird, 443 U.S. 622 (1979) (permitting minors to have abortions without parental consent only if they can demonstrate "sufficient maturity" to make abortion decision). Yet because the rationale supporting these limitations is that individuals below the age of majority are not yet fully mature and thus cannot responsibly exercise full control over their own reproductive capacities, *see Matheson,* 450 U.S. at 408, these limitations do not undercut the notion that married and unmarried adults possess a significant degree of autonomy in making decisions regarding procreation.

49. Some commentators have argued that the rights to avoid conceiving and bearing a child imply the affirmative right to procreate. *See* Robertson, *supra* note 10, at 416 & nn.30–32; Note, *Artificial Insemination: A Legislative Remedy,* 3 W. St. U.L. Rev. 48, 55–56 (1975).

50. The validity of this analysis does not hinge on the continued vitality of Roe v. Wade, 410 U.S. 113 (1973), because the individual's procreation right does not even arguably threaten a separate interest in the preservation of life.

51. *See* Hafen, *The Constitutional Status of Marriage, Kinship, and Sexual Privacy—Balancing the Individual and Social Interests,* 81 Mich. L. Rev. 463, 527–38 (1983).

52. *See supra* pp. 676–77 & notes 45–48.

53. The claim that the Supreme Court is concerned with individual autonomy rather than with limiting procreation is bolstered by the majority opinion in Roberts v. United States Jaycees, 104 S. Ct. 3244 (1984). Although the case dealt with associational freedoms, the Court termed the right to form a family a liberty basic to personal identity; Justice Brennan's opinion suggested that "the ability independently to define one's identity that is central to any concept of liberty" derives from the ability to have a family and to transmit one's own values. *Id.* at 3250. The Court implied that certain relationships are accorded constitutional protection because they create interpersonal bonds necessary to individuals' emotional and social well-being; those bonds are strongest when the relationships are familial. *See id.*

54. *See* Skinner v. Oklahoma, 316 U.S. 535, 541 (1942).

55. Weber v. Aetna Casualty & Sur. Co., 406 U.S. 164, 173 (1972) (quoting Stokes v. Aetna Casualty & Sur. Co., 257 La. 424, 433, 242 So. 2d 567, 570 (1970)).

56. Nonetheless, courts have not recognized the validity of homosexual or lesbian marriages. *See, e.g.,* Jones v. Hallahan, 501 S.W.2d 588 (Ky. 1973); *see also* J. Areen, Family Law 25 (1978) (noting further cases and relevant statutes).

57. *Cf.* Parham. v. Hughes, 441 U.S. 347, 366 (1979) (White, J., dissenting) (noting state supreme court's belief that the father of an illegitimate child suffers no real loss from that child's death); Stanley v. Illinois, 405 U.S. 645, 654–55 (1972) (finding impermissible a state's conclusive presumption that unmarried fathers are unfit parents).

Strong arguments exist for closely scrutinizing statutes that discriminate between married and unmarried parents. *See* Note, *Equal Protection for Unmarried Parents,* 65 Iowa L. Rev. 679, 704–08 (1980).

58. *See* Weinberger v. Wiesenfeld, 420 U.S. 636, 645 (1975); Frontiero v. Richardson, 411 U.S. 677, 685 (1973); *Stanley,* 405 U.S. at 654–55.

59. The Supreme Court's notion of family as a network of close emotional bonds, *see supra* note, 53, reveals a concern not with formal structures, but with underlying values and human needs. *See also* Moore v. City of E. Cleveland, 431 U.S. 494, 506 (1977) (plurality opinion) ("[T]he Constitution prevents [government] from standardizing its children—and its

adults—by forcing all to live in certain narrowly defined family patterns.");
cf. Smith v. Organization of Foster Families for Equality & Reform, 431 U.S.
816, 843 (1977) (family can exist without genetic relationship); Stanley v.
Illinois, 405 U.S. 645, 651–52 (1972) (family can exist without marriage). If
the Court were to follow this line of thought consistently, it would extend
protection to all closely knit units that are tied together by affection,
understanding, common values, and shared experience. If the law's protection of personal relationships is commensurate with the value that the
parties place on them, individuals will benefit and society will be strengthened. This understanding of family would grant unmarried persons a due
process right to procreate with the aid of reproductive technology.

60. Roberts v. United States Jaycees, 104 S. Ct. 3244, 3251 (1984). Although the majority in *Jaycees* did not specifically identify the two ends of
this "spectrum," one can surmise that the Court would place the marital
family at one extreme and large, impersonal, commercial enterprises at the
other.

61. *See supra* note 53.

62. In Moore v. City of E. Cleveland, 431 U.S. 494 (1977) (plurality
opinion), the Supreme Court emphasized blood relationship over nuclear
family structure; by the former criterion, relationships created through the
use of reproductive technology would fall within the Supreme Court's
definition of family. *Moore* also emphasized, however, that certain family
arrangements are protected because they have been traditionally approved. *See id.* at 503–04. Nonmarital procreation has clearly not been
accorded such approval.

63. *See* Kritchevsky, *supra* note 5, at 37; *cf.* Lehr v. Robertson, 103 S. Ct.
2985, 2996–97 (1983) (states may, without violating equal protection, accord
more favorable legal treatment to parents who have "continuous custodial
responsibility" for their children than to parents who have not undertaken
such responsibility).

64. Births achieved through reproductive technology are never accidental: individuals seeking to procreate by such means must plan ahead and
sacrifice their time and resources in order to conceive a child. In view of
their demonstrated desire and determination to be parents, these individuals are likely also to plan for their children's care and needs after birth.

65. *See* Eisenstadt v. Baird, 405 U.S. 438 (1972) (plurality opinion).

66. *See* Stanley v. Illinois, 405 U.S. 645 (1972). *Stanley* dealt only with
unmarried fathers' right to participate in raising their children; the decision
did not address whether unmarried persons have an affirmative right to
procreate equal to that of married persons.

67. Courts and legislatures should also be aware that allowing unmarried persons access to certain reproductive techniques but not to others
might result in unequal procreative rights for women and men. For example, because men are unable to bear their own children, an outright
prohibition of surrogate mothering would leave unmarried men the only
class of adults deprived of access to reproductive technology. Married
women could, with their husbands' consent, be artifically inseminated.

Married men could, with their wives' consent, contribute to homologous artificial insemination, or AIH (artificial insemination, husband), which is used if intercourse is impossible. *See* Wadlington, *supra* note 1, at 469. Married men and women could also participate in *in vitro* fertilization or embryo transfer. Unmarried women apparently have legal access to artificial insemination in at least one state, *see supra* note 13; and in practical terms, unmarried women may avail themselves of the procedure, even if they lack *legal* access, *see supra* note 16. Although a ban on surrogate mothering would also adversely affect women who are incapable of carrying their own children, its greatest impact would be on unmarried men.

This disparate impact would not compel a court to invalidate legislation that barred surrogate mothering, because the goal of such legislation would almost certainly be nondiscriminatory. *See infra* p. 684. Under current equal protection doctrine, a court will invalidate a law that affects men and women unequally only if the legislature intended to discriminate on the basis of gender. *See* Personnel Adm'r v. Feeney, 442 U.S. 256, 274–80 (1979). But a law's potential disparate impact on men and women should caution legislatures against enacting such sweeping measures, especially when less restrictive alternatives may be available. *See infra* p. 684.

68. A state could not deny unmarried persons access to reproductive technology on the ground that they would likely be poor and require public support. *See* Kritchevsky; *supra* note 5, at 29–30. Such a regulation would be overinclusive in that it would deny procreative rights to unmarried persons *able* to support their families, and underinclusive in that it would apply neither to unmarried persons procreating coitally nor to poor married persons. *See* Zablocki v. Redhail, 434 U.S. 374, 386 (1978); Kritchevsky, *supra* note 5, at 29–30. Moreover, people who can afford expensive reproductive techniques, *see e.g.*, L. Andrews, *supra* note 24, at 126 (discussing high cost of *in vitro* fertilization), are unlikely to require public support.

This last observation raises the difficult question whether access to reproductive technology should depend on wealth. Even if a state were to grant unmarried persons access, equal protection would probably not require the state to subsidize the access. *See* EAB Report, *supra* note 25, at 35,051; *cf.* Regan v. Taxation With Representation, 103 S. Ct. 1997, 2003 (1983) (stating that "a legislature's decision not to subsidize the exercise of a fundamental right does not infringe the right"); Harris v. McRae, 448 U.S. 297 (1980) (denying the government's obligation to fund indigents' medically necessary abortions); Maher v. Roe, 432 U.S. 464 (1977) (denying the government's obligation to fund nontherapeutic abortions). Although some commentators seem untroubled by this wealth discrimination, *see*, *e.g.*, Kritchevsky, *supra* note 5, at 29 n. 145, it seems unfair that exercise of the right to procreate should depend on economic status.

69. Society has long condemned "irresponsible liaisons beyond the bonds of marriage," Weber v. Aetna Casualty & Sur. Co., 406 U.S. 164, 175 (1972) and "illegitimate relationships," Trimble v. Gordon, 430 U.S. 762, 769 (1977). The Supreme Court's frequent lack of sympathy for the equal

protection claims of unmarried parents reflects its disapproval of both nonmarital sexual relationships and unmarried parents' failure to legitimize their children. *See* Parham v. Hughes, 441 U.S. 347, 353 (1979).

70. A state law granting unmarried persons access to reproductive technology could limit such access to persons over a certain age without offending the Constitution, just as a state may regulate marriage of a minor. *Cf.* Bellotti v. Baird, 443 U.S. 622, 637 & n.16 (1979) (state can require parental consent for marriage of minor).

71. *See supra* pp. 679–80.

72. *See* Robertson, *supra* note 10, at 418, 424.

73. An additional argument exists: even if one agreed that society should strive to decrease the number of nonmarital births, *see, e.g.,* [1 Natality] National Center for Health Statistics, Pub. Health Serv., U.S. Dep't of Health and Human Servs., Vital Statistics of the United States: 1979, at I-54 (1984) (stating that children born to unmarried women constituted 17% of all births in 1979, as compared with less than 11% in 1970), prohibiting unmarried persons access to reproductive technology is a highly underinclusive means of achieving that goal. Of course, states that actively enforce statutes outlawing fornication could claim that banning technological procreation outside marriage is part of a comprehensive legal scheme to eradicate nonmarital procreation. Yet as of 1978, only 15 states and the District of Columbia still had such laws, *see* Note, *Fornication, Cohabitation, and the Constitution,* 77 Mich. L. Rev. 252, 254 n.4 (1978), and even those states rarely enforced them, *see id.* at 270-71 & n.97. In most cases, therefore, only nonmarital technological procreation would be limited.

Such an extremely underinclusive statute would probably not survive strict scrutiny; it is less clear how narrowly a law must be drafted in order to survive intermediate scrutiny. On the application of intermediate scrutiny, see Trimble v. Gordon, 430 U.S. 762, 772 (1977), and Craig v. Boren, 429 U.S. 190, 197 (1976).

74. *See, e.g.,* Roe v. Wade, 410 U.S. 113, 149 (1973) (state can restrict "inherently hazardous [medical] procedure[s]").

75. A state health interest in screening sperm donors for genetic defects could not justify outlawing artificial insemination. Such a law would be unnecessarily restrictive because the state could simply require screening.

76. *See* EAB Report, *supra* note 25, at 35,057.

77. *See id.* at 35,044, 35,056.

78. Approximately 18,500 births result annually from the artificial insemination of married women. *See supra* note 1; *supra* p. 671.

79. A child conceived by an unmarried person using reproductive technology might often be raised by two adults—for example, infertile unmarried couples.

80. In recent years, psychologists have disputed the theory that such children are disadvantaged. *See, e.g.,* Blechman, *Are Children with One Parent at Psychological Risk? A Methodological Review,* 44 J. Marriage & Fam. 179 (1982) (arguing that methodological flaws and social biases colored

past studies, leaving unclear whether children raised by one parent are at risk); Gongla, *Single Parent Families: A Look at Families of Mothers and Children*, Marriage & Fam. Rev., Summer 1982, at 5, 11 (contending that children can develop normally in single-parent homes).

81. *See, e.g.*, N.Y. Dom Rel. Law § 110 (McKinney 1977); Pa. Cons. Stat. Ann. tit. 23, § 2312 (Purdon Supp. 1984–1985); *supra* note 5.

82. This problem is not speculative; much of surrogate mothering's notoriety has come from a few highly publicized cases of surrogates who resisted giving up their children to the contracting fathers. *See* L. Andrews, *supra* note 24, at 211–12. Courts would probably recognize that forcing surrogates to give up children could cause them psychological harm; even if a court were to hold a surrogate mothering contract valid, it would probably refuse to compel delivery of the child to the contracting party. *See* Brophy, *A Surrogate Mother Contract To Bear a Child*, 20 J. Fam. L. 263, 264 (1982).

83. A ban based on this rationale would be underinclusive if it failed to ban other practices that carry similar potential to cause mothers psychological harm. One such practice is adoption: many mothers who relinquish their children for adoption suffer from feelings of isolation, social scorn, grief, and loss. *See* Chiaradonna, *A Group Work Approach to Post-Surrender Treatment of Unwed Mothers*, Soc. Work with Groups, Winter 1982, at 47, 48, 63.

84. Similar screening is already conducted on ovum donors by the Ovum Transfer Project, a privately funded embryo transfer program conducted at the University of California, Los Angeles. *See* Brotman, *supra* note 3, at 43. Although some surrogate mothering centers already require such screening, *see* Brozan, *supra* note 31, there is currently no way to guarantee that proper precautions are taken. The legislative void in which surrogate mothering now languishes invites the private sector to take a more active role, yet such involvement might not ensure a sufficiently sensitive regard for surrogates' physical and emotional health. The state could reconcile its valid interests with individuals' fundamental right to procreate by creating a state-supervised program for surrogate parenting, perhaps one modeled after the current adoption system. *See* Wadlington, *supra* note 1, 504, 511–12. Because most women who apply to be surrogates do so at least in part out of financial need, *see* Wallis, *supra* note 2, at 53, such a program should standardize compensation for surrogates to prevent their being paid unfairly.

85. Robertson, *supra* note 10, at 424; *see id.* at 418.

8

Contraception and Public Policy:
Recognizing the Right Not to Conceive

Kim Ezra Shienbaum

Until relatively recently, birth control was an issue permeated with the imprint of the Judeo-Christian ethic which prescribed that sex was to be procreative and that procreative sex was to take place only within the institution of marriage. Hence contraception was roundly condemned by the Church as "dangerous, demoralizing and sinful."[1] Government followed suit, regarding the issue of birth control as, by and large, outside its jurisdiction.

When government did intervene, public policy reflected negative religious views which did not recognize the right of persons to regulate their own fertility. The 1873 Comstock Laws, for instance, prohibited the mailing or transportation of contraceptives or contraceptive information across state lines and most states had restrictions on the use of contraception, with the state of Connecticut outlawing the practice altogether. Thus it was left to private persons, acting privately (such as Margaret Sanger, founder of Planned Parenthood) to lay the foundations for family planning in the USA.

It was not until the 1960s that the United States government began to play a positive role in birth control and it did so then only because it was pushed in that direction by a number of factors. One of those was the influence of public opinion. Leona Baumgartner

---

Kim Ezra Shienbaum is an associate professor of political science at Rutgers University-Camden.

reported that by 1956, 65% of the U.S. population (and even 59% of Catholics) favored some kind of government action on the issue.[2] Private groups such as the Rockefeller and Ford Foundations joined the long time advocates of birth control and gave them financial support for their activities. The United Nations, particularly the Agency for International Development, together with the media, publicized the issue of a world-wide "population explosion" and the problems associated with it. As Baumgartner says:

> The pressures from the developing countries themselves, particularly those in Asia [forced] action on the United Nations and the specialized agencies and on Western leaders.[3]

By the time President Kennedy took office, a sea change took place in governmental attitudes. Unlike Eisenhower, who had emphatically stated that birth control was not a governmental issue, Kennedy regarded it as a public, and not solely a private, concern.

Nevertheless it was the U.S. Congress which first responded to the pressures for action on birth control—and then only in an international context. There was still an official unwillingness to consider the fertility of *Americans* a legitimate subject for public policy. A few years later, even Lyndon Johnson's State of the Union address in 1965 reflected this international orientation:

> I will seek ways to use our knowledge to help deal with the explosion in *world* population.[4]

In any case, the U.S. government by the mid-1960s did commit itself to cooperate with the United Nations and developing countries to assist them with their population problems. Working through AID, family planning became a major preoccupation of U.S. Foreign Assistance Programs. In 1968, the United States Congress amended the Foreign Assistance Act of 1961 to provide a specific mandate to help, through appropriate executive agencies, developing countries that sought U.S. aid to carry out projects relating to population growth and family planning. By 1969, the United States was the principal source of funding for family planning programs outside the U.S.

Contraception in the United States

By the mid-1960s, birth control, once officially taboo, had become the subject of domestic policy debate. Judicial rulings had established the right of married couples NOT to conceive (*Griswold v. Connecticut*, 1965 and *Eisenstadt v. Baird*, 1972) but it was not until 1971 that the federal government acted to: 1) officially repeal the Comstock Laws; and 2) provide birth control to poor families on a national scale. The first federally supported family planning program had actually been approved almost ten years earlier (1962) in Washington, D.C. and by 1966 family planning had become a continuing component of D.C. public health programs. In addition, Senator Joseph Clark and Representative James Scheuer tried to expand family planning programs through the Office of Economic Opportunity and the then Department of Health, Education and Welfare. OEO proved to be marginally more sympathetic than HEW and, in 1965, Clark added "family planning" as one of the specific health programs supported by OEO.

Meanwhile an institutional base for domestic policymaking was being established. A Center for Population Research was created in the National Institute of Child Health and Human Development (1966) and a Center for Family Planning Services was established within the Health Services and Mental Health Administration in 1969. Encouraged by these events, Senator Joseph Tydings introduced legislation in Congress to authorize funds for specific family planning projects to public agencies and non-profit institutions. It was not passed at that time and, in fact, a similar measure did not become law until 1970 when the *Family Planning Service and Population Research Act* was passed. It was the first time that federal funding was provided for domestic family planning programs nationally. At the same time, Congress also passed an act to establish a Presidential Commission on Population Growth and the American Future, establishing an executive interest in the subject.

Federal support for birth control was also reflected in two subsequent pieces of legislation. In 1971, Title X of the Public Health Service Act provided birth control assistance to low income recipients, while "family planning" was added to Title XIX (Medicaid) of the Social Security Act, making it possible for doctors to provide birth control in the same manner they provided other services to their clientele.

From that high point, family planning (the official euphemism for contraception) has hit several shoals, the chief of which is Congressional unwillingness to adequately fund the programs. Baumgartner notes the irony:

More recently, the tendency of the federal government seems to have been to overestimate the amount it spends on family planning. This is in sharp contrast to the pre-1962 policy of hiding any expenditures.[5]

By the 1980s, two developments had occurred. The first was a conservative moral climate which united conservative Republicans and fundamentalist Christians against the use of contraceptives by unmarried teenagers, using the argument that Congress intended to provide funds for *family* planning. This argument was made by Senator Jeremiah Denton, who chaired the 1981 Senate Oversight Hearings on Family Planning Programs under Title X of the Public Health Service Act.

The Commission noted that in ten years, the federal government had spent $1.5 billion on family planning, but that by 1980, one-third of all Title X recipients were *unmarried teens* who received contraceptives without parental consent. Denton suggested two changes in the way family planning programs were being administered: block, rather than categorical, grants given to States to spend as they saw fit, and a parental notification requirement which was eventually written into the Omnibus Budget Act of 1981. Acting on these congressional instructions, the Department of Health and Human Services issued final regulations in January 1983 requiring federally funded family planning clinics to notify parents of minors receiving birth control devices. These administrative rulings were, however, challenged and subsequently overruled by the courts, which found that they contravened the intent of Congress when it passed the original Family Planning Act in 1970.

A second development, which subsequently foundered in the new more conservative environment of the Reagan years, was an attempt to introduce legislation to establish an Office of Population Policy with the controversial goal of population stabilization. Representative Richard Ottinger, who sponsored HR 907 in the House, stated that his effort grew out of the recommendations of the Global 2000 Report to the President (the Federal Government's first comprehensive effort to project current levels of resources utilization into the future, based on population growth projections) which "forecast grim consequences if nations failed to take immediate action to confront the imbalance between population, resources and the environment."[6] The Reagan Administration opposed the initiative because it was felt it called for more, rather than less, government supervision and control and because the Administration placed a greater priority upon "technological advance and economic expansion"[7] than upon birth control. This sentiment was echoed in testimony before the House Subcommittee on Census and Population which held hearings on HR 907 in 1982. Ben Wattenberg of the American Enterprise Institute told the Committee that he would have preferred the name Office of Population Information to the Office of Population Policy, but in any case went on to condemn the thrust of the legislation:

> . . . this position of population stability . . . which is government attempting to influence the size of families in this country, is neither pro-choice nor pro-civil liberties.[8]

Thus, once again, an attempt to follow other industrialized nations with a comprehensive "population policy" foundered, in large measure, on the traditional American antipathy to Big Government and to conservative counterarguments cast in terms of support for individual rights and liberties.

The issue of contraception in the 1980s, then, is caught between several complex political issues. Even if the federal government has moved beyond the Eisenhower position that birth control was not the government's business, there is now the question of budgetary austerity, and a more conservative moral climate, which make problematic the adequate funding of those programs which do exist.

Notes

1. See Marilyn Jane Field, *The Comparative Politics of Birth Control: Determinants of Policy Variation and Change in Developed Nations.* (New York: Praeger, 1983).
2. Leona Baumgartner, "Governmental Responsibility for Family Planning in the United States in S. J. Behrman, M.D., Leslie Corsa Jr., M.D., and Ronald Freedman, Eds., *Fertility and Family Planning—A World View* (Ann Arbor: University of Michigan Press, 1976) p. 437.
3. *Ibid*, p. 439.

4. Quoted in Elihu Bergman, "American Population Policymaking: A Shift to the States" in Elihu Bergman et. al., *Population Policymaking in the American States* (Mass.: Lexington Books and D.C. Heath and Co., 1974) p. 4.

5. Baumgartner, *op. cit.*, p. 446.

6. Quoted in Richard Ottinger, "The Case for a National Population Policy" in *American Demographics*, March 1982, Volume 4, p. 32.

7. *Ibid*, p. 32.

8. U.S. House Committee on Post Office and Civil Service, Sub-Committee on Census and Population, *National Population Policy Hearings*, March 10–11, 1982, 97th. Congress, 2nd. Session, p. 197.

While environmentalists and fertility control groups supported HR 907, conservatives were by no means the only ones to oppose the bill. Hispanic groups such as the League of United Latin American Citizens voiced strong opposition on the grounds that a population policy would be viewed as a "racist effort to dictate and curtail our growth". (p. 191).

9

Tolerance and the Abortion Controversy

Mary C. Segers

The characteristic virtue of a liberal democratic society such as the United States is sometimes said to be tolerance.[1] Tolerance is necessitated by the existence of a plurality of religious, ethnic, and other kinds of groups in society; it is also justified in terms of the implicit bias of the American constitution towards the protection of civil liberties. We agree to disagree in a democratic republic; ideally we share a consensus on the importance of individual freedom, moral autonomy and respect for the rights of citizens to differ.

Yet the liberal ideal of tolerance has been subjected to great strains in recent years; and nowhere is this clearer than in the matter of public controversy over abortion. Prochoice advocates claim that "Right-to-Lifers are trying to impose their morality on the rest of us," and characterize such tactics as "Neo-Fascist".[2] For their part, prolife activists persist in depicting abortion proponents as "murderers" and "babykillers"; moreover, they resist the use of law and government to impose upon them a "secular morality" which, in their view, glorifies sexual permissiveness, ethical relativism, and an uncritical acceptance of technological advances. At the level of political discourse, discussion of the abortion issue has, at times, been positively uncivil; perhaps citizens need to be mindful of their duties to be tolerant of and respectfully attentive to the expression of opposing views in a democratic society. At the level of political and public policy, the relevance of tolerance to the abortion issue seems less certain.

Mary C. Segers is an associate professor of political science at Rutgers University-Newark.

The fundamental political and legal question is: what should public policy on abortion be in a pluralistic society profoundly and deeply divided over the morality of abortion? Some argue that government should be neutral and tolerant, and should adopt a liberal, non-coercive policy which permits involuntarily pregnant women to decide in conscience whether or not to terminate a pregnancy. Others think it is neither possible nor desirable for the state to be neutral, and that a permissive abortion policy is in fact the imposition upon them of a liberal worldview which exalts individual freedom at the price of responsibility to others. On this view, government ought not to tolerate abortion because it is immoral.

In this essay, I wish to examine the applicability of the concept of tolerance to public policy on abortion. My focus is primarily on tolerance by government of the practice of abortion, and only secondarily on tolerance by society or by the individual. There are several sub-topics. First, within the context of American politics, what are we to make of the demand that government be "neutral" in this matter? Second, what of the "hard case" concerning abortion policy, in which it is argued that abortion, though immoral, should remain legal and not be recriminalized? Here I would like to draw attention to Roman Catholic arguments for religious liberty and for limits to the use of law in the enforcement of morals. I maintain that the former comprise positive and the latter comprise negative arguments for tolerance of abortion by government.

Some Preliminary Considerations

It could be argued that it is necessary to resolve the fundamental moral question, whether the fetus is a human being and a person, before even considering the applicability of tolerance to abortion. Also the applicability of tolerance to this issue depends in a crucial sense on the definition of abortion. If abortion is defined as the direct, deliberate killing of an innocent human being, then presumably such killing cannot be tolerated (or the burden of proof is on the abortion proponent). There are limits to tolerance, and violence to others is one of the limits.

Yet, recent developments in public discussion of abortion suggest that these central definitional questions are not nearly so intractable as they may have seemed in the past. First, Mahowald has distinguished the definition of abortion as termination of pregnancy from abortion defined as termination of fetal life, and has suggested that advances in medical technology (neonatology in particular) might make this distinction practically, technically feasible in the relatively near future.[3] An advantage of this distinction, of course, is that it throws into relief the conflict between a pregnant woman's interests and those of the fetus, and suggests some partial resolution of this dilemma (although it raises other problems, such as who would have responsibility for the care of unwanted born children).

A second interesting development in the abortion controversy occurred in the course of hearings in the spring of 1981 before the Senate Subcommittee on the Separation of Powers which was taking testimony on the recently introduced human life statute. Testimony from physicians and scientists that the fetus is biologically human rather than canine or bovine life suggested a rephrasing of a central issue in the controversy. The basic question is now said to be not whether the fetus is human life (it is), but what value we wish to assign to nascent, developing human life. This question is not decided by biological facts; it is a matter of social convention and moral agreement. The answer is not automatically given by nature but must be decided by human beings who must, through common deliberation, reach a consensus.

These developments suggest a degree of fluidity in discussions of the morality of abortion and hint at the possibility of change and development. In other words, the possibility of tolerance by government and society of abortion under certain circumstances is not ruled out *a priori*. Since discussion is not foreclosed in advance, we may move on to consider the role of tolerance in the controversy over public policy on abortion.

The Argument for Government Neutrality

Tolerance, defined as "the disposition to tolerate beliefs, practices or habits differing from one's own," (Webster's Dictionary, second edition) is regarded by some liberal thinkers as the essential political norm of liberal government and society. As Charles Frankel wrote:

Translated into political and moral terms, the liberal Weltanschauung calls for making tolerance the keystone on which social cooperation depends. In education and government, in the relations between classes, in styles of culture, it favors choices that are likely to promote rational communication and criticism, a fluid social structure and a dispersion of power sufficient to give the curious and the restless room to turn around. And because liberalism's outlook is dominated by a sense of the many-sidedness of the individual and of any sophisticated society, it stresses the virtues of negotiation and compromise, within a framework of civil liberty about which there can be no compromise. It does so not simply because negotiation and compromise are 'realistic,' but because they reflect the moral respect that should be shown to people whose interests and views are different from one's own.[4]

A corollary notion to the liberal concept of tolerance is the concept of governmental neutrality. Galston notes that, "The neutral state is incontestably the leading idea of contemporary liberal theory." By 'neutral state' is meant the moral neutrality of government, "the idea that the state must be systematically neutral on questions of personal moral development and the good life."[5] Historically, of course, the neutral state in embryonic form was a product of the religious wars of Reformation and post-Reformation Europe. Tolerance by government of a plurality of religions was originally justified in negative terms, as the only possible cure for debilitating civil strife. In Locke's view, it was necessary to create a private sphere, exempt from state interference, within which individuals would be able to associate freely to worship in their irremediably diverse ways. Moreover, since it was an inward act of the mind or conscience, true religious faith could not be coerced by external, political force. Thus the state had no business invading the private realm of freely given spiritual assent.

As Galston notes, the history of liberal political thought is characterized by a steadily expanding understanding of state neutrality, as skepticism about religious truth was extended to conceptions of moral conduct and of the good life. The sphere of private, individual decisionmaking and the sphere of obligatory public neutrality were gradually enlarged throughout the eighteenth, nineteenth, and twentieth centuries. Contemporary liberal thinkers such as Rawls, Nozick, Dworkin, and Ackerman have all in one way or another stressed that government must be neutral on the definition of individual human excellence, on the question of the good life.[6]

The concept of state neutrality has figured prominently in the contemporary controversy over public policy on abortion in the United States. Prochoice advocates consistently and persistently propound it as the only sensible government policy on abortion. They contend that government should adopt a neutral, non-coercive policy which permits but does not require or prohibit abortion. With such a policy the government extends tolerance to a variety of moral beliefs on the issue, whether such beliefs are religiously-based or grounded in a non-theological ethics.

This type of argument was featured extensively in the trial court briefs of the plaintiffs in *Harris v. McRae* (1980), the suit in which abortion proponents challenged Congressional restrictions on Medicaid funding of abortion. There plaintiffs argued that the Congressionally-enacted Hyde Amendment (named after Representative Henry Hyde, R.-Illinois) violated the religion clauses of the First Amendment because: (1) it enacted into civil law a particular religious view of abortion, namely, the view that the fetus is a human being from the moment of conception; and (2) it violated the free exercise clause by funding childbirth for those women whose religious views are antiabortionist while denying funds to those women whose religious or conscience views lead them to choose to terminate pregnancies. Lawyers for the American Civil Liberties Union and the Center for Constitutional Rights maintained that:

> Catholics and Orthodox Jewish groups support an anti-abortion position while many Protestant and the majority of Jewish groups advocate the religious necessity of choice over the abortion question. Plaintiffs, who include the Women's Division of the Methodist Church, asked the Court to find that the government can have no role in enacting into law an abortion statute which clearly elevates one religious belief over another and aids those religions which forbid abortion while inhibiting those persons who hold opposite religious beliefs or no religious beliefs at all. The state must remain neutral on the abortion issue.[7]

While the U.S. Supreme Court ultimately rejected plaintiffs' legal arguments and held that the Hyde Amendment was not unconstitutional,[8] the idea or argument that government must be neutral on the abortion issue is still heard quite frequently. Abortion is held to be a religious issue, best left to the private conscience rather than to public legislation. In its public policy (so the argument runs), the state must remain neutral and not intrude upon the domains of individual liberty and conscience. Government neutrality is best achieved through the removal of restrictive abortion laws from the books (as in *Roe v. Wade*). It is assumed that government neutrality is both possible and desirable. Further, it is urged, repeal of antiabortion statutes is said to pass no judgment on the substantive ethical issues, but merely to allow individuals to make up their own minds.

One of the more interesting aspects of the abortion debate is the degree to which abortion opponents have questioned the possibility of government neutrality on this issue. Speaking of attempts to force an interpretation of life on someone else, John Garvey wrote:

> Prochoice people often accuse the antiabortion people of doing just that. In their view reasonableness requires an open-ended view of human life and its origins, one which in the absence of clear and agreed-upon definitions of humanity would allow abortion to those who choose it. It cannot be proven that fetal life is human; therefore it may be taken. But to accept this as the proper view of tolerance in a democracy is to accept a particular orthodoxy. To insist that in the absence of a proof of human life, life may be taken, is to make a moral judgment as arbitrary as any made by right-to-life people . . .[9]

Prolife advocates do not believe it is possible for government to enact a neutral public policy on abortion. They believe that a permissive policy of choice is as much the imposition of a particular worldview or metaphysics upon them as a restrictive policy is an imposition of prolife values upon abortion supporters. As one philosopher stated: "A decision to remove abortion laws from the books is no more ethically neutral than a decision to put such laws on the books or to keep them there."[10] Such an ostensibly neutral policy begs the question of the status of the fetus, or, at the least, assumes that there are no normative standards whatever for determining the rights of fetuses, except the standard that individuals are free to use or to create any standard they see fit. This frankly libertarian individualistic approach hardly seems neutral. Each of the above premises involves a philosophical judgment and has philosophical implications. A governmental decision to remove restrictive antiabortion statutes from the law and to leave the question up to individuals is an explicitly liberal rather than neutral approach.

Prolifers also believe that the view that it is possible for government to remain neutral on the abortion issue betrays a certain naiveté about the role of law in society. The Greeks recognized the educative role of the laws[11] and were aware that changes in the law not only reflect significant shifts in public moral attitudes but also affect individual moral judgments. Mohr has shown the impact in the United States of the nineteenth-century antiabortion statutes upon public attitudes regarding abortion: whereas the great majority of Americans in 1850 did not regard abortion as morally wrong, public opinion in 1950 was invariably opposed to abortion.[12] In the face of such evidence concerning the role of law as a socializing agent—at least with respect to attitudes (although not necessarily with respect to behavior)—it seems naive and disingenuous to pretend that government, law, and public policy are or can be neutral on the abortion question.

Abortion opponents question whether abortion is a religious issue, which therefore ought to be left to private conscience rather than to public legislation. They wonder what is meant by the statement that abortion is a religious issue. If it means that for some churches and some religious believers their positions are the direct result of religious teachings, this hardly entails the conclusion that the issue is thus intrinsically religious. One might as well say that racial equality is a religious issue and not subject to legislation, because there are some churches which declare racism immoral on religious grounds. That religious groups take religious positions on many issues (e.g., war, poverty, equality, capital punishment) does not exempt those problems from public legislation nor turn them into theology.

Abortion seems to be a philosophical and ethical issue, not a religious question. This does not mean the issue is therefore best left to the domain of private conscience. Every serious social issue is philosophical. Matters of war and peace, disarmament, foreign aid, race- and sex-based discrimination, fiscal and monetary policy all involve ethical issues. Questions about the meaning of justice, liberty, or equality arise all the time, and such questions are philo-

195

sophical and legal in nature. The answers to them shape public policy in a decisive fashion. That abortion is a philosophical and ethical issue, then, does not automatically put it beyond the pale of governmental consideration and relegate it to the sphere of private, personal morality. Nuclear war and racial justice are also philosophical and ethical issues; and we dare not consign them to the realm of private decisionmaking.

So to the argument that government should be neutral on the abortion issue and should enact permissive laws which leave abortion decisions in the sphere of private morality, abortion opponents respond that this picture of the neutral state is a caricature. The state cannot be neutral on the issue, and it is misguided to think that it can or ought to be. Galston states this point nicely. Addressing the question of whether the neutral state is in any sense a real possibility, he states:

> I think not . . . Every political community consists to a significant degree in shared institutions and practices, which both embody and further a specific moral understanding. Once a matter becomes a part of this common public realm, the contending parties cannot simply agree to differ. If compromise is impossible, one must prevail. Specific kinds of abortion must either be permitted or forbidden. Whatever its decision, the community must commit itself, on many levels, to specific views of human personality and conduct, as well as to a range of predictable but uncontrollable external effects on other institutions and practices. And thus, in general, contemporary liberals cannot sustain their charge that groups such as the Moral Majority are illegitimately introducing moral considerations into a public space that has heretofore been devoid of them. The battle is between two competing moral conceptions, not between morality and neutrality.[13]

If the idea of state neutrality on the abortion issue is seen for the misguided argument it seems to be, then perhaps we may withdraw charges that Right-to-Lifers, Moral Majoritarians, and other abortion opponents are intolerant fascists who are trying to impose their moral views upon the rest of us. Liberalism is as much a political philosophy, an ideology, and a moral conception as is the hodge-podge of ideas subscribed to by the Moral Majority. Rather than contend that government adopt a 'neutral' choice policy, prochoice adherents might more accurately argue that America is a liberal society which accords very high priority to individual choice, which cannot achieve public consensus on the abortion question, and which, as a result, must reluctantly leave resolution of the matter to private individual judgment. This would be a valuable clarification of the prochoice argument because it would acknowledge implicitly that there are limits to tolerance and because it would avoid the strawman caricature of the liberal as someone who identifies liberty with license. Such a useful clarification might also encourage abortion proponents to be less self-righteous and more tolerant.

Distinguishing the Morality and Legality of Abortion

I would like now to address the so-called 'hard case' concerning public policy on abortion, namely, the argument that abortion, though immoral, should be tolerated and permitted by government. For purposes of discussion, we may assume the position of an individual who considers abortion immoral under most circumstances and asks whether the law should mirror or reflect this view. Here the concern is with public policy and law, with the politically feasible and the practically possible. Let us consider the view that the law should not reflect this individual's moral judgment; that is, abortion should be legally permissible. To support this position, we may adduce what might be called 'negative' arguments concerning the relation between morals and the criminal law; we may also cite more positive arguments having to do with the centrality of freedom in American constitutional reflection as well as in recent teachings of the Roman Catholic Church concerning religious liberty.

Negative Arguments for the Legality of Abortion

The negative arguments have to do with practical limitations upon the use of the criminal law to enforce morality. I use the umbrella term or rubric, "The Prohibition Argument," to signify the contention that using the criminal sanction to legislate X may not achieve the desired, intended good (or prevent the proscribed immoral behavior) but may, instead, simply bring about a state of affairs which, on balance, is worse than that preceding enactment of X.

Prohibition is often cited as an example of the futility of attempting to use law and public policy to achieve moral reform in society. The Eighteenth Amendment and the Volstead Act did not change people's behavior—they still consumed large quantities of alcohol—but only made alcoholic consumption more dangerous and costly (in terms of social costs). Among the costs were bootlegging, an increase in the black market, an increase in the power of organized crime, widespread evasion of the law and a resulting contempt for the law on the part of average citizens. On balance, Prohibition advanced the interests of neither society nor the individual.

Can the same be said of abortion? I think the Prohibition argument does apply. Recriminalizing abortion will not deter women from seeking abortions nor reduce significantly the number of abortions performed, and it will result in a host of unintended consequences the end effect of which will be a state of affairs worse than that prior to enactment of such a restrictive law. Prior to *Roe v. Wade* (1973), restrictive antiabortion statutes did not deter women from seeking or having abortions. It seems unlikely that, after nine years of a post-*Roe* permissive policy, the reimposition of strict abortion laws will act to deter women from procuring abortions.

It could be argued that a severely restrictive statute would lessen, although not eliminate, the number of abortions performed, and that this would constitute a significant gain in the battle to prevent the deaths of innocent, unborn children. However, the evidence does not seem to support such a conclusion. For example, prolife advocates thought that the Hyde Amendment restricting Medicaid funding of abortions for poor women would significantly reduce the number of abortions performed among the poor; however, the Centers for Disease Control and other research groups report that the impact of the Hyde Amendment has not been to deter poor women from having abortions but to force them to collect the funds from private sources to pay for their abortions.[14] Cutting federal funding of abortions has not, in other words, reduced the incidence of abortion but has only made the lives of poor women more difficult (an example, if you will, of the Prohibition effect).

It is not hard to see why this is the case with antiabortion statutes. The involuntarily pregnant woman often feels desperate in the face of an unwanted pregnancy, and will go to great lengths (including resort to unsafe, illegal abortionists or to self-abortion) in order to prevent a pregnancy from progressing to term. This raises the second part of the Prohibition argument, the idea that the unintended consequences of a particular law or public policy will be a state of affairs worse than that prior to enactment of the policy. The litany of evils resulting from a severely restrictive abortion statute is well-known and includes the following: the return of the illegal abortionist operating in unsafe, unhygienic conditions (with high risk to women); widespread evasion of the law with the attendant risk of disrespect and contempt for the law; lax law enforcement on the part of police and prosecutors for whom other types of crime may have higher priority; at the other extreme, strict enforcement of the law at the expense of violating the privacy and dignity of human beings;[15] and, finally, selective, discriminatory enforcement of the law against poor women who lack the financial resources necessary to pay discreet, respectable physicians for their services.[16] Given the probability that recriminalizing abortion will lead to these unintended and undesired conditions, it seems foolish to reenact severely restrictive abortion statutes, particularly when they will also fail to achieve the unintended effect of reducing the incidence of abortion.

In countering these utilitarian, consequentialist arguments for government tolerance of abortion, prolife adherents sometimes appeal to an older conception of society, morality, and law—a conception which may be traced back to Cicero and Aristotle[17] and which has been articulated in recent years by the British jurist, Patrick Devlin.[18] According to this view, a society cannot cohere without a moral consensus. What makes a collection of individuals a society is a shared morality; moreover, this public morality is not confined to that which supports public institutions but also extends to individual behavior in private. Society cannot exist without a morality which mirrors and supplements the law's proscription of conduct injurious to others; similarly, a community or society cannot exist unless its shared morality is enforced by the law. Given the necessity, then, of a close fit between law and morality in a well-ordered society, it is argued that a society may use its legal sanction to preserve morality in the same way as it uses it to safeguard anything else that is essential to its existence.

As applied to the abortion issue, prolifers contend that society should go on record condemning abortion (defined as the deliberate termination of innocent human life) and that it should enshrine in law shared moral principles concerning the sanctity of life and the physical integrity of the human being. Whether the law is efficacious is irrelevant, for the important point is society's public pronouncement through law of its moral values. It doesn't matter that particular statutes are honored more in the breach than in the observance, because it is an essential function of the law to mirror, reflect, and enunciate basic values concerning respect for the sanctity of innocent human life. Law must promulgate these values publicly and clearly so that citizens can know what is right and wrong. Permissive abortion laws fail to do this, thereby suggesting that abortion is good or neutral, not tragic or morally unacceptable. Prolife supporters thus conceive law in functionalist, consequentialist terms (law is both a reflector and shaper of values) and tend to collapse the distinction between law and morals.

While this is a very attractive argument, even a proponent such as Lord Devlin realized the practical obstacles to its implementation. While he maintained that society has the right to pass judgment on matters of morals and the theoretical right to use the law to enforce its moral judgments, Devlin elaborated some general, elastic or flexible principles to determine in what circumstances the state should exercise its power. He held (1) that there must be toleration of the maximum individual freedom that is consistent with the integrity of society; (2) that, in law enforcement, as far as possible privacy should be respected (he recognized that there is in practice a strong reluctance on the part of judges, legislators, and police to sanction invasions of privacy and dignity in the detection of crime); and (3) that the law is concerned with the minimum and not with the maximum, that is, it is not concerned with making men morally perfect but with ensuring human behavior that is consonant with the state's duty to safeguard peace, order, safety, health and welfare. In practice, then, Devlin's pragmatic rules comprise realistic concessions to the minimalist liberal state.

There are other objections, of course, to the Devlin-type argument that a society or community cannot exist unless its shared morality (concerning, for example, the immorality of abortion) is enforced by the law. First, what if there is no shared moral consensus about a particular practice? What then are law and government to do but tolerate different moral conceptions? Second, what evidence exists to support the contention that society will, in fact, disintegrate if abortion is permitted? Japan has the most permissive abortion system in the world, but is Japanese society on the verge of collapse? And is life less sacred in Japan than, say, in Argentina, France, or the United States? Finally, the Devlin-type argument as applied to abortion is as functionalist, consequentialist, and utilitarian as is the Prohibition argument. Theoretically, therefore, it may not be much of an improvement over such arguments. Moreover, since they are utilitarian, both the Devlin and the Prohibition arguments cry out for empirical evidence to confirm or refute them. And here the evidence does not favor the Devlin-type argument. In the past, antiabortion statutes in the American states did not 'work', they did not to any great degree prevent abortions in the 1850–1950 period. They may have changed attitudes but they did not alter behavior; and they brought in their wake a train of unintended consequences. On balance, they did more harm than good. Daniel Callahan has summarized succinctly the Prohibition argument against highly restrictive abortion laws:

> They lead to a large number of illegal abortions, hazardous enough in affluent countries, but all the more so in underdeveloped countries. If they succeed in keeping down the overall number of abortions, they do so at too high a price. Unenforced and unforceable, they bring the law into disrepute. They have proved to be discriminatory. In a pluralistic society, they offend the conscience of many. They take from a woman's hands the possibility of making her own decisions, thus restricting her freedom—but in doing so offer no compensatory or justifying gain for the common good. As a means of symbolizing society's respect for unborn life, they are poor, too widely disregarded and known to be disregarded to give the symbol any real power. Society ought to have a high regard for nascent life, seeking to protect and further it, but restrictive abortion laws have not proved an effective way of exhibiting this regard.[19]

Although the Prohibition argument is plausible and persuasive, I grant that it is not the strongest type of argument that can be made to convince our hypothetical prolifer that abortion, though immoral, should not be made illegal. It is a utilitarian type of argument which looks to the effects of an antiabortion statute and contends that such a statute will do no good and will produce only negative, unintended consequences. Now there is nothing to suggest that prolifers could not use the same argument with respect to a decision (such as that in *Roe v. Wade*) to liberalize abortion laws. Could they not argue that the law will do no good and that the effects of such a permissive law will be evil (the killing of approximately one million innocent unborn children per year)? Stating the problem in this way enables us to see that stronger arguments are necessary in any putative conversation with our hypothetical pro-lifer. Principles rather than consequences must be the basis of our appeal to him or her, and principles can be supplied. They consist of a general appeal to the principle of liberty enshrined in our Constitution, and a special appeal to the principle of religious liberty enunciated at the Second Vatican Council of the Roman Catholic Church.

Positive Arguments for the Legality of Abortion

In the first section of this paper, we concluded that it is misguided to think that public policy on abortion in the United States can be neutral. Rather, it would be more accurate to recognize that America is a liberal society which accords very high priority to individual choice, which cannot achieve public consensus on the abortion question,[20] and which, as a result, must leave resolution of the matter to the judgment of private individuals. Here there are several sub-arguments. The first concerns the centrality of freedom in American constitutional reflection. This Constitution defines a democratic political process which rewards those who organize well enough to deliver the votes on their preferred issues. After the 1980 election, Right-to-Lifers, Moral Majoritarians, and other New Right activists could maintain that they had done their political homework and now had the necessary votes—and therefore the right—to enact legislation such as the Human Life Statute (S 158) and the Family Protection Act (HR 311). The political system is neutral, they could argue; power determines the outcome, and they now have the necessary power in numbers to repeal *Roe v. Wade*.

To this it can only be objected, of course, that the American political system is not neutral but is biased towards individual liberty, and that this constitutional bias limits the types of public laws and policies which may be enacted. We need not read De

Tocqueville to recall the dangers of majoritarian tyranny. Under a liberal constitution and in a pluralistic society such as ours, the majority cannot *legitimately* tyrannize over the single, lone dissenter on a civil liberties issue over which there is such profound disagreement.[21] The issue may not be resolved constitutionally by power alone because the Constitution is weighted in favor of individual freedoms. To take a specific example, the religious freedom clauses of the First Amendment set constraints upon public policy, such that a religiously-defined morality which conceives abortion as the immoral taking of another human life should not be enshrined in public law to the disadvantage of another religiously-based morality which views abortion under certain circumstances to be a moral duty. In the American constitutional arrangement, a citizen who considers abortion immoral may be said to have a duty to tolerate and respect the autonomy of those who, in obedience to a duty of responsible parenthood, think abortion moral under certain conditions. In other words, the American constitution and political system are not neutral but *liberal*, and an abortion law which permits individuals to decide whether or not to terminate a pregnancy may be the appropriate law for such a liberal polity.

The commitment to freedom characteristic of constitutional government is reflected in the Declaration on Religious Freedom promulgated by the Second Vatican Council of the Roman Catholic Church in 1965. The noted American theologian, John Courtney Murray, was principally responsible for the writing of this document, and he brought to the task his experience and understanding of what he called "the American experiment" in religious liberty and church-state relations in a pluralistic society. I call attention to these emphases within the Catholic tradition because they would seem to suggest that the prolife movement and, within that movement, Roman Catholics in particular might perhaps reconsider their involvement in political campaigns to recriminalize abortion.

The Declaration on Religious Freedom was one of the more heavily debated proposals at Vatican II; over a two-year period the schema went through five drafts before being approved on December 7, 1965.[22] The final version of the Declaration was addressed to all men and women (to Christians and non-Christians alike) in purely rational and philosophical, as opposed to theological, terms. A language was sought that would be understood by legislators and governments. In the Declaration itself, traditional appeals to reason and revelation are employed. The object of religious freedom is said to be immunity from coercion in religious matters, and its foundation is the dignity of the human person. The Declaration begins with the recognition that:

> A sense of the dignity of the human person has been impressing itself more and more deeply on the consciousness of contemporary man. And the demand is increasingly made that men should act on their own judgment, enjoying and making use of a responsible freedom, not driven by coercion but motivated by a sense of duty. The demand is also made that constitutional limits should be set to the powers of government, in order that there may be no encroachment on the rightful freedom of the person and of associations.

> . . . This Vatican Synod declares that the human person has a right to religious freedom. This freedom means that all men are to be immune from coercion on the part of individuals or of social groups and of any human power, in such wise that in matters religious no one is to be forced to act in a manner contrary to his own beliefs. Nor is anyone to be restrained from acting in accordance with his own beliefs, whether privately or publicly, whether alone or in association with others, within due limits.[23]

The right to religious freedom antedates the creation of government but is to be recognized as a civil right in the constitutional law whereby society is governed. Governments must protect, not violate, this right. Moreover, the Declaration recognizes rights of conscience as well as rights to religious freedom.

> In all his activity a man is bound to follow his conscience faithfully . . . It follows that he is not to be forced to act in a manner contrary to his conscience; nor, on the other hand, is he to be restrained from acting in accord with his conscience, especially in matters religious.[24]

While government must respect and protect the right to religious freedom, it may regulate the exercise of this right in order to safeguard the public order. The public order is said to include an order of peace, an order of justice (entailing protection for the rights of others), and an order of public morality (here the morality under discussion does not involve an agreement on all specifics of morality but rather is that basic shared morality which is necessary for people to live together in society).[25]

However, beyond minimal intervention to safeguard the public order, governments may not curtail or restrict the exercise of the right to religious liberty. In what Murray called a statement of "the basic principle of the 'free society,' " the Declaration states: "For the rest, the usages of society are to be the usages of freedom in their full range. These require that the freedom of man be respected as far as possible, and curtailed only when and in so far as necessary."[26] Finally, all persons are reminded of their duties towards tolerance:

> In the exercise of their rights, individual men and social groups are bound by the moral law to have respect both for the rights of others and for their own duties toward others and for the common welfare of all. Men are to deal with their fellows in justice and civility.[27]

Undoubtedly, the twentieth century experience of the Church and the world in the face of the threat of totalitarianism underscored for the Council Fathers the need to stress constitutional limits to the powers of government. The Vatican II Declaration reads at times like a classically liberal tract, stressing the distinction between state and society, emphasizing the necessity for limited government (limited by a fundamental law or constitution), and defining religious liberty in negative terms as immunity from governmental coercion and restraint. Government is seen as the keeper of public order rather than an interventionist positive state. Some commentators have criticized what they regard as an individualistic emphasis in the Declaration; according to one theologian, "In Murray's formulation there remains a danger that one does not give enough importance to the role of the state especially in areas of social and economic justice."[28]

Questions of welfare state liberalism aside, however, it remains to spell out the implications of this Declaration on Religious Freedom for an understanding of the relation between law and morality. Charles Curran has suggested that the Declaration provides the basis for a newer understanding of law and morality which supersedes the older, more traditional conception of the need for a close fit between natural law and positive law.[29] Noting that American jurisprudence accepts the principle enunciated in the Declaration—as much freedom as possible and as little constraint as necessary—Curran contends that this newer emphasis on freedom enables

Catholics to arrive at different opinions on abortion law. "One could give importance to the existing pluralism in our society on this question and argue for certain indications allowing abortion or even for no law against abortion." Curran himself, a theologian at Catholic University, favors a law "that would allow the real possibility of free choice to the woman, including counseling and the necessary help for her in meeting all the costs of whatever decision she decides to make." He is opposed, on theoretical and practical grounds, to attempting to amend the Constitution. "Any attempts for such amendments (e.g., a states' rights or a human life amendment) will be both divisive and futile." Yet Curran is dismayed at the number of abortions performed annually in the United States. He has advocated that the Church try to influence *society* in the matter of abortion choice by establishing a nationally coordinated program voluntarily supported by Catholics and others to publicize that the Catholic Church will guarantee for any pregnant woman the financial, psychological, medical and social assistance needed to carry her child to term and to care for that child after birth. But, out of respect for the existing pluralism of American society, he does not advise the Church to employ political action to influence the *state* to recriminalize abortion.

On another occasion Curran wrote that "Within a pluralistic society one must recognize the rights of other people who might be in disagreement about the morality of a particular action."

> In our American society, the primary purpose of the law is to protect the freedom of individual people, and the benefit of the doubt must be given to that freedom. When one is confronted with an issue in which a very large number of Americans believe they should have freedom, then one can argue on the benefit of the doubt that their rights should prevail.[30]

Pluralism also figures prominently in the views of Canadian theologian and sociologist, Gregory Baum, who views abortion as an ecumenical dilemma. "The dilemma is that there are Christians who think that a liberal position on abortion is more moral, more in keeping with God's will, than the traditional one."[31] Approaching this fact from the perspective of an ecumenical theologian, Baum states: "Even when we disagree with the view on abortion defended by many Protestant thinkers, we must respect it as part of the Christian conversation about the meaning of the gospel for modern life." On the basis of these and other reflections, he concludes that Catholics should not employ language and arguments against abortion that do not recognize the ecumenical dimension of the problem. Specifically, he writes, "One cannot approve of the language and arguments adopted by Catholics in their defense of the traditional position, which imply that the defenders of abortion are immoral, selfish, insensitive, cruel, lacking in respect for life, or worse. Yet such language is found even in statements made by bishops and popes."[32]

Theologian Richard McCormick reiterates Baum's and Curran's emphasis on the need for tolerance in the abortion controversy and the duty to respect the rights of others in a pluralistic society.[33] Baum's view really exemplifies Glenn Tinder's theoretical approach to tolerance, in which Tinder sees tolerance not as a negative, second-best norm or value but as a positive aspect of life in a free, pluralistic society. Community and communication are emphasized; for example, Baum as an ecumenist assumes there is a community of Christians conversing together regarding the meaning of the Christian gospels and that Christians of all persuasions owe respect to one another despite different views on the abortion issue.

But the most important aspect of the thinking of some Roman Catholic theologians in the post-Vatican II era is the recognition of a greater distinction between state and society and a newer understanding of the relationship between law and morality. In applying this understanding to abortion politics, "The important thing to recognize is that the difference between civil law and personal morality means that one can truly be convinced that abortion is - morally wrong, but still support legislation that allows for abortion. Curran concludes:

> In the light of the present situation, I believe it is imperative for the Roman Catholic Church to recognize as clearly as possible the relationship between civil law and morality. There is a prophetic or teaching aspect to civil law, but civil law cannot be seen primarily in terms of an application of the natural law. Rather, civil law must ensure that the 'freedom of man be respected as far as possible, and curtailed only when and insofar as necessary.' The proper role of civil law is more limited than in the older Catholic understanding. The Roman Catholic Church cannot and should not always depend

on the civil law to back up its own teachings, but, rather through education, service and other means, should strive to develop an ethos in which its own moral teachings and values can be effectively mediated to its members. Even now I think the efforts of Roman Catholics could be better directed towards this work of education and service rather than absorbed by attempts to amend the Constitution.[34]

Some Cautionary Clarifications

In drawing out the implications of the doctrine of religious liberty for the political controversy over abortion in the United States, these theologians, it should be noted, are in no way asking the Roman Catholic Church to change its doctrinal condemnation of abortion, but simply to re-evaluate its approach to law and public policy on abortion. Since 1975 the Church has been engaged in a three-fold pastoral plan of education, service, and political organizing to overturn *Roe v. Wade*. In November 1981, Cardinal Terence Cooke of New York and Archbishop John Roach testified before the Senate Subcommittee on Constitutional Amendments on behalf of a states' rights amendment which would repeal the Supreme Court decision and allow Congress and the states to legislate concerning abortion. The views of theologians, ethicists, and lawyers such as Curran, Baum, McCormick, and Robert F. Drinan suggest that the American bishops ought not to press for a constitutional amendment but should concentrate their efforts on influencing society rather than government in the matter of abortion. According to Baum,

It is the task of the moral theologian to institute a detailed critique of society in order to see more precisely how violence [the violence of abortion] is nourished by injustice. . . . We must ask what are the social injustices that make people interfere with the lifegiving process in a violent manner. The repudiation of abortion should then be accompanied by a critique of society that tries to define the contradictions operative within it that foster the violence of abortion.[35]

Baum identifies two kinds of oppression in society favoring abortion: (1) the alienation imposed on people, especially, though not exclusively, on the underprivileged, by the money- and profit-oriented, maximizing economic system; and (2) the oppression of women who are denied opportunities for the self-realization open to men because they are defined solely in terms of marriage and motherhood. Baum recommends that "Catholic theologians . . . make their rejection of violence as a licit means of birth control, a statement that is politically and culturally responsible and [one which] raises the consciousness of the community in regard to the contradictions operative in it."[36]

Curran's suggestion that the Church should try to influence society by establishing a nationally coordinated program of assistance to involuntarily pregnant women has been noted above. The advantages of such a program seem apparent. It might reduce the incidence of abortion, it would demonstrate a commitment to assisting women, and at the same time it would bear witness and be prophetic within society without causing the excessive divisiveness of futile efforts to amend the Constitution. In any case, it is important to note the reasons why these theologians oppose the use of civil law to recriminalize abortion. Respect for the freedom of those who differ on the morality of abortion, tolerance of opposing views in a pluralistic society, a strong sense of the distinction between state and society, and a renewed understanding of the relation between law and morality based on the Second Vatican Council's Declaration on Religious Freedom—all provide a basis for accepting public policy on the legality of abortion that is consonant with the particular bias of the American Constitution towards liberty.

Conclusion

In the current atmosphere of abortion politics in the United States, the hypothetical prolifer who considers abortion immoral need not abandon his principles, but he must temper his convictions with (1) an awareness of the limits of the criminal sanction in eliminating immorality (the Prohibition argument); and (2) with a sense of respect for the personal autonomy, religious liberty, and freedom of conscience of those who disagree with him. A tolerant person in a pluralistic society may support social and educational efforts (including public policies helpful to women) to reduce the incidence of abortion. But through a renewed understanding of the distinction between morality and public policy, our hypothetical antiabortionist need not conclude that abortion is moral because it is now legal.

Notes

1. Robert Paul Wolff, "Beyond Tolerance," in R.P. Wolff, Herbert Marcuse, and Barrington Moore, Jr., *A Critique of Pure Tolerance* (Boston: Beacon Press, 1969), p. 4.

2. Faye Wattleton, President of the Planned Parenthood Federation of America, is reported as stating, "Right-to-Lifers are trying to impose their morality on the rest of us," in Helen Epstein, "Abortion: An Issue That Won't Go Away," *The New York Times Magazine*, March 30, 1980, p. 67. The term "Neo-Fascist" was used by Ellen Willis to describe the Right-to-Life movement in her report of Judge Dooling's Federal District Court decision in *Harris v. McRae, The Village Voice*, January, 1980.

3. Mary Mahowald, "Abortion: Toward Continuing the Dialogue," *Cross Currents*, Vol. 29, No. 3 (Fall 1979).

4. Charles Frankel, "The Continuing Claims of Liberalism," in Dorothy James, *Outside, Looking In: Critiques of American Policies and Institutions, Left and Right* (New York: Harper and Row, 1972), p. 3. Some standard liberal writings on tolerance are, of course, John Locke's *Essay on Toleration* and John Stuart Mill's *Essay on Liberty*. See also D.J. Manning, *Liberalism* (New York: St. Martin's, 1976), chapter two; "Tolerance, A Symposium," with articles by G. Tinder, R.P. Wolff, and N.O. Keohane in *Polity*, Vol. VI, No. 4 (Summer 1974), pp. 445–487; and Glenn Tinder, *Tolerance: Toward A New Civility* (Amherst: University of Massachusetts Press, 1976).

5. William A. Galston, "Perfectionism and the Neutral State: Dilemmas of Kantian Liberalism," Paper presented at the 1981 Annual Meeting of the American Political Science Association, p. 1.

6. According to Rawls, the liberal state rests on a conception of "equality between human beings as moral persons, as creatures having a conception of the good and capable of a sense of justice . . . Systems of ends are not ranked in value . . ." Rawls, *A Theory of Justice* (Cambridge: Harvard Univ. Press, 1971), p. 19. Again, Rawls defines primary goods as "things that every rational man is presumed to want, whatever else he wants . . . These goods normally have a use whatever a person's rational plan of life." *Ibid.*, pp. 62 and 92. Robert Nozick finds it incredible that there could be one best society for everyone to live in or that one collectively specified and promoted good could be best for the enormous variety of human types; for Nozick excellence is inherently pluralistic. See his *Anarchy, State, and Utopia* (New York: Basic Books, 1974), pp. 309–12. For Ronald Dworkin, the liberal state rests on the liberal theory of equality; "government must be neutral on . . . the question of the good life . . . Political decisions must be, so far as is possible, independent of any particular conception of the good life, or of what gives value to life." See his essay, "Liberalism," in Stuart Hampshire, ed., *Public and Private Morality* (Cambridge: Cambridge Univ. Press, 1978), p. 127. And most recently, Bruce Ackerman has advanced the "Neutrality Principle" as the linchpin of liberal theory. It constrains the kinds of reasons that may validly be offered

in defense of social arrangements (that is, it operates much the way Rawls' "veil of ignorance" functions in the original position). According to the Neutrality Principle, "No reason [that purports to justify a social arrangement] is a good reason if it requires the power holder to assert (a) that his conception of the good is better than that asserted by any of his fellows, or (b) that, regardless of his conception of the good, he is intrinsically superior to one or more of his fellow citizens." Bruce Ackerman, *Social Justice in the Liberal State* (New Haven: Yale Univ. Press, 1980), p. 11. I am indebted to William Galston for these references; see his "Perfectionism and the Neutral State: Dilemmas of Kantian Liberalism," (unpublished).

7. Janet Benshoof and Judith Levin, "Current Legal Issues in Abortion Litigation," paper prepared for the Biennial Conference of the American Civil Liberties Union, Mount Vernon College, Washington D.C., June 16–19, 1979, p. 14.

8. At the Federal District Court level, Judge John Dooling rejected the argument that the Hyde Amendment represented an unconstitutional establishment of religion; however, he did recognize that women might seek to terminate a pregnancy for religious reasons or reasons of conscience, and he therefore concluded that the Hyde Amendment violated the free exercise clause of the First Amendment. In its decision in *Harris* v. *McRae* (1980) 448 U.S.———, the Supreme Court upheld Judge Dooling's ruling on the establishment argument, but dismissed appellees' arguments concerning the free exercise clause because the parties concerned lacked standing to raise a free exercise challenge to the Hyde Amendment. Justice Stewart wrote: "None alleged, much less proved, that she sought an abortion under compulsion of religious belief. . . . [The parties] therefore lack the persona stake in the controversy needed to confer standing to raise such a challenge to the Hyde Amendment." *Harris* v. *McRae*, 100 S. Ct. 2671, at 2690.

9. John Garvey, "Beyond Proof and Disproof: The Religions of Pro-choice and Pro-life," *Commonweal*, Vol. CVIII, No. 12 (June 19, 1981), p. 360.

10. Daniel Callahan, "Abortion: Some Ethical Issues," in Thomas Shannon, ed., *Bioethics* (New York: Paulist Press, 1976), p. 17.

11. Recall, for example, Socrates' argument concerning the laws in *The Crito* (Plato, *The Last Days of Socrates*, trans. Hugh Tredennick, Penguin Classics, 1969, pp. 28–39).

12. James C. Mohr, *Abortion in America* (New York: Oxford University Press, 1978), pp. 262–263.

13. Galston, "Perfectionism and the Neutral State: Dilemmas of Kantian Liberalism," p. 10.

14. See my "Governing Abortion Policy," in James Foster, Richard Gambitta, and Marlynn May, eds., *Governing Through Courts* (Los Angeles: Sage Publications, Inc., 1981) for a summary of the impact studies done to date. See also James Trussell, Jane Menken, B.L. Lindheim and Barbara Vaughn, "The Impact of Restricting Medicaid Financing for Abortion," *Family Planning Perspectives*, Vol. 12, No. 3 (May–June, 1980), pp. 120–130.

15. Representatives from Planned Parenthood, the National Abortion Rights Action League, the Center for Constitutional Rights, and the American Civil Liberties Union frequently cite the obstacles to strict law enforcement, ranging from the specter of police presence in physicians' offices to check for possible evidence of induced as opposed to spontaneous abortions, or to check for the use of contraceptives such as the intrauterine device which function as abortefacients.

16. One of the more telling arguments for legalizing abortion concerns the problem of discriminatory enforcement of antiabortion laws. Mohr has stated this argument forcefully. Noting that in the twentieth century a substantial number of American women continued to seek and to have abortions despite nineteenth century statutes designed to make them unavailable, he wrote:

"By itself, of course, the violation of a law is not an especially persuasive argument for its repeal; few people would advocate the legalization of a homicide, for example, simply because a certain number of Americans continue to kill one another each year in spite of the criminal sanctions against doing so. But the evidence about the continued practice of abortion in the United States throughout the twentieth century raised some rather more difficult problems. Wealthy women could afford to travel to those jurisdictions where the antiabortion laws were not rigidly enforced; poor women could not. Wealthy women, it was alleged, could arrange for safe and 'legal' abortions by persuading their physicians to interpret the therapeutic clauses of various anti-abortion laws very loosely, while poor women could not. The nation's antiabortion laws were thus perceived as discriminating against poor, frequently non-white, women in an era of heightened sensitivity to egalitarianism. It was also the poor who were more likely to die at the hands of the gross incompetents who preyed upon the desperation of those without sufficient funds either to terminate their pregnancy safely and discreetly or to make socially acceptable arrangements both for the period of confinement and for the subsequent care and upbringing of the child, through adoption or other means. Unenforceability, in other words, might be one thing, but discriminatory enforcement was quite another." Mohr, *Abortion in America*, p. 255.

17. See, for example, Cicero's definition of the state in *De Republica*, Book I, Ch. XXV (G.H. Sabine trans., Ohio State University Press, 1929): "The commonwealth, then, is the people's affairs; and the people is not every group of men, associated in any manner, but is the coming together of a considerable number of men who are united by a common agreement about law and rights and by the desire to participate in mutual advantages." On this view, a common consensus about what is right, a shared morality, is as essential to the definition of a state as is mutual advantage, interest, and utility.

18. Patrick Devlin, *The Enforcement of Morals* (London: Oxford University Press, 1965), especially chapter one, "Morals and the Criminal Law" which was the Second Maccabean Lecture in Jurisprudence delivered to

the British Academy in 1959. This address provoked a response by H.L. Hart, "Immorality and Treason," and a longer book by Hart, *Law, Liberty and Morality* (New York: Vintage, 1963). The so-called Hart/Devlin Debate on the use of the criminal law to enforce morals is discussed in Richard Wasserstrom's anthology, *Morality and the Law* (Belmont, Calif., Wadsworth Publishing Company, 1971).

19. Daniel Callahan, *Abortion: Law, Choice and Morality* (New York: The MacMillan Company, 1970), pp. 486–487.

20. Actually, periodic Gallup polls since 1975 have shown a fairly consistent breakdown in public opinion; approximately sixty percent of Americans think that abortion should be legally available under certain conditions, while twenty percent favor abortion under no circumstances and twenty percent favor abortion under all circumstances. There may, that is, be a sufficiently broad, extensive, shared moral consensus to justify the legality of abortion. However, public opinion on abortion has always been open to widely divergent interpretations, depending on the particular conditions in which abortions should be permitted. See for example Charles Curran, "Abortion: Legal and Public Funding Aspects," in his *Transition and Tradition* (Notre Dame, Ind.: Univ. of Notre Dame Press, 1979), pp. 232–233; Judith Blake, "The Supreme Court's Abortion Decisions and Public Opinion in the United States," *Population and Development Review*, Vol. 3, Nos. 1 & 2 (March and June, 1977), pp. 45–62; Judith Blake, "The Abortion Decisions: Judicial Review and Public Opinion," in *Abortion: New Directions for Policy Studies*, ed. E. Manier, W.T. Liu, and D. Solomon (Notre Dame, Indiana: University of Notre Dame Press, 1977) pp. 51–82; and Judith Blake, and Jorge H. del Pinal, "Predicting Polar Attitudes toward Abortion in the United States, in *Abortion Parley*, ed. James T. Burtchaell (New York: Andrews and McMeel, Inc., 1980). Also see Andrew Greeley, *The American Catholic: A Social Portrait* (New York: Basic Books, 1977), pp. 245–247, for a discussion of Catholic attitudes towards abortion.

21. The absence of a shared moral consensus in society on the abortion issue is crucial in this argument, as is the pluralistic character of society. These factors make the argument for tolerance of the lone dissenter in this case different from the case of the lone dissenter who views murder as right. There is no controversy in society over the rightness or wrongness of murder.

22. Two interesting accounts of the drafting process are John Courtney Murray's "The Declaration of Religious Freedom: A Moment in Its Legislative History," in J.C. Murray, S.J., ed., *Religious Liberty: An End and A Beginning* (New York: MacMillan, 1966), pp. 15–42; and Gregory Baum, "The Declaration on Religious Freedom: Development of Its Doctrinal Basis," in G. Baum, *Ecumenical Theology No. 2* (New York: Paulist Press, 1967), pp. 247–262.

23. Declaration on Religious Freedom of the Second Vatican Council, reprinted in J.C. Murray, *Religious Liberty: An End and A Beginning*, pp. 162 and 166–167.

24. *Ibid.*, section 3, pp. 169–170.

25. *Ibid.*, pp. 176–177 and footnote 20; this is not an official footnote in the text but an unofficial comment expressing John Courtney Murray's view.

26. *Ibid.*, section 7, pp. 177–178.

27. *Ibid.*

28. Charles E. Curran, "Civil Law and Christian Morality: Abortion and the Churches," in *Conversations* published by the Graymoor Ecumenical Institute (Graymoor/Garrison, N.Y.: Spring 1975), p. 9.

29. Charles E. Curran, "Abortion: Legal and Public Funding Aspects," in his *Transition and Tradition* (Notre Dame, Indiana: University of Notre Dame Press, 1979), p. 236; also see his "Civil Law and Christian Morality: Abortion and the Churches."

30. Curran, "Civil Law and Christian Morality," p. 15.

31. Gregory Baum, "Abortion: An Ecumenical Dilemma," in *Bioethics*, ed. Thomas A. Shannon (New York: Paulist Press, 1976), p. 28.

32. *Ibid.*, p. 27.

33. Richard A. McCormick, "Abortion: Rules for Debate," in his *How Brave A New World?: Dilemmas in Bioethics* (Garden City, N.Y.: Doubleday, 1981).

34. Curran, "Civil Law and Christian Morality," pp. 15–16.

35. Baum, "Abortion: An Ecumenical Dilemma," p. 33.

36. *Ibid.*, p. 34.

10

Biopolicy and the Courts:
Reversible Sterilization and Reproductive Choice

Robert H. Blank

There is little doubt that we are swiftly being drawn into an era in which traditional notions of human existence and the nature of human life will be severely tested. Furthermore, these challenges to what, until recently, have been accepted as given promise eventually to alter our views of what it means to be a human being. As we acquire the technical capability to intervene directly in the biological nature of our species, we will be forced to make difficult decisions as to whether or not to exercise these new-found options.

This paper examines public policy dimensions of emerging technologies in one of the most sensitive and fundamental levels of human existence—reproduction. An array of reproduction intervention techniques already are producing formidable ethical questions concerning the definition of the beginnings of human life. Procedures such as *in vitro* fertilization, cryopreservation of semen, and prenatal diagnosis and screening, although in the early stages of development, are fast becoming compelling public issues.

The policy problems raised by reproductive technology are among the most volatile and incisive issues imaginable. They do not fit the traditional mold of political issues which are resolved through a bargaining and compromise process. Instead, reproductive issues reflect fundamental value conflicts over meanings of human life and death, which themselves represent basic tenets of a variety of religious and secular ethical frameworks. Societies do not

Robert H. Blank is an associate professor of political science at Northern Illinois University.

often debate fundamental definitions, but when they do, volatility results. Moreover, the rapid pace of technological change has created these value conflicts over a very short time span whereas values themselves normally change gradually over generations through a socialization process. Although there is no doubt that these issues are difficult to deal with politically, thereby explaining the tendency of many officials to avoid them when possible, the rapid advances in technology make it mandatory that action be taken at least to discuss the issues within the political context.

In addition to influencing the development of reproductive technologies, the government might become involved in the individual or aggregate use of these techniques. The most likely forms such intervention might take include encouragement of use by provision of free services, education programs, or financial inducements, or, conversely, discouragement of use by reducing accessibility or imposing direct control. At the extremes, individual use of specific reproductive technologies might be mandated or prohibited. Examples of such action are, respectively, compulsory genetic screening programs and legal constraints on voluntary sterilization. The range of options available to the government to intervene in the procreative process is vast and, despite cultural predispositions favoring individual reproductive choice in the United States, many policy controversies will center on questions of the proper role of the government in individual applications.

The Courts and Biopolicy

Given the nature of the issues raised by reproductive technologies, it is obvious that the courts are destined to play a major role in resolving them. Questions of reproductive privacy and individual autonomy are inherent in application of these techniques as are broader concerns of due process, equal protection of the laws, and so forth. Not surprisingly, most government activity in issues of reproduction to date has been concentrated in the courts. Actual involvement of the courts in reproductive litigation has had significant policy ramifications in spite of the ongoing debate over whether or not courts ought to be or are capable of having a policy-making role. Critics argue that inherent limitations on judicial policy making preclude an active role in the policy realm of biomedical research. For Schoenberg (1979), anything with as few legal precedents and as politically controversial as the definition of "life" and "death" should be left to the elected representatives of the people to determine. More specifically, because the judicial process is passive and retrospective, it is viewed as too slow to react to rapid technological progress. Elliot L. Segall, president of the American Society of Law and Medicine, is quoted by Arehart Treichel (1980:156) as contending that the "U.S. legal system is one generation behind the medical science."

Also, because the primary function of the court is to resolve conflicts centering on the rights and obligations of the parties before it, individual cases supposedly are decided on evidence produced by the parties to each case and not on the grounds of public policy considerations. Although particular decisions might serve as implicit principles with important policy implications, the courts "generally refrain from deciding individual cases on the bases of deliberately establishing public policy controls" (Green, 1976:171). In those instances where judicial decisions have consequences beyond the immediate parties to the case, according to Nakamura and Smallwood (1980:107), there often are "serious difficulties in communicating new legal requirements to populations that are not yet within the jurisdiction of courts." As a result, decisions are episodic, unpredictable, and often inconsistent. Case-by-case adjudication across a wide variety of state and federal courts adds to the confusion. Due to the slowness of this process, Green (1967) concludes that we cannot rely on the courts to protect society against rapid technological developments. "Judgemade rules of law always come after, and usually long after, the potential for injury has been demonstrated." Nelkin (1977:71) adds that new technological developments such as fetal research "continually raise problems that require reanalysis of legal principles."

Proponents of an active role of the courts counter that especially in sensitive policy areas the courts do have a role to play. For instance, the same constraints alleged to prevent the courts from making policy in human reproduction were present in civil rights, but the courts initiated great policy changes in those areas. The common law American legal tradition allows for judicial innovation. One need only look at the broad impact of *Roe v. Wade* or at the recent "wrongful life" torts (Blank, 1982) and the pressures they exert on physicians to utilize prenatal diagnostic techniques (Powledge, 1979) to see social consequences extending beyond the original litigation. The expanding concept of fundamental rights,

217

especially as it relates to privacy and self-determination in reproductive matters, and the notion of "compelling state interest" plainly demonstrate the conceivable influence of the courts on the application of reproductive technology.

Despite the limitations of the courts, they are at this stage unmistakably involved in the resolution of individual uses of reproductive technologies. As Tribe (1973:98) suggests, at the expressive and symbolic levels the law has a potential role as a catalyst for needed changes in the system. The law dramatizes injustices and channels executive as well as legislative attention toward areas needing more systematic reform or comprehensive regulation. Although the law reflects public values, it also induces cultural and moral change through alterations in legal doctrine. Despite the fragmented, oblique and at times contradictory policy implications of the judicial system, it appears likely that the most critical reproductive issues ultimately will reach the Supreme Court for resolution. Contrarily, despite the indications that the courts by default are being cast into these issues, it is unlikely that the courts as now constituted are either capable or willing to play a critical role in setting societal priorities and goals regarding reproductive technology or in assessing the social consequences in any systematic manner.

One of the most persistent and longstanding social policy issues in reproductive choice is that of sterilization. Next to abortion, sterilization provokes intense reactions, especially when it is conducted without informed consent of the subject. New technological developments in human sterilization promise to complicate rather than resolve the constellation of constitutional, political and social problems surrounding the termination of fertility. Most prominent among this array of emerging techniques are reversible sterilization methods which are considerably less intrusive than conventional surgical techniques. This paper examines the current technical and legal context of human sterilization and explicates the ramifications of recent innovations in reversible sterilization for public law.

Sterilization Techniques and Usage

Until very recently, sterilization once performed was a permanent condition for both males and females. Although a multiplicity of techniques were available, they were all irreversible. Although no attempt is made here to detail these conventional sterilization methods (see Brown and Schanzer, 1982) they briefly are reviewed in order to (1) demonstrate the extent of their intrusiveness; (2) show why their application has elicited considerable debate; and (3) contrast them with reversible sterilization innovations.

Surgical intervention in the male to occlude the vas deferens and thereby prevent the passage of sperm from the testes is termed *vasectomy*. Although it has been performed at least since 1894, vasectomy has become a widely available and popular method of fertility control. The most common techniques for vasectomy include: (1) removing a portion of the vas and tying the ends; (2) fulgurating the ends by electrocautery; (3) applying two or more clips or staples through the vas; or (4) inserting valves or other obstructive devices in the vas. Often these techniques are used in combination to effectuate total occlusion of the vas.

There is considerably more variation in female sterilization techniques than in vasectomies. Although female sterilization lagged behind male sterilization in frequency until the 1970s, because of significant advances in and simplification of tubal sterilization techniques it now outnumbers vasectomies in the United States. Most modern methods of female sterilization concentrate on ways to block effectively the fallopian tubes so that sperm and egg can not unite. The most common methods of tubal occlusion used include: (1) ligation, in which the tube is cut and the ends tied off; (2) resection, in which a section of the tube is removed; (3) fulguration, in which the tube is cauterized; and (4) a variety of applications of clips, bands, rings and chemicals to the fallopian tube.

Further variation is added by introduction of different methods for gaining access to the fallopian tubes. The three most common approaches are through (1) an abdominal incision; (2) a vaginal incision; or (3) a transcervical route without an incision. The three major operative procedures using an abdominal method of access are the laparotomy, mini-laparotomy and laparoscopy. The laparotomy is the conventional method of access to the fallopian tube and is most commonly used with the Pomeroy technique, still the most popular method of female sterilization. In this approach, the tube is picked up near the midsection to form a loop, the base of the loop is ligated with an absorbable suture, and the top of the loop is cut off. As the suture material dissolves, the ends of the tube pull apart. The "mini-lap" and the laparoscopy utilize much smaller abdominal incisions and can, therefore, be used under local anesthesia on an out-patient basis. Other operative techniques included the colpotomy and the culdoscopy which use an incision in the posterior area of the vaginal canal behind the cervix to gain access to the fallopian tubes.

The most extreme and irreversible method of female sterilization is the hysterectomy or surgical removal of the uterus. Given the wide variety of other less extreme procedures now available, most observers reject this technique specifically for fertility control purposes and contend it should be performed for sterilization only when other gynecologic problems are present (Saidi and Zainie, 1980:44). This is especially critical in light of the recent emphasis placed on the importance of using methods which promise the highest probability of reversibility.

The Growing Demand for Reversible Sterilization

The interest over reversible sterilization can be understood best by examination of the convergence of social and technical patterns. First, voluntary sterilization has become a popular method of birth control, the only truly effective method. Studies of trends in contraception practices demonstrate a clear and definite direction toward increased use of sterilization for birth control (Westoff, 1976). Although male and female sterilization techniques were introduced a century ago, voluntary surgical sterilization was used infrequently until the 1950s and 1960s. Not until the 1970s, however, did sterilization become a major method of fertility control worldwide. Speidel and Ravenholt (1978:260) note that the confluence of a number of factors has resulted in this recent and rapid upswing in the use of sterilization. Worldwide, sterilization is now the single most used means of fertility control, while in the United States where over 13 million persons have been sterilized, it is second to the pill and gaining. The factors contributing to this upswing include: (1) liberalization of legal and policy constraints on the availability of sterilization; (2) an intense demand for a one-time effective means of fertility control; (3) greatly increased efforts to provide sterilization services; and (4) major refinements in sterilization technology, particularly female sterilization, which make it practical in a greater variety of settings than in the recent past.

Sterilization is viewed by growing numbers of Americans as a safe and sure form of contraception. The development of oral contraceptives and Intrauterine Devices (IUDs) in the 1960's gave couples increased reproductive control. Initially, both the pill and the IUD were hailed as offering safe and effective means of fertility control. By 1968, however, the public was being warned by the government that the pill was not as safe as earlier suggested and that some women were at high risk for a variety of diseases if they used the pill. The supposed final answer to reproductive control, it seems, had serious drawbacks. The IUD suffered a similar fate in that initial enthusiasm was soon dampened by evidence of serious and in some cases fatal pelvic inflammatory infections in IUD users. Ironically, in some users these infections scarred the fallopian tubes, resulting in permanent sterility. While research continues on IUDs, and this method remains the choice of a minority of women, again as with the pill, subsequent data demonstrate it is not the panacea it was first touted to be.

Long-term fertility control then is as elusive as it was two decades ago. With most couples electing to have small families, often while they are young, they are faced with upwards of 20 years of fertility control after completion of their family. Rather than using a form of contraception which at best is inconvenient and not fully effective and at worst a significant hazard to the woman's health, more couples are opting for sterilization as a permanent contraception solution.

Reinforcing and probably extending this demand by couples for a fail-safe, permanent method of contraception, a variety of organizations have expended considerable effort to provide sterilization services to individuals who desire them. The Association for Voluntary Sterilization, Inc. (AVS) and the Planned Parenthood Federation of America, Inc. have spearheaded these efforts and both have been active in calling for the elimination of statutory constraints on voluntary sterilization and the provision of such services as part of an overall population planning program. AVS emphasizes the individual's right to know about and choose sterilization through its nationwide education program. Planned Parenthood presents sterilization as one aspect of an overall population control program and has been a prime force behind the establishment of family planning clinics in the United States. These and other organizations across the nation have done much to inform the public of the options for sterilization.

The increase in demand for sterilization can also be traced to substantial refinements in sterilization techniques. This is most apparent in female sterilization procedures. What once required inpatient surgery under general anesthesia with lengthy recovery periods, now normally is available on an outpatient basis with local anesthesia and minimal inconvenience for the patient. This not only has increased the acceptability of sterilization, but also has overcome and relieved the need for scarce and expensive medical care personnel and facilities. The relative cost of sterilization vis-a-vis the long-term costs of alternative contraceptive methods has decreased as a result of these new procedures. Although most individuals choosing sterilization are reasonably certain they wish to terminate their fertility permanently, some would like a form of safety net in case of unforeseen situational changes.

A second and complicating factor which is producing an increased demand for reversible methods specifically, is the extremely high divorce-remarriage rate of the 1970s and 1980s. With heightened frequency, individuals who voluntarily and enthusiastically were sterilized during their first marriage are remarrying and then finding that their sterilized state is unacceptable under the changed marital circumstances. A renewed interest in childbearing with their new partner often results in their attempt to have the sterilization reversed. According to Brosens and Winston (1978), there are also "a substantial number of sterilized women (and men) whose main concern is not so much the restoration of childbearing but who demand reversal because they feel incomplete as women or because they feel their new consort may find them unsatisfactory as a marital partner in their sterilized state." While there is considerable disagreement over the proportion of patients regretting being sterilized, Winston, Schwykart and Kutner (1973) found the range to be between 1.3 and 15.0 percent in the 22 published studies they reviewed. Even use of the lower figure translates to approximately 200,000 persons, given the large number already sterilized. Also, there is evidence that a growing number of "career women," some of whom had been sterilized, are deciding late in life that they want children. Whatever the motivation, in each case there is a salient and accelerating demand for reversal by both men and women. This, despite the fact that most knew it would be an irreversible process when they underwent sterilization voluntarily.

Until recently, most of these individuals had no technical recourse to their plight. However, new advances in microsurgery and reconstructive techniques have led to a considerable increase in the number of reversal operations being conducted and in the success rates of these procedures. According to Brosens and Winston (1978), "There has been an explosion in the interest of microsurgery amongst gynecologists largely because of women requesting reversal." The same holds true for urologists regarding vasectomy reversals. Recent advances in sterilization procedures themselves, such as the application of tubal rings or clips which reduce trauma to the tubes, promise even greater success of reversals in the future. Social patterns, then, are combining with the development of more sophisticated sterilization and reversal procedures to make reversible sterilization a more common practice in the western world.

Although considerable strides have been made in the last decade to reverse "permanent" sterilization procedures, the Association for Voluntary Sterilization considers standard procedure to dictate that women undergoing tubal sterilization and men undergoing vasectomy continue to be advised that the procedures are intended to be irreversible. They are permanent methods of fertility control which *may* be reversible. The reason for the caution relates to the complexity of the factors influencing reversibility as well as the yet preliminary data on reversal. Even with the skills of a highly trained surgeon using the most refined instruments and newest techniques, the chances for reversal of tubal ligations and vasectomies are not high. Additionally, while some men and women are ready candidates for reversal surgery, others are not. Although the demand from women for surgical reversal is expected to increase and improved microsurgical techniques and highly trained surgeons will likely boost the success rates, current research emphasis is being directed at techniques that are designed to be reversible from the start.

Reversible Sterilization Techniques

There are many approaches to reversible sterilization currently being tested. However, the technique which appears to offer the greatest promise to drastically revise our concepts of sterilization as well as contraception is the removable silicone plug (RSP). This method, which is presently undergoing clinical trials for the Food and Drug Administration, involves the occlusion of the fallopian tubes with flexible silicone plugs. Unlike past sterilization procedures, RSP's are designed to be removed at a later date in order to "reverse" the procedure and permit childbearing (Wimberley, 1982:1).

This procedure makes use of recent developments in fiber optics to visualize the installation of the silicone in the fallopian tubes. A hysteroscope is introduced through the cervix and into the uterine cavity. A guide assembly and obturator tip are then introduced via the hysteroscope surrounding an inner tube which serves as a flow tube for the series of solutions. The tubal ostium is visualized and sealed by moving the guide tip assembly to a position parallel to the cornual section of the tube. The guide tip assembly is then filled with a diluted concentration of methylene blue which is injected into the oviduct to test whether or not there is a preexistent tubal blockage. If the methylene blue flows through the oviduct, the liquid silicone mixture is pumped through the inner tube of the guide assembly and into the oviduct where it solidifies in approximately five minutes.

Following solidification of the silicone, the inner tube is withdrawn and the obturator tip released. The final step involves removal of the outer tube, leaving the tip in place attached to the fallopian plug. This tip later serves as the means of pulling the plug if reversal of the procedure becomes desirable. Following this procedure which takes approximately 15 to 20 minutes for each oviduct, x-rays are taken to confirm the plugs' satisfactory formation. A successful procedure will result in plugs that fill the entire length of the fallopian tubes and which are of greater diameter at each end of the tube than in the center. This assures that the plugs

will remain in place until they are removed by grasping the re-
trieval loop with forceps and pulling.

The RSP procedure entails less than one hour in an out-patient
surgical facility with several followup sessions. Reversal, "pulling
the plug" is expected to be a relatively simple office procedure
although clinical testing thus far has focused only on the implantation aspect. Preliminary reports show a success rate in occluding
the fallopian tubes ranging from 73 percent (Reed and Erb, 1980) to
86 percent (Cooper, et al. 1982). Reed and Erb (1980) speculate that
there will always be a group of about 10 percent for whom this
method will be inappropriate. Conversely, with improved patient
selection and refinements in instrumentation, they estimate that 90
percent of all women will be able to use RSP.

Wimberley (1982), however, cautions that questions of reversibility are yet unanswered. While reversibility among rabbits has
been demonstrated (Erb, 1976), no trials of reversibility in humans
to date have been conducted. Although intuitively it seems reasonable that once the plugs are removed, ovulation should return, the
fallopian tubes have proven highly sensitive to intrusion. According to Wimberley (1982:5):

> At issue is whether prolonged occlusion of the fallopian tubes with
> formed-in-place silicone plugs will result in traumatic or degener-
> ative tissue changes. Only further clinical studies will resolve this
> concern.

At this point, however, this procedure shows great promise of
offering an easily reversible method of sterilization and, thereby,
challenges currently held notions of sterilization as an irreversible
process. In the least, this relatively noninvasive method of tubal
occlusion is expected to replace a variety of surgical methods of
female sterilization currently in use.

As noted earlier, there is evidence that, should a safe and effective means of sterilization be developed which is also easily reversible, there would be substantial demand by women. A recent
survey of patients of reproductive age found that the number of
women intending to be sterilized at some time in the future would
more than double if reversal could be 95 percent effective (Shain,
1979). While Henry, et al. (1980) contend that this goal of 95 percent
reversal is unrealistic for the near future, these limited findings

demonstrate how important the reversibility aspect of sterilization is to many women. As noted by Sciarra and Zatuchni (1978:274):

> . . . there seems to be a considerable demand for reversal; as reversal services become more widely available, the demand will probably be even greater. In the past whenever a service such as abortion or sterilization has been offered, demand has far exceeded the need indicated by surveys.

Once people hear that successful reversals are being achieved or that new reversible techniques are available they will be encouraged to consider reversal of their own sterilization or opt for sterilization if it can later be reversed. Initial successes, then, serve as stimuli for increased demand for reversal services. It is probably not too early for third-party payers to investigate potential demand and costs of providing these services. Responses from five of the physicians involved in FDA clinical trials on the RSP technique differed as to how long it would be before the method is widely used as a means of sterilization. Estimates ranged from two or three years to seven or eight years (Wimberley, 1982). Furthermore, although none of the respondents foresaw RSP as replacing the birth control pill as the most popular form of contraception in the near future, estimates as to how long it would be before the method is widely used as a nonpermanent contraceptive ranged from two to ten years. Even on the outside, then, the primary researchers envision the widespread use of RSP within the decade.

In addition to RSPs, a large variety of other approaches have been proposed to block the flow of the egg from the ovaries through the fallopian tube. Trials are now proceeding with many of these methods including fimbrial prothesis (Laufe, 1978), hug plastic clips (Craft, 1978), tubal hoods (El Kady, et al., 1978), teflon plugs (Meeker, 1978) and a variety of innovative procedures involving burying the fimbrial end of the fallopian tubes (Droegemueller, et al., 1978). Although theoretically these procedures may be more reversible, according to Henry, et al. (1980:C107), "there is no information available to date either on reversals performed or on subsequent pregnancy rates."

Although most attention on reversible methods is being directed currently toward women, some efforts are being made to make future male sterilization simple and reversible as well. According to

Lubell and Frischer (1976:108ff), future procedural prospects for male sterilization are: (1) non-surgical methods of chemical sterilization (transcutaneous vas occlusion); (2) pharmacological sterilizing agents; (3) vas occlusive plugs and prosthetics similar to RSP in women; and (4) reversible valves or other devices which can be switched on or off to regulate passage of the sperm through the vas. Despite the interest in reversible techniques for males, however, most research continues to focus on reversible procedures for women.

Sterilization Policy and the New Technologies

In whatever form, human sterilization clearly illustrates the distinction between individual choice and eugenic motivations for use. When based on informed and voluntary consent of the person undergoing the procedure, sterilization is the most effective means of fertility control, thereby extending reproductive choice of the user. Contrarily, nonconsensual, or in some cases compulsory, sterilization raises ominous policy questions of a basic constitutional nature. If the distinction between voluntary and nonconsensual sterilization was precise, the dilemma would be lessened considerably. Unfortunately, that is not the case and most of the controversy over sterilization centers on situations where the actual choice of the potential subject is indeterminate.

The dimension of consent is further obscured by tangential distinctions (see figure 1). These include the individual choice versus eugenic and the therapeutic versus nontherapeutic aspects of sterilization. Fully informed consent can be either present or absent in situations where sterilization is medically indicated as well as when used for fertility control. Although there is a possibility that a person might voluntarily consent to be sterilized for eugenic purposes, for instance a bearer of a dominant deleterious trait such as Huntington's disease, usually the use of the term eugenic refers to imposed social control and precludes true free consent. Failure to clarify these multiple motivations and frameworks for each type of sterilization application leads to considerable confusion in much of the literature and in court decisions. Often what appears to be a clearcut case is in actuality a complex dilemma when placed in a broader conceptual context. Although the legal and political issues

227

Figure 1 Three Dimensions of Sterilization

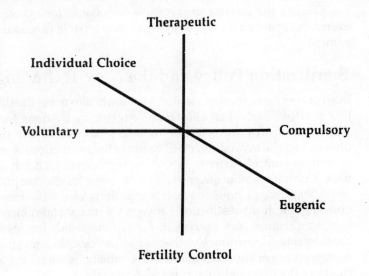

surrounding voluntary sterilization are far from resolved (Blank, forthcoming), this discussion focuses on the current legal context of nonconsensual sterilization in the United States and examines potential policy problems raised by the introduction of reversible techniques.

Non-Consensual Sterilization Policy

Initial interest in sterilization in America was based on social control not individual choice grounds. Early legislation was motivated both by medical theories which postulated that mental illness was inherited and by social elitist theories stemming from social Darwinism (see Haller, 1983). In 1907 Indiana was the first state to pass a Eugenic Sterilization Law based on the logic that retardation could be eliminated simply by sterilizing of relevant target groups of "unfit" individuals. Eventually, 30 states passed legislation that empowered mental and corrective institutions to sterilize inmates. In some states such as Washington, statutes extended punitive sterilization of certain felons, especially those convicted of rape, and to chronic alcoholics, derelicts and so forth.

The extent to which the eugenic logic dominated American society is best illustrated by Justice Oliver Wendell Holmes's affirmation in *Buck v. Bell* (1927) of the power of the state to impose sterilization as an appropriate exercise of its police power.

> We have seen more than once that the public welfare may call upon the best citizens for their lives. It would be strange if it could not call upon those who already sap the strength of the state for these lesser sacrifices, often not felt to be such by those concerned, in order to prevent our being swamped with incompetence.

Holmes's dictum that "three generations of imbeciles are enough" is a cogent reminder of the impact of even faulty medical theory on the courts. Its callous disregard for the rights of the individuals concerned was not questioned until the Court in *Skinner v. Oklahoma* (1942) held violative of equal protection a state law authorizing involuntary sterilization of particular felons. According to Justice Douglas, marriage and procreation are civil rights of man, fundamental to the very existence and survival of the race.

> The power to sterilize, if exercised, may have subtle, far-reaching and devastating effects. . . . There is no redemption for the individual whom the law touches. Any experiment which the state conducts is to his irreparable injury. He is forever deprived of a basic liberty.

Although *Skinner* did not address directly the question of eugenic sterilization, it raised procreative freedom to a fundamental right which cannot be readily violated.

Although the most glaring constitutional deficiencies have been recognized by the courts since *Skinner,* revised statutes have been upheld by a succession of courts (Sherlock and Sherlock, 1982:945). In most cases, these revisions reflect a noticeable shift in rationale for sterilization from the largely discounted eugenic arguments to a concern for the best interests of the affected individuals or their potential progeny. Three related themes are apparent in the resurgence of proposed sterilization legislation since the 1960s. The first is the presumption that the mentally retarded are incapable of being fit parents. Therefore, to protect their potential as well as actual progeny, the retarded ought to be sterilized without their consent, since informed consent on their part is impossible. A second approach is paternalistic and argues that sterilization is in the best interest of the affected person. The onset of menstrual periods and eventually pregnancy represent unnecessary burdens on the sexually active retarded and by sterilizing them we are freeing them from these emotional and physical burdens.

A third theme in some of the proposed legislation is directed toward women on public assistance and is obviously utilitarian at its base. Welfare recipients unable themselves to control their fertility, it is argued, represent a drain on the taxpayers. In order to relieve what is perceived to be an unfair burden on the state in caring for numerous children where the parents have no responsibility or ability to do so, coerced sterilization has been proposed in at least ten states. Although none of the bills based on this latter argument have passed, persons on public assistance are vulnerable to such pressures since general public sentiment is strongly in favor of such measures. Obviously, the situation is politically explosive since many of the targets of such legislation are members of minority groups.

Many such operations reportedly have been performed as welfare workers threatened recipients with a loss of benefits unless they agreed to be sterilized. If the estimate of 63,000 federally-funded sterilizations in 1977 is accurate, it would be surprising if many were not coerced in some manner. Many women purportedly have been sterilized without their knowledge while ostensibly in the hospital for abortions or other surgeries. Reports of many such abuses surfaced after passage of the 1970 Family Planning Act made sterilization available in federally-funded clinics. In response to the growing controversy in the absence of federal standards for voluntarism, the Department of Health, Education and Welfare in 1974 imposed a moratorium on the federal funding of sterilization of all minors and those considered mentally incompetent. A subsequent district court injunction permanently enjoined the government from sterilizing minors and incompetents.

The Department also went a step further and imposed guidelines on the sterilization of all other public assistance recipients. Individuals had to be informed of the nature, risks and irreversible nature of sterilization. A waiting period of at least 72 hours was required between the written consent and performance of the sterilization. The welfare recipient had to be informed before consenting that benefits could not be withdrawn if she refused to undergo the procedure. Furthermore, the sterilization had to be approved by a five-member review committee appointed by responsible authorities of the federally funded or sponsored (i.e., Medicaid) program or project.

The 1974 guidelines themselves were criticized by some for not going far enough in prohibiting such procedures. A more common set of criticisms, however, came from those who argued that reports of abuse had been exaggerated and that the stringent guidelines assured that many medically indigent were being denied sterilization on the basis of arbitrary judgments by administrators. These proponents of sterilization contended that no minimal age or parental consent should be required and that physicians ought to have full discretion in performing sterilization on their Medicaid patients. The effect of the restrictions, it was argued, was to make it difficult for those on public assistance to obtain a sterilization. This entire debate was replayed in 1979 when the Department of Human Services held hearings nationwide and further tightened the guidelines.

While the Department of Human Services had addressed the question of sterilization with federal government funds, nonconsensual sterilization of the mentally retarded is largely outside of its jurisdiction and within the domain of the 50 separate states. As a result, current practice regarding the sterilization of those deemed incapable of informed consent is inconsistent and often contradictory from one jurisdiction to the next. A flurry of court decisions in the late 1970s and early 1980s, however, appears to have provided a meaningful set of boundaries for resolving this sensitive reproductive issue. This is not to say that the signals coming from the courts are in accord or that they are unequivocal, only that they offer a reasonable framework for proceeding to even more difficult dilemmas these issues raise.

On the first reading, these recent court rulings appear to be heading in two different directions. On the one hand, in *In re Flannary* (1979) the Maryland Circuit Court held that there is no common law power in a court to order sterilization of a minor on a parent's petition. Similarly the Supreme Court (*Tulley v. Tulley*, 1979) denied review to the California Court of Appeal's decision that the state court had no power to order sterilization of mentally incompetent persons on petition of the guardian. These and other comparable rulings in various states mean that in the absence of statutory provisions, sterilization cannot be nonconsensually performed unless for therapeutic reasons.

Conversely, the Washington Supreme Court in *In re Hayes* (1980) upheld the common law power of the superior courts to issue sterilization orders on the petition of a parent and in absence of any state statute expressly authorizing the issuance of such an order. In like manner in *In re C.D.M.* (1981) the Alaska Supreme Court reversed a lower court finding of no jurisdiction and remanded the case with instructions to reconsider their holding in light of judicially created standards for sterilization of incompetent persons. In *In re Grady* (1981) the New Jersey Supreme Court also found jurisdiction to authorize sterilization of retardates in some situations.

Although these latter decisions are in conflict with *In re Flannary* and *Tulley*, in each of these cases the rulings narrowly defined the court's discretion in ordering nonconsensual sterilizations. By placing the burden of proof on the petitioners to "convincingly prove" that sterilization serves the best interest of the retardate and establishing very stringent guidelines, these decisions provide substantial procedural constraints. The *Hayes* court set down specific procedural and substantive requirements which include a court hearing with counsel, expert evaluations of the physical, mental and social state of the candidate, and evidence that the candidate is "permanently incapable of caring for a child even with reasonable assistance."

In like manner the *Grady* court reserved power to review in an adversary hearing the parental or guardian petition to sterilize. The court held that although the Constitution guarantees every person a right to procreate as well as *a right not to procreate*, mental retardation precludes exercise of either right. Under such circumstances, after *Grady* the parents may initiate sterilization proceedings, but only the court may give final approval. According to Munro (1981:24), the *Grady* court "effectively held that *only* the court may exercise a retardate's right not to procreate." Furthermore, as in *Hayes*, the court set forth explicit substantive and procedural standards to assure adequate representation of the candidate and full consideration of his or her interests and the need for sterilization. Similar rulings have come from the Wisconsin Supreme Court (*In re Guard. of Eberhardy*, 1981), the Supreme Court of Colorado (*In re A.W.*, 1982) and a Maryland Appeals Court (*Wentzel v. Montgomery General Hospital, Inc.*, 1983). According to Kindregan (1982:16),

> The last three years have seen a remarkable shift in the attitude of the courts toward petitions for the sterilization of incompetents. It is likely that the newer trend of accepting jurisdiction over these cases, together with a hesitation to act on a particular petition except in the most extreme cases, will mark the attitude of the courts in the coming years.

These most recent examples of courts asserting equitable power over nonconsensual sterilization in the absence of authorizing statutes, have placed the interests and civil rights of the retardates in first priority. Since the veil of judicial immunity was restored in *Stump v. Sparkman* (1978) the courts recognized equitable jurisdiction to authorize sterilization, but only within very limited circumstances. Moreover, they have established exacting procedural and substantive safeguards to minimize abuse that occurred without proper legal protections. Although there likely will continue to be considerable controversy over the courts' authorization of any sterilizations, there appears to be a growing move toward that end (McIvor, 1982).

During this period of conspicuous judicial activity, many state legislatures have demonstrated a renewed interest in sterilization statutes, with mixed consequences. North Carolina adopted House Bill 158 (1981) which permits parents of mentally retarded children to petition the court for permission to sterilize. This bill was a response to *In re Johnson* (1980) where the North Carolina Court of Appeals upheld the constitutionality of the statutory authorization of mentally deficient persons who are either unfit as parents or likely to produce progeny with mental deficiencies, but clarified the tests to be applied and placed the burden of proof on the state. Similarly, Virginia authorized incompetent minors to be sterilized by court order if they are between 14 and 18 years of age (Senate Bill 537, 1981). However the court must find that the candidate is so mentally impaired that he or she cannot and never will be able to make an informed decision about sterilization. The court must also be convinced that no reasonable alternative method of contraception exists and that the candidate is incapable of caring for a child. Although North Dakota ostensibly moved in the opposite direction by prohibiting the sterilization of institutionalized persons on eugenic grounds, it allows such operations if the court determines with clear and convincing evidence that it is in the best interest of the candidate.

Trends in Sterilization Policy

Current trends in policy lean toward the authorization of sterilization of the mentally incompetent, but only within narrowly defined parameters where it can be determined to be in the best interests of the candidate. The assumption here is that if the person was able to make an informed choice, he or she would voluntarily choose sterilization. Since they are not able to make that choice, it is made for them, but with their best interests uppermost in the decision. If this assumption is accepted, sterilization under such conditions probably falls somewhere between a pure voluntary situation and a pure compulsory case where it is performed against the explicit wishes of the individual. Despite continued opposition by many groups, Westoff (1976) foresees this trend continuing.

Another theme prevalent in sterilization policy which has replaced to a large extent earlier eugenic arguments is the use of sterilization to reduce the number of "unfit" parents and, therefore, implicitly to protect children who otherwise would have been born into such a situation. The presumption to this line of reasoning is that mentally retarded persons make unfit parents. According to Gostin (1979) research does not support this assumption. He argues that most mentally retarded people are capable of responsible parenting, particularly when provided with assistance. Moreover, he notes that if we accept the legitimacy of social policy designed to reduce the number of unfit parents by coerced sterilization, we ought to be prepared to sterilize individuals with past histories of child abuse, abandonment, alcoholism, and drug abuse. Actually, there probably is significant public sympathy for this broader restrictive policy. As Ludmerer (1972) notes, the public as well as decision makers historically have tended to embrace such eugenic attempts. It should be noted that the most adamant proponents of sterilization often are parents of the deinstitutionalized retarded who want their children to be free of the risk of pregnancy. They argue that their children are not competent to bear and raise children of their own.

Does society have the right to require that the retarded (or prisoners) undergo sterilization in order to be deinstitutionalized? Do children have the right to be born to sane and able parents, as Ingle (1973) argues? Retarded persons constitute only 2 percent of the population, but they produce 17 percent of retarded children (Reilly, 1977:131). According to Reed and Anderson (1973:118), the risks of retardation are "much higher among the offspring of retarded persons than among normals." Additionally, many people feel that educable retarded persons can lead relatively independent lives if they are not burdened with the care of children (Reilly, 1977: 131).

One troubling aspect of the framework of nonconsensual sterilization policy is that, with few exceptions, it is directed toward women. Sexually active retarded women, not men, are the targets of most involuntary sterilizations. Although there are some practical biological reasons for this development, it illustrates the sexist nature of most reproductive policy. Surprisingly, there has been little discussion of this point, although feminist groups are some of the most vocal opponents of nonconsenual sterilization policy. This problem needs to be addressed more adequately by the agents of sterilization as well as the civil libertarian critics of such policy.

The Policy Implications of Reversible Sterilization

Rather than clarify these issues, the probable widespread availability of safe and effective reversible methods in the near future is likely to confuse the debate over nonconsenual sterilization. Devices such as removable silicone plugs promise to revise traditional assumptions of sterilization as irreversible, but they will not resolve the difficult dilemmas raised by sterilization policy. These developments in sterilization technology are bound to alter the context within which such policy is established—the question is in what way?

The opponents of compulsory sterilization have long emphasized the irreversible nature of sterilization and given considerable weight to the "finality" of sterilization (*Skinner v. Oklahoma*, 1942). Will the new reversible techniques also reverse the trend toward more stringent regulations on its use? Certainly it is easier to justify a reversible procedure. This ultimately raises questions of who decides when to "pull the plug?" Is there much likelihood that the technically "reversible" sterilization will ever actually be reversed, or is the knowledge of that possibility enough? Should the government pay the costs of reversing sterilization if it paid for or ordered the original procedure?

As noted earlier, the 1970s reflected a renewed acceptance of sterilization for welfare recipients among many legislators. There also were many reports of sterilization of substantial numbers of the poor without full voluntary and informed consent (Spriggs, 1974; Rothman 1977). Will the introduction of reversible techniques accentuate the use of such procedures and weaken regulations designed to control them? Given current negative attitudes of the public toward those on welfare, the increased emphasis on the population problem, the scarcity of public funds for welfare programs, and the emerging focus on the competency of parents, it would not be surprising if the availability of reversible sterilization gave further impetus to pressures for widespread use of incentives (or coercion) to encourage (or force) sterilization of the poor, retarded, and those otherwise deemed "unfit." Sterilization issues, just as abortion issues, will remain critical areas of public concern because they reflect basic value conflicts in society over fundamental human rights.

Furthermore, given social and economic trends which today are in evidence among some elements in the United States, the economically-deprived especially are vulnerable to be the target of discriminatory applications of sterilization policies unless extreme caution is employed. To the extent that minority groups constitute a disproportionately high percentage of the poor, increased tension is likely to emerge between the white majority who tend to embrace these innovations as a means of expanding procreative choice and minorities who perceive, perhaps accurately, the same techniques as threats to their individual and collective interests. The contradictory uses of and reaction to reversible sterilization between the middle class majority and specific minorities is a cogent example of the volatile and emotive nature of these emerging inequities. For illustrative purposes, one difficult and potentially explosive social problem is briefly examined here.

Certainly, one of the most controversial aspects of sterilization policy relates to its use on welfare mothers. As noted above, there presently are pressures to relieve the burden of supporting children born to welfare mothers by offering, and in some reported cases, coercing, sterilization. Although paternalistic reasons frequently are cited to justify these policies, they often are based more on rigid moral or economic grounds. Conversely, opponents of sterilization of welfare mothers charge that it is the fundamental right of every woman to have children and that sterilization precludes that choice. They agree that this freedom might place a monetary burden upon society, but they argue that society exists primarily to protect the interests and rights of all classes of citizens.

Although coercive irreversible sterilization is antithetical to a free society, coercive reversible sterilization might have merits which must be considered. It might be speculated first that many children born to women on welfare are unplanned. Abortion demand among women on public assistance, which ran about 300,000 per year before the Hyde Amendment cut off federal funding in 1978, supports this assumption. Moreover, traditional educational and counseling programs and contraceptive techniques have been unsuccessful in curtailing the fertility rate of the uneducated segment of those on public assistance. If the premise is correct that there is a desire to reduce fertility among these women but an understandable aversion to permanent sterilization, then reversible techniques might be a solution. It is apparent that the pressures for some action to reduce the fertility rates of those on public assistance will persist and probably increase. The unfortunate "solutions" to date have been to terminate fertility entirely, continue to pay for abortions and hope that birth control education followup is partially effective, or to allow, encourage or force the woman to live with her fertility and produce children which will be supported monetarily by society.

This situation clearly manifests extreme features of reproductive decision making. Here we have women exercising reproductive "rights" and producing children but not exercising the corresponding obligations to support these children without direct societal support. Also, if is speculated that often the "exercise of their reproductive rights" is a sham and that in fact if they were "free" to do so they would practice fertility control. The question, of course, is whether reversible sterilization would in each particular case interfere with or guarantee the woman's reproductive choice.

On one hand, any intervention into reproduction of women on public assistance is attacked as a form of genocide. Critics vehemently argue that such action represents not only wholesale violation of the women's rights but also clear attempts to eliminate classes of people by terminating their fertility. Although stated in different terms, there is little doubt that the intention of many proponents of limiting procreation of those on public assistance is just that. Ingle (1973), for instance, feels that the gene pool is deteriorating because of increasing discrepancies between the birth rates of the educated middle class and the uneducated poor. While the middle class has reduced its fertility rate substantially in recent decades, the poor, who according to Ingle are often poor because they are genetically inferior, continue to reproduce without compunction. To Ingle and others who support his gene pool argument (Muller, 1959) the survival of society demands intervention in reproduction, especially where large classes of people do not themselves have the means nor the desire to limit the number of children they continue to produce.

Conclusions

Whatever a person's position regarding nonconsensual sterilization policy, it is likely to be intense. Human reproduction is not to be taken lightly in U.S. society. Moreover, it seems certain that the policy issues surrounding sterilization will not abate as innovations in reversible procedures are perfected but instead will increase both in magnitude and intensity. Reversible sterilization is a prime example of a new biomedical technology which offers considerable benefits but also complicates an already complex policy issue. It also demonstrates the delicate interrelationship between social trends and advances in technology and the extent to which change in one produces pressures for alteration of the other. Finally, sterilization illustrates the difficulty in making meaningful social policy in response to the rapidly changing technical and social context of human reproduction.

The courts are destined to play a critical role in defining the boundaries of reproductive choice in the United States. For over seventy years the courts intermittently have dealt with sterilization applications, both consensual and nonconsensual. Reversible techniques are likely to force reconsideration of objections based on the irreversible nature of sterilization and will require hard decisions as to whether or not uses in particular cases are justified and if so, on what constitutional grounds. As noted throughout this paper, instead of ameliorating the policy dilemmas surrounding intrusion into reproductive choice, innovations such as reversible silicone plugs often add further complexity to already difficult problems.

As the courts are drawn further into a broad array of biopolicy areas, including human reproduction, recombinant DNA applications, genetic intervention, psychosurgery, and so forth, it is crucial that the judiciary, the legal profession, and students of public law become aware of the social implications of these advances in biology and medicine. Without doubt, some of the most difficult constitutional, contractual, and tortious questions are imminent in these areas. It is not too early to recognize the potential scope and intensity of these issues that relate directly to our basic conceptions of what it is to be human. To some extent, abortion has preempted attention among issues of biopolicy and demonstrates clearly the sensitive nature of biopolicy. Although the courts' failure to resolve the abortion issue is less than encouraging, it does demonstrate the need for public law scholars to monitor closely and analyze court reaction to the emerging biopolicy issues.

Appendix A: Court Cases

1. U.S. Supreme Court Opinions

Buck v. *Bell,* 274 U.S. 200 (1927)

Skinner v. *Oklahoma,* 316 U.S. 535 (1942)

Stump v. *Sparkman,* 435 U.S. 349 (1978)

Tulley v. *Tulley* 83 Cal. App. 3d 698, 146 Cal. Rptr. 266 (Cal App. 1978), cert. denied, 440 U.S. 967 (1979)

2. Other Court Opinions

In re A.W., 637 P. 2d 366 (Colorado, 1982)

In re C.D.M., 627 P. 2d 607, 611 (Alaska 1981)

In re Flannary, C.C. Mont. Cty. Maryland (December 11, 1979)

In re Grady, 85 N.Y. 235, 426 A. 2d 467 (1981)

In re Guard. of Eberhardy, 307 N.W. 2d 881 (Wisconsin, 1981)

In re Hayes, 93 Wash. 2d 228, 234, 608 p. 2d 635, 637 (1980)

In re Johnson, N.C. App. Ct. (March 18, 1980)

References

Arehart-Treichel, J. (1980) "Questioning the New Genetics," *Science News* 116:155–156.

Blank, R. H. (1982) "Torts for Wrongful Life: Individual and Eugenic Implications." *Original Paper, No. 1*, Social Philosophy and Policy Center.

———. (forthcoming) *Redefining Human Life: Reproductive Technology and Social Policy.* Boulder: Westview Press.

Brosens, I., and R. Winston (1978) *Reversibility of Female Sterilization.* London: Academic Press.

Brown, H. P., and S. N. Schanzer (1982) *Female Sterilization: An Overview with Emphasis on the Vaginal Route and the Organization of a Sterilization Program.* Boston: John Wright-PSG, Inc.

Cooper, J. et al. (1982). "Hysteroscopic Tubal Occlusion with Formed-In-Place Silicone Plugs." Paper presented at the annual meeting of the American College of Obstetrics and Gynecology, April.

Craft, I. (1978) "Laparoscopic Sterilization Using the Hug Plastic Clip," in J. J. Sciarra, et al., eds., *Reversal of Sterilization.* Hagerstown, MD: Harper and Row.

Droegemueller, W. et al (1978) "Modern Modified Aldridge Procedure," in J. J. Sciarra et al., ed., *Reversal of Sterilization.* Hagerstown, MD: Harper and Row.

El Kady, A. A. et al. (1978) "The Tubal Hood: A Potentially Reversible Sterilization Technique," in J. J. Sciarra et al., eds., *Reversal of Sterilization.* Hagerstown, MD: Harper and Row.

Erb, R. (1976) "Silastic: A Retrievable Custom-Molded Oviductal Plug," in J. Sciarra et al., eds., *Advances in Female Sterilization Techniques.* Hagerstown, MD.: Harper and Row.

Gostin, L. O. (1979) "Consent to Involuntary and Nonmedically Indicated Sterilization of Mentally Retarded Adults and Children." Paper presented at a symposium on Sterilization of Mentally Retarded Persons, Toronto, Ontario, Canada May 24.

Green, H. P. (1967) *The New Technological Era: A View From the Law.* Washington: Program for Policy Studies, George Washington University.

―――. (1976) "Law and Genetic Control: Public Policy Questions." *Annals of the New York Academy of Sciences* 165, January 170 177.

Haller, M. H. (1963) *Eugenics: Hereditarian Attitudes in American Thought.* New Brunswick, N.J.: Rutgers University Press.

Henry, A., et al. (1980) "Reversing Female Sterilization." *Population Reports* C-8: September.

Ingle, D. (1973) *Who Should Have Children?* Indianapolis: Bobbs-Merrill.

Kindregan, C. P. (1982) "Court-Ordered Sterilization of Incompetent Persons." *1981 Rptr. H.R.L.* July–August:15–16.

Laufe, L. E. (1978) "The Fimbrial Prothesis," in J. J. Sciarra et al., eds., *Reversal of Sterilization.* Hagerstown, MD: Harper and Row.

Lubell, I., and R. Frischer (1976) "The Current Status of Male and Female Sterilization Procedures." *Procedures of the Royal Society of London* 195:93–114.

Ludmerer, K. M. (1972) *Genetics and American Society.* Baltimore: Johns Hopkins University Press.

McIvor, C. L. (1981) "Equitable Jurisdiction to Order Sterilizations." *Washington Law Review* 57:373–387.

Meeker, C. I. (1978) "A Tubal Occlusive Device in Monkeys," in J. J. Sciarra et al., eds., *Reversal of Sterilization.* Hagerstown, MD: Harper and Row.

Muller, H. J. (1959) "The Guidance of Human Evolution." *Perspectives in Biology and Medicine* 3, 1:1–43.

Munro, A. B. (1982) "The Sterilization Rights of Mental Retardants." *Washington and Lee Law Review* 39:207–221.

Nakamura, R. T., and F. Smallwood (1980) *The Politics of Policy Implementation.* New York: St. Martin's Press.

Nelkin, D. (1977) "Technology and Public Policy," in I. Spiegel-Rosing and D. deSolla Price, eds., *Science, Technology, and Society.* Beverly Hills: Sage.

Powledge, T. M. (1979) "Prenatal Diagnosis: New Techniques, New Questions." *Hastings Center Report* 9:16–17.

Reed, S. C., and V. E. Anderson (1973) "Effects of Changing Sexuality in the Gene Pool," in F. de la Cruz, and G. Laveck, eds., *Human Sexuality and the Mentally Retarded.* New York: Brunner/Mazel.

Reed, T., and R. Erb (1980) "Tubal Occlusion with Silicone Rubber: An Update." *Journal of Reproductive Medicine* 25:25–28.

Reilly, P. (1977) *Genetics, Law and Social Policy.* Cambridge: Harvard University Press.

Rothman, S. (1977) "Sterilizing the Poor." *Society* 14: 36–41.

Saidi, M. H., and C. M. Zainie (1980) *Female Sterilization: A Handbook for Women*. New York: Garland STPM Press.

Schoenberg, B. (1979) "Science and Anti-Science in Confrontation." *Man and Medicine* 4, 2:79–102.

Sciarra, J. J., and G. I. Zatuchni (1978) "Discussion Summary," in J. J. Sciarra et al., eds., *Reversal of Sterilization*. Hagerstown, MD: Harper and Row.

Shain, R. N. (1979) "Acceptability of Reversible Versus Permanent Tubal Sterilization: An Analysis of Preliminary Data." *Fertility and Sterility* 31, 1:13–17.

Sherlock, R. K., and R. D. Sherlock (1982) "Sterilizing the Retarded: Constitutional, Statutory and Policy Alternatives." *North Carolina Law Review* 60:943–983.

Speidel, J. J., and R. T. Ravenholt (1978) "The Potential of Reversible Sterilization in Family Planning Programs," in J. J. Sciarra et al., eds., *Reversal of Sterilization.* Hagerstown, MD: Harper and Row.

Spriggs, E. (1974) "Involuntary Sterilization: An Unconstitutional Menace to Minorities and the Poor." *New York University Review of Law and Sociological Change* 4, Spring:127–151.

Tribe, L. H. (1973) "Technology Assessment and the Fourth Discontinuity: The Limits of Instrumental Rationality." *Southern California Law Review* 46, June:617–660.

Westoff, C. F. (1976) "Trends in Contraceptive Practices: 1965–1973." *Family Planning Perspectives* 8:54–57.

Wimberley, E. T. (1982) "The RSP Method of Tubal Occlusion: A Review and Update." *Biomedical Bulletin* 3, 1:1–6.

Winston, R., M.A. Schwykart, and S. J. Kutner (1973) "A Reanalysis of Female Reactions to Contraceptive Sterilization." *Journal of Nervous and Mental Disorders*, 1565:354–370.

11

Social Services, the State, and the "Basic Civil Rights" of Retarded Parents:
The Uncertain Commitment

Judith A. Gran

The question, "Should the mentally retarded become parents?" is more fruitfully raised in armchair debate than in discussion of social policy. Since the great majority of mentally retarded persons cannot legally be prevented from having children (except by counseling or other voluntarily-accepted advice), they may become parents whether we like it or not. The question we, as a society, must ask is not whether persons with retardation should have children, but how to respond when they do.

The urgency of this question for retarded parents is that without support of some kind—whether from family, friends or the social service system—many risk losing custody of their children through inability to meet their children's needs from their own resources. Nor, once lost, is custody likely to be regained without support since the parent cannot "cure" her retardation. For the retarded parent, loss of custody, even when it is temporary in a formal sense, often leads inevitably to termination of parental rights, a Draconian "solution" that completely severs the parent's relationship with her child, and leaves her on the same legal footing as if she had never borne the child at all.

This chapter explores the legal and policy implications of long-

Judith P. Gran is a staff attorney at the Public Interest Law Center of Philadelphia.

term support services to retarded parents as an alternative to loss of custody or termination. Using a case study to illustrate some fundamental problems in the response of child welfare agencies to the problems of retarded parents, it argues that long-term support services are far more practical and beneficial to both parents and children than removal of the children from the parent's home.

Retarded Persons as Parents: The Historical Background

No discussion of American attitudes on the subject of parenting by retarded persons can ignore the legacy of that era of our history bounded roughly by the years 1896 and 1930. The era witnessed the founding of the Jim Crow regime in the South and of large state institutions for the mentally retarded, the passage of restrictive immigration legislation by Congress and of legislation authorizing involuntary sterilization of the retarded by the states. In that period, blacks, immigrants and retarded persons all were singled out for exclusion from society, and parallel ideologies and stereotypes were developed to justify their exclusion. The flood of immigration and America's transformation into an industrial society spawned a popular ideology of eugenicism and Social Darwinism, whose adherents considered retardation a hereditary taint and a cause of crime, vice and all manner of social ills. The retarded were considered a "menace to society and civilization . . . responsible in a large degree for many, if not all, of our social problems."[1] Among Americans of "older stock," the "menace of the feeble-minded"[2] was linked to the threat posed by blacks and immigrants to their accustomed way of life and social dominance. In the popular mind, both blacks and non-Nordic immigrants were labeled intellectually inferior; this racialist thesis was "proven" by the new "science" of IQ testing, developed originally to place retarded school children in special classes and subsequently used to rate the intellectual capacity of blacks and recent immigrants.[3]

In his opinion in *City of Cleburne, Texas v. Cleburne Living Center*[4], Justice Thurgood Marshall eloquently described the state-imposed exclusion of retarded persons from society during the early part of this century:

A regime of state-minded segregation and degradation soon emerged that in its virulence and bigotry rivaled, and indeed paralleled, the worst excesses of Jim Crow. Massive custodial institutions were built to warehouse the retarded for life; the aim was to halt reproduction of the retarded and "nearly extinguish their race." Retarded children were categorically excluded from public schools, based on the false stereotype that all were ineducable and on the purported need to protect nonretarded children from them. State laws deemed the retarded "unfit for citizenship."

Segregation was accompanied by eugenic marriage and sterilization laws that extinguished for the retarded one of the "basic civil rights of men"—the right to marry and procreate. . . . Marriages of the retarded were made, and in some states continue to be, not only voidable but also often a criminal offense. The purpose of such limitations, which frequently applied only to women of child bearing age, was unabashedly eugenic; to prevent the retarded from propagating. To assure this end, 29 states enacted compulsory eugenic sterilization laws between 1907 and 1931.

Like blacks and immigrants, retarded persons were regarded as "troublesome, backward . . . genetically inferior but capable of tremendous reproduction."[5] Fear of retarded persons' sexuality and reproductive powers was overwhelming. Unchecked procreation by the retarded, it was alleged, threatened the nation with degeneracy and indeed, had already plunged the race into a state of decline.[6] Segregation of retarded persons in remote, custodial institutions was desirable as an end in itself—to prevent the feebleminded from "contaminating" normal people with their "psychic insufficiency, moral indifference, and uncontrollable impulses"[7]—and also as a way to keep retarded persons from "producing their kind."[8] Despite lingering doubts about the constitutionality of compulsory sterilization, it was commonly regarded as a necessary adjunct to state-imposed segregation. Many advocated both segregation and sterilization (or even outright asexualization) as complementary methods for confronting "the menace of the feebleminded", and saw the ultimate goal as the gathering of all retarded persons into "industrial, celibate communities," a solution that offered the best hope of alleviating the " 'White Man's Burden' of distress, pauperism, and disease."[9]

Contempt and fear of social groups that were regarded as innately inferior was also reflected in the tradition of foster care that developed around the turn of the century, the successor system to the nineteenth century practice of placing neglected children in orphanages and asylums. Underlying this seemingly benign practice was the belief that "unfit" parents are incorrigible and that the best means to serve their children is to remove them from the home and place them with new families. The ranks of children in foster care swelled as the ethnic and Social Darwinist prejudices of the era joined the more traditional disdain for the poor as justification for the practice.[10]

In *Buck v. Bell*,[11] the United States Supreme Court upheld the constitutionality of a Virginia statute authorizing involuntary sterilization of institutionalized retarded persons. Justice Holmes's opinion for the Court endorsed the eugenicist ideology of the era; he declared that mentally retarded persons "sap the strength of the state" that to avoid "being swamped with incompetence," society must "prevent those who are manifestly unfit from continuing their kind." Sterilization, he wrote, was preferable to "waiting to execute degenerate offspring for crime, or to let them starve for their imbecility."

After 1930, the eugenicist hysteria of the era abated, and with it the reasoning behind Justice Holmes's argument for compulsory sterilization. Eugenics had always been a political and social rather than a scientific movement, and in fact it was rejected even by geneticists of the Social Darwinist era.[12] With the recognition that only a small percentage of retardation is caused by abnormal genes or chromosomes, the rationale for sterilization statutes as preventive public health measures evaporated. And with the Court's explicit holding, in *Skinner v. Oklahoma*[13] that procreation is a fundamental constitutional right, the constitutionality of sterilization statutes required more than ever, the existence of such a rationale. To pass constitutional muster, a state statute that affects the exercise of fundamental rights must be *necessary* to protect an important state interest, and *narrowly drawn* so that it does not affect persons whose rights not be abridged to protect that interest. After *Skinner*, sterilization statutes could not survive this test, and in most of the 29 states cited by Justice Marshall these statutes were either invalidated by the courts or repealed voluntarily by the legislature.[14]

Reintegration of Retarded Persons and Community Services

Beginning in the 1960s, in a struggle that in many respects parallels the struggle of black persons for equality and integration, retarded persons began at last to achieve a significant degree of reintegration into the community. As in the black civil rights movement, the milestones of equal citizenship for retarded persons are court decisions and federal legislation. In *Pennsylvania Association for Retarded Children (PARC) v. Commonwealth*,[15] a group of parents of handicapped children successfully drew upon the victory of black parents in *Brown v. Board of Education*[16] (in which the Supreme Court held that when a state creates a system of universal compulsory schooling, it must make that system available to all children equally) to establish that all retarded children have a constitutional right to education in the public schools. Three years later, *PARC* was codified in the federal Education of the Handicapped Act[17] which guarantees to all handicapped children a free, appropriate public education and the right to be educated with children who are not handicapped. Also in the 1970's, a series of lawsuits against large, segregated state retardation institutions[18] resulted in judicial recognition of the harm of segregation and the benefits to retarded persons of living in family-like settings in normal communities. And in 1973, Congress enacted Section 504 of the Rehabilitation Act,[19] whose language tracks Title VI of the Civil Rights Act of 1964[20] and guarantees to all handicapped persons, including persons with retardation, freedom from discrimination and reasonable accommodation in federally funded programs and activities.

With the development of new school and community programs for retarded persons, knowledge of how to teach retarded persons the skills they need to live and work in the community has flourished. An ample body of literature now documents the success of teaching methods that address retarded persons' particular learning styles. Retarded persons tend to think concretely, and are less apt than non-intellectually handicapped people to manipulate abstract concepts and to generalize, to transfer, to perform skills learned in one environment or with one set of materials and cues to other environments. Educators have developed simple but effective techniques for teaching persons with retardation, such as task analysis (breaking a task down into a series of small steps that can be mastered in sequence); repetition; teaching by demonstration, modelling and physical assistance, avoidance of reliance on verbal or abstract didactic instruction; and use of positive contingencies to reinforce learning. With appropriate instructional methods, it was soon learned, retarded persons can master skills they were thought incapable of learning in an earlier era, including the ability to work alongside non-handicapped people in competitive employment.[21]

Knowledge of how to teach and train persons with retardation to reach their fullest potential exists in special education programs and in specialized, community-based programs for retarded adults and children; it is found much more rarely in generic services such as child welfare programs. Outside small networks of parents, advocates and community services providers, attitudes shaped by the "regime of state-mandated segregation and degradation" persist—the belief, for example, that a retarded person's learning capacity is fixed at a certain "mental age," or that values, ethics, and relationships with other persons are not as important to retarded people as they are to "normal" people. As Justice Marshall noted, the "lengthy and continuing isolation of the retarded has perpetuated the ignorance, irrational fears, and stereotyping that long have plagued them." Unfortunately, the experience of retarded parents in the child welfare system too often reflects those archaic attitudes.

Despite the flourishing of community retardation services during the last decade, specialized training and support services for retarded parents, such as the Allegheny County Association for Retarded Citizens' Project ESPRIT are rare, not so much because the knowledge of how to teach retarded parents does not exist as because of lack of other resources, combined perhaps with a trace of the historic fears. Funding for these programs is likely to come from private sources or, if out of public mental retardation service dollars, from family resource service funds, for which "normal" parents of retarded children compete vigorously.

Empirical studies of parenting by retarded persons have shown that retarded persons can be good parents and that inadequacy among retarded parents is often caused by factors other than retardation, for example, family size, socioeconomic status, and the strength of the marriage.[22] With early intervention and enrichment programs, the children of retarded parents will likely be "on track" developmentally.[23] Retarded persons are most effective at parenting when they have access to "contextualized and nondemeaning assistance" in survival skills such as money management, housing, travel, scheduling school and medical appointments, from either natural support systems (e.g. grandparents and other family members) or formal services.[24]

But because of the paucity of social services, retarded persons who need support may not receive it unless they are part of a well-functioning natural support network, or, in some cases, already served in a community mental retardation program before the child is born. Where the retarded parent first encounters the social service system through a child welfare agency, she is likely to find that agency staff have little knowledge of the needs, the potential and the abilities of retarded persons and even less enthusiasm for referring the parent to services where that knowledge does exist. Although innovative child welfare agencies have recently begun to emphasize intensive, flexible in-home services as alternatives to foster care placement, these services have a distinct disadvantage for retarded parents. They almost always are short-term (five months or less) and are designed to aid families in a state of acute crisis rather than furnish the long-term support the retarded parent is likely to need.[25]

Dependency, Termination, and the Retarded Parent

All states have statutes allowing the state to intervene in family affairs to protect children who are abused or neglected. Statutory proceedings are of two basic types: dependency proceedings to remove a child at risk of harm from his parents' custody, and termination proceedings to sever permanently the parent-child relationship. Pennsylvania's statutory scheme is typical. "Any person" may file a court petition[26] alleging that a child is "dependent," that is, "without proper parental care or control, subsistence, education . . . or other care or control necessary for his physical, mental, or emotional health, or morals."[27] If, after a hearing, the court finds by clear and convincing evidence that the child is dependent, the court must hold a second (dispositional) hearing to decide whether the child should be permitted to remain with his parents or whether legal custody of the child should be transferred to another individual or to an agency, including the local child welfare agency.[28] Dependent children removed from their parents' custody are most commonly placed with foster families.

The more drastic measure of termination may be imposed on a parent whose child has been ordered removed from the home by a court if after six months:

> the conditions which led to the removal or placement of the child continue to exist, the parent cannot or will not remedy those conditions within a reasonable period of time, the services or assistance reasonably available to the parent are not likely to remedy the conditions which led to the removal or placement of the child within a reasonable period of time and termination of the parental rights would best serve the needs and welfare of the child.[29]

Termination may also be imposed, whether or not the child has already been removed from the home, if:

> The repeated and continued incapacity, abuse, neglect or refusal of the parent has caused the child to be without essential parental care, control or subsistence necessary for his physical or mental well-being and the conditions and causes of the incapacity, abuse, neglect or refusal cannot or will not be remedied by the parent.[30]

Parents with mental retardation are particularly vulnerable to termination under either section of the statute, for if a court finds that parental neglect is due to retardation, it may also find that the "conditions and causes" of the neglect cannot be remedied because the parent's retardation cannot be "cured."

Pennsylvania's dependency and termination procedures both require the moving party to show that services to enable the child to remain with his parent cannot reasonably be provided, the latter explicitly, the former by case law.[31]

The federal Adoption Assistance and Child Welfare Act[32] also requires that states seeking federal reimbursement for foster care and other services assure that "reasonable efforts" are made to avoid placement outside the home. Specifically, it requires that before a state may receive federal reimbursement for any individual child's foster care maintenance, a judge must rule that "reasonable efforts" have been made to prevent or eliminate the need to remove the child from the home.

Since the evidence is plain that retarded persons can be good parents, that their effectiveness can greatly be enhanced if they have support in survival and maintenance needs, should not those supports be required in cases where the retarded parent's difficulties are due to lack of skill, not moral inadequacy? The courts' answers to this question conflict. The harshest is that of Georgia Court of Appeals that in *In re S.R.J.*[33] upheld the termination of a retarded mother's parental rights although her child was not deprived and although she had "ever-present and capable help" from the child's grandmother. The test, the court held, is "whether the parent, *ultimately standing alone,* is capable of mastering and can effectively demonstrate the ability to utilize those parenting skills" (emphasis added). By this test, a parent whose child had never suffered any neglect, who was able to purchase the services her child needed, or whose spouse was able effectively to care for the child, could also have her parental rights terminated.

Only slightly less harsh is the test set forth by the Pennsylvania Supreme Court in *In re William L.*[34] There, the court terminated the parental rights of a retarded mother with respect to her sons, who had lived for 5 years in foster care (through no fault of the mother's), although she was presently caring adequately for a younger child, a daughter who had never been in foster care, with the help of county social services. Justice Nix, in dissent, noted that to satisfy the Pennsylvania termination statute, the court must find that the mother's incapacity (in this case, mental retardation) had "*caused* her child to be without essential care and control" and that the mother here had prevented that consequence by voluntarily seeking help from social service agencies to ensure that essential care would be provided. Nevertheless, the majority upheld termination because the mother's "very limited social and intellectual development" plus her five-year absence from her sons, showed that she was incapable of providing minimal care for her children.

William L. has been called a "no-fault termination case" because the mother's rights were terminated simply because of her retardation, not because she lacked a sense of responsibility or devotion to her children, nor even because the mother's retardation had ever caused the children to suffer harm or neglect.

Another Pennsylvania court reached a conclusion, in *In re C.M.E.*[35] that on its face seems to contradict *William L.*, although the two cases can be reconciled. At the termination hearing, the lower court had heard testimony from a psychologist that a mentally retarded mother, if provided an intensive educational program of up to two and a half years, would be able to learn the parenting skills she needed to care for her child. The lower court found this level of time and effort prohibitive. The Superior Court disagreed, stating that to terminate the mother's rights because the program needed to rehabilitate her was costly would be to punish her for the severity of her disability. The standard by which the mother's parenting capacity should be judged, the court held, was that of "an individual in [the] circumstances [in] which the parent under examination finds herself." Measured by that standard, the court stated, the mother had committed no wrong that would justify termination: "We refuse to punish a parent for her lack of parenting skills which is based, at least in part, on her limited intellectual capacity."

In re C.M.E. can be distinguished from *In re William L.* The court in *William L.* reached the result it did in part because the mother's relationship with her sons deteriorated drastically during the five years they were in foster care. (No effort was made to terminate Marjorie's rights with respect to her daughter, although she was not able independently to care for her, either.) Still, *William L.* illustrates the likely result of prolonged foster care for the retarded parent.

Although the court in *In re C.M.E.* did not squarely answer the question whether services or termination should be ordered when the parent is decent and caring but no amount of "rehabilitation" will enable her in the foreseeable future fully to cope on her own, it suggested the answer in its characterization of termination solely because of the parent's retardation as "punishment" for being retarded. *In re S.R.J.* and *In re C.M.E.* therefore represent opposite judicial responses to the question whether long-term support is an appropriate, and even a legally required, alternative to termination.

Other courts have recognized that it is far easier to provide support services to retarded parents and their children than it is to replicate the child's unique relationship with its parent. Judge Berman of the Colorado Court of Appeals wrote, in an opinion concurring in the reversal of an order terminating a retarded parent's rights:

> Indisputably, the [child's] welfare would be served, now and in the future by preservation and encouragement of the tender, loving relationship she enjoys with her mother, even though that may not be sufficient to supply the totality of the child's developmental needs. That relationship is, in my view, the single most significant factor in determining whether the child will become a happy, well-adjusted adult. The State can more easily supply mechanisms to meet the child's other developmental requirements than it can the love of a parent for its child, and of a child for its parent."[36]

Judge Berman's elegant, simple logic is in stark contrast to the convoluted consumer-agency and inter-agency machinations that are illustrated in the following case study.

Amanda S.: A Case Study

Amanda lacks none of the moral qualities of a good parent; she is patient and stable and indeed, has coped far better emotionally than most women would in a stressful family situation. A soft-spoken, low-key woman, somewhat hard of hearing, Amanda expresses her affection for her sons quietly but strongly. Her face lights up when a visitor praises one of the boys: "My kids was always good kids," she affirms with a rare, radiant smile.

With an assigned IQ of 71, Amanda is considered mildly retarded. She spent most of her adolescence in a state institution for retarded women in New York and was employed briefly in a textile mill before her marriage to Sam. The irony of Amanda's involvement with the child welfare system—for alleged neglect of her six sons—is her bedrock commitment to the role of full-time wife and mother. Married to Sam for 26 years (the first ten of them childless—Amanda says "the Lord answered my prayers" and enabled her to conceive), she has lived in the same home and community for nearly all her married life. A regular churchgoer who attends services twice a week, she has built her life around keeping house and nurturing her brood and says she has never wanted any other occupation. When food is scarce, as it often is since Sam became unemployed, she is always the last to eat. Putting her children's needs ahead of her own is so ingrained in her character that she cannot imagine any other way.

Amanda scarcely raises her voice to her six sons, who range in age from 3 to 17, and she certainly has never physically abused them. When, in a judicial proceeding initiated by her county's child welfare agency, the six boys were found to be "without essential parental care and control," and two of them were removed from her home, she was devastated.

It would be tempting, but too easy, to summarize the story of how Amanda came to lose custody of her children in a single sentence. Because of her intellectual limitations, Amanda, despite her love for her sons, her good intentions and the efforts of child welfare workers, was unable to provide for her children's needs. It is too easy because the real reasons lie deeper, in the irrationality and ineptitude of a service system that, like other bureaucratic systems, has an occasional tendency to give its own organizational needs priority over the needs of its clients. Unfortunately, Amanda's experience with the service system is not unique. In fact, it aptly illustrates the problems retarded parents encounter when they seek help from traditional child welfare agencies.

Amanda, who lives in a small, decaying industrial town in Pennsylvania, turned to her local welfare agency several times during the late 1970s, when she needed someone to watch her children while she was in the hospital for childbirth or surgery. Her husband Sam was employed and although the family was poor, they scraped by. Social workers' notes from that period praise Amanda as "the pillar of the family" and claimed that she was doing the best that anyone could given her "limitations." No serious problems in family functioning were noted and the case was closed.

In 1979, Sam had a breakdown on the job and became unemployed. Amanda again contacted the child welfare agency to ask their help in finding him new employment. The agency's response was to refer Sam, who is not retarded, to the county sheltered workshop. He balked, saying he did not want to work with handicapped persons (perhaps he was also aware that his wages in the workshop would be only a fraction of what they had been in competitive employment) but despite his resistance the agency persisted for at least nine months. (They never did succeed in getting him to work in the workshop.) Eventually, the illness that had triggered Sam's breakdown was diagnosed as "undifferentiated schizophrenia," and Sam began to attend a mental health program at a local hospital.

In 1983, Sam's condition worsened. He refused to attend the mental health program or to take the psychotropic medications that controlled his symptoms of psychosis. He had outbursts of temper in which he threatened the children; although he never actually harmed them, these episodes brought the family's situation dramatically to the attention of the child welfare agency once again. More important, perhaps, for overall family functioning, was that Sam now was too sick to be a parent to his sons. He was no longer able to drive the family car, to run errands, help around the house and transport the boys to school or other activities. And much more of Amanda's time and energy were now consumed by Sam's demands.

In addition, as the older boys reached adolescence and the family's poverty deepened, Amanda found it increasingly difficult to manage the household. In their cramped, two-bedroom apartment, wedged between a public parking lot and the town's major highway, the boys had no place to play and Sam had nowhere to take his frustrations. Overwhelmed and at a loss what to do, Amanda was more than willing to accept whatever help the child welfare system could deliver.

And the agency offered help in abundance—"help" that ultimately would tear the family apart. The tragedy of Amanda's story from this point on is that the more services the agency provided, the worse the family's problems seemed to become.

The case manager assigned to the family enrolled them in a new, innovative agency-funded program for parents with "mental health problems or developmental disabilities" (it was never really clear whether the basis for their enrollment was Sam's schizophrenia or Amanda's retardation—the project manager for the program was later to testify that she did not know whether or not Amanda was retarded). It was a model program, at least on paper, providing a minimum of 10 hours a week of an in-home worker's time to teach housekeeping and parenting skills.

The child welfare agency discovered that several of Amanda's and Sam's six children were in special education classes in the local schools, and that Simon, the youngest child, showed signs of developmental delay. Simon was placed in an early intervention program funded by the county office of mental health/mental retardation. A public health nurse was enlisted to monitor the family's physical health; the family was referred to the county legal aid office for help securing public benefits. Eventually, as many as seven different agencies were actively involved in the case (the child welfare agency, the family service provider agency, the mental health/mental retardation program, the early intervention provider, the public health nurse, the mental hospital, and the children's school); and in 1984 the family's case manager began convening regular monthly inter-agency meetings to discuss the family's problems.

The services provided the family, in other words, sound like a social service administrator's dream come true. Intensive in-home services; multidisciplinary, interagency cooperation and coordination. Yet despite all the intensive activity, the family seemed to get worse instead of better. Amanda made no progress in learning to manage the family's money nor in serving well-balanced meals. The boys were out of the house at all hours on school nights, and Amanda could not seem to get them to bed at a decent hour nor get them off to school in the morning.

Finally, in late 1985, the county child welfare agency filed a dependency petition, asking the court to declare that the children were "without essential parental care and control." After hearing testimony from the social service workers involved with the family, the court found all six children dependent; at a second hearing, it removed two of the older boys from their parents' custody to the custody of the child welfare agency, which then placed them in a foster home in an adjoining county. The county announced its intention of placing all six boys.

Outside experts who evaluated the family, however, were impressed with Amanda's strengths as a parent and recommended that the children remain at home with proper support services. The county's rejoinder, of course, was that they had already tried to rehabilitate the family with those services—services far more intensive than those they provided other families on their caseload. Was the county right? Had they already done everything that reasonably could be expected to enable the children to remain at home?

The problem with the services the county provided was, quite simply, that they were the wrong services. The in-home teaching sessions might well have been effective for a "normal" person, but they were inappropriate to Amanda's family situation and her retardation. First, the trainer was never there in the late evening hours and early in the morning, when Amanda most needed help with her sons. Second, when she was there, she used methods (verbal teaching, counseling) that require a "normal" person's ability to manipulate abstract concepts. If Amanda did not master a task in one or two lessons, the trainer concluded she could not or would not learn it and went on to the next task rather than repeating and reinforcing the lesson.

An example was the agency's "nutrition" lessons. After visiting Amanda's home, social service workers observed that although she was able to cook simple meals, she did not know how to serve her sons a balanced diet. Agency workers decided to remedy the problem by teaching Amanda to cook a greater variety of foods. Accordingly, the in-home worker scheduled weekly cooking lessons designed to teach her a new dish each week. The social service notes of those lessons tell a sad but ludicrous story. One week the lesson focused on "making pizza from scratch." The in-home worker noted that Amanda was cooperative but that at the conclusion of the lesson she was "not able independently to make pizza from scratch." At the next session, rather than repeating the pizza-making lesson, the trainer went on to teach Amanda how to make chicken soup from scratch. Again, Amanda was cooperative but unable to master the task in a single sitting. The trainer went through a number of dishes in this fashion before she concluded that Amanda simply could not learn to be a better cook and the lessons were dropped.

The sad part of this sequence is that while the in-home worker played Julia Child, she wasted valuable time that could have been used to teach Amanda the tasks she needed to master to feed her sons a balanced diet. Amanda did not need to know how to make chicken soup from scratch, although that might make her an "ideal," thrifty middle-class housewife. What she *did* need to know, to ensure her sons were properly fed, was much more basic: how to get a vegetable on the dinner table every single night. An effective instructional program would have set that as a specific, measurable goal ("Amanda will serve a vegetable at dinner seven out of seven times") and worked backward, analyzing all the steps Amanda and others would need to take to achieve that goal (including transportation to the store, selection, purchasing and preparation), teaching Amanda those steps in sequence with as much repetition as necessary. By teaching Amanda things she didn't need to know in ways that ensured she wouldn't learn, the in-home sessions were counter-productive and actually interfered with effective learning.

Amanda's single biggest problem with her children, in her own view as well as that of the child welfare agency, was controlling their evening comings and goings and getting them to bed on time. The in-home worker worked a nine-to-five day and relied on verbal instruction to tell Amanda how to discipline her sons in the evening when the worker was not there. The in-home worker suggested various disciplinary consequences Amanda might impose and prepared written charts (Amanda cannot read) for her to refer to when a problem arose.

The in-home program was planned as a time-limited one that would train parents to be almost fully independent within a year. Thus, the program began to pull away its support just as Amanda's family situation worsened and she began to need the support more and more.

Underlying these symptomatic problems were more serious, underlying flaws in the county's method of providing services to Amanda and her family. In four volumes of social service records on the family, it is difficult to find a single notation—either in agency assessments, statements of objectives, or progress reports—that states what Amanda could do, what she had learned, and what she was expected to learn—in terms of specific, concrete, measurable behavior. The agency's objectives for Amanda were vague: for example, "to become a more effective parent" and its efforts to assess and measure her progress were equally nebulous. The concept of stating objectives and outcomes in measurable behavior ("Simon will be in bed by 9 PM five nights a week") rather than in terms of opinions, characteristics, inner states or emotions is considered a cornerstone of teaching technology in the retardation service system. Without it, it is impossible to know what to teach, what the person needs to know, and what impact the teaching has had.

Another remarkable feature of the social service agencies' intervention is that, after working intensively with Amanda's family for more than two years, the social workers seemed to know or care so little about her as an individual. Nowhere, for example, in the social service notes was there any discussion of Amanda's hearing loss and the impact it may have had on her parenting abilities. A court-ordered evaluation later discovered that Amanda had difficulty hearing someone at the front door—a fact that surely affected her ability to control her sons' whereabouts.) Although the agencies working with the family arranged for numerous psychological and psychiatric evaluations for the children, no one even suggested a simple audiological assessment for Amanda.

Similarly, social service workers made no attempt to understand or draw upon Amanda's close ties to her church as a source of natural support for the family. The only reference in the social service records is a rather derogatory comment about the church as a "fundamentalist sect." Nor was there any effort to build upon Amanda's relationship with her mother, who lived nearby and desired more involvement with her grandchildren.

Finally, social workers apparently never considered enhancing Amanda's own social skills to help her become a more effective parent. Perhaps because she had spent most of her adolescence in an institution for the mentally retarded, Amanda was illiterate and lacked many community skills that she obviously was capable of learning, such as the ability to use public transportation. Although the local public library in Amanda's town had a free adult literacy program, the family's case manager never referred her to it or any other adult education program.

The child welfare agency treated the children's problems in isolation rather than treating the family as a whole, with regard to the needs of each of its members. Unfortunately, this is a common legacy of the era that conceptualized child welfare services as rescue of the children of the "unfit," to be raised by new and more worthy parents. That legacy is especially pronounced where the parent is retarded and whose "unfitness" therefore is presumptively established.

Although every outside expert who evaluated the family concurred that housing was by far their most pressing need—because their present housing stock was hazardous and because the limited physical space available contributed seriously to family dysfunction—none of the social service agencies serving the family made any serious effort to find better housing. The child welfare agency acknowledged the problem but felt it could not help because "if we do it for one family, then we have to do it for everybody."

Ironically, Amanda and her family, perhaps uniquely among all the child welfare agency's clients, were eligible for an excellent county-funded housing program which would also have met their need for support services, yet county agencies working with the family actually *opposed* the idea of placing them in it. Pennsylvania, like most other states, provides publicly-funded community residential programs for retarded persons, called Community Living Arrangements (CLAs). Almost all CLAs are operated by private, non-profit corporations under contract with county government agencies. In a typical Pennsylvania CLA, three retarded persons (sometimes more or fewer) live with an appropriate number of staff in a normal home in a residential neighborhood. The arrangement is designed to allow retarded persons to live as much as possible as their non-retarded neighbors do. The cost of staffing the CLA is paid by the county from state and federal funds allocated by the state. Most residents receive Supplemental Security Income benefits (as Amanda does), and pay a flat room and board charge of 72% of their monthly SSI check; county funds pay any additional housing costs. CLA staff are trained to teach housekeeping and independent living skills to retarded persons and are expected to work with each resident to carry out a set of specific, measurable objectives in an individual program plan. The program's underlying philosophy is developmental and humanistic. Its goal is to help retarded CLA residents reach their fullest potential, and its orientation is toward "the whole person." Staff work flexible hours, when CLA residents need their help, rather than nine to five. Services are long-term rather than short-term or crisis-oriented.

Amanda and at least three of her children test in the "retarded" range; her youngest son was already served in a county-funded mental retardation (early intervention) program. The family as a whole was eligible for a CLA. A CLA offered decent housing, long-term homemaker help at flexible hours, trained staff to provide tutoring and other enrichment for the children and for Amanda herself, and all at less cost to the county than the foster care arrangements the county proposed to fund instead. Why was a CLA not seriously considered?

The answer lies in a combination of interagency "turf" issues and fiscal disincentives, and it is also likely that, at some level, county social service workers simply felt that Amanda and her family did not deserve a CLA. Although CLA programs are designed to be "the functional equivalent of a biologically-related family,"[37] the idea that CLA residents might actually *be* a biologically-related family (the vast majority of CLA residents are single adults) was regarded as radical, not only by the county child welfare program but by the county mental health/mental retardation program as well. Actually, a CLA was first proposed, in an early interagency meeting on the family, by a minor staff person as an economical way to "consolidate" the services presently being provided by numerous different agencies. A representative of the county mental health/mental retardation program responded that the family was "ineligible" to receive such a program under its auspices (without, however, making the formal determination of eligibility required by the agency's regulations) and the subject was dropped. Pressed for reasons why the family was considered ineligible, the mental retardation administrator (whose program has a limited number of state-funded "slots" for a long list of eligible clients) told the family's case manager that Amanda was ineligible for mental retardation services because her IQ was one point too high, 71 instead of 70 (no such cut-off exists in agency regulations).

The county child welfare agency, which already was committed to spending more funds on foster care for the children than a CLA for the entire family would have cost, could easily have purchased a CLA program for the family from one of the local private service providers, but refused to do so. The agency's reasoning was, again, that "if we provide a CLA for one family, we'll have to do it for everyone." (Clearly, the agency saw a CLA as a more desirable service than foster care and hence one that would be demanded by eligible families if they knew the service existed.) A deeper but unspoken reason was that the child welfare agency feared it could not obtain state reimbursement for funds spent on a CLA, while reimbursement was unquestionably available for foster care.[38] (Nothing, however, would prevent the agency from spending *county* dollars to purchase the service.) The agency's refusal to spend its funds on non-reimbursable services, regardless of whether those services genuinely benefited the family, illustrates the service dilemma a noted community mental retardation administrator in another state has called the "ethics of funding" issue. In her words, a mature social service system must at some point resolve explicitly that the services it provides will be driven by client needs, rather than by the conditions imposed by funding streams.[39]

Committed to its own imperative of conserving county dollars, the child welfare agency nevertheless refused to press the mental health/mental retardation program to serve Amanda's family. Contrary to all accepted canons of social work, the family's case manager declined even to pursue a determination of the family's eligibility for county mental retardation services. An agency representative candidly confessed that this was because Child Welfare did not want to disturb its smooth relationship with the Mental Health/Mental Retardation. "After all, we may need their help in our next case."

It was only when two multidisciplinary teams, one procured by the parents' attorneys and one ordered by the court, had recommended that the children remain with Amanda and Sam and that the family be provided with a CLA or other service combining adequate housing and long-term homemaking support, that the county agreed seriously to discuss support services as an alternative to foster care.

Conclusion

Amanda's experience represents many of the problems faced by retarded parents in the service system. Those problems may briefly be summarized as follows:

1. Historic perceptions of retarded persons as inherently "unfit" to be parents influence retarded parents' experience in the child welfare system.

2. Knowledge of the learning capacities of retarded persons, and of the instructional and service technology that allows retarded persons to fulfill their potential, is not widely received or utilized in the child welfare system.

3. Because social service consumers whose needs do not fit squarely within the rubric of a single agency's jurisdiction may not receive services at all, retarded persons tend to become victims of interagency turf squabbles when, as parents, they enter the child welfare system.

4. The tendency of bureaucratic social service agencies to pursue their own interests rather than those of their clients has an especially negative impact on retarded parents in the child welfare system, insofar as they lack effective advocacy and are devalued by persons who work in that system.

4. Agencies' tendency to allow funding sources, rather than client needs, to dictate the services that will be provided also impacts adversely on retarded parents since there is no funding source targeted especially to their needs.

Although knowledge of the human capabilities and potential of persons with retardation has progressed considerably since the Social Darwinist era, traces of the old belief that retarded persons are inherently "unfit" to be parents linger in our attitudes and our service delivery systems. Until we rid ourselves of those beliefs, we will continue to do disservice to retarded parents and their children. No reason exists not to transfer the knowledge, the assumptions, and the expectation that retarded persons can develop given proper support from the community retardation system to the child welfare system. Only then will we overcome "the irrational fears and the stereotyping" that long have plagued the retarded parent.

Notes

1. H. Goddard, "The Possibilities of Research as Applied to the Prevention of Feeblemindedness," *Proceedings of the National Conference of Charities and Correction* 307 (1915), *cited in* A. Deutsch, *The Mentally Ill in America* 360 (2d ed. 1949).

2. This phrase appeared frequently in popular pamphlets of the era, published to alert the public to the "dangers" of allowing retarded persons to remain at large and the necessity of segregating them in custodial institutions. *See, e.g.,* C. Frazier, *The Menace of the Feeble-Minded in Pennsylvania* (1913); Connecticut School for Imbeciles, *The Menace of the Feeble Minded in Connecticut* (1915); Juvenile Protection Association of Cincinnati,

The Feeble-Minded, Or the Hub to Our Wheel of Vice (1915). *See also* "The Menace of the Feeble-Minded" (editorial), 62 *Journal of the American Medical Association* 938 (1915).

3. For the use of intelligence testing during this period as a political tool to justify the segregation of blacks and retarded persons and to exclude immigrants of non-Nordic backgrounds, *see* S. Gould, *The Mismeasure of Man* (1981) and L. Kamin, *The Science and Politics of IQ* (1974).

4. 105 S.Ct. 3249, 3266–67 (1985).

5. P.L. Tyor and L. V. Bell, *Caring for the Retarded in America: A History* 104 (1984).

6. "The Problem of the Feeble-Minded" (editorial), 58 *Journal of the American Medical Association* 785 (1912) (reporting eugenecist Charles Davenport's views).

7. Punton, "The Segregation and Treatment of the Feeble-Minded," 222 *Illinois Medical Journal* 299 (1912).

8. C. S. Yoakum, *Care of the Feebleminded and Insane in Texas, Bulletin of the University of Texas No. 369* at 46 (Humanistic Series No. 16, November 5, 1914) (on file in Pamphlet Collection, Texas State Archives, Austin, Texas).

9. "Editorial," 3 *Journal of Psycho-Aesthenics* 144 (1899), *cited in* Tyor, *supra* n. 5 at 104.

10. Edna McConnell Clark Foundation, *Keeping Families Together: The Case for Family Preservation* 2 (1985).

11. 274 U.S. 200 (1927).

12. This fact is amply documented in K. M. Ludmerer, *Genetics in American Society* (1972).

13. 316 U.S. 535 (1942).

14. Note, "Involuntary Sterilization of the Mentally Retarded: Blessing or Burden?" 25 *South Dakota Law Review* 55 (1980).

15. 343 F.Supp. 279 (E.D. Pa. 1972).

16. 347 U.S. 583 (1954).

17. 20 U.S.C. 1400–1415.

18. The leading cases are collected in *Association of Retarded Citizens of North Dakota v. Olson* 561 F.Supp. 473 (D.N.Dak. 1982), *aff'd*, 713 F.2d 1391 (8th Cir. 1983).

19. 29 U.S.C. 794.

20. 42 U.S.C. 2000d.

21. For an overview of instructional technology for retarded persons, including the most severely handicapped, *see, e.g.*, W. Sailor, B. Wilcox, & L. Brown, *Methods of Instruction for Severely Handicapped Students* (1980); M. E. Snell (ed.), *Systematic Instruction of the Moderately and Severely Handicapped* (1978); P. Wehman & P. J. McLaughlin, *Program Development in Special Education: Designing Special Education Programs* (1981). For vocational technology emphasizing competitive employment, *see* P. Wehman, *Competitive Employment: New Horizons for the Severely Disabled Individual* (1981).

22. A. G. Zetlin, T. S. Weisner, & R. Gallimore, "Diversity, Shared Functioning, and the Role of Benefactors: A Study of Parenting by Re-

tarded Persons," in S. K. Thurman (ed.), *Children of Handicapped Parents: Research and Clinical Perspectives* 68, 70–71 (1985); Note, "Retarded Parents in Neglect Proceedings: The Erroneous Assumption of Parental Inadequacy," 31 *Stanford Law Review* 785 (1979).

20. "Help for Retarded Parents: Child-Care Lessons Ease The Burden and the Pain," *Newsweek*, June 23, 1986 at 62 (quoting Marsha Blanco of the Allegheny County Association for Retarded Citizens).

24. Zetlin, *et al.*, *supra*, n. 22 at 90–91.

25. *See, e.g.*, the programs described in National Clearing House for Home Based Services to Children and their Families, *Alternatives to Foster Care: Planning and Supervising the Home Based Family Centered Program* (1980).

26. 42 Pa. C.S.A. 6334 (1982).

27. 42 Pa. C.S.A. 6302 (1982).

28. 42 Pa. C.S.A. 6531 (1982).

29. 23 Pa. C.S.A. 2511(a)(5) (Supp. 1985).

30. 23 Pa. C.S.A. 2511(a)(2) (Supp. 1985).

31. *Interest of K.B.*, 419 A @d. 508, (Pa Super. 1980).

32. P.L. 96-272, 94 Stat. 501 (1980), *codified at* 42 U.S.C. 670–676. Although a federal appellate court has held that the rights created by the Act are enforceable by a private right of action in federal court, *Lynch v. Dukakis*, 719 F.2d 504 (1st Cir. 1979), there are problems in using the Act to force the provision of social services. First, federal regulations implementing the Act fail to define "reasonable efforts" or to specify whether "reasonable efforts" require only that existing services be provided or that new services be created. This distinction should be critical if the services needed were specialized services for retarded parents. What constitutes "reasonable effort", therefore, is determined largely by the states. Edna McConnell Clark Foundation, *supra*, n. 10 at 15–17.

Second, the requirement that family court judges and magistrates make a judicial determination (usually on a standard form that is provided for the magistrate to check off so that federal reimbursement can be obtained) each time a child is placed in foster care that "reasonable efforts" have been made to avoid placement tends in practice to water down the "reasonable efforts" standard tremendously. Further—and this is important because parents have no right in many states to counsel in dependency and termination proceedings—unless the lower court's decision is appealed, the finding that "reasonable efforts" have been made will become *res judicata* and prevent the parent from challenging the decision later on in a federal court proceeding.

33. 337 S.E. 2d 444, 445 (Ga. App. 1985).

34. 383 A.2d 1228 (Pa. 1978), *cert. denied*, 439 U.S. 880 (1978).

35. 448 A.2d 59 (Pa. Super. 1982).

36. *People v. C.A. K.*, 638 P. 2d 136 (Colo. App. 1981), rev-d, 652 P. 2d 603 (Colo. 1982).

37. This phrase has been used to describe the essential character of a CLA in *Hopkins v. Zoning Hearing Board of Abington Township* 423 A. 2d 1082

(Pa. Cmwlth. 1980) and other zoning cases.

38. State regulations forbid the state to reimburse county children, youth and family programs for "the cost of mental health or mental retardation treatment services." 55 *Pa. Code* 3140.21(c)(1).

39. Interview with Lyn Director, Executive Director of Region V Community Retardation Services, Nebraska, June 19, 1986.

Section Two:

Sexual "Deviancy" and Social Policy

12

Feminism, Pornography and Law

Eric Hoffman

Since *Roth v. United States*,[1] the Supreme Court has maintained that "obscenity is not protected by the freedoms of speech and press."[2] This means that, consistent with the usual procedural constraints,[3] state and federal governments can regulate obscene books, photographs, and movies.[4] At the same time, the Court has developed a restrictive definition of obscenity that, in effect, limits obscenity regulation to hardcore pornography.[5]

First amendment theorists have widely criticized obscenity law.[6] Their arguments tend to focus on the problem of defining obscenity, and some criticize any attempt to define or regulate obscenity.[7] The theorists' legal arguments are informed by their perceptions of pornography and its social significance; these perceptions may be broadly categorized as either conservative or liberal.[8] The Court's current position represents a compromise between the conservative and liberal positions, a position that satisfies neither side.[9]

Recently, a new voice entered the obscenity law debate. Feminists have begun to articulate their opposition to pornography,[10] to organize and demonstrate,[11] and to secure the passage of antipornography laws.[12] Not all feminists oppose pornography or view it as an important issue,[13] but those who do have advanced argu-

---

Eric Hoffman practices law and wrote this article while a student at the University of Pennsylvania Law School. It first appeared in the University of Pennsylvania Law Review, 1985.

269

ments informed by a perspective that differs fundamentally from both the conservative and the liberal positions.[14]

Feminist arguments against pornography focus on its role in reinforcing sexist views and attitudes, which, on one level, simply fail to treat women as serious human beings and, on another level, sanction and perhaps promote violence against women.[15] These arguments reflect and are part of a broader attack on the character of sexual relationships in sexist societies. The arguments do not presuppose that sex itself is necessarily degrading or dehumanizing. Feminist criticisms of pornography instead focus upon its ideological role in maintaining gender relations that harm the status of women generally as well as the individual women victimized by the violence that is sanctioned and encouraged by pornographic materials.[16]

This essay evaluates the feminist argument and considers whether it can or should be used to justify the legal regulation of pornography. Parts I and II contrast the liberal and conservative perspectives represented in judicial opinions and scholarly analysis with the emerging feminist perspective. Part III articulates the legal proposals generated by the feminist perspective, and Part IV evaluates these proposals.

Evaluation of feminist arguments does not lead to a simple acceptance or rejection of feminist proposals. Feminist arguments against pornography push very hard in the direction of legal regulation; in some instances, efforts to shape the law in accordance with feminist concerns have already been made.[17] This essay argues that insofar as the law plays a role in defining and shaping social values, pursuit of feminist antipornography laws may well have some value. From a political perspective, however, feminists should probably avoid endorsing state regulation of pornography. Feminists have reasons for being suspicious of the power of the state, which has historically been, and seems likely to remain, male-dominated. Thus the potential value of feminist antipornography laws may well be offset by considerations of political strategy as well as first amendment principles.

Obscenity Law

Legal Doctrine and First Amendment Theory

The first amendment protects freedom of speech primarily to foster two values: truth, which is supposed to be served by free exchange in the "marketplace of ideas," and political participation, which requires a public forum for the speech of citizens.[18] Some scholars argue that these values, and therefore the scope of protected speech, should be narrowly construed; others argue for a broad construction on the grounds that first amendment values can be fully served only by more extensive protection of free expression.[19]

The linchpin of obscenity law since *Roth v. United States*[20] has been its holding that "obscenity is not protected speech."[21] Although the definition of obscenity has changed somewhat since *Roth*, characterization of a work as obscene has consistently meant that it is not protected by the first amendment, with the consequence that the government has authority to regulate its distribution.[22]

The legitimacy of this authority is grounded primarily in the idea that pornography is harmful, or at least that it is reasonable for legislatures to believe that it is harmful.[23] The Court's opinions also possess a strain emphasizing dignity, decency, order, and virtue, suggesting that, even if pornography causes no direct harm, its corrupting influence harms both the quality of life and the quality of the democratic citizenry.[24]

A doctrinal defense of *Roth*'s exclusion of obscenity from first amendment protection must rely on an interpretation of obscenity that explains why it should not be considered speech within the meaning of the first amendment.[25] Writing for the Court in *Roth*, Justice Brennan argued that the history of the first amendment implicitly rejects protection for obscenity because it is "utterly without redeeming social importance."[26] This conclusion was largely premised upon the Court's judgment, made in *Chaplinsky v. New Hampshire*,[27] that obscene utterances "are no essential part of any exposition of ideas, and are of such slight social value as a step to truth that any benefit that may be derived from them is clearly outweighed by the social interest in order and morality."[28] Because the aim of the first amendment is to protect the marketplace of ideas, it follows that obscenity cannot be protected speech.[29]

Assuming that obscenity justifiably may be excluded from the protection of the first amendment, the crucial problem is to distinguish the obscene from the nonobscene. The evolution of the definition of obscenity culminated in *Miller v. California*,[30] which held that material is obscene if,

(a) . . . 'the average person, applying contemporary community standards' would find that the work, taken as a whole, appeals to the prurient interest. . . ; (b) . . . the work depicts or describes, in a patently offensive way, sexual conduct specifically defined by the applicable state law; and (c) . . . the work, taken as a whole, lacks serious literary, artistic, political, or scientific value.[31]

For the most part this definition classifies as legally obscene only what might intuitively be thought of as hard-core pornography.[32] Its narrow scope can be demonstrated by contrasting four of its features with alternative formulations that would permit more extensive government regulation of obscene materials. First, the definition refers to the "average person" rather than to children or to the easily corrupted.[33] Second, the definition requires that the work be "taken as a whole" and does not permit parts to be evaluated out of context.[34] Third, the definition requires that the depictions be "patently offensive," which means that not all sexually explicit material will be obscene.[35] Fourth, the work itself must be relatively worthless; "serious" work is protected.[36]

Although the *Miller* standard is relatively narrow in scope, it requires courts and juries confronting obscenity questions to evaluate the content of the work at issue. They must decide whether a work "appeals to the prurient interest," whether it depicts sexual conduct "in a patently offensive way," and whether it "lacks serious literary, artistic, political, or scientific value." These inquiries are aesthetic because their resolution requires analysis and judgment of the content of images and its effect on an audience.[37] Liberal Justices and commentators tend to place aesthetic judgments beyond the scope of the judiciary's proper role in the determination of first amendment issues.[38] Yet, there is little doubt that judges consciously make such judgments in the realm of obscenity law.[39]

Many commentators believe that obscene works should not be excluded from first amendment protection.[40] Some believe that the first amendment protects expressive nonverbal conduct as well as verbal speech.[41] Others argue that even hard-core pornography has sufficient cognitive content to be considered speech within the meaning of the first amendment.[42] Underlying all of these objections is the notion that obscenity law's two-tier approach, which distinguishes valued or protected speech from worthless or unprotected speech,[43] is inconsistent with the principle that government should refrain from evaluating speech.[44]

Conservative and Liberal Approaches to Pornography

Liberal and conservative positions on pornography can be distinguished by their responses to three issues.[45] The first issue is the nature and meaning of sex. The second is the function of sexual imagery, and the third is the proper role of law in the regulation of sexually-oriented materials.

Characterization of the conservative position on pornography begins with its reliance on a traditional view of sexuality.[46] In this view sex is legitimate, proper, and moral only within marriage and, even then, only for the purpose of procreation.[47] This account of sexuality derives from a fundamentally religious strand of Western culture that generally denigrates the corporeal in favor of the spiritual[48] and that until recently strongly influenced social mores. Current mores perhaps embody less extreme versions of this account, but the notion that sex is somehow wrong, dirty, or sinful unless it is redeemed by some legitimating circumstance like marriage or love remains a force in our culture. This notion is part of a larger conservative emphasis on virtue, self-control, and dignity as the basic elements of a moral and social perspective.[49]

In the conservative view, images of sex are inevitably isolated from the context of love, commitment, and decency that legitimate sexuality. Thus the tendency of such images is to arouse a nonspecific desire for sex rather than a desire for sexual interaction with a specific person and to degrade a private activity by making it public.[50] The consequence of allowing sexually arousing images to become a part of public life is the corruption of community values. Ultimately, virtue is sacrificed, and the quality of social life declines.[51]

The scope of the conservative view may sweep beyond what is normally thought of as pornography. With respect to literature and other media, the conservative critique may extend to materials that use strong language or approve of indecent activities. Conservative opposition to pornography may be politically related to the opposition to sex education, birth control, civil rights for homosexuals, or abortion. The unifying theme is virtue expressed in terms of sexual restraint and maintenance of the family as an institution.[52]

Finally, the conservative perspective is generally sympathetic to the use of law, as an expression of collective morality, to reflect and enforce fundamental values.[53] In the conservative view the law is a means of protecting social decency and the quality of life. Conservatives would conclude that pornography is not something that ought to be protected by the first amendment because it depraves and corrupts its audience, indirectly causes widespread social decay, and particularly harms the family.

In contrast the liberal view tolerates, and sometimes even approves of, a wide variety of sexual activity. The desire to have sex is seen as healthy rather than as shameful or sinful. Liberals thus argue that the only legitimate restraint on sexual activity is the informed consent of the participants;[54] any further restriction is an exercise in moralism and paternalism. In fact liberals argue that the very constraints approved by conservatives are the cause of the "perversions" that conservatives condemn.[55]

For the liberal, images of sex may serve a variety of important social functions, but they reveal an individual's fundamental taste.[56] The fact that a variety of legitimate tastes exist is confirmed by the existence of a market for a variety of sexually-oriented materials.[57] Thus, although some liberals may believe that some sexually-oriented materials are disgusting and offensive, the problem is seen as an issue of taste, not morality.

Once this conclusion is reached, it seems illegitimate to prefer one set of tastes to another. It then follows that pornography, however defined, should be protected by the first amendment.[58] Thus, just as liberals argue that the law should not restrain the sexual activities of consenting adults, they also argue that the law should protect consenting adults who produce and consume sexually-oriented materials.[59]

Conservative and Liberal Elements in Obscenity Law

Obscenity law is fundamentally conservative, but its details represent a compromise with liberalism. This conservatism is primarily evident in the denial of first amendment protection to obscenity. The Supreme Court has premised its obscenity holdings on its concern for maintaining public decency and avoiding obscenity's perceived harms.[60] Despite its conservative premises, the Court has made concessions to liberalism by employing a relatively narrow definition of obscenity.[61] This definition nonetheless embodies conservative assumptions. The conservative bias is evident in the Court's concern with "prurience," which, despite some attempts to limit its meaning,[62] seems to refer simply to a work's intent to produce sexual arousal.[63] Use of the capacity for sexual arousal as the main test for obscenity expresses the conservatives' basic disapproval of sex. The Court's requirement that a work have some serious value further amplifies this bias. This requirement implies that a work that produces sexual arousal can be redeemed[64] if it, as a whole, contains some serious value that encourages the reader's detachment from any sexual response. Finally, the "patently offensive" requirement seems to presume a set of shared values that define clearly what should offend any decent person.

The legal standards distinguishing the obscene from the non-obscene therefore reflect a conservative bias by preferring the tastes of those who are offended by sexually-arousing materials to the tastes of those who enjoy them. In contrast liberals would consider legitimate, even socially important, a work having sexual arousal as its primary purpose.[65] A distinction may be drawn between works that serve this purpose well or badly, but erotica itself is not inherently suspect. Thus, evaluating these works is a job for cultural critics, not judges.

The specific elements of the Court's definition of obscenity, and the concerns underlying them, have long been the object of a liberal attack.[66] With respect to the Court's worries about corruption, liberals emphasize the right of citizens in a free society to corrupt themselves. They also emphasize the inappropriateness of any government efforts to define corruption in the area of consensual sexual relations.[67] Expanding on these arguments, liberals submit that pornography is produced, distributed, and consumed by willing participants, none of whom feel harmed. Liberals further believe that there is little evidence that pornography causes any actual harm.[68] In their view pornography seems as likely to have beneficial as harmful effects given its educational, cathartic, and liberating functions.[69] Liberals would put the burden of proof upon those who would restrict the liberty of those who desire to produce and consume sexually-oriented materials.[70] Finally, liberals argue that even if the Court believes pornography's participants *are* being harmed, by sacrificing their dignity for money or by weakening the self-control required for virtuous citizenship, its decision to "protect" the participants through obscenity regulation is plainly paternalistic.[71] The liberal position therefore concludes that the most sound course is to defend liberty against moralism and paternalism.

Liberal accusations of paternalism are met with conservative accusations of anarchy and license.[72] Conservatives defend the Court's underlying moral position by arguing that liberty divorced from virtue is not worthy of political commitment. Conservatives also dispute the empirical issues, arguing that there is evidence showing pornography to be harmful.[73] Although the evidence may be inconclusive, they point out that long-term and indirect effects are difficult to verify experimentally. Yet, such effects may be crucial to the argument.[74] Finally, conservatives are incredulous that anyone could believe that sexually-oriented materials have no effect. "If you believe that no one was ever corrupted by a book," writes Irving Kristol, "you also have to believe that no one was ever improved by a book . . . and that, consequently, all education is morally irrelevant."[75]

Liberals and conservatives do agree on the parameters of their disagreement. Both believe that people's varying reactions to sexually-oriented material are informed by the observer's underlying philosophy of sexuality. Liberals and conservatives also agree that the legal treatment of sexually-oriented materials depends on aspects of social philosophy as well as on empirical research into the effects of pornography. Because feminists question these assumptions, their views challenge the comfortable dialogue that has determined the parameters of obscenity law. The starting point for understanding the feminist challenge is an examination of the feminist account of pornography.

The Feminist Account of Pornography

Feminists[76] differ considerably from both conservatives and liberals in their responses to all three of the issues delineating political positions on pornography. These differences are largely attributable to the fact that the focal point of the feminist view is neither virtue nor liberty but, instead, equality. This different focus produces a crucial insight: only from a male perspective, whether liberal or conservative, does pornography seem to be primarily about sex. Feminists emphasize equality in sexual relations and evaluate sexually-oriented materials in that light. Pornography, so viewed, is not so much about sex as it is about power.[77]

This distinction between sex and power is complicated, however, by the existence of issues of power throughout the realm of sexuality. Sexuality has long been a means by which men have expressed and exercised power over women.[78] Historically, sexual repression has been disproportionately enforced upon women, while male "sinfulness" and "indiscretion" have been legally and socially tolerated.[79] The feminist commitment to sexual equality extends further than a simple desire for expanded opportunities for women's sexual expression, however. Many feminists sense that sexuality itself has been so distorted by male dominance that women cannot participate equally unless eroticism is redefined.[80]

This emphasis on equality is an important aspect of feminist perceptions of sexual images. Feminists distinguish between liberating, egalitarian images and degrading images; images within the first category are erotic, whereas images within the second category are pornographic.[81] Pornography thus "objectifies, degrades and brutalizes a person in the name of sexual stimulation or entertainment."[82]

Feminist suspicions that sexuality has been distorted by male dominance are confirmed by their finding that the vast majority of sexually-oriented materials produced in this society are pornographic rather than erotic.[83] The sexual imagery of the pornography industry, an industry in which men produce images of women for other men,[84] objectifies and degrades women. It portrays them as requiring some coaxing, after which they always become eager for sexual submission—even for violence and torture. Pornography approves male domination of women by portraying it as pleasurable both to men and women. Feminists argue that pornography thereby increases the probability and social acceptability of violence against, and exploitation of, women. Ultimately, this pornographic ideology tends to make both men and women discount women's perspective, interests, and will.[85]

The effects of pornography can be understood only in light of the history of gender inequality and exploitation. In general, women have been excluded from culture and relegated to the private sphere of domesticity from which they have been permitted to escape only on the condition that they accept male-defined terms. Women's perspectives have thus been systematically neglected, distorted, and undervalued.[86] Hence, an insistence on the value of women's experience is the bedrock of any feminist analysis.[87] And sensitivity to male power and female powerlessness is characteristic of a developed feminist perspective.[88]

These principles suggest that the feminist attempt to define an aesthetic that does not suffer from one-sidedness of the dominant male view requires the articulation of women's experience of pornography.[89] However, taking such a perspective on pornography would mean feeling oneself imaginatively to *be* the women portrayed by a medium that "begins by annihilating the real female self and replacing this self with a false self."[90] This annihilation is achieved both by the very existence of pornography and by its actual content.

In form, pornography is the marketing of images of women by men for men. This objectifies women; they are manipulated and are thereby robbed of their subjectivity and their capacity to define reality in their own terms.[91] This formal characterization is reinforced by the anonymity of pornography,[92] its emphasis on parts of the woman's body,[93] its thematic focus on fetishism,[94] and its general lack of feeling.[95] The subjectivity that women do express in pornographic images is predominantly one of pleasure in being objectified. Women are portrayed as desiring fulfillment by serving as an object that perfectly inspires, responds to, and fulfills male sexual desires.[96] Pornography's most brutal forms portray women as enjoying being beaten, raped, bound, or otherwise abused.[97]

Women *do* resist in pornography, but their resistance is of two basic stereotyped kinds. First, there is false, moralistic resistance. Once this resistance is overcome, whether by force or seduction, the woman often adopts a nymphomaniacal attitude.[98] Second, there is more serious resistance generated by a desire for independence or control. This resistance tends to mark the woman as a "bitch," "feminist," or "lesbian"; in any case, she is not a "real woman." Her fate is often grisly.[99]

Once women's experience is taken seriously, pornography appears as neither perversion nor entertainment, but as a genre expressing threats and hostility aimed at the maintenance of male power over women. It portrays for men the pleasures of power and the dangers of losing control; it reveals to women the dangers of any attempt independently to explore their own sexuality.[100]

The pornography industry, rather than simply catering to a tiny minority of our society, sells a product that is widely desired and socially significant. The industry is larger than the legitimate film and record industries combined, and the combined circulation of *Playboy* and *Penthouse* exceeds that of *Time* and *Newsweek*.[101] Assuming that the feminist account of pornography is correct and recognizing that pornography has a wide audience, we are led to conclude that pornography is an integral part of an ideological system that advocates and legitimates male domination of women. In both instrumental and symbolic ways, feminists argue, pornography affirms male sexual rights over women and female sexual duties (sometimes disguised as rights or desires) to men. Feminists therefore conclude that pornography should be regulated because it violates women's rights to equality.

This focus on equality differentiates feminists from conservatives, who focus on virtue. Feminists charge that pornography helps to stabilize the male-dominated social order, whereas conservatives charge that it corrupts the citizenry and thereby destabilizes social order.[102] The feminists' connection of pornography with equality places the problem in a context of changeable social circumstances and thereby leaves open the possibility of nonpornographic erotic materials.[103] Conservatives base their opposition on principles they assume to be common to all decent societies, thus placing pornography in a context of an unchangeable order of virtues that does not allow for any possibility of nonpornographic erotic materials.

Although feminist and liberal positions on the issue of regulation tend to differ, their overall differences are fewer and more subtle than those between feminists and conservatives. Historically, feminism has been connected with liberal or progressive movements,[104] and feminists and liberals are often allies in other causes.[105] The compatibility between liberals and feminists breaks down, however, with liberals' willingness to subordinate women's sexual equality to the pornographer's individual liberty. Feminists—particularly radical feminists—perceive this difference as evidence of a profound male bias or insensitivity in liberalism.[106]

The bias may reflect a fundamental difference between female and male moral frameworks, such as that suggested by Carol Gilligan.[107] Gilligan characterizes the moral framework of women in terms of care and responsibility rather than in terms of rights and rules. This suggests that a feminist moral evaluation of pornography will emphasize the kind of community it helps to create. In contrast, a male evaluation of pornography, whether conservative or liberal, will tend to emphasize abstract principles.[108]

Feminist Approaches to the Legal Regulation of Pornography

Arguments in Support of Regulation

Feminist arguments posit three interests in the regulation of pornography. First, women participate in the pornography industry itself, primarily as models and performers. By some criteria, their participation is voluntary.[109] Yet, strong social forces such as poverty, responsibility for childcare, and a general socialization to "femininity," may well motivate women's participation, and the presence of these forces suggests that the participation of women is less voluntary than may first appear. Considering these forces together with the personal and commercial exploitation common in the pornography industry, it seems reasonable to view women as harmed by their participation in the production of pornography.[110] At the least it would seem necessary to guarantee better wages, working conditions, and job security; more ambitiously, it seems important to eliminate the social and economic forces that motivate women to participate in pornography.[111]

Second, pornography indirectly functions as an influential form of propaganda vividly advocating male domination of women.[112] This propaganda is all the more effective because its ideological nature is generally denied; the popular view that pornography is primarily about sex rather than power conceals its male supremacist ideology and provides a basis for its social acceptance. In this respect pornography differs from explicit racist, or even sexist, propaganda, which is more likely to be viewed as socially unacceptable.[113] This propaganda works to shape and maintain attitudes and behaviors that stabilize structures of male domination and increase the likelihood that society will tolerate violence against women.[114]

The third concern, related to the second, is that pornographic images of women tend to damage women's reputation as women.[115] The reputation of women can be damaged in ways that men's cannot. Images of individual women who emerge from the private sphere generalize easily to all women; the token woman represents her gender. In contrast, the actions and qualities of individual men are not so easily generalized. Men are persons, whereas women are women.[116] Pornographic portrayals of individual women thus harm all women.

Feminists argue that if these considerations about women's interests in pornography are taken more seriously than conventional male-biased moral theory would take them, a strong and unambiguous condemnation of pornography is justified.

Feminist Theories for the Regulation of Obscenity and Pornography

Defining Pornography

Pornography is currently regulated by excluding obscenity from first amendment protection. The legal definition of obscenity makes it clear that regulation is oriented towards conservative concerns.[117] The use of a feminist definition of pornography would make the regulation of pornography more sensitive to feminist concerns.

By choice, feminists define pornography rather than obscenity. Obscenity is a relatively subjective term, connoting an offense to decency, whereas pornography denotes a relatively specific and popularly identified class of materials.[118] Because the feminist argument emphasizes the role of such materials in maintaining male domination, rather than its offensiveness, the term pornography is preferred.

One feminist attempting to redefine pornography advocates defining pornography as "verbal or pictorial material which represents or describes sexual behavior that is degrading or abusive to one or more of the participants *in such a way as to endorse the degradation*."[119] Although this definition undoubtedly requires

281

some clarification, particularly as to the meaning of "endorse" and "degradation," it is arguably no more vague than the current definition of obscenity. From a feminist perspective its virtue is that it directs attention to the endorsement of degradation and the approval of male domination, rather than to the arousal of prurient interest. It thus reflects the feminist argument that pornography concerns power rather than sex.

Some municipalities have recently considered antipornography laws incorporating a feminist sense of the obscene. These proposals define pornography in terms of the manner in which women are presented by the materials.[120] However, much of the material within this definition is protected under current laws.[121] The question thus posed by feminist arguments is whether there are persuasive reasons to prefer this definition to the now-prevailing *Miller* standard.

Feminist Theories Supporting Legal Regulation of Pornography

Feminist concerns regarding pornography generate three theories supporting regulation: that pornography causes failures of the marketplace of ideas, that it causes harms, and that it libels women as a group.[122] Feminists argue that women have generally been excluded from the marketplace of ideas, which the first amendment is designed to protect.[123] Men dominate the sphere of public speech, often with the aid of law.[124] The marketplace of ideas cannot produce truth or democracy when historical injustices handicap half the population.[125] Based upon this theory, women may legitimately demand some special consideration aimed at promoting their participation in the marketplace of ideas or at protecting them from the abuse and exploitation permitted by a marketplace that ignores their concerns.

This failure of the marketplace may justify state regulation of pornography. Feminists argue that pornography is a male preserve, a criticism no less valid because it can be applied to almost all aspects of culture.[126] In fact, recognizing that pornography is a part of sexist society actually strengthens the feminist argument that the marketplace of ideas truly has failed. Sexism is articulated, expressed, and endorsed by the cultural phenomenon of pornography. This male preserve in which women are abused and exploited plays a crucial role in the silencing of women. Certainly discussion of sexuality is dominated and distorted by pornographic images that bar the articulation of a genuine female sexuality.[127] The feminist argument thus leads to the conclusion that the suppression of pornography would remove a barrier to women's participation in the marketplace of ideas.

A second doctrinal argument in support of regulation is that pornography harms women. This argument differs from the usual harm-oriented conservative justification for regulation in that it emphasizes different harms and different mechanisms by which the harms occur. Thus far, liberals and conservatives have ignored women's interests in pornography. When these interests are systematically considered in light of the evidence regarding pornography's harms, it is plausible that the government's interest in suppressing pornography is strong enough to override any first amendment values served by the pornographer's freedom of expression.[128]

Although feminists should be reluctant to accept a two-tier or multitier theory of the first amendment or a narrow construction of what kind of speech the first amendment protects, if these arguments are accepted, feminist considerations add weight to the view that pornography is harmful. At the least, if the feminist account of pornography is more plausible than the conservative account, there is greater reason than is now offered to deny pornography the protection of the first amendment. In fact, the feminist emphasis on violence as the causal link between pornography and harm may well be more plausible than the conservative emphasis on prurience.[129]

Feminist criticism of pornography leads to a third theory of regulation: that pornography libels women as a group. In *Beauharnais v. Illinois*[130] the Supreme Court upheld a group libel law against a first amendment challenge. The challenged law made it unlawful to publish or exhibit a portrayal of "depravity, criminality, unchastity, or lack of virtue of a class of citizens, of any race, color, creed or religion" that would expose that group to "contempt, derision, or obloquy."[131] The Court held that instances of group libel affect the reputation of the groups defamed and thereby harm individual members of the group.[132] Thus it was permissible for the Illinois legislature to enact the law as part of its attempt to deal with problems fostered by racial and religious tensions and violence.[133]

Beauharnais has not been explicitly overruled, but most commentators[134] and some lower courts[135] have questioned its continued validity. Some recent work, however, has argued that group libel doctrine is not, or should not be, dead.[136] Group libel theory justifies the regulation of vilifying speech that is aimed at vulnerable, historically oppressed groups on the theory that such speech operates "nonrationally" and therefore cannot be effectively counteracted by opposing speech,[137] particularly speech by or on behalf of the vilified group.[138] This theory depends on controversial, but plausible, psychological assumptions and suggests that the law should countenance civil or criminal sanctions against the dissemination of hate literature aimed at disadvantaged groups.[139]

Feminist arguments characterize pornography as a species of hate literature, parallel to pamphlets vilifying blacks or Jews. It falsely portrays women as finding self-fulfillment in sexual submission to the violent will of men and conveys this image in a manner that bypasses the critical faculties of its audience. By portraying women as whores,[140] it thereby encourages both men and women to take women's interests less seriously than men's.[141] This is a denial of women's humanity, dignity, and self-respect.[142]

Forms of Legal Regulation

There are many ways in which the law could regulate pornography. To the extent that pornography is not protected by the first amendment, outright suppression through criminal laws is the most obvious possibility.[143] Some sort of regulatory scheme, involving licensing or taxes, is also possible.[144] The direct involvement of the state in any regulatory scheme would involve first amendment problems similar to those posed by criminalization, but, to the extent that regulatory schemes may be viewed as time, place, or manner restrictions, their permissible scope may be somewhat wider than that of criminal statutes.[145] First amendment procedural requirements[146] are likely to make such regulatory schemes unworkable, however.

In terms of feasibility and political strategy, civil actions may provide a preferable approach. The strength of legislatively designed tort actions, such as the Minneapolis ordinance,[147] lies in their form as amendments to municipal civil rights laws. They treat pornography as "a form of discrimination based on sex."[148] The state role is confined to adjudication, and the factual presentation of the cases is left to those who claim to be harmed. This allows feminist plaintiffs to exercise some control over the development of claims under the statutes.

An Evaluation of the Feminist Approach

Questions About the Feminist Account of Pornography

Three challenges can be made to the feminist interpretation of pornography. The first is a challenge to the feminists' universalization of "men" and "women." Proponents of this challenge de-emphasize gender and instead emphasize that responses to pornography vary according to the individual and that many women respond positively to pornography whereas some men respond negatively.[149] This argument misses the feminists' point, however. Gender-conscious analysis is appropriate for a number of reasons. First there appear to be empirical differences in male and female responses to pornography.[150] Moreover, because individual perceptions of pornography may depend on psychological pre-dispositions, it is important to view empirical data critically.[151]

A defense of the feminist analysis leads to more serious challenges concerning feminist assumptions about sexuality. The feminist account assumes that sex can be divorced from violence and domination, yet this may not be true. A conservative analysis of this issue would link male sexuality to aggression and dominance by arguing that a man's potency depends on feelings of power and control, perhaps even hostility.[152] Female sexuality is correspondingly passive and submissive; hardly considered to be a sex drive at all.[153] Thus the conservative argument concludes that pornography depicts sex as it is and has to be for men. Applying this conclusion to the issue of regulation, the conservative would then argue that sexuality and sexually-oriented materials must be controlled because the liberation of male sexuality is the liberation of hostility and antisocial feelings, particularly feelings against women. Conservative opposition to sexuality and sexually-oriented materials can therefore be seen as motivated by a form of respect for women.[154] In contrast, a liberal analysis of the claim that there is a necessary connection between aggression and sexuality would point to the intensity of the desires aroused in sex.[155] Thus this view also argues that sexual activity must have a tinge of aggression. Similarly, this account of the matter concludes by charging that feminists merely want sex to be sensuous cuddling, devoid of passion.[156]

Although a full answer to this criticism would require consideration of sexological research beyond the scope of this essay, suffice it to say that feminists flatly deny that male and female sexuality are necessarily dominant and submissive,[157] and they attribute any sadomasochistic elements of sex[158] to socialization rather than genetics. Feminists may acknowledge that sex has a passionate dimension, particularly for men as they have been socialized. Yet, they would further argue that to the extent that sex may be intrinsically "violent" the violence ought to be equally distributed among men and women, in contrast to current pornography.[159]

A final challenge to the feminist account of pornography builds on the doubts raised by the preceding challenge.[160] The argument is that men and women do indeed have different sexual styles.[161] These styles are in part genetic, but they are reinforced and amplified by a culture that is undeniably biased in favor of men. Pornography is a genre of male fantasy in which women are portrayed as having a male sexuality; that is, they are aroused by what arouses men. Male fantasies *are* somewhat aggressive and degrading to women, and this is unfortunate, but pornography is nonetheless part of a legitimate masculine style, a style which is more visual, less tactile, more instrumental, less expressive, more lustful, less loving. These differences are ultimately irreducible, although some women have masculine styles, and vice versa. The difference in sexual styles may be illustrated by comparing pornography to what is often considered the parallel phenomenon for women: romance.[162] Romance differs from pornography in that its eroticism is emotional, diffuse, and inexplicit rather than functional, pointed, and explicit. Yet, what excites women's fantasies in romance is the very same male power that pornography glorifies. Here, too, no attractive image of sexual equality is either portrayed or sought.[163] This analysis therefore concludes that a greater equality between men and women must be achieved if we are to overcome the sense that the masculine style is the only style. With greater equality, masculine and feminine sexual styles will remain different but will be equal.[164]

This interpretation of pornography undermines the feminist position. It acknowledges that current pornography is too violent and degrading to women but suggests that pornography is a fantasy genre tailored to a legitimate erotic style. In response to this challenge, many feminists may be willing to modify their positions.[165] Many others, however, will argue that although masculine and feminine sexual styles do exist, they are a product of male-dominated society rather than of genetics.

Questions About the Use of Law to Regulate Pornography

The Liberal Critique of the Feminist Position

Although it is not absolute, first amendment protection is broad in scope.[166] The courts have not, however, wholly refrained from limiting speech. Regulation must be pursued in the least restrictive manner possible,[167] but some inhibitions of first amendment freedoms have been permitted.[168] The strongest doctrinal criticisms of the feminist position therefore flow from the work of liberal commentators rather than the courts.[169] These criticisms are all traceable to the liberal position that regulations on speech should be minimal, if they are legitimate.[170] As a result, liberal evaluations of specific feminist proposals all tend to generate the criticism that they necessitate government evaluation of the content of works.

The liberals' main problem with the feminist argument, then, is that it interprets pornography as political speech, and hence, inadvertently implies that it must be given full first amendment protection.[171] In addition, it is settled law that the advocacy of what some legislature believes is a dangerous ideology cannot be made illegal.[172] Furthermore, it is difficult to argue that individual pieces of pornography, however much they implicitly endorse the degradation of the women portrayed, advocate clearly that all women should be or are degraded. Thus feminists would have to grant the government the power to interpret the message expressed in a wide range of materials in order to identify materials that advocate harm to women.[173]

Feminists justify government intervention primarily by reference to the market failure theory, arguing that something needs to be done to help end the silencing of women and equalize the voices of men and women in the marketplace of ideas. A preliminary response to this theory might attack its factual premises by denying that pornography dominates and distorts the articulation of women's sexual sensibility. One can point to the romance industry[174] and to publications that study and discuss women's sexual perspective as evidence that the marketplace has not failed to accommodate women's voices.[175] Another response might be to point out the degree to which other aspects of culture are male monopolies. Feminists must explain what distinguishes pornography from other expressions of male dominance.[176]

Even accepting the feminist account of pornography as a market failure, the theory is problematic because it justifies government intervention to assure equal or adequate access to the marketplace of ideas.[177] Equality and adequacy, however, remain vague; specification of their meaning will usually presuppose some conception of what a properly functioning marketplace would look like. Market failure theory therefore grants the government authority to decide how the marketplace of ideas should look.

This criticism of the feminist account of the market failure theory also applies to the feminist argument that the harms of pornography justify its suppression. If pornography is viewed as an expression of political ideology,[178] its regulation should be subject to the "clear and present danger" test. Because the harms of pornography are still disputed and its consequences, even by the feminist account, are indirect, pornography does not pose a "clear and present danger" under the standards that the courts have thus far established. If pornography is nonetheless suppressed by reason of its harms, the standards governing such regulations will have been diluted. The danger of political expression will no longer have to be clear or present in order for its suppression to be justified, and the government will be able to identify other dangerous ideologies to be suppressed.

Feminists might respond, at this point, that if pornography is political speech, its politics are implicit, not explicit.[179] Only when it is analyzed and understood, which it almost never is, can its women-hating message be seen. This response, however, puts feminists in a dilemma by forcing them to choose between this view and the group libel theory. Futhermore, the materials to which a group libel law could be applied would have to clearly vilify the group in question,[180] yet pornography does not meet this standard of clarity. Attempts to identify individual pieces of pornography that do meet this standard of clarity would again engage the government in evaluating the content of speech.

Alternate Conceptions of Regulation

The crux of the liberal critique of feminist theories is that by advocating regulation of pornography feminists condone the use of government to evaluate speech. Feminists may respond by arguing nonneutrally that pornography should be subject to legal restriction because it really is dangerous, whereas advocacy of socialism, for example, is not. This kind of argument has some attraction, particularly for feminists who are conscious of the extent of private coercion that has been exercised against women under the legal regime of public neutrality.[181]

Feminists would replace this regime of public neutrality with a regime oriented towards their vision of true neutrality, expressed in terms of equality. Feminists, like conservatives, are willing to subordinate individual liberty to a particular vision of the good community. As has been noted,[182] however, the feminist vision of community differs from the conservative vision. Not all nonliberal theories are conservative.[183] Although feminists and conservatives both argue that liberty can be realized only in a community that socializes its members to share certain values,[184] conservatives argue that liberty entails virtue while feminists argue that it entails equality.[185]

In the feminist account current noninterference with individual liberties is not really neutral; rather, it is an endorsement of the status quo. The status quo thus endorsed is more than a failed marketplace of ideas; culture itself is a male construct that inhibits the equality of women.[186] Feminists therefore challenge the neutrality that protects the sex industry by linking their use of legal regulation to a conception of social change. In the feminist vision regulation of pornography is part of a larger goal of actively promoting women's participation in culture and protecting women from being perpetually silenced.

Thus, the feminist argument is not that the government should determine whether or not a given book is presenting women as whores by nature; rather, it is that the government should be helping to eradicate the view that women are whores by nature by regulating works that present this view.[187] The result of such regulation would be the transformation of culture into a sphere sufficiently shared by men and women that the neutral principle of noninterference would truly be effective. However, this argument for the legal regulation of pornography is open to some serious objections regarding the wisdom of its underlying political assumptions.

Strategic Considerations Regarding the Use of Law

Invoking the law to suppress the dissemination of pornographic images raises difficult political issues for feminists. Freedom of expression, particularly freedom of sexual and political expression, is crucial to any feminist program of social reform.[188] Furthermore, the state has long been an instrument of male domination.[189] Thus an evaluation of the use of legal regulation cannot focus simply on traditional doctrinal arguments but must also consider broader questions of political strategy.

Strategic considerations regarding feminist opposition to pornography begin with the decision of whether the issue should be addressed at all. Pornography may not be as important as feminists claim; perhaps it is more an effect than a cause of male domination. If this is the case, then feminists should turn their attention to basic causes of pornography, such as inequality in family and work. Their elimination may cause pornographic expressions of male domination to wither away. In the meantime, emphasizing pornography diverts energy away from more important issues and alienates liberal allies of feminism. This argument merits consideration by feminists as an important strategic issue, but it does not threaten their basic moral argument. Even if pornography is primarily a cultural symptom, it nonetheless plays a role in reproducing male dominance and merits condemnation on that account.

Strategic objections to the feminists' legal arguments have considerably more force than objections to their account of pornography and its social role. The first strategic objection is that male-dominated legal institutions are unlikely to be sensitive to the feminist perspective on pornography and are certain to be sensitive to what they perceive to be first amendment values. Furthermore, even if the law can be made attentive to feminist concerns, the legal principles on which feminists need to rely are dangerously vague or overbroad and tend to approve exercises of government power that may be more dangerous to women's liberation than pornography.[190] If feminists argue that the dangerous ideas expressed in pornography justify suppression of it, they must accept the possibility that the government's notion of dangerousness will differ · from theirs. In fact, viewed in historical context, a relaxation of constitutional protection for "dangerous ideas" is far more likely to open feminists and their allies to legal harassment than to promote their political success.

Such harassment seems particularly likely given that, in our society, feminists do not generally express widely shared values, particularly on pornography. Enduring nonneutral principles must rest on a community's shared values.[191] Feminists may argue, along lines similar to traditional "Marxist" ones,[192] that their values may become shared once the government enforces them. After a period of such enforcement, the argument goes, other members of the community would become enlightened and would see pornography as feminists do.

There may be circumstances in which the end justifies the means in the way that this argument requires, but these do not seem to obtain in the case of pornography. It is more plausible when, as Marx imagined, the entire working class—the majority of society—actively participates in the exercise of state power. Moreover, Marx advocated total change, change for which it may be necessary to employ drastic means. In cases of one isolated cultural phenomenon, such as pornography, the Marxist argument loses force. It therefore seems wiser to think that pornography will wither away as feminist values somehow become more widely shared than to think that governmental enforcement of feminist values in the form of anti-pornography laws will cause them to be more widely shared.[193]

Does this mean, especially given the nagging question of how to facilitate the sharing of feminist values, that feminists should eschew legal regulation completely? The arguments considered above may take the law too seriously as an instrument of certain ends and not seriously enough as a symbolic expression of social values. Thus there may be some value in the symbolic and educational effect of compelling the government to grapple with the feminist analysis as it is presented through statutory proposals and litigious discourse.[194] The Minneapolis ordinance made headlines and caused people to consider why a City Council found it plausible to think that pornography is a form of sex discrimination. The law does not simply stand outside controversies over basic values; it is inevitably a participant.

Justice Brandeis once observed that "[f]ear of serious injury alone cannot justify suppression of free speech. . . . Men feared witches and burnt women. It is the function of speech to free men from the bondage of irrational fears."[195] The long silence about the concerns that animate feminist opposition to pornography is evidence that neither men nor women are yet free from the bondage of irrational fears expressed in pornography. As Brandeis suggested, use of the law to debate our basic values may be a crucial strategy[196] by which feminists can make their voices heard.

Notes

1. 354 U.S. 476 (1957).
2. *Id.* at 481.
3. *See* F. Schauer, The Law of Obscenity 206–27 (1976).
4. Most states regulate obscenity. For a categorization of obscenity statutes, see New York v. Ferber, 458 U.S. 747, 755 n.7 (1982). Federal regulation in the area includes provisions regulating the use of the mails, *see* 18 U.S.C. § 1461 (1982); 39 U.S.C. §§ 3001, 3008, 3010 (1982), common carriers, *see* 18 U.S.C. § 1462 (1982), interstate transportation, *see* 18 U.S.C. § 1465 (1982), and importation into the United States, *see* 18 U.S.C. § 1462 (1982); 19 U.S.C. § 1305 (1982). For a discussion of the history of federal obscenity regulation and a description of current federal law in the area, see F. Schauer, *supra* note 3, at 169-91.
5. *See infra* notes 32–36 and accompanying text.
6. *See infra* notes 66–71 and accompanying text (discussing views of liberal theorists).
7. *See infra* notes 40–44 and accompanying text.
8. *See infra* notes 45–59 and accompanying text.
9. *See infra* notes 60–64 and accompanying text.
10. *See, e.g.,* A. Dworkin, Pornography: Men Possessing Women (1981);

S. Griffin, Pornography and Silence (1981); Take Back the Night: Women on Pornography (L. Lederer ed. 1980).

11. Several feminist antipornography groups, including Women Against Pornography, formed in 1979 in New York, and Women Against Violence in Pornography and Media, formed in 1976 in San Francisco, have appeared in recent years. These groups have organized demonstrations, conferences, and workshops. Occasionally, these groups have taken direct action against particular films, theaters, and bookstores. *See* Boler, Lake & Wynne, *We Sisters Join Together . . .*, in Take Back the Night: Women on Pornography, *supra* note 10, at 19; Gever & Hall, *Fighting Pornography*, in *id.* at 261–85; LaBelle, Snuff—*The Ultimate in Women-Hating*, in *id.* at 272; Lederer, *Introduction*, in *id.* at 15; Lederer, *Women Have Seized the Executive Offices of Grove Press . . .*, in *id.* at 267.

12. The first such effort took place in Minneapolis, Minnesota. *See Ordinance Amending Title 7 of Minneapolis Code of Ordinances Relating to Civil Rights, (Dec. 30, 1983) (vetoed Jan. 5, 1984). Despite the veto of the Minneapolis ordinance, the City-County Council of Indianapolis, Indiana passed a similar measure. See* City of Indianapolis and Marion County City-County General Ordinance 24, 1984 (passed April 23, 1984) (copy on file at University of Pennsylvania Law Review); City of Indianapolis and Marion County City-County Ordinance 35, 1984 (passed June 11, 1984) (copy on file at University of Pennsylvania Law Review). A federal district court declared this ordinance unconstitutional in November 1984. *See* American Booksellers Ass'n, Inc. v. Hudnut, no. IP 84-791C (S.D. Ind. Nov. 19, 1984).

13. *See, e.g.,* Willis, *Feminism, Moralism, and Pornography*, in Beginning To See The Light: Pieces of a Decade 219 (1981); Ellis, *I'm Black and Blue from the Rolling Stones and I'm Not Sure How I Feel About It: Pornography and the Feminist Imagination*, Socialist Rev., May–Aug., 1984, at 103; English, Hollibaugh & Rubin, *Talking Sex: A Conversation on Sexuality and Feminism*, Socialist Rev., July–Aug. 1981, at 43, 56–62. Philipson, *Beyond the Virgin and the Whore*, Socialist Rev., May–Aug. 1984, at 127; Weir & Casey, *Subverting Power in Sexuality*, Socialist Rev., May–Aug., 1984, at 139, 146; *cf.* B. Faust, Women, Sex, And Pornography (1980) (agreeing that pornography is an important issue but criticizing feminist analysis).

14. The issue of censorship tends to dominate discussions of pornography. Feminists, however, are concerned primarily with encouraging people to think differently about what pornography means. *See, e.g.,* A. Dworkin, *supra* note 10, at 9; Russell, *Pornography and the Women's Liberation Movement*, in Take Back the Night: Women on Pornography, *supra* note 10, 303–04.

15. Insensitivity to feminist concerns also implicates a general critique of prevailing legal theory. Conservative legal theory perceives the harm of pornography to be in its effects upon morality rather than in its other effects on women. Liberal legal theory moves too quickly from the conclusion that pornography should not be censored as a relativism in morality and aesthetics that sets a taste for pornography beyond the scope of rational criticism.

16. A well-known formulation of the feminist position argues that "[p]ornography is the theory, and rape the practice." Morgan, *Theory and Practice: Pornography and Rape,* in Going Too Far 163, 169 (1977). For more extensive discussions of this thesis, see S. Griffin, *supra* note 10, at 111–19 (discussing both general and individual harms); Jacobs, *Patterns of Violence: A Feminist Perspective on the Regulation of Pornography,* 7 Harv. Women's L.J. 5, 9–23 (1984) (discussing both general and individual harms); LaBelle, *The Propaganda of Misogyny,* in Take Back the Night: Women on Pornography, *supra* note 10, at 174 (pornography functions as propaganda against all women); Russell, *Pornography and Violence: What Does the New Research Say?,* in Take Back the Night: Women on Pornography, *supra* note 10 at 218 (recent studies have revealed harms to individual women).

17. *See supra* note 12.

· 18. Considerable debate has been focused on identifying the basic values that freedom of speech is meant to promote. *See* Redish, *The Value of Free Speech,* 130 U. Pa. L. Rev. 591, 591–93 (1982). The values of truth, emphasized in J.S. Mill, On Liberty (1859) and of political participation, emphasized in A. Meiklejohn, Political Freedom (1960), appear uncontroversial, although there remains disagreement about how they are to be defined, *see, e.g.,* Baker, *Realizing Self-Realization: Corporate Political Expenditures and Redish's* The Value of Free Speech, 130 U. Pa. L. Rev. 646 (1982); Redish, *Self-Realization, Democracy, and Freedom of Expression: A Reply to Professor Baker,* 130 U. Pa. L. Rev. 678 (1982), and whether these values are the proper focus for first amendment analysis, *see, e.g.,* Baker, *Scope of the First Amendment Freedom of Speech,* 25 UCLA L. Rev. 964, 990–91 (1978) [hereinafter cited as Baker, *Scope of the First Amendment*].

19. *Compare, e.g.,* Bork, *Neutral Principles and Some First Amendment Problems,* 47 Ind. L.J. 1, 20 (1971) ("Constitutional protection should be accorded only to speech that is explictly [sic] political.") *with* T. Emerson, The System of Freedom of Expression 6–7 (1970) (arguing that freedom of expression is essential for assuring individual self-fulfillment, advancing knowledge, allowing participation in decision-making, and achieving a more adaptable, and hence, more stable community).

20. 354 U.S. 476 (1957).

21. *Id.* at 486. *See also* Miller v. California, 413 U.S. 15, 23 (1973) (reaffirming that obscene material is unprotected under the first amendment).

22. A distributor may increase her chances of prosecution by pandering; that is, marketing materials openly advertised to appeal to a customer's prurient interest. See Ginzburg v. United States, 383 U.S. 463, 470–71 (1966). And the Supreme Court recently held that distribution of certain nonobscene films and other visual representations involving children may be restricted to discourage production of such materials. *See* New York v. Ferber, 458 U.S. 747, 760–61 (1982).

23. *See* Paris Adult Theater 1 v. Slaton, 413 U.S. 49, 61 (1973) (stating that legislature may act "to protect *'the social interest in order and morality' "*) (quoting *Roth* 354 U.S. at 485, which had quoted Chaplinsky v. New

Hampshire, 315 U.S. 568, 572 (1942)) (footnote omitted and emphasis supplied in *Roth*).

24. *See, e.g.*, Paris Adult Theater I v. Slaton, 413 U.S. 49, 58–63 (1973).

25. It could be argued that, even if obscenity is speech, the balance of interests favors its suppression. In contrast to the Court's more formalistic approach, this argument would have to rely on some empirical proof that pornography is harmful. Findings of fact based upon empirical data are not unknown to constitutional adjudication, *see, e.g.*, Brown v. Board of Educ., 347 U.S. 483, 494 & n.11 (1954), but the Court has tended to avoid confronting the empirical issues implicated by obscenity cases. *But see* New York v. Ferber, 458 U.S. 747, 758, n.9 (1982) (citing studies of harms caused by use of children as subjects in pornography).

26. *Roth*, 354 U.S. at 484. *But cf.* Miller v. California, 413 U.S. 15, 24 (1973) ("We do not adopt as a constitutional standard the '*utterly* without redeeming social value' test.") (quoting plurality opinion in A Book Named "John Cleland's Memoirs of a Woman of Pleasure" v. Attorney General, 383 U.S. 413, 419 (1966)) (emphasis supplied in *Miller*).

27. 315 U.S. 568 (1942).

28. *Id.* at 572 (footnote omitted), *quoted in Roth*, 354 U.S. at 485 (emphasis supplied in *Roth*).

29. Professor Schauer forcefully articulates the premises of this argument. According to Schauer, "Sex in and of itself is not protected by the first amendment. . . . Underlying all of the words of [the Supreme Court's obscenity cases] is the assumption that hardcore pornography *is* sex." Schauer, *Speech and "Speech"—Obscenity and "Obscenity": An Exercise in the Interpretation of Constitutional Language*, 67 Geo. L.J. 899, 926 (1979) [hereinafter cited as Schauer, *Speech*]. Because conduct in and of itself is not protected by the first amendment, his identification of pornography as conduct rather than speech removes it from the amendment's protection. The scope of the argument is limited, however, by its reliance upon a narrow construction of obscenity. Only hard-core pornography, most of which is pictorial, can plausibly be thought to have solely a physical effect and no cognitive content. It also does not follow that obscenity ought to be suppressed, but only that its suppression would not violate anyone's right to freedom of speech. *See id.* at 933; *see also* Finnis, *"Reason and Passion": The Constitutional Dialectic of Free Speech and Obscenity*, 116 U. Pa. L. Rev. 222, 242 (1967); Schauer, *Response: Pornography and the First Amendment*, 40 U. Pitt. L. Rev. 605, 617 n.47 (1979). Another interpretation of the *Roth* argument is that pornography expresses ideas—but not ideas having any social importance.

30. 413 U.S. 15 (1973).

31. *Id.* at 24 (citation omitted) (quoting Kois v. Wisconsin, 408 U.S. 229, 230 (1979) which had quoted *Roth*, 354 U.S. at 489).

32. Although the *Miller* standard appears to be tailored towards hardcore materials, it ultimately relies upon the application of *local* community standards. *See Miller*, 413 U.S. at 30–34. This reliance on community stan-

dards can be seen as a conservative element of the definition, tending to restrict the availability of materials, although it also has been argued that a national standard would have inhibitory effects. *See id.* 32 n.13.

33. *See* F. Schauer, *supra* note 3, at 69–95.

34. *Id.* at 27–28, 105–09.

35. *Id.* at 102–05.

36. *Id.* at 136–53.

37. Kaplan, *Obscenity as an Esthetic Category,* 20 Law & Contemp. Probs. (1955), provides a discussion of aesthetic considerations of obscenity. Kaplan argues that pornography cannot really be subjected to an aesthetic analysis because such analysis requires "distance," and pornography is "not itself the *object* of an experience, . . . but rather a stimulus *to* an experience." *Id.* at 548. *But see* S. Sontag, *The Pornographic Imagination,* in Styles of Radical Will 35, 38–48 (1969) (arguing that literary pornographic works do exist but critics' view of literature by definition excludes pornography).

38. *See, e.g.,* Schauer, *Speech, supra* note 29, at 927. *See also* A Book Named "John Cleland's Memoirs of a Woman of Pleasure" v. Attorney General, 383 U.S. 413, 427 (1966) (Douglas, J., concurring) ("We are judges, not literary experts."); Paris Adult Theater I v. Slaton, 413 U.S. 49, 96–97 (1973) (Brennan, J., dissenting) (arguing that state suppression should be limited to materials utterly lacking in social value).

39. Indeed, *Miller* states that the trier of fact should consider "whether the work, taken as a whole, lacks serious literary, artistic, political or scientific value." *See Miller,* 413 U.S. at 24. *See also,* New York v. Ferber, 458 U.S. 747, 762 (1982) ("We consider it unlikely that visual depictions of children performing sexual acts would often constitute an important and necessary part of a literary performance. . . ."); A Book Named "John Cleland's Memoirs of a Woman of Pleasure" v. Attorney General, 383 U.S. 413, 450 (1966) (Clark, J., dissenting) (finding *Fanny Hill* to be "utterly without redeeming social importance"); *Roth,* 354 U.S. at 498 (1957) (Harlan, J., concurring in part) (obscenity judgments involve judicial evaluation of the works in question).

40. Most commentators seem to accept a broad enough conception of first amendment values to encompass protection for obscenity. *See, e.g.,* Richards, *Free Speech and Obscenity Law: Toward a Moral Theory of the First Amendment,* 123 U. Pa. L. rev. 45, 73, 91 (1974).

41. Professor Baker is perhaps clearest in advocating first amendment protection for a "broad realm of nonviolent, noncoercive activity." Baker, *Scope of the First Amendment, supra* note 18, at 990. *See also* Feinberg, *Pornography and the Criminal Law,* 40 U. Pitt. L. Rev. 567, 576 (1979) (arguing that regulation of expressive conduct may contravene first amendment guarantees).

42. *See* Richards, *supra* note 40, at 81 (pornography advocates "pornotopia"—a vision of society and social relationships); Gerety, *Pornography and Violence,* 40 U. Pitt. L. Rev. 627, 649–51 (1979) (supporting obscenity regulation but advocating pornographic works that "agitat[e] for social,

political, economic, cultural or artistic change.") *But see supra* note 29 (outlining arguments against protecting pornography). Ironically, the feminist analysis of pornography gives it a claim to cognitive content and even to status as political speech. *See, e.g.,* S. Brownmiller, Against Our Will: Men Women and Rape 440 (1975) ("Pornography is the undiluted essence of antifemale propaganda.") Some pornographers view themselves as advancing a form of "porn liberation." *See, e.g.,* Schipper, *Filthy Lucre: A Tour of America's Most Profitable Frontier,* Mother Jones, April 1980, at 31, 60.

43. The two-tier terminology was first used by Kalven. *See* Schauer, *supra* note 32, at 899 n.3 (citing Kalven, *The Metaphysics of the Law of Obscenity,* 1960 Sup. Ct. Rev. 1, 10). However, the analysis itself can be seen in Chaplinsky v. New Hampshire, 315 U.S. 568, 571–73 (1942) ("fighting words"), and Beauharnais v. Illinois, 343 U.S. 250, 255–58 (1950) (group libel).

44. *See, e.g.,* Richards, *supra,* note 40, at 79–80.

45. Although it is clearly an oversimplification to define only two positions on the issue of pornography, this simplification imposes some order on an otherwise bewildering array of opinions. For the purposes of this Comment, the simplification is not misleading; most of the nonfeminist analyses fall within the parameters of the conservative and liberal positions here delineated.

For examples of the conservative and liberal positions and the contrast between them, see United States Commission on Obscenity and Pornography, Report of the United States Commission on Obscenity and Pornography (1970) (liberal) [hereinafter cited as Commission Report]. *Compare id.* at 379 (statements of Morris A. Lipton and Edward B. Greenwood) (liberal) *with id.* at 383 (statements of Morton A. Hill and Winfrey C. Link) (conservative). For a more vitriolic statement of the conservative position, see *id.* at 511 (statement of Charles E. Keating, Jr.).

46. *See, e.g.,* L. Zurcher & R. Kirkpatrick, Citizens for Decency 113 (1976); Berns, *Beyond the (Garbage) Pale or Democracy, Censorship and the Arts,* in Censorship and Freedom of Expression 49, 58–59 (H. Clor ed. 1971); Christenson, *It's Time to Excise the Pornographic Cancer,* 25 Christianity Today, Jan. 2, 1981, at 20,22.

47. For a description of the traditional view, see *Introduction,* Philosophy and Sex 1–7 (R. Baker & F. Elliston eds. 1975).

48. *Id.*

49. *See* L. Zurcher & R. Kirkpatrick, *supra* note 46, at 20–23; Berns, *supra* note 46, at 60–62; Kristol, *Pornography, Obscenity and the Case for Censorship,* in Philosophy of Law 165, 169–70 (J. Feinberg & H. Gross eds. 1975). *See generally* T. Williams, See No Evil: Christian Attitudes Toward Sex in Art and Entertainment (1976) (discussing popular arguments against pornography usually invoke the necessity for decency and virtue in the face of licentiousness, vice, and corruption).

50. Berns, *supra* note 46, at 58; Clor, *Obscenity and Freedom of Expression,* in Censorship and Freedom of Expression, *supra* note 46, at 97, 102–05; Williams, *Offensiveness, Pornography, and Art,* in Pornography and Cen-

sorship 185, 188–89 (D. Copp & S. Wendell eds. 1983) ("Pornography crosses the line between private and public. . . .").

51. *See* Berns, *supra* note 46, at 63–69; Kristol, *supra* note 49, at 169–70; Williams, *supra* note 50, at 189–90; *see also* Bickel, *On Pornography II: Dissenting and Concurring Opinions,* 22 The Pub. Interest 25, 25–26 (Winter 1971), *quoted in* Paris Adult Theater I v. Slaton, 413 U.S. 49, 59 n.9 (1973): *Smut, Pornography, Obscenity—Signs the Tide is Turning,* U.S. News & World Rep., May 7, 1973, at 39–44.

52. It would be very important, in other contexts, to distinguish among conservatives adopting stronger or weaker versions of the sexual philosophy described in the text. Some would limit their opposition to a narrowly confined class of materials whereas others would oppose a broader class. *See, e.g.,* Christenson, *supra* note 46, at 20–21.

53. *See, e.g.,* P. Devlin, The Enforcement of Morals (1965). Empirical studies found a significant correlation between approval of strong law enforcement procedures and disapproval of pornography. *See, e.g.,* Birkelbach & Zurcher, *Some Socio-Political Characteristics of Anti-Pornography Campaigners,* 4 Soc. Symp. 13, 13–22 (1970); Peek & Brown, *Pornography as a Political Symbol: Attitudes Toward Commerical Nudity and Attitudes Toward Political Organizations,* 58 Soc. Sci. Q. 717, 717–23 (1978).

54. *See, e.g.,* Baumrin, *Sexual Immorality Delineated,* in Philosophy and Sex, *supra* note 48, at 116, 119–20; Elliston, *In Defense of Promiscuity,* in *id.* at 222, 232–240.

55. These views are primarily attributable to the influence of Freud and psychoanalysis. *See, e.g.,* Freud, *The Sexual Life of Human Beings,* in Introductory Lectures on Psychoanalysis 303, 310 (J. Strachey ed. 1966); *see also* Gaylin, *Obscenity is More than a Four-Letter Word,* in Censorship and Freedom of Expression, *supra* note 46, at 153, 160–62.

56. *See, e.g.,* Ginzburg v. United States, 383 U.S. 463, 491 (1966) (Douglas, J., dissenting); *see also* Feinberg, *Pornography and the Criminal Law,* 40 U. Pitt. L. Rev. 567, 568 (1979) (arguing that although pornography may be offensive, it is not harmful). *But cf.* Clark, *Liberalism and Pornography,* in Pornography and Censorship, *supra* note 50, at 45, 51–58 (arguing for reconceptualization of what is "harmful"); Gerety, *Pornography and Violence,* 40 U. Pitt. L. Rev. 627, 632–34, 652–60 (1979) (insisting that violent pornography is harmful, even to "bystanders").

57. *See, e.g.,* Baier, *Response: The Liberal Approach to Pornography,* 40 U. Pitt. L. Rev. 619, 624–25 (1979) (arguing that obscenity is protected by the first amendment, which "guarantees the freedom to express, advocate, extol, and defend alternative ideals and standards of purity"). This does not necessarily mean that all liberals approve of any and all sexually-oriented materials or of their unrestricted distribution. *See, e.g.,* Commission Report, *supra* note 45 at 51–60 (Although the Commission recommended the abolition of obscenity laws, it approved restrictions on young persons' access to sexually explicit materials.).

58. *See* Miller, 413 U.S. at 40–41 (Douglas, J., dissenting) (obscenity involves questions of taste). "Neutrality" is central to many versions of

liberalism. *See* B. Ackerman, Social Justice in the Liberal State 10–12 (1980) (authority cannot be vindicated by reference to "a privileged insight into the moral universe"); Feinberg, *supra* note 56, at 568 (Liberalism permits regulation only for the purpose of preventing harm or nuisance to others): Wechsler, *Toward Neutral Principles of Constitutional Law,* 73 Harv. L. Rev. 1 (1959). The feminist argument takes issue with the liberal stance of neutrality. *See infra* notes 186–87 and accompanying text.

59. This does not mean that pornography may not be regulated to avoid unnecessary offense or exposure of children but that regulation would have to meet the familiar time, place, and manner constraints of the first amendment. Consistent with its tolerance of the activities of *consenting* adults, the Commission Report, *supra* note 45, at 51–56, recommends the abolition of all obscenity laws but would restrict the access of "explicit sexual materials to young persons," *id,* at 66. *See also id.* at 56–60. In the same vein, the report sanctions restrictions on the public display and unsolicited mailing of explicit materials. *See id.* at 60–62. Liberal concerns for the protection of unwilling audiences are considered by Feinberg, *supra* note 56, at 567–72, and Scanlon, *Freedom of Expression and Categories of Expression,* 40 U. Pitt. L. Rev. 519, 542–50 (1979).

60. *See, e.g.,* Paris Adult Theatre I v. Slaton, 413 U.S. 49, 69 (1973).

61. *See* supra text accompanying notes 33–36.

62. *See, e.g., Roth,* 354 U.S. at 487 n.20; F. Schauer, *supra* note 3, at 96–102.

63. For a pre-*Roth* defense of this element of the definition, see F. Schauer, *supra* note 3, at 98; *see also* Gardiner, *Moral Principles Toward a Definition of the Obscene,* 20 Law & Contempt. Probs. 560. 562–71 (1955).

64. The phrase "utterly without redeeming social importance" was first used in *Roth. See Roth,* 354 U.S. at 484. It was relied upon most directly in A Book Named "John Cleland's Memoirs of a Woman of Pleasure" v. Attorney General, 383 U.S. 413, 418–21 (1966); *see also* Jacobellis v. Ohio, 378 U.S. 184, 191 (1964). *Miller* replaced the test with a formulation exempting works without "serious literary, artistic, political or scientific value" from first amendment protection. *See Miller,* 413 U.S. at 24–25.

65. *See, e.g.,* E. Kronhausen & P. Kronhausen, Pornography and the Law (1959); S. Sontag, *The Pornographic Imagination,* in Styles of Radical Will 38–48 (1969); Richards, *supra* note 40, at 79–80.

66. The liberal attack on the Court's position has been mounted perhaps most authoritatively by the Commission on Obscenity and Pornography. *See* Commission Report, *supra* note 45; United States Comm'n on Obscenity and Pornography, Technical Reports of the Comm'n on Obscenity and Pornography (1971) (five volumes of empirical research) [hereinafter cited as Technical Reports].

67. Liberal responses to the Court's concerns are traceable to John Stuart Mill's philosophy granting the government authority to restrict individual freedoms only to prevent harm to others. *See* J. S. Mill, *supra* note 18; Feinberg, *supra* note 56, at 567–68; Scanlon, *A Theory of Freedom of Expression,* 1 Phil. & Pub. Aff. 204, 213 (1972); Scanlon, *supra* note 59, at

528–37. Chief Justice Burger has explicitly rejected Mill's principle. *See* Paris Adult Theatre I V. Slaton, 413 U.S. 49, 63–69 (1973).

68. This is the most often cited conclusion of the Commission Report, *supra* note 45, at 27 ("The Commission cannot conclude that exposure to erotic materials is a factor in the causation of sex crime or sex delinquency."). For a survey of empirical research since the Commission Report, see Daniels, *The Supreme Court and Obscenity: An Exercise in Empirical Constitutional Policy-Making*, 17 San Diego L. Rev. 757 (1980). See also *infra* note 97.

69. Support for the liberal view that pornographic materials serve a cathartic function is usually drawn from the research performed for the Commission on Obscenity and Pornography. *See* Technical Reports, *supra* note 66. For criticism of the liberal view, see, for example, Clark, *Liberalism and Pornography*, in Pornography and Censorship, *supra* note 50, at 45, 56–58; Griffin, *Sadism and Catharsis: The Treatment is the Disease*, in Take Back the Night: Women on Pornography, supra note 10, at 141.

70. *See, e.g.*, Berger, *Pornography, Sex, and Censorship*, in Pornography and Censorship, *supra* note 50, at 83, 99.

71. *See* Dworkin, *Paternalism*, in Philosophy of Law, *supra* note 49, at 174–84 (discussing types of government interference that can be considered paternalistic).

72. *See, e.g.*, Kristol, *supra* note 49, at 168–69.

73. *See* L. V. Sunderland, Obscenity: The Court, the Congress and the President's Commission 71–84 (1974); *Hill-Link Minority Report*, *supra* note 45, at 390–412.

74. *See* L. V. Sunderland, *supra* note 73, at 84; *Hill-Link Minority Report*, *supra* note 45, at 390–412.

75. Kristol, *supra* note 49, at 165.

76. It should not be assumed that all feminists would agree on the importance of pornography as a women's issue or on specific elements of the feminist account as it is described here. *See supra* note 13 and accompanying text. There is, however, a significant body of feminist literature that comprises a relatively unified account of pornography; this work provides the basis for the feminist arguments presented in this Comment. It should be further noted that this Comment assumes that feminists are expressing the interests of women generally. Hence no distinction will be drawn between feminists' interests and women's interests. Needless to say, this is a controversial assumption. *See, e.g.*, B. Ehrenreich, The Hearts of Men: American Dreams and the Flight From Commitment 144–68 (1983) (describing women's antifeminist movements); Ehrenreich, *The Women's Movements: Feminist and Antifeminist*, 15 Radical Am. 93, 99–100 (1981) (same).

77. "The major theme of pornography as a genre is male power, its nature, its magnitude, its use, its meaning." A. Dworkin, *supra* note 10, at 24. *See* Diamond, *Pornography and Repression: A Reconsideration of "Who" and "What,"* in Take Back the Night: Women on Pornography, supra note 10, at 187–

92 (arguing that pornography expresses norms about male power and domination).

The feminist identification of pornography as a problem of power rather than sexuality parallels feminists' identification of rape as a crime of violence rather than an act of lust. *See* S. Brownmiller, *supra* note 42. This insight clarifies Robin Morgan's assertion that pornography is the theory and rape the practice. *See* R. Morgan, *supra* note 16, at 163.

78. *See* S. Brownmiller, *supra* note 42; Foa, *What's Wrong With Rape,* in Feminism and Philosophy 347, 347–51 (M. Vetterling-Braggin, F. Elliston, & J. English eds. 1977); Peterson, *Coercion and Rape: The State as a Male Protection Racket,* in *id.* at 360, 360–67.

79. The inequitable distribution of sexual repression is perhaps best seen in the double standard that has long been applied to male and female sexual behavior. Because it is based on the notion that men's sexual drives are greater than women's, the double standard creates the need for "bad" women with whom men can have sex. The result is a distinction between "good" and "bad" women, for which the criterion is sexual activity; this distinction is unique to women's struggles. *See, e.g.,* D. Dinnerstein, The Mermaid and the Minotaur 38–75 (1976); A. Dworkin, *supra* note 10, at 203–209; S. Griffin, *supra* note 10, at 20–24.

80. *See* S. Hite, The Hite Report 304–57 (1976); E. Willis, *Hard To Swallow: "Deep Throat,"* in Beginning to See the Light: Pieces of a Decade 68–70, 73–75 (1981); Willis, *Feminism, Moralism, and Pornography,* in *id.* at 219.

81. *See* Steinem, *Erotica and Pornography: A Clear and Present Difference,* in Take Back the Night: Women on Pornography, *supra* note 10, at 37–38; Tong, *Feminism, Pornography and Censorship,* 8 Soc. Theory & Prac. 1, 2–4 (1982) (distinguishing "erotica" from "thanatica"). *But see* A. Dworkin, *supra* note 10, at preface (erotica is currently merely a subcategory of pornography); Griffin, *supra* note 10, at 11 (speaking of "two social movements . . . [one] reclaiming [the] erotic life as a part of human nature" and the other expressing fear and hatred of eros); *cf.* Willis, *supra* note 13, at 222–23.

82. Women Against Pornography flyer (undated) (on file at University of Pennsylvania Law Review).

83. This is clearly the assumption of most antipornography feminists, and thus it is not surprising that they find it to be the case. The seeming circularity of the analysis does not undermine its validity, however; rather, it reflects the interrelationship between pornography and sexuality. The distinction between egalitarian and degrading sexual imagery is unique to feminist theory and has not often been used as a basis for scientific experiment; it is therefore difficult to offer empirical support for the feminists' conclusions that most of what is produced by the pornography industry is degrading to women. At the very least, studies have indicated that a substantial share of pornography depicts violence against women, necessarily involving domination of them. *See infra* note 114 and accompanying text.

84. The exception—gay male pornography—is produced by men for men. These materials account for approximately 10% of the adult book market and a similar percentage of the film market. Commission Report, *supra* note 45, at 15–17. For information on the business of pornography, *see id.* at 73–137; Schipper, *supra* note 42, at 31; Smith, *All-American Sex*, Phila. Inquirer, Jan. 15, 1984 (magazine), at 17.

85. *See, e.g.,* S. Griffin, *supra* note 10, at 89–93; *cf.* Lederer, *Then and Now: An Interview With A Former Pornography Model,* in Take Back the Night: Women on Pornography, *supra* note 10, at 57 (pornography industry ignores the interests and personhood of models); Russell, *Pornography and Violence: What does the New Research Say?,* in *id.* at 220–21 (discussing pornographic article purporting to substantiate the notion that women enjoy rape). The argument that pornography is related to the discounting of women's interests is reinforced by the feminist account of liberals' refusal to acknowledge the oppressive aspects of the pornographer's liberty. *See infra* note 186–87 and accompanying text.

86. *See, e.g.,* S. Griffin, *supra* note 10, at 243–49; Markovic, *Women's Liberation and Human Emancipation,* in Women and Philosophy 145, 154–64 (C. Gould & M. Wartofsky eds. 1976); Law, *Rethinking Sex and the Constitution,* 132 U. Pa. L. Rev. 955, 967–69 (1984).

87. Although there may be widespread endorsement of the abstract principle that men and women are equal, this is a far cry from actually accepting women's experience to be as equally valuable as men's experience. *See* D. Dinnerstein, *supra* note 79; W. Farrell, The Liberated Man: Beyond Masculinity 256–57 (1974) (discussing housework of male consciousness-raising group); Frye, *Male Chauvinism: A Conceptual Analysis,* in Philosophy and Sex, *supra* note 48, at 65.

88. This does not mean that male power is the only element in the feminist perspective of power. In the process of feminist consciousness-raising, awareness of women's victimization is a prelude to empowerment. *See* Bartky, *Toward a Phenomenology of Feminist Consciousness,* in Feminism and Philosophy, *supra* note 78, at 22, 27;1 *See also* MacKinnon, *Feminism, Marxism, Method, and the State: An Agenda for Theory,* 7 Signs: J. Women Culture & Soc. 515, 535–44 (1982) ("Consciousness-raising is [feminism's] quintessential expression.").

89. As a matter of empirical fact, however, men and women appear to differ in their responses to pornography. This difference is only partly explicable in terms of differences in the amount of exposure men and women have had to pornography. *See, e.g.,* Commission Report, *supra* note 45, at 163–215; H. Eysenck & D. Nias, Sex, Violence and the Media 221–25 (1978). *But see* Fisher & Byrne, *Sex Differences in Response to Erotica?,* 36 J. Personality & Soc. Psychology 117, 123–24 (1978) (suggesting that men and women respond similarly but that women perceived movies to be more pornographic than did men).

In the feminist perspective, measured responses to pornography are not central to an evaluation of pornography because responses may be influenced by socialized moral and sexual attitudes. This does not mean that empirical research is irrelevant but that its results must be weighed in light of the forces that may shape responses. Thus the crucial question is how pornography would be viewed by a developed feminist consciousness.

90. S. Griffin, *supra* note 10, at 217. *See also id.* at 204–17. Examination of pornography with a feminist consciousness is exemplified by Dworkin's analysis of individual pornographic works. *See* A. Dworkin, *supra* note 10, at 27–30 (describing photograph in which a woman is tied naked to the roof of a car, as if she had been hunted); *id.* at 138–43 (describing *Playboy* photographs of a woman bound to a pole and held stationary by lasers; the accompanying text calls her a "volunteer").

The effect of this analysis upon the consciousness of the observer is described by Dworkin: "If a woman has any sense of her own intrinsic worth, seeing pornography in small bits and pieces can bring her to a useful rage. Studying pornography in quantity and depth . . . will turn that same woman into a mourner." Dworkin, *Pornography and Grief,* in Take Back the Night: Women on Pornography, *supra* note 10, at 286.

91. *See, e.g.,* A. Dworkin, *supra* note 10, at 101–28; S. Griffin, *supra* note 10, at 36–46.

92. This anonymity is part of what makes it plausible to see pornography as being about women per se.

93. *See, e.g.,* Ordinance Amending Title 7 of Minneapolis Code of Ordinances Relating to Civil Rights § 3 (Dec. 30, 1983) (vetoed Jan. 5, 1984).

94. *See* A. Dworkin, *supra* note 10, at 123–27.

95. *See* S. Griffin, *supra* note 10, at 56–59.

96. *See, e.g.,* A. Dworkin, *supra* note 10, at 115, 129–32. The perpetuation of this view of women's sexual fulfillment is a basis of feminists' objections to even the "milder" pornographic publications.

97. There is some disagreement about how much of pornography is violent. Few studies have focused on quantifying the amount of violence in pornography. One study examined 428 adult books easily accessible to the general public and found that in approximately one-third of the sex episodes force was used to obtain women's participation. *See* Smith, *The Social Content of Pornography,* 26 J. Com., 16 (1976). Another studied cartoons and pictures in *Playboy* and *Penthouse* magazines from 1973 to 1977. It found a "clear and consistent" increase in violence with respect to pictorials over the five-year period. Overall, ten percent of the cartoons and five percent of the pictures appearing in 1977 were considered violent. Malamuth & Spinner, *A Longitudinal Content Analysis of Sexual Violence in the Best-Selling Erotic Magazines,* 16 J. Sex Research 226 (1980). This low figure is not surprising given that the two magazines chosen are among the mildest forms of pornography available.

A consistent flaw in the numerous experiments designed to test the sociological and psychological effects of pornography is the lack of control over the content of films used in experiments. *See, e.g.,* Sapolsky & Zillmann, *The Effect of Soft-Core and Hard-Core Erotics on Provoked and Unprovoked Hostile Behavior,* 17 J. Sex Research 319 (1981) (criticizing lack of content control in prior pornography research). A distinction between hard-core and soft-core pornography usually is maintained, but the effect of such factors as violence, coercion of women, and mutuality of desire among participants is rarely isolated or controlled. *Id.* For discussions of other biases and flaws in pornography studies, see generally Bart & Jozsa, *Dirty Books, Dirty Films, and Dirty Data*, in Take Back the Night: Women on Pornography, *supra* note 10, at 204; Copp, *Introductory Essay*, in Pornography and Censorship, *supra* note 50, at 15, 34–38; Diamond, *Pornography and Repression: A Reconsideration of "Who" and "What"*, in Take Back the Night: Women on Pornography, *supra* note 10, at 187–203; McCormack, *Machismo in Media Research: A Critical Review of Research on Violence and Pornography*, 25 Soc. Probs. 544 (1978): Russell, *Pornography and Violence: What Does the New Research Say?*, in Take Back the Night: Women on Pornography, *supra* note 10, at 218–39. For a critique of the use of social science research to determine public policy, see, for example, Wilson, *Violence, Pornography and Social Science*, in The Pornography Controversy 225 (R. Rist ed. 1975).

98. *See, e.g.*, E. Kronhausen & P. Kronhausen, *supra* note 65, at 195–200. Although the authors do not emphasize the points that feminists do—the book was written in 1959—their analysis can provide support for feminist arguments. *Compare id.* at 203–06 (discussing the rape of virgins) *with* S. Griffin, *supra* note 10, at 20–24 (discussing male power through money and sex) *and* S. Brownmiller, *supra* note 42, at 389–404 (discussing characteristics of rapists and rape victims). The false moralism theme in pornography is often explicitly antireligious, even sacrilegious. *See, e.g.*, S. Griffin, *supra* note 10, at 69–80; E. Kronhausen & P. Kronhausen, *supra* note 65, at 216–19. This tendency allies pornographers with one dimension of liberalism.

99. *See* A. Dworkin, *supra* note 10, at 30–36. When the "feminist" emerges victorious, Dworkin argues, the outcome stands as a clear reminder to male readers that it is very dangerous to let women out of their control. The growth of this theme in recent years, together with the general increase in explicit violence in pornography, is taken by feminists to be part of a backlash against feminism. *See, e.g.*, Russell & Lederer, *Questions We Get Asked Most Often*, in Take Back the Night: Women on Pornography, *supra* note 10, at 27–28.

100. Pornography, as a product of the male imagination, may be analyzed by drawing on psychoanalytic sources. Some feminists, who have so examined pornography, conclude that it betrays a deep fear of women's power, particularly of women's sexual power. Its basis lies in resentment against the mother, generalized to all women, and layered over with a socialization to the prerogatives of masculinity. This fear is expressed in a desperate need to control women's sexuality and in anger against any hint of genuine independence. *See, e.g.*, A. Dworkin, *supra* note 10; S. Griffin, *supra* note 10; Chesler, *Men and Pornography: Why They Use It*, in Take Back the Night: Women on Pornography, *supra* note 10, at 155; Lurie; *Pornography and the Dread of Women*, in id. at 159; *see also* N. Chodorow, The Reproduction of Mothering (1978): D. Dinnerstein, *supra* note 79, 91–114.

101. Average circulation per issue for the last six months of 1982 totalled 7,556,206 for *Time and Newsweek;* 8,873,397 for *Playboy and Penthouse.* IMS, IMS '83 Ayer Directory of Publications, at 1130, 1133 (1983). Sales of records, tapes, and legitimate movie box office receipts totalled ₡6,506,000,000 in 1981. *Leisure Time: Basic Analysis,* 150 Standard & Poor's Indus. Surv. §§ 2, L22, L31 (Sept. 16, 1982). Estimates of the sales volume of legal pornography vary considerably. The recent demand for pornographic home video cassettes alone has increased sales by several billion dollars. It is estimated that half of all video cassettes sold are pornographic. Serrin, *Sex Is a Growing Multibillion Dollar Business,* N.Y. Times, Feb. 9, 1981, at B6, col. 2. The New York Times estimated that total pornography sales in 1980 were $5,000,000,000 primarily generated by over 20,000 adult bookstores around the country. *See id.* at col 1. More recent estimates put the total volume at $10,000,000,000 for 1983. *See* Smith, *All-American Sex,* Phila. Inquirer, Jan. 15, 1984 (Magazine), at 18, vol. 1. See generally Schipper, *supra* note 42.

102. To the extent that the social order defended by conservatives is male-dominated, these two views are direct opposites. Feminists view pornography as defending traditional values, *see, e.g.,* S. Griffin, *supra* note 10, at 1–35, whereas conservatives view it as undermining them, *see, e.g.,* Berns, *Beyond the (Garbage) Pale, or Democracy, Censorship and the Arts,* in The Pornography Controversy, *supra* note 97, at 40.

103. *See, e.g.,* B. Faust, *supra* note 13, at 21–24, 189–94; Garry, *Pornography and Respect for Women,* 4 Soc. Theory & Prac. 395, 413–16 (1978).

104. *See, e.g.,* S. Evans, Personal Politics (1980); J. Freeman, The Politics of Women's Liberation (1975).

105. *See* Clark, *Liberalism and Pornography,* in Pornography and Censorship, *supra* note 50, at 45 ("Since at least the mid-nineteenth century, the fight for women's rights has largely been fought under the banner of liberalism.") *But see id.,* at 45, 46–52 (liberal emphasis on negative liberties is inconsistent with aspects of women's equality). *See generally* L. Kanowitz, Women and the Law: The Unfinished Revolution (1973).

106. *See e.g.,* S. Brownmiller, *supra* note 42, at 438, 441–45; A. Dworkin, *supra* note 10, at 207–09; Clark, *Liberalism and Pornography,* in Pornography and Censorship, *supra* note 50.

107. *See* C. Gilligan, In a Different Voice: Psychological Theory and Women's Development (1982). Gilligan's work is in part a response to Lawrence Kohlberg's theory of moral development, *see id.* at 18–23; it is also responsive to a long tradition in psychology and social theory that views women as morally inferior to men. *See, e.g.,* Freud, *Femininity,* in New Introductory Lectures on Psychoanalysis, 112, 134 (1965) ("The fact that women must be regarded as having little sense of justice is no doubt related to the predominance of envy in their mental life. . . ."); Weisstein, *Psychology Constructs the Female,* in Radical Feminism 178 (A. Koedt, E. Levine & A. Rapone ed. 1973); *see also* S. Okin, Women In Western Social and Political Thought (1980); Gould, *The Woman Question: Philosophy of*

Liberation and the Liberation of Philosophy, in Women and Philosophy, *supra* note 86, at 5.

108. *See* C. Gilligan, *supra* note 107, at 19 ("This [female] conception of morality . . . centers moral development around the understanding of responsibility and relationships, just as the [male] conception of morality . . . ties moral development to the understanding of rights and rules.")

Although many conservative arguments on pornography refer to its impact on the community, the feminist position relies on a different conception of community. Conservatives tend to rely on abstract principles about community, for example ideas about *a priori* structures such as male dominance. *See* B. Ehrenreich, *supra* note 80, at 180–82; C. Gilligan, *supra* note 107, at 173–74.

109. Pornographer Robert Guccione believes that women have an exhibitionistic drive that is satisfied by appearing in pornographic works. *See* Polman, *Guccione,* Philadelphia Inquirer, Oct. 9, 1984, at 4-E, cols. 1–3 ("[V]ery few women won't take their clothes off. They *luuuhv* doing it. . . .").

110. *See* K. Barry, Female Sexual Slavery (1979). For an insight into the lives of pornography models, see L. Lovelace, Ordeal (1980); Lederer, *Then and Now: An Interview with a Former Pornography Model,* in Take Back the Night: Women on Pornography, *supra* note 10, at 57; Weene, *Venus,* Heresies: A Feminist Publication on Art & Politics #12, 1981, at 36 (Sex Issue); Schipper, *supra* note 42, at 32–33.

The Minneapolis ordinance creates a cause of action against producers, sellers, exhibitors, and distributors for "any person who is coerced . . . into performing for pornography." Ordinance Amending Title 7 of Minneapolis Code of Ordinances Relating to Civil Rights, § 4 (Dec. 30, 1983) (vetoed Jan. 5, 1984) The Ordinance makes it extremely difficult to negate a finding of coercion. *See id.* § 4(m).

111. This analysis parallels the feminist treatment of prostitution. *See* K. Barry, *supra* note 110; Millett, *Prostitution: A Quartet for Female Voices,* in Women and Sexist Society 60) (V. Gornick & B. Moran eds. 1971); *see also* Ericsson, *Charges Against Prostitution: An Attempt at a Philosophical Assessment,* 90 Ethics 335, 348–55 (1980) (arguing that attitudes against prostitution ought to be abandoned or modified because they are damaging and are based on beliefs prejudiced against women); Wendell, *Pornography and Freedom of Expression,* in Pornography and Censorship, *supra* note 50, at 167 (assessing the extent to which coercion in production can justify regulation).

112. *See* LaBelle, *The Propaganda of Misogyny,* in Take Back the Night: Women in Pornography, *supra* note 10, at 174.

113. *See* S. Brownmiller, *supra* note 42, at 442–45.

114. *See id.* at 395–96; Morgan, *Theory and Practice: Pornography and Rape,* in Take Back the Night: Women on Pornography, *supra* note 10, at 134. Some feminists have incorporated empirical findings into their formulations of this argument. *See, e.g.,* Bart & Jozsa, *Dirty Books, Dirty Films, and*

Dirty Data, in Take Back the Night: Women on Pornography, *supra* note 10, at 204; Diamond, *Pornography and Repression,* in *id.,* at 187; Russell, *Pornography and Violence: What Does the New Research Say?,* in *id.,* at 218; *see also* McCormack, *supra* note 97. For empirical studies regarding this issue, see Donnerstein, *Pornography and Violence Against Women: Experimental Studies,* in Pornography and Censorship *supra note 50, at 219;* Donnerstein & Berkowitz, *Victim Reactions in Aggressive Erotic Films as a Factor in Violence Against Women,* in *id.* at 233; Kutchinsky, *The Effect of Easy Availability of Pornography on the Incidence of Sex Crimes: The Danish Experience,* in *id.* at 295; Malamuth & Check, *Penile Tumescence and Perceptual Responses to Rape as a Function of Victim's Perceived Reactions,* in *id.* at 257; Russell, *Research on How Women Experience the Impact of Pornography,* in *id.* at 213; Zillman, Bryant, Comisky & Medoff, *Excitation and Hedonic Violence in the Effect of Erotica on Motivated Intermale Aggression,* in *id.* at 2275; see also H. Eysenck & D. Nias, *supra* note 89; Gray, *Exposure to Pornography and Aggression Toward Women: The Case of the Angry Male,* 29 Soc. Probs. 387 (1982). *See generally* G. Byerly & R. Rubin, Pornography: The Conflict over Sexually Explicit Materials in the United States: An Annotated Bibliography (1980); C. Wilson, Violence Against Women: An Annotated Bibliography 85–99 (1981).

115. S. Griffin, *supra* note 10, 111–19; Tong, *supra* note 81, at 10–12.

116. *See* Garry, *supra* note 103, at 407–10.

117. *See supra* notes 60–64 and accompanying text.

118. Richards, *supra* note 40, at 47–51, 55–56. Richards discusses the etymology of the words "obscene" and "pornography" and concludes that to label something obscene is to condemn it, whereas to label it as pornographic is, to a greater extent, merely to describe it. *See id.* at 47–51, 55–56.

119. Longino, *Pornography, Oppression, and Freedom: A Closer Look,* in Take Back the Night: Women and Pornography, *supra* note 10, at 43. Some feminists use far looser definitions. *See, e.g.,* Yeamans, *A Political-Legal Analysis of Pornography,* in Take Back the Night: Women on Pornography, *supra* note 10, at 248 (defining pornography as "any use of the media which equates sex and violence"). These are some suggestions that feminist objections to pornography are partly based on the fact that it is *sold* for the sake of sexual stimulation. This parallels the pandering ideas elaborated in Ginzberg v. United States, 383 U.S. 463, 467–71 (1966). *See, e.g.,* Ordinance Amending Title 7 of Minneapolis Code of Ordinances Relating to Civil Rights § 4 (Dec. 30, 1983) (Jan. 5, 1984); Russell & Lederer, *supra* note 99, at 27 ("Pornography is not made to educate but to sell, and . . . what sells in a sexist society is a bunch of lies about women and sex.") Some criticism from within the feminist movement can be found in English, Hollibaugh & Rubin, *supra* note 13, at 56–57.

120. *See supra* note 12. The Minneapolis ordinance begins by defining pornography as "the sexually explicit subordination of women graphically depicted, whether in pictures or in words." Ordinance Amending Title 7 of Minneapolis Code of Ordinances Relating to Civil Rights § 3(gg)(1) (Dec.

30, 1983) (Jan. 5, 1984). The definition is complicated, however, by the statute's delineation of nine components, of which one or more must be present in pornographic works:

> (i) women are presented as sexual objects, things, or commodities; or (ii) women are presented as sexual objects who enjoy pain or humiliation; or (iii) women are presented as sexual objects who experience sexual pleasure in being raped; or (iv) women are presented as sexual objects tied up or cut up or mutilated or bruised or physically hurt; or (v) women are presented in postures of sexual submission; or (vi) women's body parts—including but not limited to vaginas, breasts, and buttocks—are exhibited, such that women are reduced to those parts; or (vii) women are presented as whores by nature; or (viii) women are presented being penetrated by objects or animals; or (ix) women are presented in scenarios of degradation, injury, abasement, torture, shown as filthy or inferior, bleeding, bruised, or hurt in a context that makes these conditions sexual.

121. Compare the feminist definitions with the standard delineated by the Supreme Court in Miller v. California, 413 U.S. 15, 24–25 (1973).

122. It should be noted that these three theories are interrelated in their reliance upon the feminist account of the silencing of women and their concerns, particularly in the sphere of sexuality. *See generally* A. Dworkin, *supra* note 10; S. Griffin, *supra* note 10. To the extent that this account is the basis of the argument that the marketplace of ideas has failed, that theory underlies the other two.

123. *See supra* note 86 and accompanying text; Dworkin, *For Men, Freedom of Speech; for Woman, Silence, Please,* in Take Back the Night: Women on Pornography, *supra* note 10, at 256–58. *See generally* J. Elshtain, Public Man, Private Woman (1981); S. Griffin, *supra* note 10.

124. *See, e.g.,* L. Kanowitz, Women and the Law: The Unfinished Revolution 4–5 (1969). Although there are no direct prohibitions of women's participation in the public sphere, disproportionate burdens in the private sphere make it impossible for women to participate equally; housework, childcare, and the emotional maintenance of personal relationships is work done almost entirely by women. *See* A. Oakley, The Sociology of Housework (1974); Mothering: Essays in Feminist Theory 135–65 (J. Trebilcot ed. 1984); Hartmann, *The Family as the Locus of Gender, Class, and Political Struggle: The Example of Housework,* 6 Signs: J. Women Culture & Soc. 366, 377–86 (1981).

125. Karst articulates a theoretical justification for treating equality as a value served by the first amendment. Karst, *Equality as a Central Principle in the First Amendment,* 43 U. Chi. L. Rev. 20, 23–26 (1975). He construes the principle to undermine "content discrimination" and obscenity laws in particular, *See id.* at 19–32. *But see* Redish, *The Content Distinction in First Amendment Analysis,* 34 Stan. L. Rev. 113, 135–139 (1981).

126. *See, e.g.,* S. Griffin, Woman and Nature: The Roaring Inside Her

(1978); Rich, *Afterword,* in Take Back the Night: Women on Pornography, *supra* note 10, at 313.

127. Bonnie Klein, the director of the feminist antipornography movie, *Not A Love Story: A Film About Pornography,* originally set out to make an erotic film but found that "woman's sexual imagery had been co-opted by the 'male entertainment industry." This discovery prompted her to make the documentary. *Off Our Backs,* April 1982, at 20. Dworkin, emphasizes the similarities between pornographers and sexologists. A. Dworkin, *supra* note 10, at 178–98.

128. This is especially true if a "positive" conception of freedom is adopted, as feminists urge. S. Griffin, *supra* note 10, at 1; Longino, *supra* note 119, at 51–53; Russell, *supra* note 99, at 29; *see also* Clark, *Liberalism and Pornography,* in Pornography and Censorship, *supra* note 50, at 45.

129. The link between media violence and behavior is far better substantiated than any link between media sexuality and behavior. *See* H. Eysenck and D. Nias *supra* note 89.

130. 343 U.S. 250 (1952).

131. *Id.* at 251 (quoting Ill. Ann. Stat. ch. 38, § 471 (Smith-Hurd 1949) (repealed 1961)).

132. *See Beauharnais,* 343 U.S. at 262.

133. *Id.* at 259–62.

134. *See, e.g.,* F. Haiman, Speech and Law in a Free Society 90–99 (1981). Haiman argues that *Beauharnais* found group libel theory to be valid by relying upon analogies to individual libel and fighting words. These doctrines, he reasons, have since been undermined by New York Times Co. v. Sullivan, 376 U.S. 254 (1964) (libel), Cohen v. California, 403 U.S. 15 (1971) (fighting words), and Gooding v. Wilson, 405 U.S. 518 (1972) (fighting words). *But cf.* Smolla, *Let The Author Beware: The Rejuvenation of the American Law of Libel,* 132 U. Pa. L. Rev. 1, 11 (1983) (arguing that doctrinal confusion is one of the causes of the recent rejuvention of American libel law).

135. *See, e.g.,* Collin v. Smith, 578 F.2d 1197, 1205 (7th Cir.) (discussing abrogation of *Beauharnais* and holding that that case does not make first amendment inapplicable to prohibition of Nazi march), *cert. denied,* 439 U.S. 916 (1978).

136. *E.g.,* Note *Group Vilification Reconsidered,* 89 Yale L.J. 308 (1979) (distinguishing group libel from group vilification by relying primarily on Meiklejohn's narrow first amendment theory); *cf.* Delgado, *Words that Wound: A Tort Action for Racial Insults, Epithets, and Name-Calling,* 17 Harv. C.R.-C.L. L. Rev. 133 (1982) (endorsing tort action over first amendment objections).

137. *See* Delgado, *supra* note 136, at 135–49; Note, *supra* note 136, at 317–22.

138. Paradoxically, in cases involving a group in particular need of protection, because of the listener's tendency to believe that the group is somehow inferior, this belief also prevents the listener from taking the

group's views seriously. For a discussion of women's experience in this area, see Frye, *supra* note 87, at 74–79.

139. This nonneutral principle, as articulated here, depends in part on the market failure argument. *See supra* notes 123–27 and accompanying text.

140. *See* A. Dworkin, *supra* note 10 (especially chapters 6 and 7. The word pornography derives from Greek in which it meant the "depiction of the lowest whores." *Id.* at 200. *See also* Ordinance Amending Title 7 of Minneapolis Code of Ordinances Relating to Civil Rights § 3 (Dec. 30, 1983) (vetoed Jan. 5, 1984).

141. Tong, *supra* note 81, at 4; *see* Garry, *supra* note 103, at 397–405, 413–16.

142. *See* Hill, *Servility and Self-Respect*, 57 The Monist 87 (1973).

143. This is the form of most present-day obscenity laws. *See supra* note 4; *see also* Feinberg, *supra* note 56, at 567–68.

144. It might even be possible to compel the pornography industry to support shelters for battered women or rape crisis centers by some sort of tax transfer scheme. It appears that no one has ever proposed such a plan.

145. *See e.g.,* New York v. Ferber, 458 U.S. 747 (1982) (upholding statute prohibiting promotion of sexual performances by minors); FCC v. Pacifica Found., 438 U.S. 726 (1978) (upholding statute forbidding broadcasters from using "any obscene, indecent, or profane language" on radio); Young v. American Mini Theatres, 427 U.S. 50 (1976) (upholding portions of zoning ordinance regulating "adult" movie theaters).

146. *See* F. Schauer, *supra* note 3, at 206–227.

147. *See* Ordinance Amending Title 7 of Minneapolis Ordinances Relating to Civil Rights (Dec. 30, 1983) (vetoed Jan. 5, 1984) The Minneapolis ordinance would have created a cause of action for any person coerced into pornographic performances, for any person who has pornography forced upon him or her, and for any person assaulted in a way directly caused by pornography. *See id.* §§ 5–7. The Ordinance would have also created a cause of action for any woman "as a woman acting against the subordination of women." *Id.* § 4.

148. *Id.* § 3. The doctrinal justification offered in support of this treatment of pornography is similar to that usually given for affirmative action or for legislation under section five of the fourteenth amendment. Such an argument would begin by positing that we face a conflict between two constitutional values—equality and liberty. The argument would then propose that the conflict be resolved in favor of equality because the alleviation of women's oppression must take precedence over the rights of pornographers.

149. This raises the issue of whether women's participation in the pornography industry is truly voluntary. *See, e.g., supra* note 111 and accompanying text.

150. *See supra* note 89 and accompanying text.

151. The point here is not simply that perspective influences experience, but that some perspectives may be better than others. Although

there will always be disputes about the relative superiority or inferiority of perspectives, this argument does not imply that all perspectives are equal. It necessarily entails that the issue cannot be settled only by reference to data on people's experience.

152. This theory is at least partially embodied in the language. *See generally* Sexist Language: A Modern Philosophical Analysis (Vetterling-Braggin ed. 1981) (examining sexist language and its relation to male domination and female subordination); R. Lakoff, Language and Woman's Place (1975) (analyzing sexist language as indicative of the speaker's true feelings regarding women); Baker, *"Pricks" and "Chicks": A Plea for "Persons"*, in Philosophy & Sex, *supra* note 48, at 45.

153. This view of sexuality was certainly the dominant one before Kinsey; perhaps it still is. *See* B. Faust, *supra* note 13, at 6.

154. *See* Garry, *supra* note 103, at 396–97 (distinguishing the respect for women that conservatives support from that urged by feminists).

155. *See, e.g.*, Mitzel, *The District Attorney is a Girl's Best Friend: Feminists and the Anti-Porn Crusade*, Gay News, Aug. 7, 1981, at 17.

156. *See* B. Faust, *supra* note 13, at 49 (discussing Kinsey); E. Willis, *Feminism, Moralism, and Pornography*, in Beginning to See the Light: Pieces of a Decade 223–25 (1981).

157. *See, e.g.*, S. Hite, The Hite Report: A Nationwide Study of Female Sexuality (1976) (especially 465–770); Powers of Desire (A. Snitow, C. Stansell & S. Thompson eds. 1983); 3 Heresies: A Feminist Publication on Art & Politics #12, 1981 (Sex Issue); 5 Signs: J. Women Culture & Soc. 569 (special issue); 6 Signs: J. Women Culture & Soc. 1 (1980).

158. The view that sex is inevitably sadomasochistic is sometimes attributed to Sartre, although the sadomasochism is not inevitably male-female. *See* Collins & Pierce, *Holes and Slime: Sexism in Sartre's Psychoanalysis*, in Women and Philosophy, *supra* note 107, at 112; Oaklander, *Sartre on Sex*, in Philosophy of Sex 190 (A. Soble ed. 1980).

159. *See supra* note 97. *But see* English, Hollibaugh, & Rubin, *supra* note 13, at 57–58.

160. This argument follows that of B. Faust, *supra* note 13.

161. *Id.* at 45–59.

162. B. Faust, *supra* note 13, at 98.

163. *See* English, Hollibaugh & Rubin, *supra* note 13, at 54–55.

164. Faust and Safilios-Rothschild express concern about whether men and women are fundamentally incompatible. *See* B. Faust, *supra* note 13, at 187–204; C. Safilios-Rothschild, *supra* note 161; *see also* Rapaport, *On the Future of Love: Rousseau and the Radical Feminists*, in Women and Philosophy, *supra* note 107, at 185.

165. *See, e.g.*, English, Hollibaugh, & Rubin, *supra* note 13, at 54–55 (more female pornographers would break down harmful pornographic gender hierarchy).

166. *See, e.g.*, Abood v. Detroit Bd. of Educ., 431 U.S. 209, 234 (1977) (employees' right to refuse to associate sufficient to prevent union from spending dues on political activities unrelated to collective bargaining);

Southeastern Promotions, Ltd. v. Conrad, 420 U.S. 546, 552–58 (1975) (holding unconstitutional denial of use of municipal auditorium based on content of program); NAACP v. Button, 371 U.S. 415, 429 (1963) (litigation by NAACP to further objectives of racial equality is protected political expression). *But see* Kairys, *Freedom of Speech,* in The Politics of Law: A Progressive Critique 140, 141 (D. Kairys ed. 1982) (broad right of free speech is a relatively recent development).

167. *See, e.g.,* Cantwell v. Connecticut, 310 U.S. 296, 303–04 (1940).

168. *See, e.g.,* Board of Educ. v. Pico, 457 U.S. 853, 869–72 (1982) (plurality opinion) (partially limiting school board's discretion to remove books from library); Brandenburg v. Ohio, 395 U.S. 444, 447 (1969) (speech intended to incite or produce imminent lawless action and likely to incite or produce such may be restricted).

169. *See, e.g.,* Baker, *supra* note 19. *But see* Roth v. United States, 354 U.S. 476, 508–14 (1957) (Douglas, J., dissenting) (arguing that freedom of speech and press be given broadest possible application).

170. *See supra* notes 40–41.

171. *See* Kaminer, *Pornography and the First Amendment: Prior Restraints and Private Action,* in Take Back the Night: Women on Pornography, *supra* note 10, at 246.

172. *See* Brandenburg v. Ohio, 395 U.S. 444, 447–48 (1969); Yates v. United States, 354 U.S. 298, 312–27 (1957).

173. *See infra* notes 188–96 and accompanying text.

174. B. Faust, *supra* note 13, at 146–56 (discussing romantic fiction directed at women readers).

175. *See, e.g.,* L. Barbach, For Yourself: The Fulfillment of Female Sexuality (1975); B. Dodson, Liberating Masturbation (1974); N. Friday, My Secret Garden: Women's Sexual Fantasies (1973); S. Hite, The Hite Report (1976); S. Kitzinger, Women's Experience of Sexuality (1984); 3 Heresies: A Feminist Publication on Art & Politics #12, 1981 (Sex Issue). Sex also seems to have become a legitimate subject in women's magazines in recent years. *See* B. Faust, *supra* note 13, at 157–69.

176. *See, e.g.,* English, Hollibaugh & Rubin, *supra* note 13, at 55, 60–61.

177. Professor Baker distinguishes four versions of market failure models. *See* Baker, *supra* note 19, at 981–85. The argument that follows repeats Baker's analysis.

178. Although feminists certainly want to claim that pornography expresses an ideology, it is not clear whether it is properly characterized as a *political ideology.* This is a general problem with "women's issues"; hence the feminist slogan, "the personal is political." *See* Nicholson, *"The Personal Is Political": An Analysis in Retrospect,* 7 Soc. Theory & Prac. 85 (1981); *cf.* J. Elshtain, *supra* note 123, at 320–23 (arguing for preservation of a purely personal sphere).

179. This is part of the basis for arguing that it "bypasses the conscious faculties of its hearer." Note, *supra* note 136, at 317–18.

180. *See* W. Prosser, Handbook of the Law of Torts 750–51 (4th ed. 1971)

(limitations on tort of group libel include requirement of showing "some reasonable personal application of the words" to the specific persons claiming injury).

181. Dworkin is particularly outspoken in her analysis of the hypocrisy of those who neutrally defend freedom of speech. *See* A. Dworki, *supra* note 10.

182. *See supra* note 102 and accompanying text.

183. *See, e.g.,* R. Unger, Knowledge and Politics (1975).

184. Longino, *Pornography, Oppression, and Freedom: A Closer Look,* in Take Back the Night: Women on Pornography, *supra* note 10, at 50–53; *see also* S. Griffin, *supra* note 10, at 88–93 (discussing pornographer's definition of liberty).

185. For the classical argument against such conceptions of positive liberty, see Berlin, *Two Concepts of Liberty,* in Four Essays on Liberty 118 (1969); *see also* Karst, *supra* note 125.

186. *See, e.g.,* S. Griffin, *supra* note 11; Ortner, *Is Female to Male as Nature Is to Culture?,* in Women, Culture & Society 67 (M. Rosaldo & L. Lamphere eds. 1974).

187. For an example of such a regulation, see Ordinance Amending Title 7 of Minneapolis Code of Ordinances Relating to Civil Rights § 3 (Dec. 30, 1983) (vetoed Jan. 5, 1984).

188. In fact obscenity laws have often been used against materials feminists would endorse, such as those of birth control advocate Margaret Sanger. *See* Alschuler, *Origins of the Law of Obscenity,* 2 Technical Reports, *supra* note 66, at 65, 79 (antiobscenity laws historically connected with legal sanctions against other sexual conduct).

189. *See* MacKinnon, *Feminism, Marxism, Method, and the State: Toward Feminist Jurisprudence,* 8 Signs: J. Women Culture & Soc. 635 (1983); MacKinnon, *Feminism, Marxism, Method, and the State: An Agenda for Theory,* 7 Signs: J. Women Culture & Soc. 515 (1982); MacKinnon, *Toward Feminist Jurisprudence,* 34 Stan. L. Rev. 703, 717–19, 723–37 (1982).

190. Legislative or judicial control of pornography is simply not possible without breaking down the legal principles and procedures that are essential to our own right to speak. . . . We must continue to organize against pornography . . . , but we must not ask the government to take up our struggle for us. The power it will assume to do so will be far more dangerous to us all than the "power" of pornography.

Kaminer, *Pornography and the First Amendment,* in Take Back the Night, *supra* note 10, at 247. *See also* Willis, *Feminism, Moralism, and Pornography,* in Beginning to See the Light: Pieces of a Decade, *supra* note 13, at 226.

191. *See* R. Unger, *supra* note 183.

192. *See, e.g.,* Marx, *Critique of the Gotha Program,* in The Marx-Engels Reader 382 (1972). It is debatable whether Marx would have endorsed the theory outlined in the text.

193. *But see* Baker, *The Process of Change and the Liberty Theory of the First Amendment,* 55 S. Cal. L. Rev. 293 (1982). Professor Baker insightfully

explores this underdeveloped area in first amendment theory and concludes that arguments like that made in the text generally should be rejected.

194. *See* Comment, *On Letting the Laity Litigate: The Petition Clause and Unauthorized Practice Rules*, 132 U. Pa. L. Rev. 1515, 1520–28 (1984) (discussing relationship between government legitimacy and process of entertaining legal claims).

195. Whitney v. California, 274 U.S. 357, 376 (1927) (Brandeis, J., concurring).

196. Although feminists do not necessarily agree on the strategy that should be adopted to address the issues raised by pornography, *see supra* note 13 and accompanying text, a host of strategies have been suggested. *See, e.g.,* S. Brownmiller, *supra* note 42, at 438–45; Garry, *Pornography and Respect for Women*, in Pornography and Censorship, *supra* note 50, at 61; Gever & Hall, *Fighting Pornography*, in Take Back the Night: Women on Pornography, *Supra* note 10, at 279; Morgan, *How to Run the Pornographers Out of Town (And Preserve the First Amendment)*, Ms. Nov. 1978, at 55.

13

"Not the Law's Business":
The Current Predicament for Sexual Minorities

Meredith Gould

There must be a realm of private morality or immorality which is, in brief, not the law's business.—*The Wolfenden Report, Section 61.*

Discrimination affects every aspect of social life, both public and private, for lesbians and gay men in ways it simply does not for other minorities. To be sure, employment and housing discrimination, child custody battles, immigration challenges, and capricious military discharge are experienced by women and racial-ethnic minorities. Sexual minorities are, however, distinguished from other oppressed groups by the extent to which prejudice and discrimination invade personal life without legal relief or remedy. Laws have gradually evolved to protect the civil rights of women and racial-ethnic minorities. Few such legal means are available to gay people. Today, overt expressions of racism and sexism are largely unacceptable. The same cannot be said for overt expressions of heterosexism and homophobia. Heterosexism, a belief in the superiority of heterosexuality, and homophobia, the hatred and fear of homosexuality, are rarely perceived as bigotry. Heterosexism is viewed as normative and permissible. Homophobia is frequently perceived as an indication of moral purity, sexual health, and a properly aligned gender identity. This last point is par-

---

Meredith Gould is project manager of the Business/Humanities Project at the New Jersey Department of Higher Education.

ticularly important. Lesbians and gay men are women and men who choose to relate socially and sexually with same-sex partners. The only thing that distinguishes these women and men is sexual preference. However in our society, where women and men are socialized into specific roles according to sex status, distinctions between sex, gender and sexuality are often blurred. Consequently, any discussion about the legal status of sexual minorities is not simply about sexual activity, but also about appropriate social roles for women and men.

A critical sociological examination of the laws and public policies affecting lesbians and gay men reveals the tenacity of gender stereotypes. The legal problems faced by gay people derive from a pernicious sexism, one that constrains important civil liberties. This is particularly apparent in family law. In this chapter, I discuss what lesbians and gay men face in the area of domestic relations. My focus on the family is based on several factors. First, the family is a social and legal institution of almost sacred proportions in the United States. The right to marry, contracept, have children or choose abortion are protected by the United States Constitution. These have been declared, often after protracted constitutional adjudication, fundamental rights protected by the first, ninth and fourteenth amendments to the United States Constitution. Second, as a social institution, the family is central to our identity as social actors. No matter how we modify the family, the fact remains that we all experience membership in this institution regardless of sex, race, ethnicity, or sexual preference. Third, the family is a gendered institution in which a sexual division of labor can be observed and sex specific social roles are taught. Finally, despite its role as the subject of social policy and the object of legal regulation, the family is generally considered a private sphere by its members and outside observers alike. Questions about the validity of legal intrusion into private life are highlighted when family issues are involved.

Many of the problems faced by lesbians and gay men in the area of family law illustrate the way discrimination against sexual minorities is based on stereotypes about male and female behavior. And because our cultural attitudes about gender, the family, and homosexuality share the same religious roots, this chapter begins with a brief description of that heritage before discussing the legal barriers to family life faced by sexual minorities.

316

The Religious Roots of Homophobia

The Scriptures are a powerful body of myth and legend which have significantly shaped the sexual ideologies of Western civilization. All sexual attitudes, and especially those encoded in the common law tradition, have been deeply affected by western religious culture. The religious texts of Judaism and Christianity form the foundation for the sex-negative moral code we call the Judeo-Christian ethic. This ethical stance is based on the assumption, and indeed prescription, that sexual activity must be procreative. Reproduction is the only valid and legitimate outcome of human sexual conduct. All other sexual activities such as masturbation, cunnilingus, fellatio, and anal intercourse are "unnatural" because they do not lead, at least not directly, to the "natural" outcome of pregnancy. All such sexual activities are therefore fundamentally heretical and sinful. In addition, marriage is the only legitimate setting for procreative sexuality. According to the Judeo-Christian ethic, reproductive sexuality is granted moral status only within the institution of marriage.

Throughout history, these moral and religious teachings have been advanced most vociferously by fundamentalist religious sects. Legal proscriptions about sexuality derive from religious doctrine. When Church and State doctrine merged into one system of law, as they did by the fourth century A.D., "unnatural" sexuality became simultaneously a crime against God and the State. Heresy became synonymous with treason. Male homosexuality was declared a capital crime by the early Christian emperor Constantius.

Historical evidence suggests that women and men endured different prohibitions and punishments at different historical moments. For the most part, prohibitions against same-sex sexual activity in the Old and New Testaments were directed against men who were perceived as acting out female, and hence degraded, sexual roles. Such roles were considered especially detestable because they were not procreative. The Penitentials, which catalogued punishments for sexual sins during the fourth century, referred only briefly to lesbianism by the end of the fifth century. As secular law emerged, the torture, mutilation and immolation of suspected lesbians and homosexuals abated somewhat, although

317

sodomy remained a male criminal offense punishable by death in England during the sixteenth century. Lesbianism was not explicitly named, although some feminist scholars argue that the thousands of women burned as witches must have included lesbians who were perceived as having repudiated traditional female roles.[1] Cultural proscriptions against homosexuality and lesbianism endured even after sodomy was no longer a capital crime, sustained by developing medical science and, much later, by psychiatry.[2]

Early Christian teachings about sexuality in general, and homosexuality in particular, are encoded in the statutory language of law. As sociologists John DeLamater and Patricia McCorquodale point out, "the laws governing sexual conduct in this country were derived from and still reflect Christian theology; to the extent that legal institutions influence sexual expression, they reinforce the impact of religious ones."[3] It is not difficult to find historical and contemporary examples of statutes that illustrate the influence of the Judeo-Christian ethic. One blatant example can be found in the anachronistic language of a North Carolina statute which in its original version read:

> Any person who shall commit the abominable and detestable crime against nature, not to be named among Christians, with either mankind or beast, shall be adjudged guilty of a felony, and shall suffer death without the benefit of clergy.[4]

Indeed the presence and influence of organized religion continues to be a major block to the legal reform of statutes that seek to regulate "buggery," "unnatural or perverted sexual practices," and "crimes against nature." Such medieval language still exists in many state statutes today, nearly forty years after the famous Kinsey studies demonstrated that human sexuality involves a wide range of activity.

The role of marriage in granting moral legitimacy to sexual activity is also encoded in law. Wisconsin is one state that is quite explicit about the role law should play in sustaining the Judeo-Christian ethic. In 1983, Wisconsin added this to its section on "Crimes Against Sexual Morality":

> The state recognizes that it has a duty to encourage high moral standards. Although the state does not regulate the private sexual

activity of consenting adults, the state does not condone or encourage any form of sexual conduct outside the institution of marriage. Marriage is the foundation of family and society. Its stability is basic to morality and civilization, and is of vital interest to society and this state.[5]

In addition, despite ample historical and cross-cultural evidence about the nature and prevalence of homosexuality, stereotypes still dominate public attitudes. Gay men, who are usually indistinguishable from heterosexual men, get defined as either "effeminate," or "promiscuous" or "child molesters." Lesbians get stereotyped as aggressive and masculine. American society is ill equipped to deal with human variation. The result is homophobia, an irrational fear of homosexuality, which is sanctioned and perpetuated by an administration of justice tainted by covert religiosity.

At this point in time, the United States remains one of the few countries in the world where the State actively seeks to define and regulate the non-coital activity of its adult citizens. Recommendations of the National Association for Mental Health, the Task Force on Homosexuality of the National Institute of Mental Health, and the National Commission on Reform of Federal Criminal Laws led to the decriminalization of consensual sodomy between adults in the Model Penal Code drafted by the American Law Institute in 1955. This section of the code has not been uniformly adopted. Individual states, in fact, have the constitutional right to establish their own statutes, and do so in terms that leave no doubt as to the religious roots of legalized homophobia or the moral imperatives of marriage as seen in the Wisconsin legislation. These laws do much more than advance sex-negative religious ideologies. They also support a gender system, one in which women and men are viewed and treated differently. Gay people are not exempt from gender stereotyping and are, perhaps, most victimized by it. Gender inequalities deeply affect the lives of lesbians and gay men.

Gender Differences

The imputation of particular social meanings to sex status is termed gender by sociologists and refers to the constellation of behaviors and attitudes labeled masculine and feminine in this society. Dimensions of masculinity and femininity are socially, culturally, and psychologically produced sets of characteristics; behavior deemed the social property of females and males. These characteristics are "fixed" only insofar as society can control their definition. Anthropological research has demonstrated how social standards for femininity and masculinity vary cross-culturally. Social historians have documented how attitudes about gender have varied historically. In the contemporary United States, social standards for femininity and masculinity have shifted somewhat in the past decade. Rock stars and couturiers notwithstanding, some gender stereotypes remain impervious to change; especially those about sexuality and sexual minorities.

The legal discrimination suffered by all gays is tied to the gender meanings and expectations of this society, as well as traditional attitudes about sexuality. Obscured by these laws and policies is the fact that homosexuals, like heterosexuals, are a heterogeneous group. There are gay people in all classes, religions, and racial-ethnic groups. Gay people embrace a variety of lifestyles and political affiliations. Lesbians and gay men no more organize the entirety of their lives around sexual conduct than do heterosexuals. In addition, they are socialized into gender roles like everyone else; behaviors and identities often evince what Gagnon and Simon have called "a conformity greater than deviance."[6]

The rigidity of genderized expectations for behavior is highly visible in discussions of homosexuality and lesbianism. Lesbianism and homosexuality fundamentally challenge gender expectations and the social institutions that buttress gender roles even when the gay social actor lives a conventional life. Gender expectations shape the legal response to issues somewhat differently for lesbians and gay men. Understanding gender helps explain why some substantive areas of law have traditionally had an impact on the lives of gay men; others more so on the lives of lesbians. Two brief examples will help illustrate this point.

First, the undetected and undetectable participation of gay men in the military repudiates the stereotype of homosexual effeminacy. Dishonorable discharge from the armed services for homosexuality is discriminatory because it prevents these men from participating in an important institution of secondary socialization and a traditional source of job training. Second, motherhood is a revered status for adult women. Although many lesbians are, and choose to become mothers, lesbianism repudiates the traditional image of motherhood as a heterosexual institution. Lesbians are women who experience another layer of discrimination in the areas of divorce and child custody. The parameters of potential discrimination against gay people have expanded as more women enter the labor force and more men become actively involved in parenting. This is particularly visible in cases involving child custody where either the mother or the father is self-identified as gay because assumptions about the relationship between gender and sexuality are challenged. A look at the history of child custody reveals the gender assumptions in this area of family law.

Legal Standards for Child Custody

Under English common law, children belonged to their fathers. Scholars speculate this may have been due to antiquated notions of women as mere incubators of the homunculus, or the strength of primogeniture and the corresponding need to clearly trace a line of inheritance and descent.[7] As late as 1880, the United States Bureau of Education suggested a paternal preference rule in cases where both parents sought custody, also noting that the "welfare of the child" should be the outstanding criterion for custody awards.[8] By the 1920s, women were increasingly winning custody battles. In 1925, jurist Benjamin Cardozo introduced what is now called the "best interests" standard in *Finlay v. Finlay.*[9] This standard had the effect of establishing a maternal preference for child custody. The "tender years" presumption, upon which the "best interests standard" was built, reified a particular image of women in family law. In sociological terms, sex and gender were conflated. Social stereotypes about women's unique capacity to mother were given the weight of law in custody cases.

In response to what had become an almost inviolable maternal presumption, an unfitness challenge developed, bringing into sharp relief the strength of cultural images and social stereotypes about women as mothers. To challenge the "tender years" presumption, ex-husbands would charge mothers with unfitness. Virtually any deviation from traditional mothering norms could result in shifting custody to the father whose own case was strengthened by remarriage, especially if the next wife was willing to be a full-time mother.

In 1973, Goldstein, Freud and Solnit published *Beyond the Best Interests of the Child*, giving a strong boost to the reemerging notion of paternal entitlement. Their proposed "psychological parent" standard emphasized the importance of family continuity and deemphasized the biological parent.[10] Now fathers whose children resided with them for any length of time were not automatically expected or required to relinquish custody to their ex-wives when challenged. By the mid-1970s, women who had to move from the marital home for job-related, economic, or even personal preference reasons, had to consider that such a move could be interpreted as a break in the continuity of family life.

In addition, Goldstein, Freud and Solnit invoked psychological data to argue for fathers' quality in lieu of quantity parenting. "Best interests," it was argued, might also be defined economically, thus perpetuating gender disparities between women and men as mothers and fathers.[11] The "least detrimental alternative"[12] sustained the traditional mothering role by impugning a woman's parental fitness if she had a career, while redefining "best interests" in lifestyle terms that she, as a single parent, in all probability could not provide without working.

In 1981, a new standard for child custody was developed in *Garska v. McCoy*:[13] the court in this case stated that "the best interests of the children are best served in awarding them to the primary caretaker parent, regardless of sex."[14] The custody of minor children is awarded to the parent who provides primary care and nurturing during the ongoing marriage. The range of activities outlined by the *Garska* Court, from getting a child ready for school in the morning to tucking that child in at night, with all associated trips and events in between, describes a traditional mothering role. Proponents of this standard argue, however, that it is sex-neutral; presumably men could provide primary nurturing. The "primary caretaker parent" standard has not, as yet, been adopted nationally and the dominant "best interests" standard is clearly bound in with cultural images and social stereotypes about women and men as parents. Without a doubt, gender shapes parenting in the United States. This is true regardless of either parent's sexual preference. And yet when lesbian mothers and gay fathers turn to the courts for custody and visitation rights, another aspect of gender discrimination is revealed. Not only are gay parents treated differently, but the expressed concerns about their role as parents differs as well.

Lesbian Mothers

Lesbian motherhood seems to embody contradictory images that courts have difficulty sorting out. Sexist law intuitively confers custody on the female parent under the "tender years" presumption, while heterosexist law views lesbian custody as morally impossible. Lesbians are considered morally suspect because of distorted stereotypes about the gender roles of women-identified women. Such stereotypes include images of the lesbian as being masculinized, sexually aggressive, severely neurotic, emotionally unstable, immature, and compulsive. The law has traditionally viewed lesbianism as synonymous with unfitness, the only characterization that can undermine and invalidate the "tender years" presumption.

Family courts tend to approach lesbian custody in a variety of ways. Traditionally, courts have been blunt about the relationship between a woman's lesbianism and the "best interests" of her children. The child's "best interests" in these cases has been consistently interpreted as being more about morality than either continuity, psychological parenting, or financial stability. Until the mid-1970s, courts would sometimes award child custody to a lesbian mother if she and her partner agreed to separate their households. In essence, courts would recognize the lesbian family unit, then dismantle it. By the end of the 1970s, this changed somewhat and for a while it seemed that lesbianism was being removed as an issue. However, recent case law suggests that courts have only become more subtle in sustaining discrimination against this particular group of women. Courts in many jurisdictions have claimed to dismiss the impact of lesbianism as irrelevant while in practice custody is removed from the mother on other grounds. Sometimes this sleight of law is easy to see, often times it is not.

In 1979, the Superior Court of New Jersey awarded custody to a lesbian mother in *M.P. v. S.P.*,[15] rejecting plaintiff's argument that the wife's sexual lifestyle would embarrass the children:

> If defendant retains custody, it may be that because the community is intolerant of her differences these girls may sometimes have to bear themselves with greater than ordinary fortitude. But this does not necessarily portend that their moral welfare or safety will be jeopardized. It is just as reasonable to expect that they will emerge better equipped to search out their own standards of right and

wrong, better able to perceive that the majority is not always correct in its moral judgments, and better able to understand the importance of conforming their beliefs to the requirements of reason and tested knowledge, not the constraints of currently popular sentiment or prejudice. . . . We conclude that the children's best interests will be disserved by undermining in this way their growth as mature and principled adults.[16]

Closer inspection of this case reveals that the court ruled for the lesbian mother in part because her ex-husband's sexual behavior was "so far out of the ordinary . . . [that it] . . . would create the most acute anxieties about entrusting so troubled and deviant a personality with the responsibility of creating an environment for the upbringing of two young girls."[17] For this court, discerning the "best interests" required balancing one form of conduct against another and deciding that, in this case at least, lesbianism was the lesser of two evils.[18]

In cases where both parents are considered equally fit, lesbianism does become an issue and may still be characterized as immoral and/or illegal. In *Jacobson v. Jacobson,*[19] the Court argued that sexual preference could indeed be factored in if other factors were equal:

Because the trial court has determined that both parents are "fit, willing and able" to assume custody of the children we believe the homosexuality of Sandra is the overriding factor. . . . despite the fact that the trial court determined the relationship between Sandra and Sue to be a "positive one," it is a relationship which, under the existing state of the law, never can be a legal relationship.[20]

In this case, the trial court was reversed and the children were removed from their mother's custody and awarded to their father.

Jacobson is interesting because it illustrates the way courts factor lesbianism into the "best interests" standard, and also because it illustrates the current trend in such cases. By the 1980s, courts that had originally awarded custody to lesbian mothers living alone or separately from their lovers, transferred custody to fathers if a lesbian household was established after custody was initially determined.

In 1982, for example, the Oklahoma Supreme Court ruled in a case of first impression, that the mother's cohabitation with her female lover was a change in circumstance warranting a change of custody to the father. In *M.J.P. v. J.G.P.*[21] the court, agreeing with expert testimony, found that "it is in the child's best interests to be taught the prevailing morals of society, and that it is generally considered immoral for two women to engage in a homosexual lifestyle."[22]

While there may be nothing subtle about this reasoning and the language that describes it, there has indeed been a shift in the way courts distinguish between lesbian and heterosexual mothers. Now, instead of focusing on the mother's sexuality, courts declare her sexuality irrelevant and claim to focus exclusively on the interests and welfare of the child. Once refocused, courts will say, as they did *In Matter of Jane B.*,[23] that:

> respondent here can have her own life style but she cannot impose it on her child who is a ward of the court. . . . The issue . . . is not homosexuality; it is solely the best interest and welfare of the child. . . . The court here is not abridging respondent's fundamental rights or privacy but concerns itself solely with the well-being of the child and the questions as to whether the present environment is a proper one for this child and in her best interests.[24]

In Jacobson, the court noted that the mother's decision to establish a lesbian household was, unlike her lesbianism, under her control, and argued:

> It may be argued that to force her to dissolve her living relationship in order to retain custody of her children is too much to ask. However, we need no legal citation to note that concerned parents in many, many instances have made sacrifices of varying degrees for their children.[25]

By shifting the focus from identity to lifestyle,[26] courts make substantively the same decisions under the guise of a new, albeit thinly disguised, objectivity. No matter how it is articulated by the courts, lesbianism jeopardizes a woman's chance to maintain child custody because it is viewed as either an identity or a lifestyle that is at odds with the gender expectations for women who are mothers in this society. According to the Judeo-Christian ethic, sexuality is a reproductive activity. Stereotypically, women relinquish all sexuality upon becoming mothers. For gay people in general, the law conflates gender and sexuality. When lesbians enter the legal system, gender stereotypes about women are eclipsed by stereotypes about gay sexuality. The lesbian mother is seen as unfit because she violates both gender and sexual norms for women. For gay fathers, the sexual stereotypes are articulated somewhat differently although the result is substantively the same.

Gay Fathers

There has been reported case law on visitation and custody claims by gay fathers since 1952, but it is sparse. This probably reflects larger realities: 1) divorce cases, especially those involving minor children, are not routinely reported; 2) there is empirical data to support the contention that men who do challenge custody usually win;[27] and 3) men who do receive child custody after a court battle usually relinquish custody to the mother within three years.[28]

Courts rely on traditional masculine stereotypes when making decisions affecting family life. The roles men play within the family as husband, father, and breadwinner (even in families where both adults work) are conflated and conceptually subsumed under one status, that of breadwinner. Men who succeed in gaining custody, do so primarily on the grounds that they are able to provide for the child in ways the single mother cannot. The traditional view holds that men are expected to make a pecuniary rather than emotional contribution to domestic life. Courts routinely assume that men hold the master status of breadwinner within the contemporary American family; less emphasis is placed on nurturing. This breadwinner status eclipses all others, shaping the way courts evaluate men's parental competency.

As is the case with lesbian mothers, the few reported cases involving gay fathers focus on these fathers' gay identity and lifestyle. For the lesbian mother, sexuality eclipses stereotypes about maternal nurturing. For the gay father, assumptions about sexuality eclipse expectations about providing. But not always. In 1974, the New Jersey Superior Court drastically restricted visitation for one gay father in part because of his "obsessive preoccupation" with the gay movement, an involvement that the Court thought had economic consequences. In *J.S. v. C.*[29] the court made a point of noting that:

> In the past defendant has earned a substantial income which was utilized to help support the children. He has now decided to forego this income in favor of the gay rights movement.[30]

While this father's reduced income was not the sole determining factor in this case, it was nevertheless enough of a feature to be mentioned by the Court.

Most cases having to do with gay fathers focus on the father's sexuality. For the courts, gay sexuality is synonymous with promiscuity and it is also not unusual for courts to make reference to sexual molestation. In *J.L.P. v. D.J.P.*[31] the Missouri Court of Appeals rejected experts' testimony that most child molestation is perpetrated by heterosexual men, saying that "Every trial judge, or for that matter, every appellate judge, knows that the molestation of minor boys by adult males is not as uncommon as the psychological experts' testimony indicated".[32] In this case the Court upheld the trial court in denying the gay father overnight visitation, also barring him from taking his son to gay activist social gatherings and to a gay-oriented church.

The tension between competing stereotypes about masculinity is interesting in these cases. The dominant stereotype about male sexuality is that it is voracious and indiscriminate. This stereotype is intensified for gay men and persists in the face of evidence to the contrary. In almost all reported gay father cases, the father was living with a lover in a stable household. This situation is reduced to the genital by the courts. In case after case, courts condition custody and visitation on the father's not sharing a bedroom with his lover when the child is around. In *Roe v. Roe*[33] the Virginia Supreme Court went even further:

> The trial court was . . . seriously concerned as to the impact of the father's conduct upon the child, but took the position that its worst features could be allayed by ordering him out of his lover's bedroom. We are not so persuaded. The child's awareness of the nature of the father's illicit relationship is fixed and cannot be dispelled. The open behavior of the father and his friends in the home can only be expected to continue. . . . We conclude that the best interests of the child will only be served by protecting her from the burdens imposed by such behavior. . . . this necessitates not only a change of custody to the mother, but also a cessation of any visitations in the father's home, or in the presence of his homosexual lover, while his present living arrangements continue.[34]

In a 1985 case reported in the *New York Law Journal*, the New York Appellate Division modified a Supreme Court decree and allowed visitation in the gay father's home with the lover present, arguing

327

that "excluding the lover as a condition of visitation serves no real purpose other than as a punitive measure against the father."[35] The child in this case was restricted from participating in gay activities or publicity. In Massachusetts, two foster children were removed from a gay male couple who had lived together for almost a decade, by the Department of Human Services. In defense Governor Michael Dukakis stated that "we're talking about what's in the best interest of the children."[36] Clearly assumptions about sexual abuse are persistent and gay fathers are in no better position than lesbian mothers to gain access to their children. Distorted stereotypes about the male role as father and the sexual behavior of gay men make such access difficult, if not impossible.

Creating Public Policy

Courts today are, for the most part, sophisticated enough to avoid blatantly discriminatory language when dealing with lesbians and gay men who seek child custody or visitation rights. No longer do the words "perversion," "abomination," or "revulsion" feature in published court opinions. Nevertheless, there is an underlying tone to these cases, one that alerts the reader: lesbianism and homosexuality are unacceptable variations in human sexual conduct.

In addition to the gender stereotypes used by courts to determine what constitutes proper mothering and fathering, two legal arguments are used to justify court imposed limits on child custody and visitation for gay people. One argument is about the legal status of same-sex couples. Another is about the felonious nature of sodomy. Each argument bears closer examination since all could be dealt with legislatively if the private character of intimate, family life were constitutionally protected for all citizens.

The argument about sodomy is based on the fact that in many states it is considered a felony to engage in anything other than penis-vagina intercourse with a marital partner. Sodomy statutes have traditionally been catch-alls for any and all sexual behavior, including activity between two consenting adults. During the early 1970s several lower courts challenged the traditional statutory language as "fatally vague" and therefore unconstitutional. It is now the mid-1980s and this has not yet been resolved. In fact, several states, Arizona, Arkansas, Oklahoma and most recently, Texas, have rewritten their laws to specify the criminalization of homosexuality.

Gay couples who present themselves to the court as being in an intimate, on-going relationship are denied custody and visitation in part because they are in direct violation of criminal law. An admission of lesbianism or homosexuality is simultaneously an admission of intent; that intent is criminal. Courts argue that they cannot grant custody and visitation to criminals. The gay father in *J.S. v. C.*, in fact, argued unsuccessfully that because bank robbers were allowed full visitation he should also be allowed visitation.

The argument about the legal status of same-sex couples is closely aligned with the sodomy argument just described. Courts have relied on previous cases denying or restricting custody to a parent engaged in a heterosexual nonmarital relationship in the child's presence. Courts consistently refer to such relationships as "illicit" and "immoral." This is extended quite easily to gay couples which, by law, cannot ever be solemnized by marriage. *Roe v. Roe* clearly illustrates the way these arguments are used in tandem. In this case the Virginia Supreme Court said:

> The father's continuous exposure of the child to his immoral and illicit relationship renders him an unfit and improper custodian as a matter of law. Indeed, the mother . . . points out that, as an illustration of the relative degree of abhorrence by which our society regards such conduct, adultery is a class four misdemeanor in Virginia . . . which is seldom prosecuted, while the conduct inherent in the father's relationship is punishable as a class six felony . . . which is prosecuted with considerable frequency and vigor. . . ."[37]

This conundrum could be solved: first, by decriminalizing sodomy, and second, by recognizing the validity of homosexual and lesbian marriage. As of this writing, the impact of the fundamentalist New Right has had a serious deleterious effect on the decriminalization of this victimless crime. In light of the recent AIDS hysteria it is unlikely that such revisions in the states' criminal codes will be forthcoming. One might think that homosexual marriage would appear more desirable as a consequence of these recent phenomena. Monogamous marriage for gay people might appeal to those who advocate a containment policy for this sexual minority. In the past when same sex couples have attempted to marry, states have denied a license because "marriage has always been considered as the union of a man and a woman and we have been presented with no authority to the contrary."[38] In most states, the law will not condone a marriage whose very consummation is illegal. The City Council of West Hollywood, California recently passed a domestic partnership ordinance that would presumably establish the legal equivalent of a spousal relationship for gay couples and other cohabitors. This ordinance, which has yet to be tested in the courts, illustrates a creative approach.

Of course the larger issue is one about sexism and heterosexism in a society that ignores distinctions between gender and sexuality. Civil rights for lesbians and gay men is only part of a larger picture of contemporary society in the United States. Discrimination against gay people is as much about gender as it is about sexual practice. The whole community suffers when public policy is sociologically naive.

Notes

1. See Mary Daly, *Gyn/Ecology* (Boston: Beacon Press, 1978) and Andrea Dworkin, *Woman Hating* (New York: E. P. Dutton, 1974).

2. See Wainwright Churchill, *Homosexual Behavior Among Males: A Cross Cultural and Cross Species Investigation* (Englewood Cliffs, N.J.: Prentice Hall, 1967).

3. See John DaLamater, and Patricia MacCorquodale, *Premarital Sexuality: Attitudes, Relationships, Behavior* (Madison: University of Wisconsin Press, 1979) p. 264.

4. The North Carolina Statute was revised in 1964 to read: "Crimes against nature: If any person shall commit the crime against nature with mankind or beast, he shall be guilty of a felony." (Section 14-177 N.C. Criminal Code).

5. Wisconsin State Ann. § 944.01 (West 1983).

6. John H. Gagnon and William Simon, "A Conformity Greater Than Deviance: The Lesbian" in *Sexual Conduct: The Social Sources of Human Sexuality* (Chicago: Aldine Books, 1973) p. 176–216.

7. For historical perspective see M.A. Glendon, *State, Law and Family* (1977); L. C. Halem, *Divorce Reform: Changing Legal and Social Perspectives* (1980); Lenore T. Weitzman, *The Marriage Contract* (1981).

8. Ibid.

9. 148 N.Y. 429, 148 N.E. 624 (1925)

10. J. Goldstein, A. Freud, and A.J. Solnit, *Beyond the Best Interests of the Child* (1973, 1979).

11. Lenore T. Weitzman and Dixon, "Child Custody Awards: Legal Standards and Empirical Patterns for Child Custody, Support and Visitation After Divorce", *University of California at Davis Law Review* 473 (1979).

12. Supra note 6, at 53.

13. 278 S.E. 2d 337 (W. Va 1981).

14. Id. at 361.

15. 169 N.J. Super. 425 (1979)

16. Id. at 438–9.

17. Id. at 438.

18. For the past two decades, sociologists have become increasingly critical of the concept of deviance as a category of behavior. Today, most agree that behavior is not deviant *per se*, but comes to be labeled deviant through a process of social interaction and societal reaction. See, for example, S.L. Hills, *Demystifying Social Deviance* (1980) and E.M. Schur, *Labelling Deviant Behavior* (1971) and *Interpreting Deviance* (1979).

19. 314 N.W. 2d 78 (1981)

20. Id. at 80-1

21. 640 P 2d. 966 (1982)

22. Id. at 969.

23. 85 Misc. 2d. 515 (1975).

24. Id. at 524–5.

25. Supra note 15, at 81

26. It is also important to note that activity is not identity or lifestyle. An actor might engage in homosexual acts without assuming the label "homosexual". See L. Humphreys, *Tearoom Trade: Impersonal Sex in Public Places* (1970, 1975); A.C. Kinsey, W.B. Pomeroy, and C.E. Martin, *Sexual Behavior in the Human Male* (1948) and A.C. Kinsey et al., *Sexual Behavior in the Human Female* (1953).

27. See Lenore T. Weitzman, *The Marriage Contract* (New York: The Free Press, 1981). In the second situation, women do not usually have the economic resources to appeal the decision.

28. In the third instance, the mother having "won" does not generally go back into court. See Weitzman and Dixon, "Child Custody Awards: Legal Standards and Empirical Patterns for Child Custody, Support and Visitation After Divorce", *op. cit.*

29. 129 N.J. Super 486, 324 A 2d. 90 (1974).

30. Id. at 95.

31. Mo. Ct. App. West. Dist. 12/14/82.

32. 9 FLR 2164

33. *Roe v. Roe* Va. Sup. Ct. No. 832044 1/18/85

34. 11 FLR 1156.

35. *Gottlieb v. Gottlieb*, NYADI Dept 488 4/30 NYS 2nd 180, 108 AD 2d 120—Divorce 301 (1985)

36. *New York Times*, 5/25/85 p. 24.

37. 11FLR 1156.

38. *Jones v. Hallahan* 501 5. W 2d. 588 (1973).

14

AIDS, Power and Reason

Ronald Bayer

Introduction

At the conclusion of his magisterial history, *Plagues and Peoples*, William McNeill asserted: "Ingenuity, knowledge and organization alter but cannot cancel humanity's vulnerability to invasion by parasitic form of life. Infectious disease, which antedates the emergence of humankind, will last as long as humanity itself, and will surely remain as it has been hitherto one of the fundamental parameters and determinants of human history" (McNeill, 1976:291). Written ten years ago, these observations seemed, at the time, somewhat overdrawn, especially with reference to the advanced technological societies. Now in the fifth year of the AIDS epidemic, as American political and social institutions seek to fashion a response to the HTLV-III retrovirus, McNeill's observations seem prescient.*

Since 1981, when the Centers for Disease Control determined that a pattern of extraordinary illnesses had begun to appear among young gay men on the West Coast, America has been compelled to confront a challenge that is at once biological, social, and political. What some had believed might be a short-lived episode, like toxic shock syndrome or Legionnaires' disease, has proved to be quite otherwise, and no end is in sight. Predictions as to the ultimate toll over the next decade range into the hundreds of thousands. However this modern epidemic is brought under control, it is clear that no critical dimension of American social and

---

Ronald Bayer is a Fellow at the Hastings Law Center. This article first appeared in the Milbank Memorial Fund Quarterly, 1986. © 1986, Milbank Memorial Fund Quarterly.
*Editor's note: HTLV-III has been renamed HIV (Human Immunodeficiency Virus)

political life will remain untouched. AIDS has become a "fundamental parameter" of contemporary history.

Like the epidemics of prior eras, AIDS has the potential for generating social disruption, for challenging the fabric of social life, the more so since it has been identified with those whose sexual practices and use of drugs place them outside the mainstream. As the disease spreads more rapidly among heroin users, the color of those who fall victim will darken, thus adding another dimension to the perceived threat to society posed by the bearers of the HTLV-III retrovirus.

In the face of an extended microparasitic siege, will American social institutions respond on the basis of reason guided by a scientific understanding of how HTLV-III transmission occurs, or will anxieties overwhelm the capacity for measured responses? Will the threat posed by AIDS elicit Draconian measures, or will fear of such measures immobilize those charged with the responsibility of acting to protect the public health? Will our capacity for social reason allow us to traverse a course threatened by irrational appeals to power and by irrational dread of public health or other measures? Will reason, balance and the search for modest interventions fall victim to a rancorous din? At stake is not only the question of how and whether it will be possible to weaken, if not extirpate, the viral antagonist responsible for AIDS, but the kind of society America will become in the process.

Private Acts, Social Consequences

The central epidemiological and clinical feature of AIDS and the feature that makes the public health response to its spread so troubling for a liberal society, is that the transmission of HTLV-III occurs in the context of the most intimate social relationships, or in those contexts that have for nearly three-quarters of a century proven refractory to effective social controls. The transmission of AIDS occurs in the course of sexual relationships and in the course of intravenous drug use. In both realms, and fueled by struggles on the part of women, gays and racial minorities, the evolution of our constitutional law tradition as well as our social ethos over the past two decades has increasingly underscored the importance of privacy and of limiting state authority—at times for reasons of practicality, at times for reasons of political philosophy.

It is no accident that the Supreme Court discovered the "penumbral rights of privacy" in a landmark case overturning Connecticut's efforts to limit the use of birth control devices (*Griswold* v. *Connecticut*, 381 U.C. 479, 1965); that issues of privacy loomed so large in the early abortion decisions; that so many of the procedural rights of criminal suspects enunciated by the Warren court emerged out of drug control cases. In each instance, attempts to enforce the law required the intrusive reliance upon the police in ways that offended the liberal understanding of the appropriate limits of state authority. Furthermore, the very effort to enforce the criminal law in such private realms was held to be inherently corrupting of law enforcement agencies, the result a "crisis of overcriminalization" (Kadish, 1968).

An ideology of tolerance emerged to reflect the new perspective on the limits of the criminal law (Packer, 1968) and on the capacity of all agencies of social control to compel adherence to standards of personal behavior where no complainants existed. When framed in the diction of sociology, the ideology of tolerance focused on the impact of "labeling" upon deviants (Schur, 1971); when framed by concerns of law enforcement, it centered upon "victimless crimes" (Schur, 1965).

This was the legal-social context within which AIDS intruded upon America, forcing a consideration of how profoundly private acts, with dire implications for the commonweal, might be controlled.

The only effective health strategy for limiting or slowing the further spread of HTLV-III infection is one that will produce dramatic, perhaps unprecedented changes in the behavior of millions of men and women in this country. Such changes will demand alterations in behaviors that are linked to deep biological and psychological drives and desires. They will demand acts of restraint and even deprivation for extended periods, if not for the lives of those infected and those most at risk for becoming infected.

The transmission of HTLV-III has as its first and most obvious consequence a private tragedy: the infection of another human being. But to conceive of such transmission between "consenting adults," as some have argued, as belonging to the private realm alone is a profound mistake (Mohr, 1985). Each new carrier of HTLV-III infection is the potential locus of further social contamination. When few individuals in a community are infected the prospect of undertaking individual and collective measures designed to prevent the spread of AIDS is enhanced. When, however, the levels of infection begin to approach a critical mass, when a level of saturation is approached, the prospect for adopting programs of prophylaxis is diminished. At stake here is a matter of extraordinary social moment. It has been estimated, we cannot be sure with what degree of accuracy, that the levels of HTLV-III infection by mid-1986 among gay men in San Francisco were something over 50%. Similar levels of infection have been cited for New York City. (Among intravenous drug users in New York and New Jersey the figures are, if anything, more grim.) Therefore, in New York and San Francisco, the likelihood of a gay or bisexual man avoiding an encounter with an infected male partner has virtually disappeared (Kuller & Kingsley, 1986). Only the practice of great care in the conduct of one's sexual behavior is left as a mode of protection against infection or reinfection. That is not now the case in many cities across the country, particularly in America's midsection. As a clinical intervention would seek to block viral replication, the public health challenge is to prevent the replication of New York and San Francisco.

In some important respects the problem posed by AIDS is like those problems posed by a host of behavior-related diseases, e.g., lung cancer, emphysema, cirrhosis, with which health policy has had to deal explicitly since the Surgeon General issued his first report on smoking (U.S. Department of Health, Education & Welfare, 1984). Ironically, at the very moment that an ethos of privacy was being enunciated, founded on philosophical individualism, the collective significance of each person's acts began to attain public recognition. Both in the Lalonde *Report* (1975) issued in Canada and *Healthy People* (U.S. Department of Health, Education & Welfare, 1979), public officials have argued that many private acts have indisputably social consequences, and that public intervention to limit social costs—characterized by economists as negative externalities—was a matter of the highest priority.

In the debate that has raged over the past two decades, about measures to promote health, particularly over mandatory seatbelt and helmet laws, the specter of Big Brother has been evoked in an effort to thwart public health regulations designed to limit morbidity through the modification of personal behavior (Moreno & Bayer, 1985). But in contrast to the difficulties that would be posed by efforts to limit the transmission of HTLV-III infection, those presented by attempts to modify smoking, alcohol consumption and vehicular behavior are simple. In each of these cases we could, if we chose to, affect behavior through product design, through pricing and taxation mechanisms, through the regulation and control of essentially public acts. Invasions of privacy would be largely unnecessary. With the transmission of HTLV-III the public dimension of the acts that are critical for public health is exceedingly limited. Closing gay bathhouses in San Francisco or New York, the subject of acrimonious debate on both coasts—to the dismay of some traditional advocates of public health, who viewed such settings simply as "nuisances"—may have important symbolic meaning. But the bathhouse is not the Broad Street pump, so crucial in the history of the effort to control cholera in Great Britain. Attempts to control the public dimension of HTLV-III transmission, whether through bathhouse closings or the repression of male and female prostitution, even if it could be achieved, will only have the most limited impact on the spread of AIDS.

Public Policy, Civil Liberties, and the Modification of Behavior

The central public problem before us is how to alter behavior that occurs in the most private settings. Can that be done? Can it be done in a way that will not involve levels of intrusion into privacy that are morally repugnant? Can it be done in ways that do not require surveillance of Orwellian proportions? Can it be done in ways that acknowledge the importance of civil liberties to the structure and fabric of American social life?

It is important to underscore at this point a matter of direct relevance to these questions. The ethos of public health and that of civil liberties are radically distinct. At the most fundamental level, the ethos of public health takes the well-being of the community as its highest good, and in the face of uncertainty, especially where the risks are high, would limit freedom or restrict, to the extent possible, the realm of privacy in order to prevent morbidity from taking its toll. The burden of proof against proceeding, from this perspective, rests upon those who assert that the harms to liberty would, from a social point of view, outweigh the health benefits to be obtained from a proposed course of action.

From the point of view of civil liberties the situation is quite the reverse. No civil libertarian denies the importance of protecting others from injury. The "harm principle," enunciated by John Stuart Mill, is in fact the universally acknowledged limiting standard circumscribing individual freedom. For 20th century liberals and civil libertarians, that principle has typically accorded considerable latitude to measures taken in the name of public health. But since the freedom of the individual is viewed as the highest good of a liberal society, from a libertarian point of view, measures designed to restrict personal freedom must be justified by a strong showing that no other path exists to protect the public health. The least restrictive alternative, to use a term of great currency, is the standard against which any course of action must be measured. When there are doubts the burden of proof is upon those who would impose restrictions.

These two great abstractions, liberty and communal welfare, are always in a state of tension in the realm of public health policy. How the balance is struck in a particular instance is, in part, a function of empirical matters—how virulent is a particular viral agent, with what degree of ease can it be transmitted, can therapeutic interventions blunt the consequence of infection—and in part a function of philosophical and political commitments. In the case of AIDS, the capacity of American culture to tolerate, over an extended period, the social stress engendered by the pattern of morbidity and mortality will determine how such empirical matters and philosophical concerns are brought to bear on the making of public health policy.

The Appeals and Limits of Power

Faced with the presence of a new infectious and deadly disease, one whose etiological agent has already infected 1–2 million individuals, there is an understandable tendency to believe that the public health response ought to reflect the gravity of the situation. A deadly disease demands a forceful and even a Draconian response. In fact, however, the public health departments in the two cities most affected by AIDS, New York and San Francisco, have responded over the past five years with considerable restraint. What better indication is there of the effort to balance a commitment to public health with an appreciation of the importance of civil liberties than the lengthy, perhaps tortured, discussion of whether or not to shut the gay bathhouses? At the federal level, the recommendations of the Centers for Disease Control throughout the epidemic have been designed to limit the impulse towards rash and scientifically unfounded interventions (Centers for Disease Control, 1985a, 1985b, 1985c). But to those who are alarmed, restraint appears as an apparent failure on the part of public health officials. The unwillingness to put forth "tough" policies on AIDS has provoked charges of timidity (Starr, 1986), an unconscionable capitulation to gay political pressure, the subversion of the ethos of public health by that of civil liberties (Restak, 1985).

Accusations against public health officials for their failure to move aggressively against disease and for their capitulation to special interests are not new. Charles Rosenberg has noted that in the 19th century, physicians who were too quick to discover the presence in their communities of epidemic diseases were often the targets of censure (Rosenberg, 1962:27). Since such diagnoses could well produce financial disaster for local commercial interests, public health officers sometimes sought to silence those who warned of the imminence of epidemics and to restrain the over-zealous. A contemporary critic said of the New York Board of Health that "it was more afraid of merchants than of lying" (Rosenberg, 1962:19). In the case of AIDS—despite the professionalization in the 20th century of those responsible for public health—anxiety has surfaced over whether political motivations have colored not only the willingness to press for forceful measures, but prevailing official anti-alarmist pronouncements about the threats posed by HTLV-III. Have public health officials been too reassuring about the modes of transmission? Have they underplayed the potential role of female-to-male transmission? Have they failed to adopt standard venereal disease control measures like sexual contact tracing because of an unbalanced concern for civil liberties? Has a commitment to privacy and confidentiality thwarted sound public health practice, thus placing the community at risk?

Such AIDS-specific fears have merged with an undercurrent of populist distrust for scientific authority that has been amplified in recent years by the politically charged debates among scientists over environmental and occupational health policy. These factors have contributed to the volatility of public opinion polls regarding matters like quarantine and isolation. Eleanor Singer (1986) has found that as many as one-third of surveyed Americans favor the use of quarantine against those with AIDS or those who "carry AIDS," though they know a great deal about the modes of HTLV-III transmission and appear to accept the findings of the CDC on such matters.

Because of the potential abuse of power and authority that could well attend the implementation of public policies designed to halt the spread of HTLV-III infection, less attention has been given to the ways in which a failure to take appropriate public health measures could produce the popular bases for more drastic action. Writing about the Black Death, McNeill noted: "In Northern Europe, the absence of well-defined public quarantine regulations and administrative routines—religious as well as medical—with which to deal with plagues and rumors of plagues gave scope for violent expression of popular hates and fears provoked by the disease. In particular, long-standing grievances of poor against rich often boiled to the surface" (McNeill, 1976:172).

We have thus far not experienced the kind of anomic outbursts described by McNeill, though reported increases of assaults on gay men (New York City Gay and Lesbian Antiviolence Project) and strikes by parents seeking to keep school children with AIDS from the classroom may be viewed as functional (but pale) equivalents (Nelkin & Heilgartner, 1986). More to the point, however, have been the calls in the press, in state legislatures, and from insurgent candidates for elective office—all still restricted to the most extreme political right—for the quarantine of all antibody-positive individuals (Intergovernmental Health Policy Project, 1985). One such proposal is to be found in the March 1986 issue of the *American Spectator:*

> There are only three ways that the spread of lethal infectious disease stops: it may be too rapidly fatal, killing off all its victims before the disease can spread; the population affected may develop natural or medically applied immunity; it may not be able to spread because uninfected individuals are separated sufficiently well from those

340

infected. [At this point the only way] to prevent the spread of the disease is by making it physically impossible. This implies strict quarantine, as has always been used in the past when serious—not necessarily lethal—infections have been spreading. Quarantine in turn implies accurate testing.

The authors then lament the failure of nerve on the part of Americans.

Neither quarantine nor universal testing is palatable to the American public where AIDS is concerned, yet both have been used without hesitation in the past.

What is so striking about such proposals is that they would enforce a deprivation of liberty upon vast numbers for an indefinite period (the duration of HTLV-III infection) because of how infected individuals might behave in the future. Unlike the transmission of some infections, where one's mere presence in public represents a social threat, the transmission of HTLV-III infection requires specific, well-defined acts. Hence, the quarantine of all HTLV-III infected persons would rest upon a willingness to predict or assume future dangerousness and would be the medical equivalent of mass preventive detention. Even were such a vast and thoroughgoing rejection of our fundamental constitutional and moral values tolerable, and even if it were possible to gather broad-based political support for such measures, the prospects for so enormous and burdensome a disruption of social life makes mass quarantine utterly unlikely.

Rarely do those who propose quarantines suggest how all antibody-positive individuals would be identified, how they would be removed to quarantine centers, how they would be fed and housed, how they would be forcefully contained. Indeed, it is one of the remarkable features of proposals for mass quarantine as a public health response to AIDS, and an indication of the profound irrationality of such suggestions, that they treat with abandon both matters of practicality and history. Because proponents of quarantine speak of mass removal as if it were an antiseptic surgical excision, they can assume that their ends could be achieved without grave social disruption. A vision of benign quarantine measures is informed by recent memories of health officers imposing isolation on those who suffered from diseases such as scarlet fever.

341

But when quarantine has been imposed upon those who viewed themselves as unfairly targeted by the state's agents, the story has sometimes been quite different. Judith Leavitt's description of how German immigrants in Milwaukee responded to efforts at the forced removal and isolation of those with smallpox provides ample evidence of what might be expected were even local and confined efforts to isolate large numbers of HTLV-III-infected individuals undertaken: "Daily crowds of people took to the streets, seeking out health officials to harass" (Leavitt, 1976:559).

But the irrationality and potentially disruptive dimensions of quarantine are no guarantee against future impulsive efforts to move in such a direction were social anxiety over AIDS to continue to mount in the next years. During the drug scares of the 1960s, both New York and California sought to meet that crisis by the establishment of mass civil commitment programs for addicts (Kittrie, 1973). Such efforts failed to stop the spread of drug use, though many were incarcerated in the process. Folly by great states is not reserved to the international arena.

Apparently more tolerable and more practicable are calls for the mandatory screening and identification of all high-risk individuals so that they might be compelled to face their antibody status, adjusting their behavior accordingly. Since it is impossible to know who is, in fact, a member of a high-risk group, calls for mandatory screening of risk group members would require universal screening. Such a program would, in turn, require the registration of the entire population to assure that none escaped the testing net. Finally, since one-time screening would be insufficient to detect new cases of infection, it would be necessary to track the movements of all individuals so that they might be repeatedly tested. The sheer magnitude of such an undertaking makes its adoption implausible. Modified versions of universal mass screening might take the form of governmentally mandated workplace testing. Though such efforts would eliminate the need for geographical dragnets, they would still pose enormous problems. To suggest that such mass screening might be undertaken, with the sole purpose of education and counseling, is inconceivable. The logic of universal mandatory screening for an infectious disease without cure leads ineluctably to mass quarantine.

Of a very different order are proposals for the quarantine of individuals—male and female prostitutes, for example—who though seropositive continue to behave publicly in a way that exposes others to the possibility of HTLV-III infection. Both criminal and health law provide ample authority for the control of such individuals. Though the moral, legal and constitutional impediments to the imposition of state control over all antibody-positive individuals does not arise in such cases, it is abundantly clear that the strategy of isolating such persons could have very little impact on the spread of HTLV-III infection.

Though there is an historical precedent for such measures in the efforts to control venereal disease by the mass roundups of prostitutes during World War I in the United States (Brandt, 1985), anyone who has examined the more finely tuned attempts to impose isolation or quarantine upon "recalcitrants" or "careless consumptives" (Musto, 1986), for example, will attest to the administrative difficulties that are entailed when even a modicum of procedural fairness is employed. More important, such efforts, directed as they are at the most obvious sources of infection, would fail to identify and restrict the many hundreds of thousands of infected individuals who in the privacy of their bedrooms might be engaged in acts that involve the spread of HTLV-III infection. If the quarantine of all antibody-positive individuals is overinclusive, the quarantine of public recalcitrants is underinclusive. That is the price of living in a constitutional society committed to the rudimentary principles of law, privacy and civil liberties. It is also a restriction placed upon us by reality.

The Appeals and Limits of Education

Confronted by the legal, moral and practical costs of mass quarantine and the limited possibilities of selective quarantine, there has been an understandable embrace of education as the way of seeking to meet the social threat posed by AIDS. Teaching members of high-risk groups about how to reduce the prospect of infecting others, or of becoming infected, is viewed as the appropriate social strategy, one that is compatible with our legal, moral and political institutions. Education must produce the critical and dramatic alteration in the sexual and drug using practices of individuals, it is argued. That has been the program of gay rights and self-help

343

groups, as well as of local and federal agencies (Silverman & Silverman, 1985). What well-funded and aggressively pursued education might attain it is still too soon to know. Despite the paeans to education governmental efforts have been limited by profound moralism. To speak directly and explicitly about "safe" or "safer" sexual practices would require a tacit toleration of homosexuality (McGraw-Hill, 1986). For those committed to a conservative social agenda such a public stance is intolerable.

The turn to education is, of course, compatible with the liberal commitment to privacy, to voluntarism, and to the reluctance to employ coercive measures in the face of behavior that occurs in the private realm. But the commitment to education in the case of AIDS occurs against a background of controversy about the efficacy of efforts to achieve the modification of personal behavior by health promotion campaigns. Attempts to encourage changes in vehicular behavior, smoking and alcohol consumption by education alone have had only the most limited success. Campaigns to encourage seatbelt use in automobiles in the United States, Canada, Great Britain and France all faltered, and ultimately necessitated the enactment of statutes mandating their use (Warner, 1983). More to the point is the failure of sex education to affect demonstrably the levels of teenage pregnancy in many urban centers. Finally, the historical legacy of efforts to control venereal disease through moral education in the period prior to penicillin provides little basis for optimism (Brandt, 1985). So skeptical are some about the prospects of health education, that they charge that such campaigns represent a diversion, from the more complex and difficult choices that need to be made (Faden, 1986).

Nevertheless, the shock wave sent through the gay community by the rising toll of AIDS cases, coupled with the extraordinary and inventive efforts by gay groups at reaching large numbers with information about "safer sex" and the transmission of HTLV-III have apparently had a dramatic effect, at least in the short run. Anecdotal reports, quasi-systematic surveys and, most important, the declining incidence of rectal gonorrhea, all have suggested to some that in the face of AIDS an unprecedented change has occurred in sexual behavior in a relatively brief period. Not only have gay men reduced the extent to which they engage in sexual activity with strangers, but so, too, have they reduced the extent to which they engage in anal receptive intercourse, the most "risky" of risky behaviors.

A longitudinal study conducted at the New York Blood Center, however, provides a sobering antidote to such educational enthusiasm, and is compatible with what we have come to expect from health promotion campaigns (Stevens, 1986). Though it, like other studies, found a dramatic change in the extent to which gay men engage in social receptive intercourse, just less than half of those in the study population continued to engage in that practice. Needless to say, we know almost nothing about how education might affect the behavior of intravenous drug users, even were such efforts to be undertaken. In the absence of a natural social support constituency, the provision of education might well be utterly ineffective.

Conclusion

Faced with a fatal illness that has the potential for grave social disruption, the appeal of coercive state power as an approach to the interruption of the spread of HTLV-III infection is understandable. But to yield to its seduction would be socially catastrophic. Confronted with the unacceptable specter of gross violations of privacy and civil liberties, many have embraced the promise of education. Here the risk is that the politically attractive will be confused with the socially efficacious. The illusions of both power and voluntarism must be rejected. Instead of the grand vision of stopping AIDS we must settle for the more modest goal of slowing its spread. As we attempt to fashion policies directed at that goal it will be important, at each juncture, to acknowledge the fundamental limits of our capacity to fight an infectious disease like AIDS.

We are hostage to the advances of virology and immunology, and will be so for many years. As the AIDS-associated toll mounts, so, too, will the level of social distress. In this protracted encounter with a microparasitic threat, it will be critical to preserve a social capacity for reasoned analysis and public discourse. That is a capacity that may be subverted by those who would generate hysteria and repressive moves as well as by those whose fears of such a turn result in irrational charges of "totalitarianism" at the very mention of public health (Ortleb, 1985, 1986). A failure to defend reason in the face of AIDS may not only hinder our efforts to limit the exactions taken by this epidemic, but will leave a dreadful imprint upon the social fabric. The history of earlier epidemics should serve as a warning.

References

Brandt, Allan, "No Magic Bullet: A Social History of Venereal Disease in the United States Since 1880" (New York: Oxford University Press, 1985).

Centers for Disease Control, a) *Morbidity & Mortality Weekly Reports*, "Education and Foster Care of Children Infected with Human T-Lymphotropic Virus Type III/Lymphadenopathy-associated Virus," (August 30, 1985), p. 517; b) *Morbidity & Mortality Weekly Reports*, "Recommendations for Preventing Transmission of Infection with Human T-Lymphotropic Virus Type III/Lymphadenopathy-associated Virus in the Workplace," (November, 1985), p. 681; c) *Morbidity & Mortality Weekly Reports*, "Recommendations for Assisting in the Prevention and Perinatal Transmission of HTLV-III/LAV and Acquired Immunodeficiency Syndrome," (December 6, 1985).

Faden, Ruth, "Ethical Issues in Government Sponsored Public Health Campaigns," *Health Education Quarterly* (1986).

Grutsch, James F and Robertson, A.D.J., "The Coming of AIDS: It Didn't Start with Homosexuals and It Won't End with Them," *The American Spectator* (March 1986), p. 12.

Intergovernmental Health Policy Project, George Washington University, "A Review of State and Local Government Interactions Affecting AIDS," (November 1985).

Kadish, Sanford, "The Crisis of Overcriminalization," *American Criminal Law Quarterly* (1986), p. 18.

Kittrie, Nicholas, *The Right to Be Different* (Baltimore: Penguin Books, 1973).

Kuller, Lewis and Kingsley, Lawrence, "The Epidemic of AIDS: The Failure of Public Health Policy," *Milbank Memorial Fund Quarterly,*

Lalonde, Marc, *A New Perspective on the Health of Canadians* (Ottowa: Government of Canada, 1975).

Leavitt, Judith, "Politics and Public Health: Smallpox in Milwaukee, 1894-5, *Bulletin of the History of Medicine*, 1976, p. 553.

McGraw-Hill's *Washington Report on Medicine and Health*, "No 'Show & Tell' for AIDS Education, CDC Says," (January 13, 1986).

McNeill, William, *Plagues and Peoples* (Garden City NY: Anchor Press, 1976).

Mohr, Richard, "AIDS: What to Do—and What Not to Do," *Philosophy & Public Policy* (Fall, 1985), p. 6.

Moreno, Jonathan and Bayer, Ronald, "The Limits of the Ledger in Health Promotion," *Hastings Center Report* (December 1985), p. 37.

Musto, David, "Quarantine and the Problem of AIDS," *Milbank Memorial Fund Quarterly*, 1986).

Nelkin, Dorothy and Heilgartner, Stephen, "Disputed Dimensions of Risk: A Public School Controversy over AIDS," *Milbank Memorial Fund Quarterly,*

New York City Gay and Lesbian Antiviolence Project, cited in *The New York Times*, November 16, 1985, p. 31.

Ortleb, Charles, "The AIDS Prophet of Doom," *The New York Native* (October 14–20, 1985).

————, "Heil Bayer!!," *The New York Native* (June 2, 1986), p. 4.

Packer, Herbert, *The Limits of the Criminal Sanction* (Stanford CA: Stanford University Press, 1968).

Restak, Charles, "Worry About Survival of Society First; AIDS Victims' Rights." *Washington Post*, September 8, 1985, C1, C4.

Rosenberg, Charles. *The Cholera Years* (Chicago IL: University of Chicago Press, 1962).

Schur, Edwin, *Crimes without Victims* (Englewood Cliffs NJ: Prentice Hall, 1965).

————, *Labeling Deviant Behavior* (New York: Harper & Row, 1971).

Silverman, Mervyn F. and Deborah, B., "AIDS and the Threat to Public Health," *Hastings Center Report* (August 1985), p. 19.

Singer, Eleanor and Rogers, Theresa F., "Public Opinion about AIDS," *AIDS & Public Policy Journal* (July 1986).

Starr, Paul, "AIDS and Public Policy" unpublished presentation, American Association for the Advancement of Science, May, 1986.

Stevens, Cladd, Taylor, Patricia and Zang, Edith et al., "Human T-Cell Lymphotropic Virus Type III Infection in a Cohort of Homosexual Men in New York City," *Journal of the American Medical Association* (April 25, 1986), p. 2167.

U.S. Department of Health, Education & Welfare, *Healthy People: The Surgeon General's Report on Health Promotion and Disease Prevention* (Washington DC: U.S. Government Printing Office, 1979).

————, Public Health Service, *Smoking and Health,* (Washington DC: Public Health Service Publication, 1964).

Warner, Kenneth, "Bags, Buckles, Belts: The Debate over Mandatory Personal Restraints in Automobiles," *Journal of Health Policy, Politics & Law* (Spring 1983), p. 51.

15

The Constitutional Rights of AIDS Carriers

Harvard Law Review

The United States Public Health Service has called Acquired Immune Deficiency Syndrome (AIDS) the nation's number one health priority.[1] Attempts to safeguard the public by controlling the spread of AIDS may make the syndrome a significant source of legal inquiry as well. Already regulations have required closing gay bathhouses,[2] refusing AIDS patients certain jobs,[3] denying carriers the opportunity to serve in the military,[4] and suspending the rights of children who carry AIDS to attend public schools.[5] Unfortunately, AIDS-control laws may be enacted in response to public misconceptions about transmission of the virus[6] and inappropriate assumptions about the moral culpability of its victims.[7] Under the guise of concern for public health, some authorities may attempt to restrict unduly the freedom of gays.[8] The courts must determine how far legislators may go to protect the public whenever new policies impair the civil rights and liberties of AIDS patients and members of high-risk groups.

In the United States, AIDS primarily affects urban residents in two population groups: seventy-three percent of AIDS patients[9] are gay or bisexual men and seventeen percent are heterosexual intraveous drug users.[10] The virus that causes AIDS destroys the body's ability to fight disease. The virus is difficult to contract—sexual and bloodstream-to-bloodstream contact with a carrier are the only proven methods of transmission[11]—but those who develop AIDS

This article first appeared as an Editorial Note in the *Harvard Law Review*, 1986.

© 1986, *Harvard Law Review Association.*

seem to have no chance of recovery. From the time AIDS was identified in 1981, through January 1986, more than 17,000 individuals were diagnosed as having AIDS.[12] The number of AIDS patients in the United States doubled during 1985. Based on this rate of growth, medical experts predict 40,000 new cases of AIDS in the next two years.[13] Doctors believe that for every case of AIDS reported, there are five to ten cases of AIDS-related complex (ARC), a milder immune system depression. Studies of blood samples suggest that an additional 400,000 to 1,000,000 Americans are symptomless carriers: they may not know they have the virus, and they may pass it on to others.[14]

This essay considers how courts should respond to threats to individual rights and liberties arising from public health regulation enacted in response to AIDS. Part I presents a history of relevant public health law in the courts in the twentieth century and concludes that, given the subsequent development of constitutional protections of individual rights and of medical technology, early cases provide little guidance to modern courts evaluating AIDS regulation. Part II applies constitutional analyses to five types of regulation: quarantines, restrictions on the association of gay men, mandatory testing and reporting requirements, public employment prohibitions, and bans on public school attendance. The first, fifth, and fourteenth amendments offer substantial protection to individuals likely to be affected by such policies. In most cases only narrowly tailored, medically compelled restrictions should be sustained by the courts—a conclusion that also applies to AIDS-control regulation not discussed here.

Early Epidemics and Public Health Precedent

In the early years of this century, courts often ruled on public health regulations that restricted the freedom of individuals. These cases established the preservation of public health as a proper concern of state legislatures.[15] Beyond this basic holding, early public health decisions prove to be poor precedent, outdated by a half-century's medical advances and by progress in the way courts evaluate civil rights infringements.

Early twentieth-century courts considered public health regulation under the minimum scrutiny standard applied to economic regulation and civil rights infringement alike. This standard presumes legislation valid unless it bears no reasonable relationship to the achievement of a proper governmental objective.[16] Using this test, courts allowed popularly held beliefs about the spread of disease to support the medical soundness of a regulation[17] and rarely found regulation enacted to protect public health to be "unreasonable," "arbitrary" or "oppressive,"[18] the limiting principles articulated in 1905 by the Supreme Court in *Jacobson v. Massachusetts.*[19]

Courts' treatment of public health regulation has changed very little since the turn of the century. Although in the 1920s courts began to require some showing of medical necessity as the science of public health advanced,[20] they continued to allow class membership alone to justify public health restrictions when a disfavored class, such as prostitutes, was the subject of the regulation.[21] These judicial opinions assumed that victims were to blame for their illnesses.[22] The attitude that the diseased are a "menace" to both health and morals survived through the 1950s and 1960s, when incarcerated tuberculosis patients challenged state authority to quarantine;[23] such an attitude could easily reappear when AIDS cases come to court.

Although the courts' formulations of public health law have not advanced a great deal since the early part of this century, both judicial construction of the Constitution and medical science have evolved significantly. In the last two decades, the Supreme Court has expanded and redefined the scope of constitutionally protected individual rights. Important medical developments now allow more closely targeted efforts to control communicable disease. Most public health precedent predates the developments in both these areas.

Before the 1960s, courts rarely evaluated government actions under the standard of strict scrutiny, which allows a law to stand only if it is narrowly tailored to promote a compelling state interest.[24] Most legislation was subject only to the minimum rationality test applied in early public health cases,[25] and like early public health law, met that unexacting standard with little difficulty.

Equal protection decisions in the 1960s established that laws infringing fundamental rights would be held to the more demanding standard of review—"strict scrutiny"—once reserved for classi-

351

fications based on race, national origin, and alienage. The Court also introduced a middle tier to equal protection analysis—"intermediate scrutiny"—which requires that legislation burdening certain "quasi-suspect" classes or impairing important, but not fundamental, rights be substantially related to an important state interest.[26] In determining whether a classification merits heightened scrutiny, a court may consider the way the class is treated by others, the relationship of class members to one another, and the relevance of the class's defining characteristics to class members' abilities to participate in society.[27]

Although no one characteristic is determinative, political powerlessness, stigmatization, a history of unequal treatment, and the inability of individuals to control their membership in the class may identify the class as a "discrete and insular minorit[y]" deserving of special treatment.[28] Gays, intravenous drug users, and AIDS carriers—all likely victims of irrational discrimination—arguably share many of these characteristics.[29]

The unenumerated substantive due process right of privacy has also undergone significant development in the last decades. The Court in the 1960s and 1970s expanded the scope of the interests protected by the privacy right beyond the traditional sphere of marital privacy.[30] The Supreme Court has held that the privacy right encompasses both a general "individual interest in avoiding disclosure of personal matters" and an "interest in independence in making certain kinds of important decisions."[31] Regulation to control AIDS affects both of these interests when it seeks either to restrain sexual activity or to identify AIDS carriers.

Revolutionary innovations in methods of disease control since the early years of this century have paralleled the development of constitutionally protected individual rights. The current state of scientific knowledge has made it possible to develop a basic biological understanding of AIDS in a fraction of the time it would have taken even twenty years ago.[32] Such advances in scientists' understandings of viral etiology now allow closely targeted efforts to stop the spread of disease. Fifty years ago, quarantine may indeed have been the least restrictive means of controlling some communicable diseases, but large-scale quarantine is now rarely justified.[33] Research, education, and individual treatment characterize the modern approach to public health policy, and courts now commonly rely on medical rather than popular assessments of the necessity of public health actions.[34] It would be inappropriate to use early twentieth-century law to evaluate state attempts to control AIDS without considering the implications of the last half-century's medical and constitutional developments.

The Constitutional Status of the AIDS-Afflicted: Rights Versus Regulation

Public apprehension that AIDS will continue to spread throughout the population is legitimate. Concern that efforts to control its transmission may infringe the civil rights of AIDS carriers and members of high-risk groups is, however, equally well-justified. AIDS regulation affects the rights of these individuals to liberty, privacy, property, free association, and free expression. When constitutionally challenged, such regulation should be subject to a series of inquiries. First, the purpose of the regulation should be evaluated under the proper standard of scrutiny to see if the state interest at stake is compelling, important, or legitimate. If the regulation meets the purpose test, then the relationship between the state's objective and the means employed to achieve it should be considered.[35]

Regulation geared to the control of AIDS will almost certainly meet the proper purpose requirement, whether at the strict, intermediate, or minimum level of scrutiny.[36] Courts have generally found preservation of the public health to be a compelling interest;[37] AIDS' potential to spread at an exponential rate suggests that protection of the public against AIDS merits equal deference.[38] Quieting the unsubstantiated fears of the voting public, however, is not a compelling, nor important, nor legitimate state interest.[39] Neither does the state have a legitimate interest in discriminatory laws, cloaked as public health regulation, that are actually designed to oppress gay people.[40]

The stigma attached to AIDS carriers—because of the disease's close association with both homosexuality and intravenous drug use—suggests that improper purpose should be a concern of courts, especially when important civil rights are at issue. Although courts have not often been willing to inquire into the motives of legislators,[41] the Supreme Court has held that courts,

353

especially in equal protection cases, should not "accept at face value assertions of legislative purpose, when an examination of the legislative scheme and its history demonstrates that the asserted purpose could not have been a goal of the legislation."[42] The failure of a state to target a regulation accurately also undermines the claim that the compelling purpose—AIDS control—is the rule's true objective.[43] Even under minimum scrutiny, the Court has looked closely at state-articulated justifications and evaluated them for their credibility, factual foundation, and logical consistency, and has struck down a rule that rested on "irrational prejudice."[44]

Although this inquiry into purposes is important and may even be dispositive of challenges to some AIDS-control legislation, this Part puts aside the purpose test and examines the constitutionality of five types of regulation under the assumption that a proper purpose of protecting public health has been established. In each case, this Part will discuss the level of scrutiny that should be applied and whether the relationship between the regulation's means and ends is likely to meet constitutional standards.

Quarantines

More than one in four Americans favors putting people with AIDS "into quarantine in special places to keep them away from the general public."[45] The Centers for Disease Control has begun to look into federal authority to quarantine,[46] and at least one state, Virginia, has planned a quarantine program to isolate AIDS patients who continue to have sexual relations.[47] Few, if any, quarantine actions, however, will be targeted narrowly enough to pass constitutional tests, despite their potential popularity with the public.

Any AIDS-control regulation that restricts the movement and personal contacts of individuals impinges on fundamental rights and should be evaluated under strict scrutiny. The Supreme Court has recognized repeatedly that involuntary confinement for any purpose constitutes a significant deprivation of liberty[48] that may not be abridged without a showing of compelling necessity.[49] The involuntary incarceration involved in a quarantine would impair other fundamental rights as well, including freedom of association,[50] the right to privacy[51] (including the right to cohabit with one's spouse and family),[52] and the right to travel interstate.[53]

Subjecting quarantine regulation to strict scrutiny would not prevent the state from safeguarding public health. The state, however, would be required to use the least intrusive means of accomplishing this objective. To identify less restrictive policy options, a court should first define the types of state action likely to control disease with sufficient efficacy and then assess their intrusiveness and the number of people affected. The option that impairs the fewest people's rights or impairs rights to the smallest degree would be constitutionally permissible,[54] as long as it does not go beyond certain basic limits.[55]

Laws quarantining members of high-risk groups are not targeted sufficiently closely to survive heightened scrutiny. A quarantine of gay men, for example, would clearly be unconstitutionally overinclusive, as only a minority of gay men have AIDS, and not all AIDS carriers are gay. Quarantines of AIDS carriers raise more difficult issues, but in general, they too should fail when they limit contacts that do not involve the transfer of bodily fluids, unless significant new medical evidence demonstrates that AIDS can be transmitted by casual contact.

Medical uncertainty prevents quarantine from being a constitutional alternative for controlling AIDS. Physicians are not yet able to determine when an AIDS carrier is infectious, and no cure or vaccine is available. Furthermore, tests now available to detect antibodies produce a significant number of falsely positive results, creating problems of overinclusiveness. Given these gaps in medical knowledge, a quarantine of AIDS carriers could require the lifelong confinement of a healthy individual who does not even carry the virus. Such a law would undoubtedly deter many carriers from seeking tests or treatment[56] and would be neither an effective nor a constitutional means of protecting the public from disease.[57]

A quarantine aimed at AIDS carriers who are considered unable or unwilling to refrain from sexual contacts or from sharing intravenous needles may appear, on its face, to be targeted sufficiently narrowly. Nonetheless, even these quarantines should not be upheld. It would be virtually impossible to identify the dangerous individuals in a pool of one million carriers of the virus.[58] Determinations would necessarily be based on predictions of future behavior that either could not be substantiated, or could not be made with sufficient certainty to meet the tests of close fit and least

355

restrictive means; an individual could face indefinite confinement simply because of assumptions about what he might do in the future. Such an individual would be considered not merely ill, but lacking in self-control, prone to engage in unacceptable behavior, and a danger to society. Under such a regulation, an individual who did not commit a crime could be involuntarily confined and permanently stigmatized without receiving the safeguards of a criminal trial.[59]

Finally, it is likely that any quarantine law would be enforced arbitrarily, with those people who are dependent upon public health facilities for medical assistance most likely to come to the attention of government authorities. Such randomness would violate the spirit of the equal protection clause, and would render any quarantine both unworkable and unconstitutional.[60]

Restrictions on the Association of Gay Men

The high percentage of gay men among AIDS victims has made gay meeting places, particularly bathhouses, targets of government regulation.[61] Closing bathhouses on the theory that they facilitate the spread of AIDS, however, raises the question of the proper scope of protected associational rights. The Court has recognized two types of association enjoying constitutional protection: collective engagement in activities protected by the first amendment and intimate personal relations.[62] Because gay sexual activity by consenting adults is central to the identities of gay people and analogous to protected heterosexual intimate activity not engaged in for procreative purpose, it should be accorded constitutional protection.[63]

Even if the Court does find that the right to privacy extends to adult, consensual gay sexual activity, however, that right would probably not protect sexual activity in commercial bathhouses. Courts have upheld the right of states to prohibit sexual activity in public[64] and in view of spectators.[65] The Supreme Court has suggested that the highly personal relationships that must be protected from unwarranted state interference "are distinguished by such attributes as relative smallness, a high degree of selectivity in decisions to begin and maintain the affiliation and seclusion from others in critical aspects of the relationship."[66] Bathhouse encounters—which often involve anonymous and multiple-partner sex[67]—seem to resemble more the Court's definition of public, unprotected activity than protected intimacies.[68]

Even if a bathhouse closing were subject to heightened scrutiny, a court should not invalidate the action for lack of a close fit between means and ends or for failure to select the least restrictive alternative.[69] There is arguably a close fit based on evidence that the sexual activity in bathhouses is a major contributor to the spread of AIDS. Moreover, a ban on bathhouses is not unduly restrictive, because it would not prevent gay men from engaging in intimate association elsewhere. Even under a heightened level of scrutiny, a bathhouse closing should be upheld[70] if the promulgator of the rule has not exceeded its statutory authority and if the rule is limited to only those public places exclusively or primarily intended to accommodate frequent, anonymous, and public sexual encounters.[71]

It would be extremely improper to use AIDS as a reason to restrict the freedom of gay organizations that have expressive, political, or social functions, especially at a time when gay rights are likely to be threatened by fear of AIDS. In order to overcome the difficult burden that is imposed when first amendment rights are implicated,[72] the state would have to show that the proposed regulation is necessary to prevent the spread of AIDS. This burden would not be met as long as there was no evidence that nonintimate contact could transmit AIDS. Even if nonintimate contact were found to be a significant method of AIDS transmission, regulation restricting the meetings of gay groups not organized for sexual activity would be overbroad. The majority of gay people do not carry AIDS,[73] and other forms of regulation would offer more direct means of protecting the public from those who do.[74] Therefore, these types of associational restrictions on gay organizations should be found constitutionally inadequate.

Mandatory Testing and Reporting Requirements

Mandatory blood testing, although a minor personal invasion, would infringe the individual's protected privacy "interest in avoiding disclosure of personal matters."[75] The bodily intrusion inflicted in mandatory blood tests is similar to that of compulsory immunizations, which have long been upheld by the courts. But unlike a vaccination, a positive AIDS blood test could have a devastating impact on an individual's life. Blood tests currently available are designed to protect the blood supply, not to diagnose carriers, and are likely to be hypersensitive. Significant psychological trauma might accompany a false diagnosis.[76] An individual's most intimate personal relationships could be affected by a positive test. Disclosure of the results to third parties could also have serious results. A positive reading might be construed falsely as proof that an individual is gay or a drug user. As one Florida court recognized, "AIDS is the modern day equivalent of leprosy. AIDS, or a suspicion of AIDS, can lead to discrimination in employment, education, housing and even medical treatment. If the donors' names were disclosed . . . they would be subject to this discrimination and embarrassment. . . ."[77] Nothing short of compelling necessity can justify forcing individuals to submit to blood tests that might cause such personal anguish.

Only if a state could show that a mandatory blood test requirement were necessary to advance the public health could it justify such a measure.[78] Yet it is difficult to conceive of a scenario in which the protection of public health would require compulsory AIDS blood tests,[79] as AIDS is not spread by casual contact.[80] Furthermore, given widespread knowledge of the demographics of AIDS patients, those individuals most at risk probably are already aware of the odds that they carry AIDS. In very few cases would compulsory blood tests substantially advance the goal of public health.

Requirements that physicians report cases of AIDS to a public health authority raise problems similar to those raised by mandatory testing, but may be permissible with appropriate confidentiality safeguards. The principle of notifying authorities about cases of communicable diseases has been upheld since 1887,[81] and required reporting of infectious disease has rarely been challenged in the courts.[82] When an AIDS-reporting regulation requires the disclosure of identity, however, it threatens the individual's privacy as well as his liberty interest in his "good name, reputation, honor, or integrity."[83] As with mandatory testing, the state will have difficulty providing sufficient safeguards that information will not be disclosed publicly, made accessible to unauthorized persons, or used to deprive an individual of government benefits.[84]

In light of these difficulties, inclusion of carriers' names in physicians' reports does not provide additional public benefit sufficient to justify the increased infringement of liberty and privacy.[85] The risk of disclosure might discourage some individuals from seeking tests, thus undermining research progress by diminishing the representativeness of the sample of known AIDS patients. Nor would the inclusion of names significantly increase opportunities either to provide counseling, or to facilitate the dissemination of information about medical treatment, should a cure be discovered. The significant likelihood of false positives reinforces the need for confidentiality. In sum, regulations requiring that names be provided to a governmental authority should not be upheld in light of the significant privacy interests at stake and the negligible gain to the public.

Public Employment

Protection for AIDS carriers against employment discrimination may be found in statutes banning discrimination against the disabled and in other civil rights laws.[86] Regulation denying AIDS carriers employment in most government jobs may also be unconstitutional.[87] When a discrete class is deprived of the opportunity for public employment, liberty interests are implicated.[88] Governmental firings of AIDS carriers or members of high-risk groups who have ongoing "contracts," "tenure," or "assurances" of continued employment deprive them of property interests as well.[89] When a regulation deprives a sensitive, although not necessarily suspect, class—such as AIDS carriers—of significant liberty interests or vital government benefits, courts have applied heightened scrutiny.[90] Even if barring AIDS carriers from public employment receives only minimum scrutiny, such a bar should not be upheld.

Excluding AIDS carriers from public employment that requires no participation in activities through which the virus could be transmitted is not substantially or even rationally related to the protection of public health. The Federal Centers for Disease Control has concluded that "[e]mployees with AIDS should work to the extent of their physical capacity."[91] Medical experts agree that even AIDS-infected food handlers pose no threat to the public.[92] Even the risk of transmission from patient to health care worker has been found to be negligible.[93] No case is known in which an individual with AIDS transmitted the disease to a household member who is not a sexual partner.[94] Opposition from co-workers or clients may make an employer reluctant to keep an AIDS carrier on the staff. But where important civil rights of an unpopular group are at stake, mere uneasiness cannot justify denial of public employment. Unless new medical discoveries or changes in the etiology of the disease suggest that AIDS carriers actually do pose a threat through nonintimate contacts, blanket restrictions on their employment in significant sectors of the economy should not be upheld.

Public School

The central importance of education in American society[95] has prompted the Court to require that statutes imposing "lifetime hardship on a discrete class of children not accountable for their disabling status" by depriving them of public education further a substantial goal of the state.[96] If public education is provided to the restricted child at home or in separate classrooms, however, the court may apply only minimum scrutiny to the regulation.[97] In these states, a regulation need only be rationally related to the legitimate state interest of protecting the public health. Children with AIDS, however, should not be barred from public schools merely to ease the minds of other students' concerned parents. Even under minimum scrutiny, "irrational prejudice" is not a permissible basis on which to rest restrictive state action.[98]

In *District 27 Community School Board v. Board of Education*,[99] the court upheld New York City's policy of considering AIDS-carrying children on a case-by-case basis, correctly relying on medical determinations and not on "unsubstantiated fears of catastrophe."[100] The court found that the Board had undertaken an extensive investigation into medical opinion and that the policy was in fact supported by the general body of medical knowledge and all but one of the expert witnesses at trial.[101]

Infected children could be prevented from attending public school if authorities had medical evidence that AIDS-infected children pose a health threat.[102] A court may not weigh conflicting opinions and simply substitute its judgment for that of the policymaker.[103] But when scientific evidence suggests that the "health hazard" posed by the children is no more than a "remote possibility," a regulation excluding infected children from public school should be found unconstitutional.[104] It is unlikely that a policy to exclude all AIDS-carrying children could be found to be based legitimately on current medical authority. No child is known to have contracted AIDS in school or in a day care center.[105] The Centers for Disease Control has recommended that schools restrict only preschool-aged children with AIDS and those school-aged children with AIDS who lack control of body secretions, are prone to biting others, or have exposed skin lesions.[106] Although even the most rational parents may feel uneasy knowing their children attend school with an AIDS carrier, it is the real, not the perceived, health hazard that courts must consider.

The public school question exposes the tensions that underlie almost every proposed AIDS-control measure. Each regulation discussed here affects some interest central to the lives of individuals: liberty, privacy, freedom of association, the right to work, and the right to be educated. Each threatens to stigmatize those affected: as gay, as a drug user, or merely as an AIDS carrier, a public menace. Perhaps in no other instance would singling out AIDS carriers have as severe consequences as with children in school, and perhaps no other groups of carriers is considered less blameworthy. At the same time, perhaps no other concerns of those calling for restrictions are more understandable than the worries of parents whose children spend their days with an AIDS carrier. Yet even in this emotionally charged context, the Constitution requires that policymakers ground their decisions in reality and allow AIDS carriers to attend school when they present virtually no risk to other students.

Conclusion

Legislators will play an important role in handling the AIDS crisis. In response to public pressure, they may advance overboard rules that appear at first glance to benefit many and disadvantage few. When challenged in court, such new regulation should be evaluated in light of significantly updated public health law. More sophisticated medical knowledge now makes it realistic for courts to require very close fits between means and ends. The last few decades' developments in constitutional analysis compel such close fits; when personal freedoms are at stake, courts may no longer assume that rulemakers have done their jobs with sufficient attention to medical necessity.

The threat that legislatures will impose severe restrictions of personal freedom on AIDS carriers poses both practical and legal dangers. Such restrictions might actually discourage high-risk individuals from reporting for testing and treatment, thereby undermining research efforts and defeating gains that might otherwise be made in slowing AIDS transmission. Legislators interested in AIDS control should encourage widespread testing, education, and research—not state-imposed restrictions. In the end, self-restraint may prove the most effective, and least restrictive, way to control AIDS.

Notes

1. *See* U.S. Public Health Service, Facts About AIDS 1 (1984). For general information about AIDS, see A. Fettner & W. Check, The Truth About AIDS: Evolution of an Epidemic (1985); Landesman, Ginzburg & Weiss, *Special Report: The AIDS Epidemic* 312 New Eng. J. Med. 521 (1985).

2. In October 1985, the state of New York empowered local health officials to close gay bathhouses in New York City, see N.Y. Times, Oct. 26, 1985, at 1, col. 4, and the House of Representatives voted 417 to 8 to allow the Surgeon General to use AIDS research funds to close any bathhouse or massage parlor that facilitates the spread of AIDS, *see* 131 Cong. Rec. H8030-33 (daily ed. Oct. 2, 1985).

3. For example, Miami recently enacted a law requiring food service workers to obtain certification that they do not carry infectious disease. *See* N.Y. Times, Oct. 26, 1985, at 30, col. 1.

4. The Defense Department now screens all military personnel for the AIDS virus and discharges those individuals who have AIDS. *See* N.Y. Times, Oct. 19, 1985, at A1, col. 1.

5. Children with AIDS have been barred from public schools in jurisdictions as dissimilar as Kokomo, Indiana, and Queens, New York. *See* N.Y. Times, Feb. 22, 1986, at 6 col. 1; N.Y. Times, Oct. 19, 1985, at A30, col. 6.

6. For example, the President of the Newark City Council stated that although there is no proof that AIDS can be transmitted by food workers, the law he had proposed requiring AIDS tests for foods workers would give "some people a psychological lift." *See* N.Y. Times, Oct. 26, 1985, at 30, col. 1. The public may overestimate the risk of well-publicized and potentially fatal dangers—such as AIDS—over which they believe they have little control. *See* Allman, *Staying Alive in the 20th Century,* Science 85, Oct. 1985, at 31. A nonhemophiliac, heterosexual American who does not take drugs intravenously has only a minute chance of contracting AIDS, *see* Langone *AIDS Special Report*, Discover, Dec. 1985, at 28, 31, yet over a third

of the respondents in the poll believe AIDS is as contagious, or more contagious, than the common cold. *See* Wash. Post Nat'l Weekly Ed., Dec. 23, 1985, at 37, col. 1.

7. Openly anti-gay groups are supporting a proposed Houston ordinance requiring food service employees to be tested for AIDS twice yearly. *See* N.Y. Times, Oct. 26, 1985, at 30, col. 1. Rep. William Dannemeyer (R-Calif.), a leading proponent of AIDS legislation, stated on the House floor that "God's plan for man was Adam and Eve, not Adam and Steve." *See* 131 Cong. Rec. H7986 (daily ed. Oct. 1, 1985). Patrick Buchanan, former White House director of communications, made public his view that gays "have declared war upon Nature, and now Nature is exacting an awful retribution." N.Y. Post, May 24, 1983, *quoted in* Bayer, *AIDS and the Gay Community: Between the Specter and the Promise of Medicine,* 52 Soc. Research 581, 589 (1985).

8. For example, the Massachusetts House of Representatives reversed its 1983 vote in favor of a gay rights bill in 1985, after an "emotional debate marked by frequent references to AIDS," *see* Boston Globe, Sept. 24, 1985, at A1, col. 3, despite the fact that lesbians, who would be protected by the bill, are among the groups least at risk for AIDS, *see* A. Fettner & W. Check, *supra* note 1, at 246. Anti-gay groups raised the AIDS issue in court as a justification for upholding criminal anti-sodomy laws. *See* Baker v. Wade, 106 F.R.D. 526 (N.D. Tex. 1985), *supplementing* 553 F. Supp. 1121 (N.D. Tex. 1982), *aff'd on other grounds,* 743 F.2d 236 (5th Cir. 1984), *rev'd,* 769 F.2d 289 (5th Cir. 1985), *reh'g denied,* 774 F.2d 1285 (5th Cir. 1985).

9. In this Note, "AIDS patients" refers to individuals who have been diagnosed as having the syndrome. "AIDS carriers" refers to AIDS patients, AIDS-related complex (ARC) patients, and symptomless carriers.

10. *See Update: Acquired Immunodeficiency Syndrome—United States,* 35 Morbidity and Mortality Weekly Rep. 18 (1986). Eight percent of gay or bisexual AIDS patients are also intravenous drug users. An additional one percent of diagnosed AIDS patients are also hemophiliacs; one percent are heterosexual sex partners of AIDS carriers; and another two percent are recipients of blood transfusions. Ninety-three percent are men. As of January 1986, 231 children had been diagnosed as having AIDS. *See id.* at 19. Most AIDS-afflicted children contracted the virus in the womb or were infected during medical treatment with blood or blood products. *See Education and Foster Care of Children Infected with Human T-Lymphotropic Virus Type III/Lymphadenopathy-Associated Virus,* 34 Morbidity and Mortality Weekly Rep. 517, 518 (1985) [hereinafter cited as *Education and Foster Care*].

11. *See Heterosexual Transmission of Human T-Lymphotropic Virus Type III/Lymphadenopathy-Associated Virus,* 34 Morbidity and Mortality Weekly Rep. 561 (1985) [hereinafter cited as *Heterosexual Transmission*]. Medical experts have found no evidence that the virus can be passed through casual contact or through the air. *See Prospective Evaluation of Health-Care Workers Exposed via Parenteral or Mucous-Membrane Routes to Blood and Body Fluids of Patients with Acquired Immunodeficiency Syndrome,* 33 Morbidity and Mortality Weekley Rep. 182 (1984). Although scientists have isolated the AIDS

virus in saliva and tears at extremely low levels, no case of AIDS has been documented as having been transmitted through either medium. *See Education and Foster Care, supra* note 10, at 518.

12. *See* N.Y. Times, Feb. 6, 1986, at B7, col. 1.

13. *See* Landesman, Ginzburg & Weiss, *supra* note 1, at 523. Experts estimate that the first 10,000 AIDS cases cost the United States $6.3 billion in hospital expenses and earnings lost because of disability and premature death. *See* N.Y. Times, Jan. 10, 1986, at A15, col. 1.

See AIDS: A Growing Threat, Time, Aug. 12, 1985, at 40, 42; Landesman, Ginzburg & Weiss, *supra* note I, at 522.

15. *See,* e.g, Jacobson v. Massachusetts, 197 U.S. II (1905) (upholding compulsory vaccination of adults against small pox even though the statute infringed on personal liberty).

16. *See* Miller v. Wilson, 236 U.S. 373, 380 (1915).

17. *See Jacobson,* 197 U.S. at 35 (stating that " 'the legislature has the right to pass laws which, according to the common belief of the people, are adapted to prevent the spread of contagious diseases,' " and that a " 'common belief, like common knowledge, does not require evidence to establish its existence, but may be acted upon without proof by the legislature and the courts' " (quoting Viemester v. White, 179 N.Y. 235, 72 N.E. 97 (1904)).

18. *See,* e.g, Jacobson, 197 U.S. at 27, 38 (upholding compulsory vaccination of adults); People *ex rel.* Barmore v. Robertson, 302 Ill. 422, 427, 134 N.E. 815, 817 (1922) (upholding a quarantine order). *But see* Jew Ho v. Williamson, 103 F. 10, 18 (N.D. Cal. 1900) (invalidating the quarantine of 15,000 Asians after nine deaths from bubonic plague in the community had been reported).

19. 197 U.S. at 25, 38.

20. *See, e.g.,* Robertson, 302 Ill. at 432–33, 134 N.E. at 819 (stating that quarantine regulations are "sustained on the law of necessity, and when the necessity ceases the right to enforce the regulations ceases").

21. *See, e.g.,* Ex parte Clemente, 61 Cal. App. 666, 215 P. 698 (1923) (holding that a quarantine was justified because information about a woman's acts of prostitution furnished a reasonable ground to believe she carried disease); *accord* Huffman v. District of Columbia, 39 A.2d 558, 562 (D.C. 1944); *cf.* People *ex rel.* Krohn v. Thomas, 133 Misc. 145, 147–49, 231 N.Y.S. 271, 274–75 (Sup. Ct. 1928) (upholding a statute authorizing examination for venereal disease of persons arrested for vagrancy).

22. *See, e.g.,* Ex parte Dayton, 52 Cal. App. 635, 199 P. 548 (1921) (justifying the jailing of a woman until she submitted to a physical examination for disease "on the ground that she is a lewd and dissolute person, and, in fact, a prostitute"); *Ex parte* Company, 106 Ohio St. 50, 57, 139 N.E. 204, 206 (1922) (stating that "those who by conduct and association contract such disease as makes them a menace to the health and morals of the community must submit to such regulation as will protect the public").

23. *See, e.g.,* Moore v. Draper, 57 So. 2d 648, 649 (Fla. 1952).

24. *See* Dunn v. Blumstein, 405 U.S. 330, 343 (1972). Strict scrutiny

requires the state to prove that the chosen action was the least restrictive alternative; the state must show that the legislation is drawn with precision, that it is closely tailored to serve the objective, and that there is no other reasonable way to achieve the goal with a lesser burden on constitutionally protected activity. *See id.*

25. *See supra*, p. 1276.

26. *See, e.g., Craig v. Boren*, 429 U.S. 190, 197 (1976) (treating gender classification as quasi-suspect); *Bell v. Burson*, 402 U.S. 535 (1971) (subjecting a law depriving individuals of driver's licenses to intermediate scrutiny).

27. *See* City of Cleburne v. Cleburne Living Center, 105 S. Ct. 3249, 3255–56 (1985) (holding that mental retardation is not a quasi-suspect classification); Mathews v. Lucas, 427 U.S. 495, 506 (1976) (denying illegitimate children suspect status); Frontiero v. Richardson, 411 U.S. 677, 688 (1973) (giving heightened scrutiny to gender-based classification); San Antonio Indep. School Dist. v. Rodriguez, 411 U.S. 1, 28 (1973) (declining to apply heightened scrutiny to poverty-based classification); Graham v. Richardson, 403 U.S. 365, 372 (1971) (treating aliens as a suspect class).

28. United States v. Carolene Prods., 304 U.S. 144, 152 n.4 (1938); *see* cases cited *supra* note 27.

29. Although the Supreme Court has neither granted nor refused gays quasi-suspect or suspect status, commentators have made a strong case for heightened scrutiny of classifications based on sexual preference. *See, e.g.,* Note, *The Constitutional Status of Sexual Orientation: Homosexuality as a Suspect Classification*, 98 Harv. L. Rev. 1285, 1297–1305 (1985); Note, *An Argument for the Application of Equal Protection Heightened Scrutiny to Classifications Based on Homosexuality*, 57 S. Cal. L. Rev. 797, 816–366 (1984).

30. *See, e.g., Roe v. Wade*, 410 U.S. 113, 153 (1973); Eisenstadt v. Baird, 405 U.S. 438, 453 (1972).

31. Whalen v. Roe, 429 U.S. 589, 599–600 (1977).

32. *See* Harv. Med. Sch. Health Letter, Dec. 1985, at 5, col. 2.

33. *See* Note, *Fear Itself: AIDS, Herpes and Public Health Decisions*, 3 Yale L. & Pol'y Rev. 479, 480 (1985) (chronicling twentieth-century developments in medicine and public health case law); *see also* Morgenstern, *The Role of the Federal Government in Protecting Citizens from Communicable Diseases*, 47 U. Cin. L. Rev. 537, 543–44 (1978) (outlining the history of federal public health programs).

34. *See, e.g.,* New York State Ass'n for Retarded Children, Inc. v. Carey, 612 F.2d 644, 650–51 (2d Cir. 1979) (granting the state leave to return to court with a plan executed "in light of the most current medical information"); LaRocca v. Dalsheim, 120 Misc. 2d 697, 710, 467 N.Y.S.2d 302, 311 (Sup. Ct. 1983) (declining, after consideration of a medical opinion, to require that a prison protect healthy prisoners from AIDS, but granting leave to renew claims as the state of scientific knowledge and hygienic procedures evolved).

35. *See* Kramer v. Union Free School Dist., 395 U.S. 621, 633 (1969).

36. Under strict scrutiny, the state carries the burden of advancing a

compelling justification for its action. Intermediate scrutiny requires the state to show that the legislation serves an "important" state objective. Under minimum scrutiny, legislation is presumed valid if it advances any legitimate state interest. *See The Supreme Court, 1984 Term*, 99 Harv. L. Rev. 120, 161–62 (1985).

37. *See, e.g.,* Brown v. Stone, 378 So. 2d 218 (Miss. 1979) (finding the state's interest in compulsory vaccination of school children sufficiently compelling to override parents' religious interests), *cert. denied*, 449 U.S. 887 (1980).

38. *See* City of New York v. New Saint Mark's Baths, No. 43640-85, Motion No. 114, slip op. (N.Y. Sup. Ct. Jan. 6, 1986).

39. *See* City of Cleburne v. Cleburne Living Center, 105 S. Ct. 3249, 3259 (1985) (holding that negative attitudes or unsubstantiated fears are not permissible bases for treating a home for the mentally retarded differently from other multiple dwellings).

40. *Cf.* O'Connor v. Donaldson, 422 U.S. 563, 575 (1975). ("Mere public intolerance or animosity cannot constitutionally justify the deprivation of a person's physical liberty.")

41. *See Developments in the Law—Equal Protection*, 82 Harv. L. Rev. 1065, 1092–1101 (1969).

42. Weinberger v. Wiesenfeld, 420 U.S. 636, 648 n.16 (1974); *cf.* Hunter v. Erickson, 393 U.S. 385, 392 (1969) (rejecting a city's articulated justification for a racially discriminatory rule).

43. *See* New York State Ass'n for Retarded Children, Inc. v. Carey, 612 F.2d 644, 650 (2d Cir. 1979) (finding that the identification and quarantine of some but not all children carrying hepatitis B suggested "that the Board did not regard its own evidence of risk as particularly convincing"). This type of inquiry should prove useful in determining the true purpose of AIDS-control regulations; the classes of people who pose the greatest health threat to the population rarely have been singled out for specific action. For example, intravenous drug users pose the most direct threat to the heterosexual majority, *see Heterosexual Transmission, supra* note 11, at 561, and make up a growing percentage of the AIDS patients in New York, *see* N.Y. Times, Oct. 20, 1985, at A51, col. 1. Nevertheless, gays are more often singled out as culpable and dangerous. *See* Bayer, *supra* note 7, at 586–95. American jurisdictions have all but ignored eliminating a significant medium of exposure to AIDS—shared intravenous needles. In the United States, where needles can be purchased only by prescription, 26% of AIDS patients have been intravenous drug users; in Canada, where needles are sold over the counter and are thus in such ready supply that few persons are likely to be tempted to share needles, the figure is 0.5%. *See* Harv. Med. Sch. Health Letter, Nov. 1985, at 3, col. 2.

44. *See* City of Cleburne v. Cleburne Living Center, 105 S. Ct. 3249, 3260 (1985). Courts have questioned the validity of some rules' purported purpose of controlling venereal disease and AIDS. *See, e.g.,* Gay Student Servs. v. Texas A & M Univ., 737 F.2d 1317, 1330 (5th Cir. 1984) (finding the argument that recognition of a gay student group would result in an

"increase in the number of persons with the psychological and physiological problems . . . prevalent among homosexuals," to be "precisely the kind of 'undifferentiated fear or apprehension' that the Supreme Court has repeatedly held 'is not enough to overcome the right to freedom of expression,' " (quoting Tinker v. Des Moines Indep. School Dist., 393 U.S. 503, 508 (1969)), *cert. denied*, 105 S. Ct. 1860 (1985); Baker v. Wade, 106 F.R.D. 526 (N.D. Tex. 1985) (denying a motion to set aside, on the basis of new evidence about AIDS, a ruling that an anti-sodomy statute was unconstitutional, because the legislative history of the statute showed that the legislature had rejected the arguments before the court).

45. *See* Washington Post Nat'l Weekly Ed., Dec. 23, 1985, at 37, col. 1.

46. *See* Boston Globe, Oct. 7, 1985. at 47, col. 1.

47. *See* Washington Post, Nov. 9, 1985, at D3, col. 1.

48. *See* Addington v. Texas, 441 U.S. 418, 425 (1979) (evaluating the standard of proof required for civil commitment of the mentally ill).

49. *See* Korematsu v. United States, 323 U.S. 214, 218 (1944) (finding that nothing short of apprehension by proper authorities of the gravest imminent danger to public safety can justify a curfew or forced removal from one's home).

50. *Cf.* Shelton v. Tucker, 364 U.S. 479, 488–90 (1960) (finding that a statute requiring disclosure of organizational memberships to violate the fundamental right of association).

51. *Cf.* Griswold v. Connecticut, 381 U.S. 479, 482–86 (1965) (finding that a law forbidding use of contraceptives impaired the right of privacy).

52. *See* Moore v. City of East Cleveland, 431 U.S. 494, 499 (1977) (invalidating a statute regulating family living arrangements).

53. *Cf.* Shapiro v. Thompson, 394 U.S. 618, 634 (1969) (holding that durational residency requirements for welfare benefits impinge unconstitutionally on the fundamental right to travel interstate).

54. *See* Dunn v. Blumstein, 405 U.S. 330, 343 (applying strict scrutiny to durational residency voting requirements).

55. For example, a regulation that inflicts criminal punishments on individuals simply because of their status as AIDS carriers would be unconstitutional, regardless of what alternative policies exist. *Cf.* Robinson v. California, 370 U.S. 660, 666 (1962) (holding unconstitutional the criminalization of the status of heroin addiction).

56. Laws permitting involuntary quarantines of AIDS carriers might also discourage individuals from participating in scientific studies. *Cf.* Brief Amici Curiae American Psychological Association and American Public Health Association in Support of Respondents at 24, Bowers v. Hardwick, 106 S. Ct. 342 (1985) (No. 85-140) [hereinafter cited as Brief Amici Curiae, *Hardwick*].

57. If a quarantine regulation were upheld, the restriction still would have to include procedural due process safeguards. Written notice, detailing the grounds and facts on which the quarantine was sought, would have to be given. *See* Greene v. Edwards, 263 S.E.2d 661, 663 (W. Va. 1980) (elaborating due process requirements for the incarceration of tuberculosis

victims). Proposed targets of a quarantine must be allowed a prior hearing, because fundamental freedoms and rights are at stake, a clear risk of erroneous deprivation exists, the government has no interest in depriving nondangerous individuals of their freedom, and the administrative burden of screening individuals should not be prohibitive. *See* Mathews v. Eldridge, 424 U.S. 319, 334–35 (1976). The state must justify the confinement with "clear and convincing" evidence that commitment is warranted. *Cf.* Addington v. Texas, 441 U.S. 418, 427–33 (1979) (discussing the standard of proof for involuntary commitment of the mentally ill); Annot., 97 A.L.R.3d 780 (1980).

58. Two classes that may be singled out as "unable or unwilling" to control themselves—intravenous drug users and prostitutes—are a threat because they are engaged in conduct which is already illegal.

59. Many jurisdictions already impose criminal liability on persons carrying venereal disease who have sexual intercourse. *See, e.g.,* N.Y. Pub. Health Law § 2307 (McKinney 1977); Tex. Stat. Ann. art. 4445, § 10(1) (Vernon 1976). Civil actions by individuals who contract venereal disease or herpes have been sustained by some courts. *See, e.g.,* Kathleen K. v. Robert B., 150 Cal. App. 3d 992, 996, 198 Cal. Rptr. 273, 276 (1984). They have recognized full disclosure by the carrier, however, as a defense. *See id. See generally* Note, *HERPES—A Legal Cure—Can the Law Succeed Where Medicine has Failed?*, 61 U. Det. J. Urb. L. 273 (1984).

60. *Cf.* Kolender v. Lawson, 461 U.S. 352, 361–62 (1983) (holding a criminal statute requiring loiterers to carry identification to be unconstitutionally vague because it encouraged arbitrary enforcement).

61. *See supra* notes 2, 8 & 10 and accompanying text.

62. *See* Roberts v. United States Jaycees, 104 S. Ct. 3244, 3249 (1984).

63. *See* Brief for Respondent at 9–14, Hardwick v. Bowers, 106 S. Ct. 342 (1985) (No. 85-140) [hereinafter cited as Brief for Respondent, *Hardwick*]; J. Baer, Equality Under the Constitution 231 (1983); L. Tribe, American Constitutional Law § 15-13, at 941–48 (1978); Richards, *Homosexuality and the Constitutional Right to Privacy,* 8 N.Y.U. Rev. L. & Soc. Change 311, 313–14 (1979). The Supreme Court has yet to rule definitively whether gay sexual activity by consenting adults enjoys constitutional protection. In Doe v. Commonwealth's Att'y, 403 F. Supp. 1199 (E.D. Va. 1975) (three-judge court), the court held that a criminal statute proscribing consensual sodomy did not violate the constitutional right of privacy. The Supreme Court affirmed the decision without opinion, *see* 425 U.S. 901 (1976), but the Court has indicated that it regards the privacy issue as unsettled. *See* Carey v. Population Servs. Int'l, 431 U.S. 678, 688 n.5, 694 n.17 (1977). The two circuits that have ruled on the issue have split. *See* Baker v. Wade, 769 F.2d 289 (5th Cir. 1985) (rejecting the privacy argument and upholding a Texas anti-sodomy statute); Hardwick v. Bowers, 760 F.2d 1202, 1211 (11th Cir.) (subjecting Georgia's anti-sodomy statute to strict scrutiny on privacy grounds), *cert. granted,* 106 S. Ct. 342 (1985). The Court ultimately rejected the privacy argument in 1986. [Editor].

64. *See* Paris Adult Theatre I v. Slaton, 413 U.S. 49, 66 n.13 (1973)

("[T]here is no necessary or legitimate expectation of privacy which would extend to marital intercourse on a street corner or a theater stage.").

65. *See* Lovisi v. Slayton, 539 F.2d 349, 351–52 (4th Cir. 1976).

66. Roberts v. United States Jaycees, 104 S. Ct. 3244, 3250 (1984) (holding that a private men's civic club lacked characteristics that would constitutionally justify its decision to exclude women from membership).

67. *See* N.Y. Times, Oct. 24, 1985, at A19, col. 1.

68. A court might, however, accept the argument that bathhouses have a symbolic, expressive quality such that their closing would warrant heightened scrutiny. *See* Bayer, *supra* note 7, at 596 (stating that "[t]he gay bathhouse has emerged as a powerful symbol of the struggle for greater social toleration for homosexuality"); *cf.* Schad v. Borough of Mount Ephraim, 452 U.S. 61, 66 (1981) (finding that nude dancing is entitled to first amendment protection).

69. *See* City of New York v. New Saint Mark's Baths, No. 43640-85, slip op. (N.Y. Sup. Ct. Jan. 6, 1986). *But see* Note, *Preventing the Spread of AIDS by Restricting Sexual Conduct in Gay Bathhouses: A Constitutional Analysis*, 15 Golden Gate U.L. Rev. 301, 319–24 (1985) (arguing that gay sexual activity in bathhouses is a protected privacy right and that bathhouse closings as a response to AIDS should be invalidated under strict scrutiny).

70. Public policy considerations, however, may argue against closing bathhouses. Opponents of bathhouse closings contend that bathhouses are a useful forum for educating the individuals most at risk who will be driven "underground and . . . beyond the reach of advice on how to avoid AIDS." N.Y. Times, Oct. 19, 1985, at A26, col. 1. Following a San Francisco educational campaign to discourage "unsafe" sexual practices, the proportion of gay and bisexual men who reported that they were monogamous or celibate or that they engaged in "unsafe" sexual practices only with steady partners increased from 69% to 81% in eight months. *See Self-Reported Behavioral Change Among Gay and Bisexual Men—San Francisco*, 34 Morbidity and Mortality Weekly Rep. 613 (1985).

71. This analysis does not extend to statutes justified on AIDS grounds that proscribe private acts of sodomy. Such regulations should be examined under heightened scrutiny because of their intrusion into intimate relationships and private homes, *see* Brief for Respondent at 7–17, *Hardwick, supra* note 63, and should be struck down as an overbroad and overly restrictive approach to AIDS control. *See* Brief Amici Curiae at 20–21, *Hardwick, supra* note 56. The likelihood of contracting AIDS is already a significant deterrent to participation in "unsafe" sexual practices; criminal sanctions against sodomy offer little if any additional deterrent effect and would certainly discourage individuals from identifying themselves as persons at risk for AIDS. *Cf.* State v. Saunders, 75 N.J. 200, 218, 381 A.2d 333, 342 (1977) ("To the extent that any successful program to combat venereal disease must depend upon affected persons coming forward for treatment, the [criminal fornication] statute operates as a deterrent to such voluntary participation."). Moreover, sodomy statutes are overinclusive when they restrict sexual activities of lesbians and others not in at-risk

groups, and underinclusive in allowing vaginal intercourse by AIDS carriers. Finally, like quarantines, sodomy statutes probably would be enforced only rarely and selectively. *See supra* p. 1284.

72. *See* Gay Lib v. University of Missouri, 558 F.2d 848, 854–55 & n.13 (8th Cir. 1977).

73. Assuming that about 70% of symptomless carriers are gay men, between 3.5% and 9% of the 8 million adult gay men in the United States carry the virus. *See* Landesman, Ginzburg & Weiss, *supra* note 1 at 522; *supra* notes 10 & 14 and accompanying text. Virtually no cases of AIDS exist in the lesbian community. *See supra* note 8.

74. *See* Gay Student Servs. v. Texas A & M Univ., 737 F.2d 1317, 1330 (5th Cir. 1984).

75. Whalen v. Roe, 429 U.S. 589, 599 (1977).

76. At present, the medical community is divided in the debate over whether blood donors who test positive should be informed of their results. *See* Curran, *AIDS Research and "The Window of Opportunity,"* 312 New Eng. J. Med. 903, 904 (1985).

77. South Fla. Blood Serv., Inc. v. Rasmussen, 467 So. 2d 798, 802 (Fla. Dist. Ct. App. 1985).

78. Although courts have upheld laws requiring individuals seeking marriage licenses to submit to blood tests for venereal disease, *see, e.g.,* Peterson v. Widule, 157 Wis. 641, 147 N.W. 966 (1914), attempts to use the state's power to regulate marriage licensing for other purposes generally have failed. *See, e.g.,* Zablocki v. Redhail, 434 U.S. 374 (1978). Mandatory AIDS testing can be distinguished from routine marital blood tests by the much more severe implications of a positive AIDS test.

79. Even in a public school setting, compulsory disclosure of the identities of AIDS carriers is not necessary to protect against any theoretical risk of transmission. *See* Respondents' Post-Trial Memorandum of Law at 62, District 27 Community School Bd. v. Board of Educ., No. 14940-85 (N.Y. Sup. Ct. Feb. 11, 1986).

80. Regulation requiring individuals to take affirmative measures to protect their own health has been held unconstitutional by at least one court. *See* State *ex rel.* Hawks v. Lazaro, 157 W. Va. 417, 437, 202 S.E.2d 109, 123 (1974) (finding a statute that permitted involuntary hospitalization of an individual in need of treatment unconstitutional).

81. *See* J. Tobey, Public Health Law 133 (1947).

82. *See* Damme, *Controlling Genetic Disease Through Law,* 15 U.C.D. L. Rev. 801, 807 (1982).

83. Wisconsin v. Constantineau, 400 U.S. 433, 437 (1971); *see* Board of Regents v. Roth, 408 U.S. 564, 573 (1972). *But see* Paul v. Davis, 424 U.S. 693, 697–99 (1976) (holding that police circulation of a picture inaccurately identifying the plaintiff as an "active" shoplifter implicated no protected rights).

84. *See* Bayer, *supra* note 7, at 600. California and Wisconsin were among the first states to pass laws to protect the confidentiality of those who take the antibody test and to prevent the use of the test by employers or

insurance companies. *See* Act of Apr. 3, 1985, Assembly Bill No. 488, 1985 Cal. Legis. Serv. ch. 23, at 27 (West); Act of Nov. 14, 1985, ch. 146 § 025, 1985 Wis. Legis. Serv. Act 73, at 45 (West). A Florida statute authorizes state officials to ban use of the test by employers or insurers, Act of May 30, 1985, § 381.606(5), 1985 Fla. Sess. Law Serv. ch. 85-52, at 118 (West). Efforts by employers and insurers to use questions about sexual orientation to identify those at risk for AIDS should similarly be prohibited.

85. Longitudinal studies may require that some identifying number be assigned to an individual, who could still remain anonymous in government records. Colorado is the only state that mandates the reporting of names of individuals found to carry the AIDS antibody. *See* N.Y. Times, Sept. 30, 1985, at B8, col. 3.

86. The Department of Labor Office of Contract Compliance considers AIDS patients disabled under the Vocational Rehabilitation Act of 1973, which makes it illegal for most federally funded employers or employers with government contracts to fail "reasonably [to] accommodate" AIDS patients who are able to work. *See* Nat'l L.J., Sept. 16, 1985, at 30, col. 2. Cancer patients have been accepted as handicapped under several state fair employment statutes. *See, e.g.,* Chrysler Outboard Corp. v. Dilhr, 14 Fair Empl. Prac. Cas. (BNA) 344, 345 (1976). *But see* Kubik v. CNA Fin. Corp., 29 Fair Empl. Prac. Cas. (BNA) 698, 700 (1981) (holding that colon cancer was not a physical handicap, because it did not bar the plaintiff from performing major life functions). For a detailed guide to statutory authority prohibiting AIDS discrimination in New York, *see* Lambda Legal Defense and Education Fund, Inc., AIDS Legal Guide: A Professional Resource on AIDS-related Legal Issues and Discrimination (1984). The City of Los Angeles has explicitly prohibited discrimination against AIDS patients, or people perceived to have AIDS, in housing, employment, education, and use of city facilities and services. *See* Los Angeles, Cal., Ordinance 160, 289 (Aug. 16, 1985). *See generally* Leonard, *Employment Discrimination Against Persons with AIDS*, 10 U. Dayton L. Rev. 681 (1985) (examining possible statutory protections against discrimination of AIDS carriers).

87. Courts may, however, accord greater deference to military employment decisions than to policies of other public employers. *Cf.* Rostker v. Goldberg, 453 U.S. 57, 66 (1981) (rejecting a constitutional challenge to Congress's decision not to draft women).

88. *See* Hampton v. Mow Sun Wong, 426 U.S. 88, 102 (1976) (finding a rule barring noncitizens from civil service employment of "sufficient significance to be characterized as a deprivation of an interest in liberty").

89. *See* Board of Regents v. Roth, 408 U.S. 564, 576–78 (1972) (stating that individuals may have property interests in employment when they are statutorily or otherwise entitled to continued employment).

90. *Cf.* L. Tribe, *supra* note 63, § 16–31, at 1090 ("In sum, either a significant interference with liberty or a denial of a benefit vital to the individual triggers intermediate review.").

91. *See* N.Y. Times, Aug. 18, 1985, at E18, col. 1.

92. *See Summary: Recommendations for Preventing Transmission of Infection*

with Human T-Lymphotrophic Virus Type III Lymphadenopathy-Associated Virus in the Workplace, 34 Morbidity & Mortality Weekly Rep. 681, 693 (1985).

93. *See id.* at 684; Sande, *Transmission of AIDS: The Case against Casual Contagion,* 314 New Eng. J. Med. 380, 381 (1986).

94. *See* Sande, *supra* note 93, at 381.

95. *See* Brown v. Broad of Educ., 347 U.S. 483, 493 (1954).

96. Plyler v. Doe, 457 U.S. 202, 223–24 (1982).

97. *See* San Antonio Indep. School Dist. v. Rodriguez, 411 U.S. 1, 36 (1973) (subjecting to minimum scrutiny a statute that provided for funding of public education).

98. *See* supra p. 1281.

99. No. 14940-85, mem. at 49 (N.Y. Sup. Ct. Feb. 11, 1986).

100. *Id.* at 49. After a five-week trial, characterized by "distress and acrimony," the court found that the policy not to exclude automatically AIDS carriers had a rational basis, that the Board was under no statutory duty to keep AIDS carriers out of public school, and that to exclude them would violate the Rehabilitation Act of 1973 and the equal protection clause, because no rational basis existed for excluding identified AIDS carriers but not those carriers who had not been tested. Similar cases are pending in several states. In Kokomo, Indiana, after local health officials allowed a child with AIDS to attend classes, a circuit court judge issued a temporary injunction barring the child from school until the court could decide whether a state statute for controlling communicable diseases covered AIDS. *See* N.Y. Times, Feb. 22, 1986, at 6, col. 1.

101. *See District 27,* at 11–24, 45.

102. *Cf.* Zucht v. King, 260 U.S. 174, 175–77 (1922) (holding that requiring vaccination as a prerequisite to public school attendance is a proper exercise of state power).

103. *See District 27,* at 43.

104. *Cf.* New York State Ass'n for Retarded Children, Inc. v. Carey, 612 F.2d 644, 650 (2d Cir. 1979) (invalidating a plan to segregate retarded children carrying the hepatitis B virus, because the school board was unable to show that the health hazard they posed was more than a remote possibility); *accord* Community High School Dist. 155 v. Denz, 124 Ill. App. 3d 129, 463 N.E. 2d 998 (1984).

105. *See Education and Foster Care, supra* note 10, at 519.

106. *See id.*

Conclusion:
The Administration of Morality

Ervin Shienbaum

In addition to the moral and constitutional issues raised by recent sexual/reproductive issues, governmental intervention entails use of public mechanisms for defining and enforcing governmental strictures. Governmental stances on the panoply of issues such as procreation, pornography, sexual behavior, and abortion would be rendered hollow without effective definitional standards and enforcement measures. Thus, we must look to the available forms for public action and the ensuing consequences in order to come to terms with the imposition of standards of morality on recent sexual/reproductive issues.

Government involvement is predicated upon the assumption that public standards of personal and institutional conduct would remain simply pious proclamations without use of the coercive capabilities of the state. At the birth of the country, James Madison articulated the common wisdom that government authority rests upon the perceived imperfectability of man: "If men were angels, no government would be necessary. If angels were to govern men, neither external nor internal controls on government would be necessary."[1] Leaving aside the question of the proper dividing line between legitimately imposed public morality and the publicly-sanctified right to privacy (an issue of extreme importance), once public action has been deemed proper, what parameters of action does government possess?

Three primary institutional mechanisms exist that serve to define

---

Ervin Shienbaum is a Research Analyst at the New Jersey Government Study Commission on State, County and Municipal Government.

and enforce existing public standards. They are: 1) the legal system, which sanctions what can and can not be done; 2) the regulatory and administrative agencies, whose jurisdictions extend to such matters; and 3) the police organs of the state, agencies specifically entrusted with enforcing existing codes and statutes. The success of governmental involvement in sexual/reproductive matters largely depends on the jurisdictional efforts forthcoming from these three public spheres of authority.

Fragmented Government Authority

The nature of the relationship among these three centers of governmental action is quite complex, fitting into a governmental landscape of functionally and geographically diffused responsibility and constitutionally dispersed powers that run the gamut from the national level to local governments. Not only is authority pertaining to sexual/reproductive matters dispersed, but, in addition, determination of these questions is the unintended byproduct of commingled intergovernmental and interinstitutional efforts.

Thus, for instance, on an issue such as the rights of AIDS victims, the 11th Circuit Court of Appeals, basing their decision on Section 504 of the 1973 Rehabilitation Act which prohibits discrimination against the handicapped for any program receiving federal financing, ruled in September of 1985 that contagious diseases, such as AIDS, constitute a handicap. This ruling was contravened by a Justice Department opinion (an action binding on the federal bureaucracy), some six months later, which challenged the Act's application to government health officials' broad powers to prevent the spread of communicable diseases.[2] The point here is that the courts, legislative branches, and executive officials frequently produce rulings and policies which run at crosspurposes to one another; in addition to which, the national government, states, and localities often counteract one another's efforts in addressing these issues.

This continual process of refinement of policy and law serves to weaken the ability of government to act decisively on sexual/reproductive questions. Even the use of the term "government" is a misnomer since what we are talking about is a national government, 50 state governments, and over 70,000 local government units which may involve themselves in some of these issues. Government in this area reflects a general political order intentionally designed by the founding fathers to be fragmented and is founded upon a pluralistic society deeply divided in its opinions on sexual/reproductive issues.

Given the disconnectedness of the governmental framework and diversity of the population represented, such disjunctions negate the possibility of policy and administrative coherency in formulating and realizing precisely defined goals and treating all citizens equitably. Instead, the application of federal, state, and local policies to different geographical areas serves to differentiate populations, imposing different restrictions and requirements on residents of different geographic areas in regard to sexual/reproductive questions. Since policies, laws, and court rulings are intergovernmentally conjoined, rather than based on jurisdictions which override one another, public action generally is the resultant of decisions made by various public institutions with differing purposes in mind.

Functioning in a pervasively open federal system, in which jurisdictional concerns are often shared intergovernmentally, agencies with particular responsibilities commonly find their roles partially defined by other levels of government. Particularly when program funding is forthcoming from the national government or there is national policy involvement, state and local policy authority becomes altered to accommodate federal goals.

The interactive effect of the courts, administrative and regulatory agencies, and law enforcement agencies' involvement on sexual/reproductive issues, overall, blunts the established objectives of individual governmental institutions. Rationally-established courses of action for a specific agency become circumscribed and altered by the requirements forthcoming from other institutions with authority on the matter. The range of agency self-possessed authority becomes truncated as a result, with the objectives of other spheres of government incorporated into the agency's administrative-enforcement processes.

The Role of the Courts on Abortion as Illustration

An examination of the courts' role in the issue of abortion is instructive for what it reveals both about the patterns of interaction between courts and state government, and the shifting standards on sexual/reproductive issues when the field of play is in the courts. With roughly 1.5 million abortions being performed annually, the issue is of direct consequence to many in American society. At the heart of the abortion controversy lie two competing claims: the right to life and that of privacy. In its decisions, the court has given primacy to the latter claim, but left enough of an opening for right-to-lifers to use sympathetic state governments to circumscribe the conditions under which a pregnant woman may have an abortion.

The landmark court decision on abortion, *Roe v. Wade* (1973), affirmed the rght of a woman to have an abortion, basing that right on the principle of an individual's right to privacy on matters pertaining to sex, marriage, and reproduction.[3] The Supreme Court also set constraints on allowing government involvement in the second and third trimesters of a pregnancy. The Supreme Court decision was the logical extension of a previous ruling in which the Court overturned a Connecticut law prohibiting use of contraceptives,[4] basing their decision on the sanctified "right of privacy" within the institutions of marriage and the family.

As is the case with other sexual/reproductive issues over which society is deeply divided, the main strategy against a clearly-defined government policy is not a frontal assault directed at dismantling or nullifying the measure, but rather an effort at enveloping it in a series of stipulations which undermine the policy until it is rendered meaningless. With 50 state governments and numbers of bureaucracies involved in defining and administering policy, ample opportunity exists to hem in disliked court decisions by pressing for passage of state laws and administrative rules which undercut the effects of court rulings.

In the matter of abortion, several state laws were passed restricting the conditions under which abortions could be given and the procedures involved in undertaking an abortion. These restrictions encompassed: 1) consent requirements by persons related to the pregnant woman 2) curtailment of federal funding for abortions and 3) the imposition of procedural requirements in granting an abortion.

Consent requirements were initially the most common state approach to deter women from having abortions. Consent requirements have generally been struck down by the Supreme Court. These cases included: *Planned Parenthood of Missouri v. Danforth* (overturned), which required the consent of the husband for a married woman and parental consent for an unmarried woman under the age of 18;[5] the Florida case of *Poe v. Gerstein* (overturned), which also required written consent of the husband for a wife's abortion;[6] *Bellotti v. Baird* (overturned), a Massachusetts law requiring parental consent for teenage girls or in the case of refusal by one of the parents, consent based on good cause by a superior court judge;[7] *M.L. v. Matheson*, a Utah case which was upheld, requiring that parents had to be notified in order to perform an abortion on a teenage girl who lived with her parents.[8]

In contrast to the difficulty of attaching consent requirements as a means of restricting the use of abortions, anti-abortion activists have been greatly successful in placing limitations on public funding for abortion. Here, the effort has been directed at deterring poor women from having abortions by denying use of Medicaid as a source of public monies. Thus, in *Maher v. Roe*, a Connecticut case, the Supreme Court upheld the state's right to provide Medicaid funding for childbirth, but withhold it for abortions.[9] The most notable of the funding restrictions is the Hyde amendment, passed by Congress to prohibit the use of Medicaid funding to finance abortions. This act constituted a major victory for foes of abortion, restricting on a nation-wide basis what had previously been limited to individual states. The Hyde amendment was upheld by the courts in *Harris v. McRae*.[10]

Another attempted roadblock by foes of abortion has been procedural requirements curtailing the conditions under which an abortion may be performed. These have included residency requirements, allowing abortions only in hospitals accredited by the Joint Commission of Accreditation of Hospitals (JCAH), requirements of prior medical staff approval, and prior consultation by more than one practitioner.[11] These have all been found to be unconstitutional.

An examination of the shifting posture of one of the most active states, Pennsylvania, in curtailing access to abortions is revealing in how states have sought to exploit potential gaps in Supreme Court decisions to limit abortions. In passing the Pennsylvania Abortion Control Act, the state legislature sought to partially counteract *Roe v. Wade* by requiring the written consent of the woman's husband or the parents in the case of a minor. When these provisions were declared unconstitutional by the Supreme Court,[12] the Pennsylvania legislature then moved on to denying Medicaid funding for abortion. Under Title XIX of the Federal Social Security Act, participating states have responsibility for establishing "reasonable standards . . . for determining . . . the extent of medical assistance" under state Medicaid plans.[13] As in other Supreme Court challenges concerning state denial of Medicaid funding for abortion, this action was upheld by the Court.

This was followed by the 1982 Pennsylvania Abortion Control Act which required doctors to counsel women seeking abortions on the full risks and alternatives. In addition, two doctors' presence was required at late term abortions with the procedure most likely to yield a live birth required. This law was narrowly struck down by the Supreme Court in a five to four decision.[14] The slim margin of the majority opinion and the issues raised by some of the dissenting opinion, raises questions about the future viability of abortion as a fundamental right.[15]

The above patterns of action and counteraction are revealing in what they tell us about sexual/reproductive policies. First, the heterogeneity of forces in the political system provide a constant source for redefinition and refinement in the scope and direction of policy. While, legally, women may possess close to an unabridged right to have an abortion, in practice, numbers of barriers can be erected which make the right difficult to realize.

Second, address of outstanding sexual/reproductive issues is not undertaken comprehensively, but rather the outcome of subissues and the pirouette of technical points ends up defining the overall concern. Thus, for the abortion question, there has been no national government effort to fully address the issue of abortion. This has allowed the states to pull in different directions, with the result of differentiated treatment of citizens from different states. The one common thread, and it has been of major importance, is the Supreme Court's affirmation of the basic right of a woman to have an abortion.

The effort to achieve rights for homosexuals has followed a pattern similar, in many respects, to that of abortion. Faced with an unsympathetic Supreme Court, which has upheld state anti-sodomy laws,[16] gay activists have sought passage of national legislation, the Civil Rights Amendments Act of 1981 as an amendment to the 1964 Civil Rights Act, outlawing discrimination based on sexual orientation. Successful passage of such a measure would have been equal in stature to the women's movement success in having the Supreme Court affirm abortion as a basic right.

With their lack of success at the national level, the gay rights movement has been able to eliminate biases against homosexuals at the state and local level, the same way that the anti-abortion movement has been able to achieve its goals in numbers of state governments. Though homosexual acts presently constitute a crime in 24 states,[17] in the last 20 years over 20 states have repealed laws prohibiting homosexual acts between consenting adults and over a dozen have reduced the penalty for the crime from a felony to a misdemeanor.[18] In addition, numbers of localities, such as New York City and San Francisco, have passed legislation outlawing discrimination against homosexuals.

The success of the gay rights movement in passing civil rights laws for homosexuals is revealing about the nature of the policy process on sexual/reproductive issues as questions of controversy. It amounts to almost a dictum that the further one goes down the levels of government, the greater the likelihood of achieving clearcut policies. To some extent at the state level, and certainly at the national level, controversial issues are subject to the tug and pull of roughly-balanced opposing forces. At the local level, situations tend to crystallize, with one of the antagonists clearly dominant. Such a political climate affords the opportunity for an unambigious policy to emerge on issues which become mired in continual controversy at the state and national levels. This has been the pattern for gay rights and also generally holds true for issues such as pornography and the emerging public response to AIDS.

The growing attention given to sexual/reproductive issues is, in major part, an outgrowth of advances in medical technology and the advent of new diseases that stem from increased sexual contact in society. The social disruption caused by these changes has led to a new societal re-examination of the proper demarcation between the private arena and the public arena. In part, segments of society are reacting to the destabilizing effects and the uncertainly caused by the rapid and disquieting changes. Furthermore, those in the frontiers of medical technology need government regulation to institutionalize the use of such technologies.

If we take surrogate mothering as an example, there is a need for statutes that codify standards governing the obligations and rights of the various parties involved in the process. Certainly, the donor, recipient and the involved medical practitioner would be more likely to proceed if they were covered under a legal framework that made clear obligations and rights.[19] Artificial insemination by donor, a technique of common usage that has preceded surrogate mothering on a commercial basis by almost 50 years, still awaits adequate legal address. That those involved avidly seek such coverage was made clear by a New England Journal of Medicine editorial in 1979 appealing for legislation establishing rights and conditions of liability.[20] At present, only 24 states have artificial insemination by donor laws in place.[21]

The application of statute to newly emerging reproduction issues would standardize these newly-adopted procedures. While establishing rights and conditions of liability, they also impose constraints on individual and institutional behavior as well. Hospitals, medical practitioners, and private parties would be bound by government codes and regulations. For those seeking the available medical technology, this poses a dilemma. On the one hand, rights are sanctified, thus providing the security of protected rights in seeking use of the available reproductive technology; on the other, those involved find their freedom circumscribed.

Public institutionalization of medically-adopted reproduction procedures thus supersedes private contracts in defining personal and institutional obligations and technology use. Such actions further brings together the spheres of public authority and private choices. Regulations on these matters follows a distinct historical pattern from late 19th century economic regulation to the social regulation of the late 1960's and early 1970's which concerned largely environmental and workplace safety issues, to the concerns of personal behavior, grounded in issues of sexuality and human reproduction.

Given the vagaries of state, court, and administrative involvement, one can expect varied public responses to emerge regarding these issues. Certainly, states will approach these issues differently. The centrality of sexuality and reproduction in human life ensures that these questions will remain subject to passionate examination in the foreseeable future. At stake is a determination of the future social fabric of society and the definition of rights of citizens within that society.

Notes

1. Alexander Hamilton, James Madison, and John Jay, *The Federalist* (Cambridge, Mass.: Harvard University Press, 1961), p. 356.
2. *New York Times* June 23, 1986.
3. Roe v. Wade, 410 U.S. 113 (1973).
4. Griswold v. Connecticut 381 U.S. 479 (1965).
5. Planned Parenthood v. Danforth 428 U.S. 52 (1976).
6. Poe v. Gerstein, 517 F. 2d 787 (1975).
7. Bellotti v. Baird, 443 U.S. 622 (1979).
8. H.L. v. Matheson, 450 U.S. 398 (1981).
9. Maher v. Roe, 432 U.S. 464 (1977).
10. Harris v. McRae, 448 U.S. 297 (1980).
11. Doe v. Bolton, 410 U.S. 179 (1973).
12. Doe v. Zimmerman, 405 F. Supp. 534 (1975).
13. Beal v. Doe, 432 U.S. 438 (1977).
14. See *New York Times* June 12, 1986 for Thornburgh v. American College of Obstetricians and Gynecologists.
15. *Ibid.*
16. As illustration, see Doe v. Commonwealth's Attorney, 425 U.S. 901 (1976), a case challenging Virginia's anti-sodomy laws.
17. Eric Goode, *Deviant Behavior* 2nd ed. (Englewood Cliffs, N.J.: Prentice-Hall, 1984).
18. H. Chase and C. Ducat, *Constitutional Interpretation* 1156 (1979).
19. In the absence of such statutes, private contracts have been commonly used. See, as illustration, Katie Marie Brophy *Journal of Family Law* Vol. 20, No. 2 (1981–82), pp. 263–291.
20. S. J. Behrman, "Artificial Insemination and Public Policy," 300 *New England Journal of Medicine* 619, 620 (March 15, 1979).
21. Illinois Legislative Council, Research Memorandum File 9-302, "Artificial Insemination and Surrogate Mother Agreements: Legal Concerns," November 1, 1982, p. 5. As reported by Andrea Bonnicksen in her "In Vitro Fertilization, Artificial Insemination, and Individual Rights" article in this volume.